Arata
THE LEGEND

We are Man, born of Heaven and Earth,
Moon and Sun and everything under them.

Eyes, Ears, Nose, Tongue, Body, Mind...

Purity will pierce evil and
open up the world of darkness.

All life will be reborn and invigorated.

Appear now.

STORY & ART BY
Yuu Watase

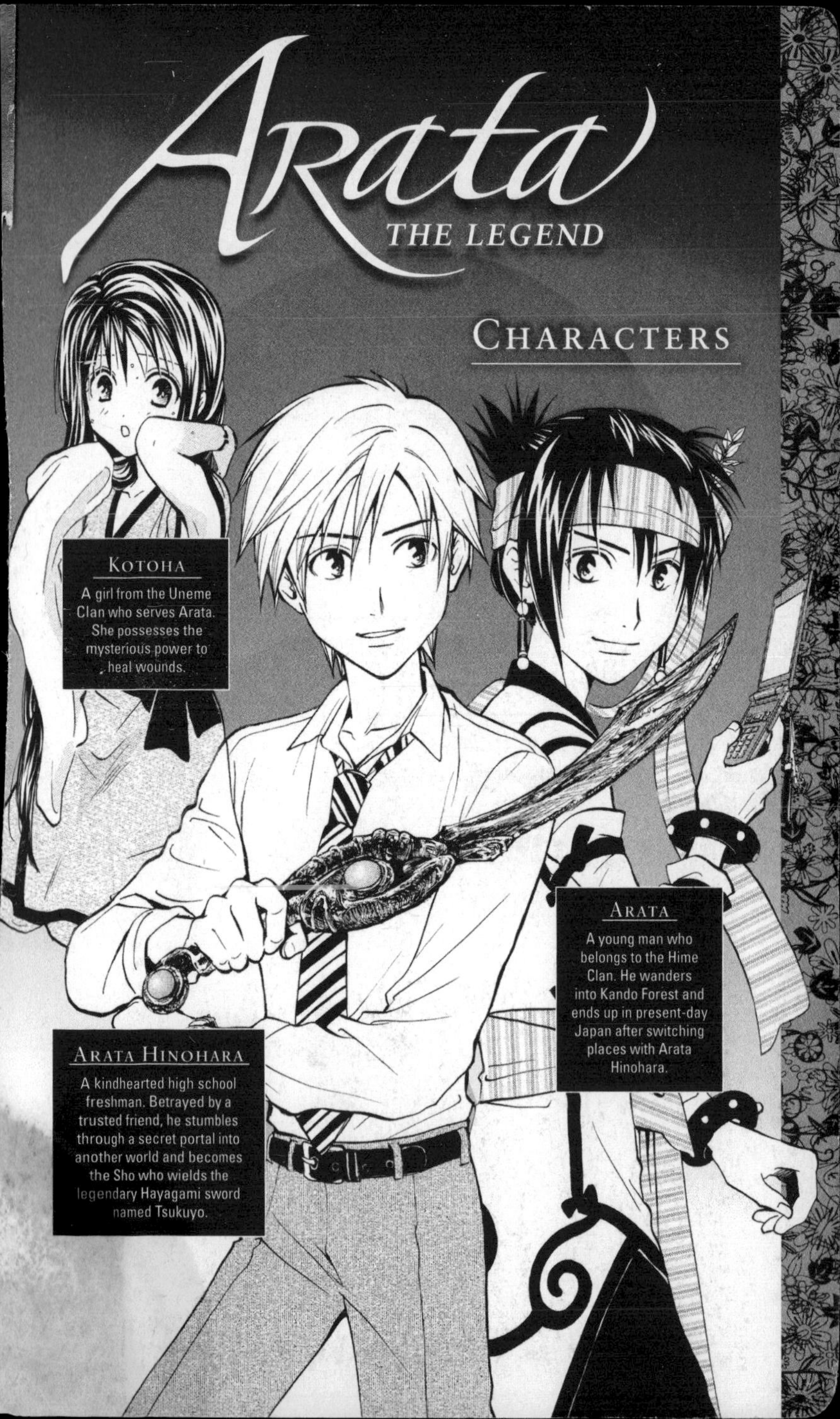
Arata
THE LEGEND
CHARACTERS
KOTOHA
A girl from the Uneme Clan who serves Arata. She possesses the mysterious power to heal wounds.
ARATA
A young man who belongs to the Hime Clan. He wanders into Kando Forest and ends up in present-day Japan after switching places with Arata Hinohara.
ARATA HINOHARA
A kindhearted high school freshman. Betrayed by a trusted friend, he stumbles through a secret portal into another world and becomes the Sho who wields the legendary Hayagami sword named Tsukuyo.

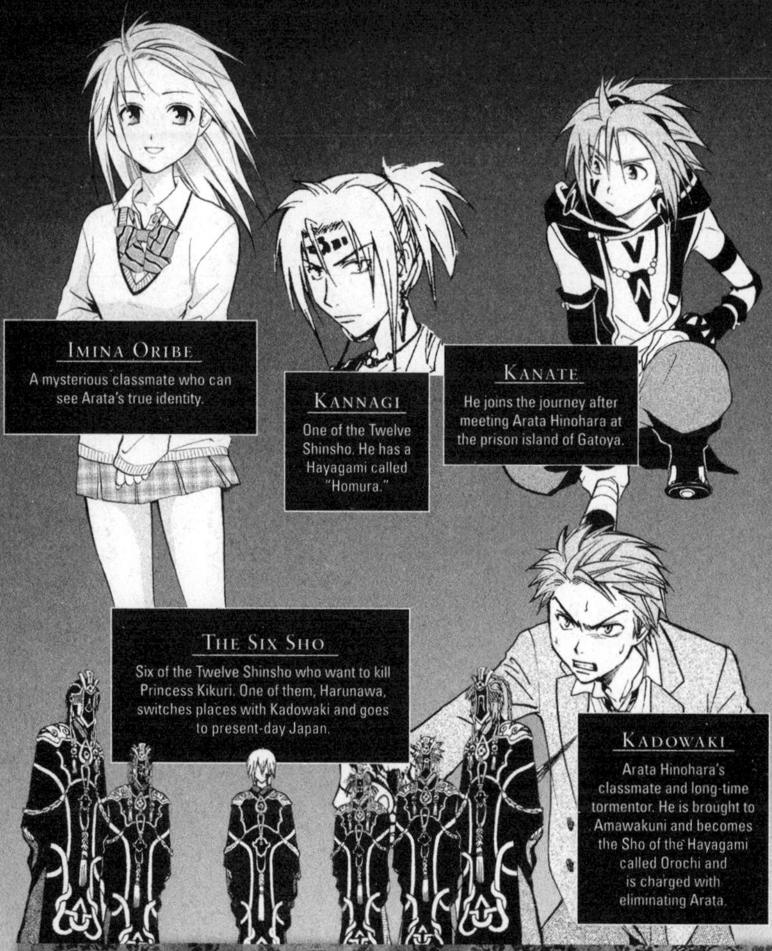
IMINA ORIBE
A mysterious classmate who can see Arata's true identity.
KANNAGI
One of the Twelve Shinsho. He has a Hayagami called "Homura."
KANATE
He joins the journey after meeting Arata Hinohara at the prison island of Gatoya.
THE SIX SHO
Six of the Twelve Shinsho who want to kill Princess Kikuri. One of them, Harunawa, switches places with Kadowaki and goes to present-day Japan.
KADOWAKI
Arata Hinohara's classmate and long-time tormentor. He is brought to Amawakuni and becomes the Sho of the Hayagami called Orochi and is charged with eliminating Arata.

THE STORY THUS FAR

Betrayed by his best friend, Arata Hinohara—a high school student in present-day Japan—wanders through a portal into another world where he and his companions journey onward to deliver his Hayagami sword to Princess Kikuri.

While the battle for the throne rages on, Arata Hinohara resolves to change the world—not through force but by changing the hearts of the Sho. He reveals his true identity to Kotoha, and she accepts him. But now the Six Sho, a mysterious subgroup of the Twelve Shinsho, plot to prevent the revival of Princess Kikuri. In order to destroy Arata, they bring his nemesis, Kadowaki, to Amawakuni...

6
Arata
THE LEGEND

CONTENTS

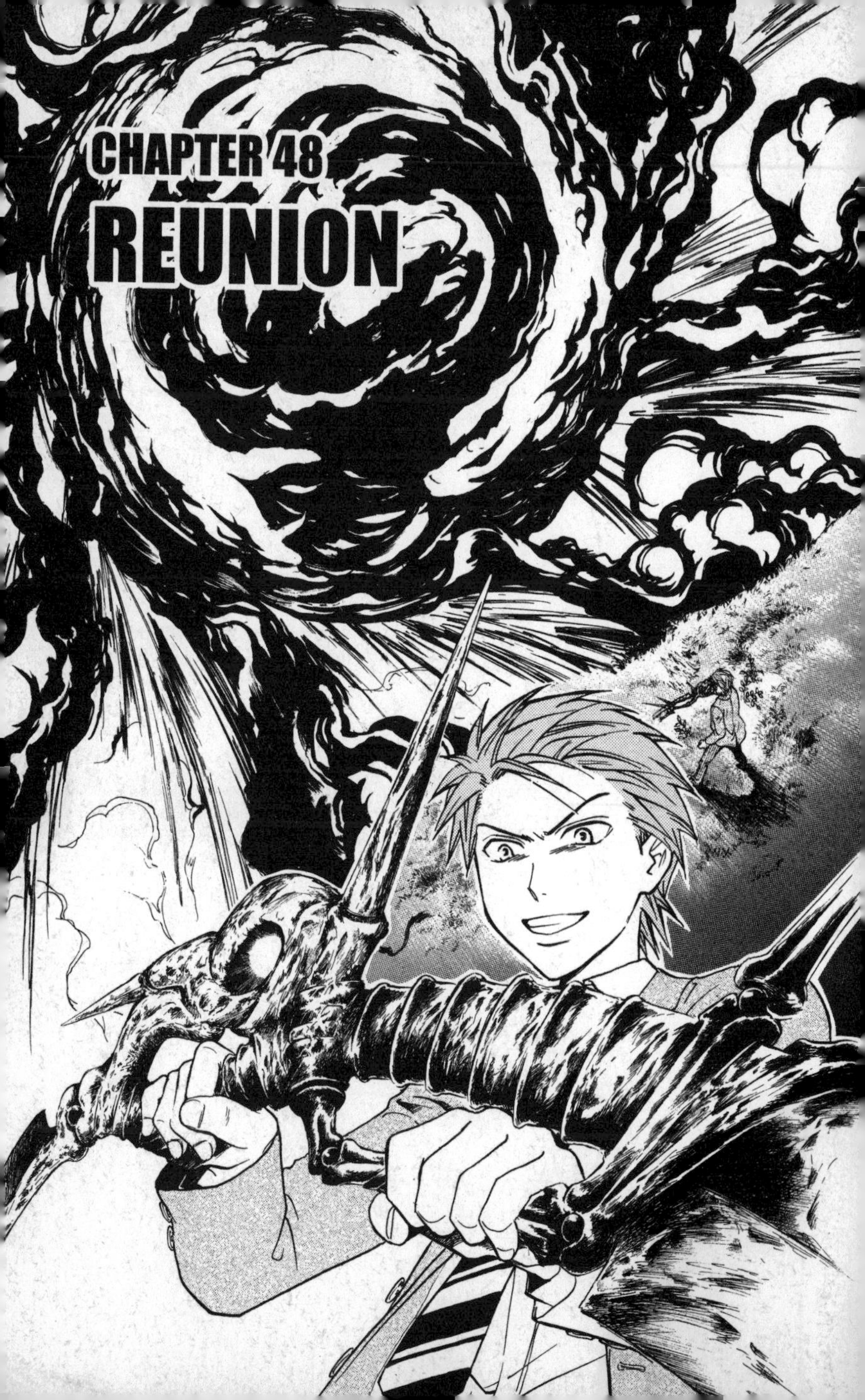
CHAPTER 48
REUNION

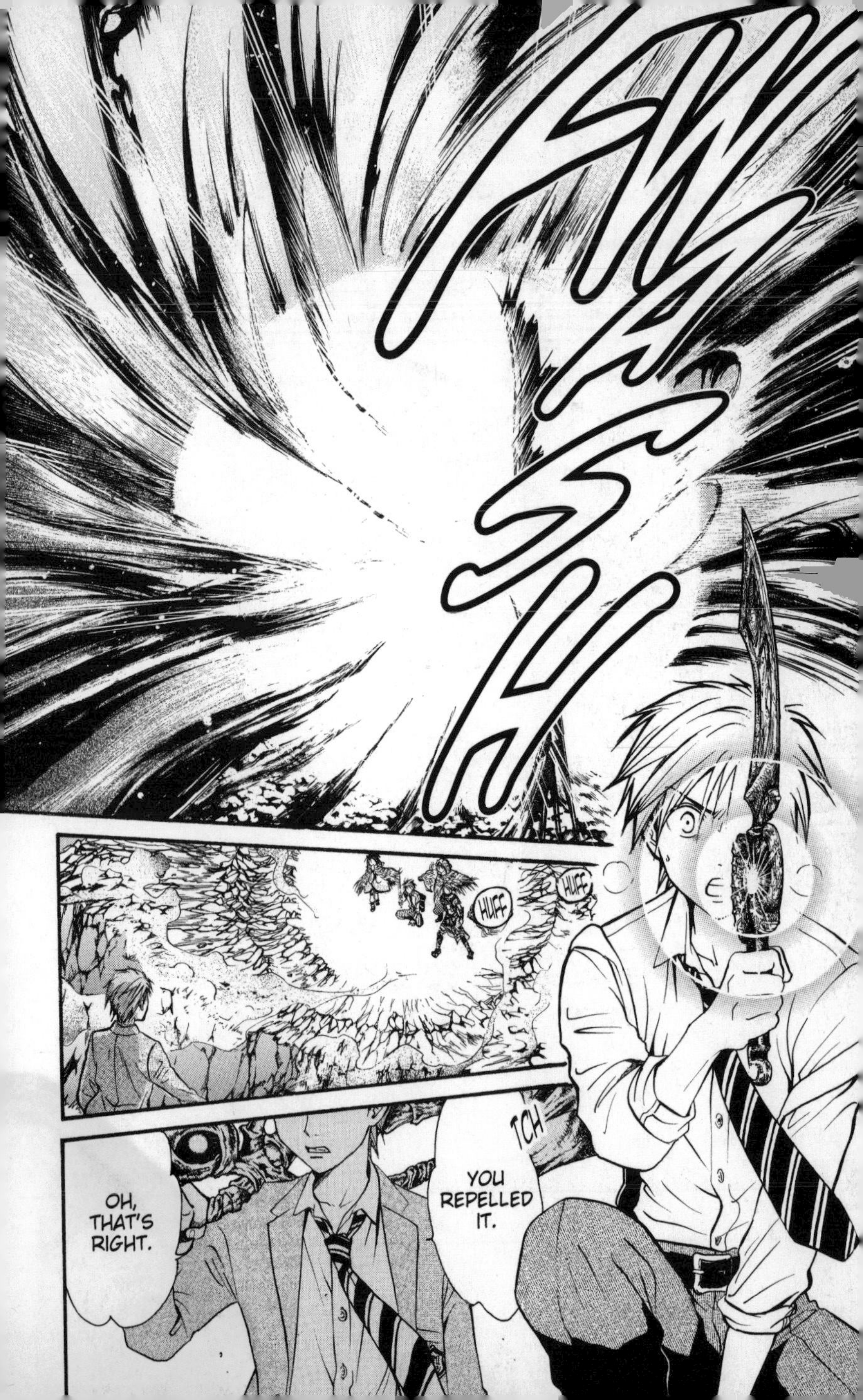
FLASH
HUFF
HUFF
TCH
YOU REPELLED IT.
OH, THAT'S RIGHT.

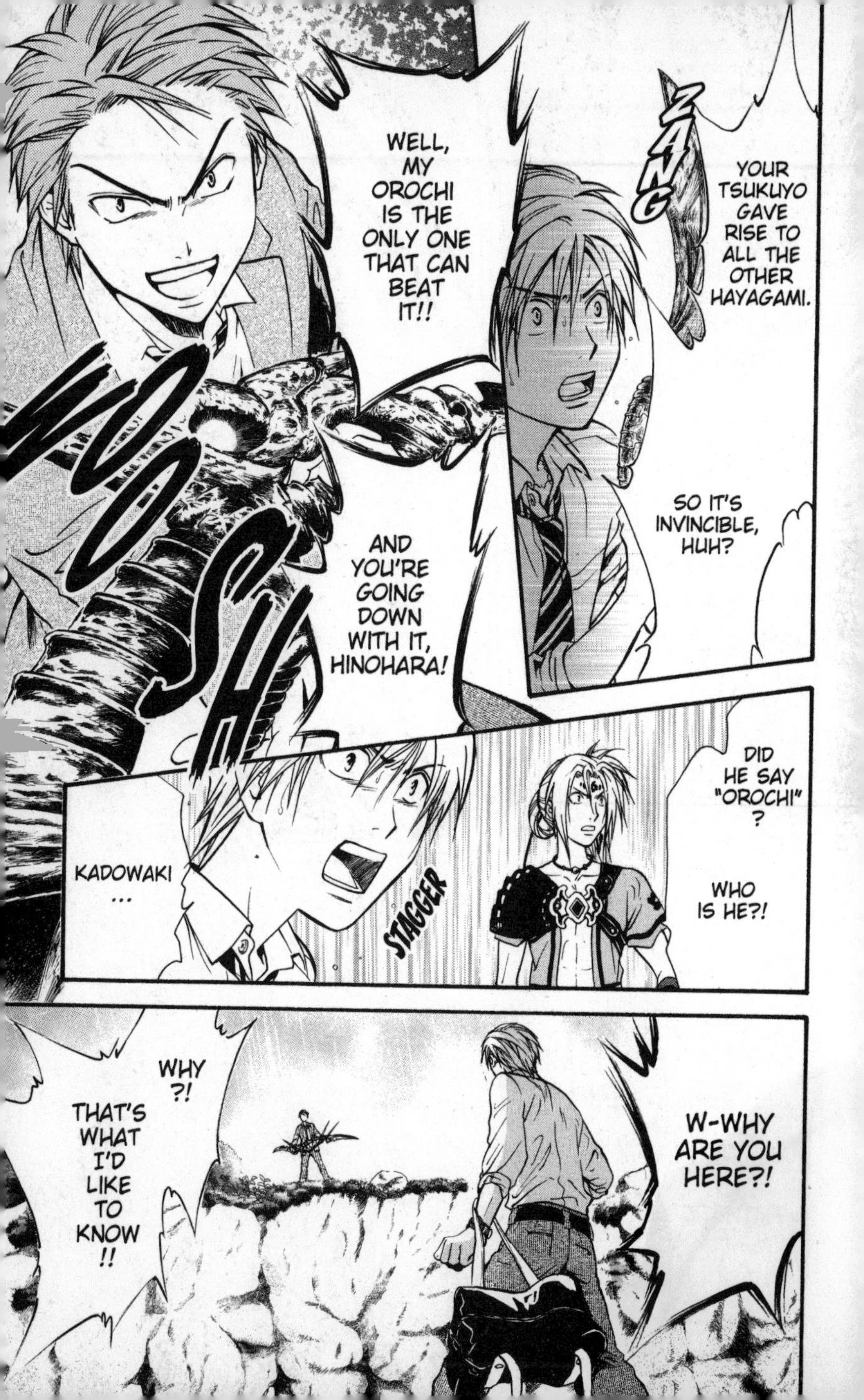

ZANG
YOUR TSUKUYO GAVE RISE TO ALL THE OTHER HAYAGAMI.
SO IT'S INVINCIBLE, HUH?
WELL, MY OROCHI IS THE ONLY ONE THAT CAN BEAT IT!!
AND YOU'RE GOING DOWN WITH IT, HINOHARA!
DID HE SAY "OROCHI"?
WHO IS HE?!
STAGGER
KADOWAKI ...
W-WHY ARE YOU HERE?!
WHY?!
THAT'S WHAT I'D LIKE TO KNOW!!

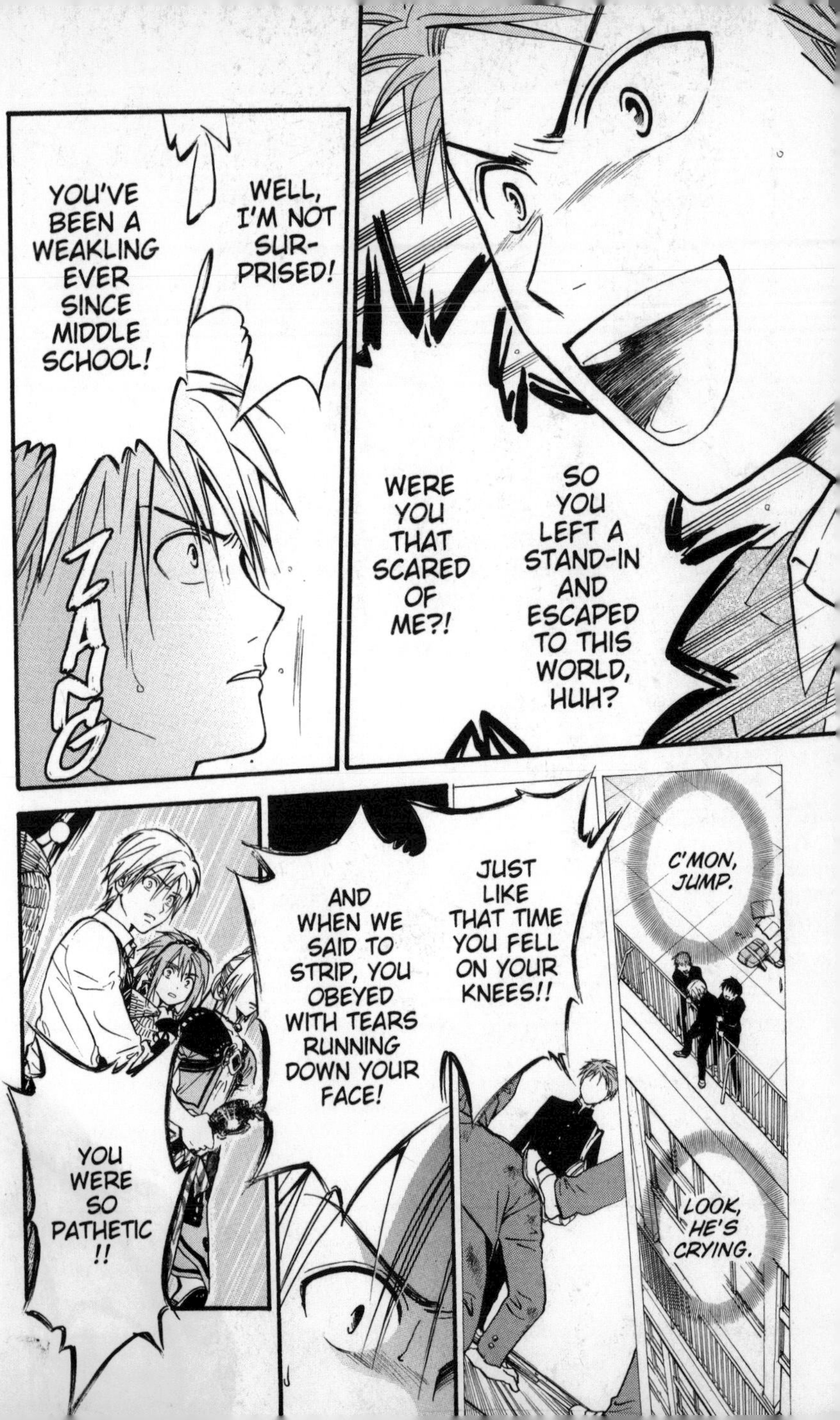
SO YOU LEFT A STAND-IN AND ESCAPED TO THIS WORLD, HUH?
WERE YOU THAT SCARED OF ME?!
WELL, I'M NOT SURPRISED!
YOU'VE BEEN A WEAKLING EVER SINCE MIDDLE SCHOOL!
C'MON, JUMP.
LOOK, HE'S CRYING.
JUST LIKE THAT TIME YOU FELL ON YOUR KNEES!!
AND WHEN WE SAID TO STRIP, YOU OBEYED WITH TEARS RUNNING DOWN YOUR FACE!
YOU WERE SO PATHETIC!!

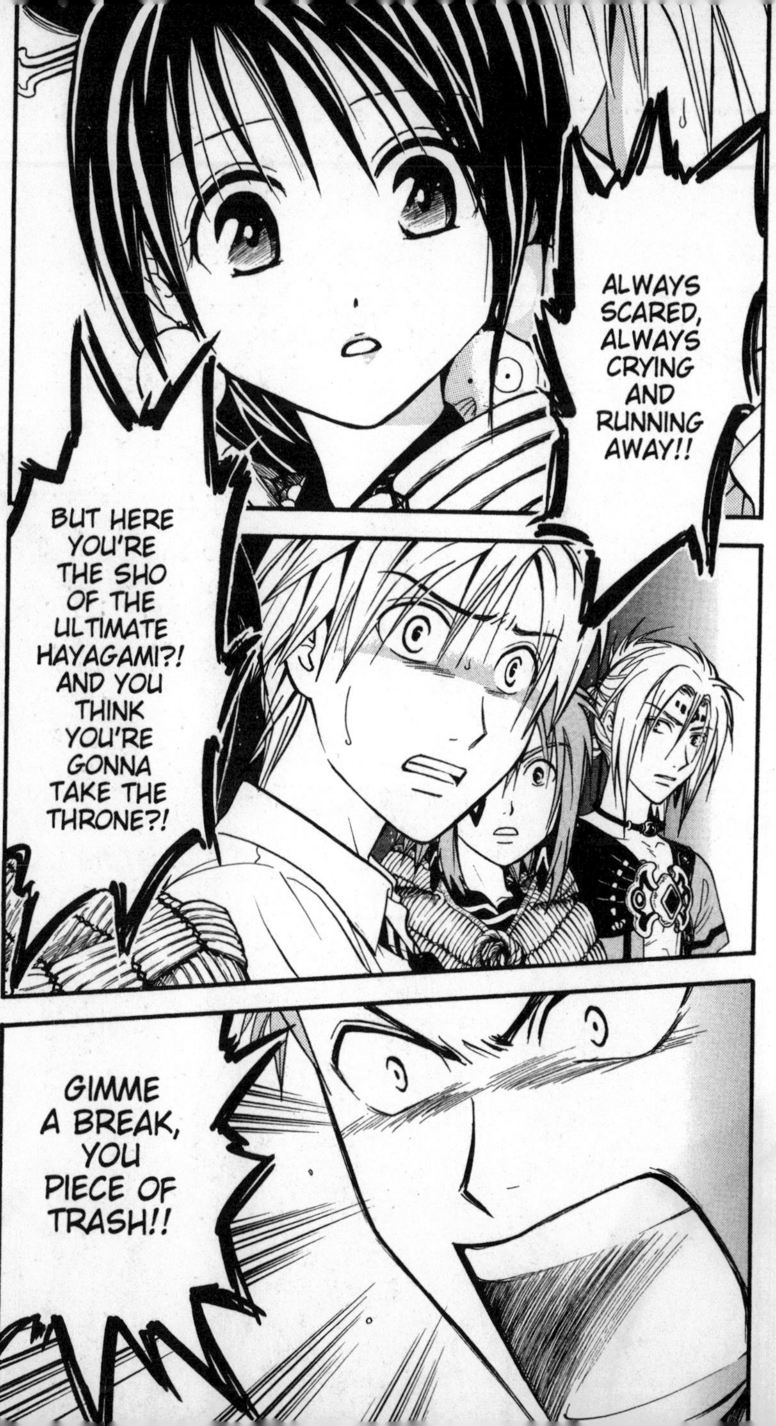
ALWAYS SCARED, ALWAYS CRYING AND RUNNING AWAY!!
BUT HERE YOU'RE THE SHO OF THE ULTIMATE HAYAGAMI?! AND YOU THINK YOU'RE GONNA TAKE THE THRONE?!
GIMME A BREAK, YOU PIECE OF TRASH!!

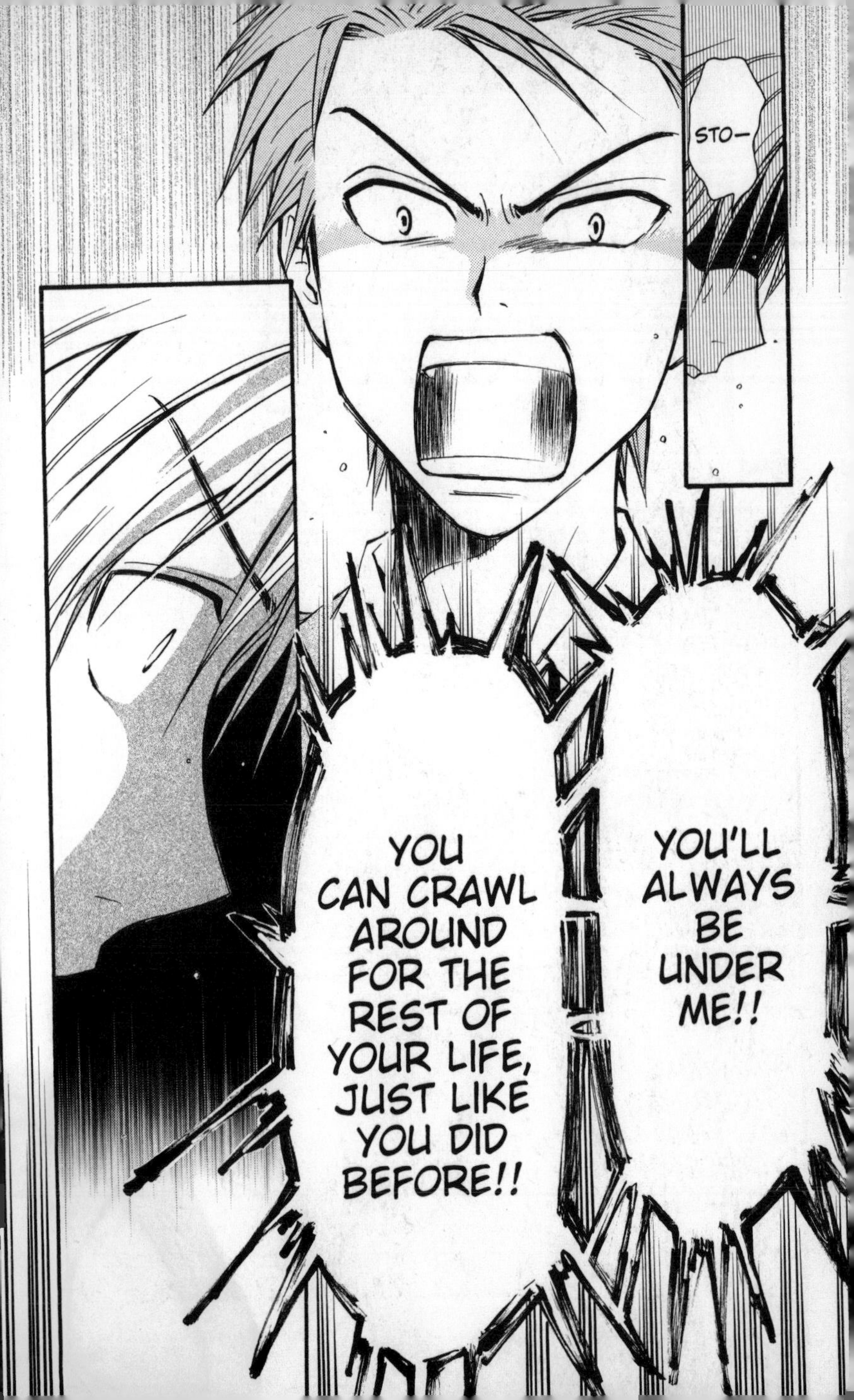
STO—
YOU'LL ALWAYS BE UNDER ME!!
YOU CAN CRAWL AROUND FOR THE REST OF YOUR LIFE, JUST LIKE YOU DID BEFORE!!

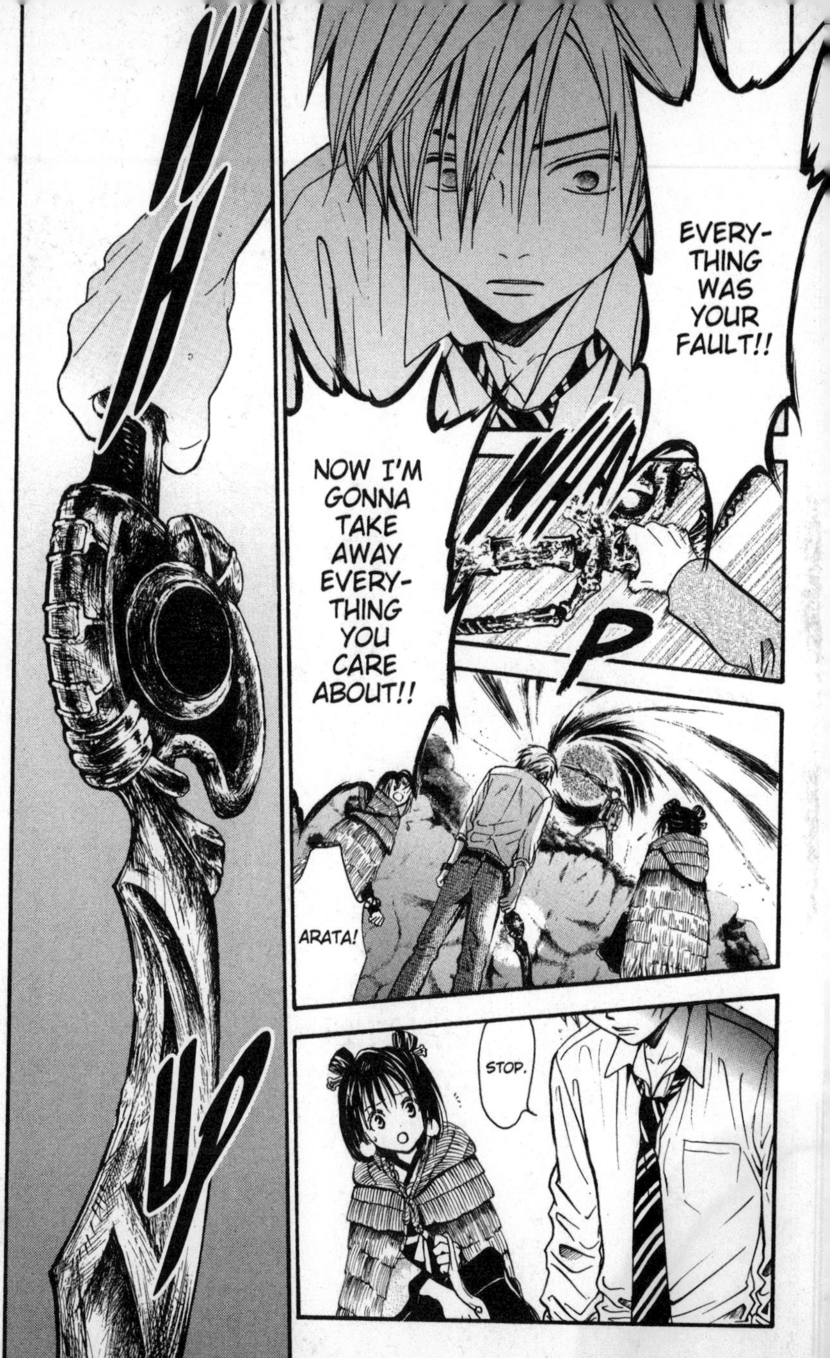
EVERY-THING WAS YOUR FAULT!!
NOW I'M GONNA TAKE AWAY EVERY-THING YOU CARE ABOUT!!
WHAP
ARATA!
STOP.

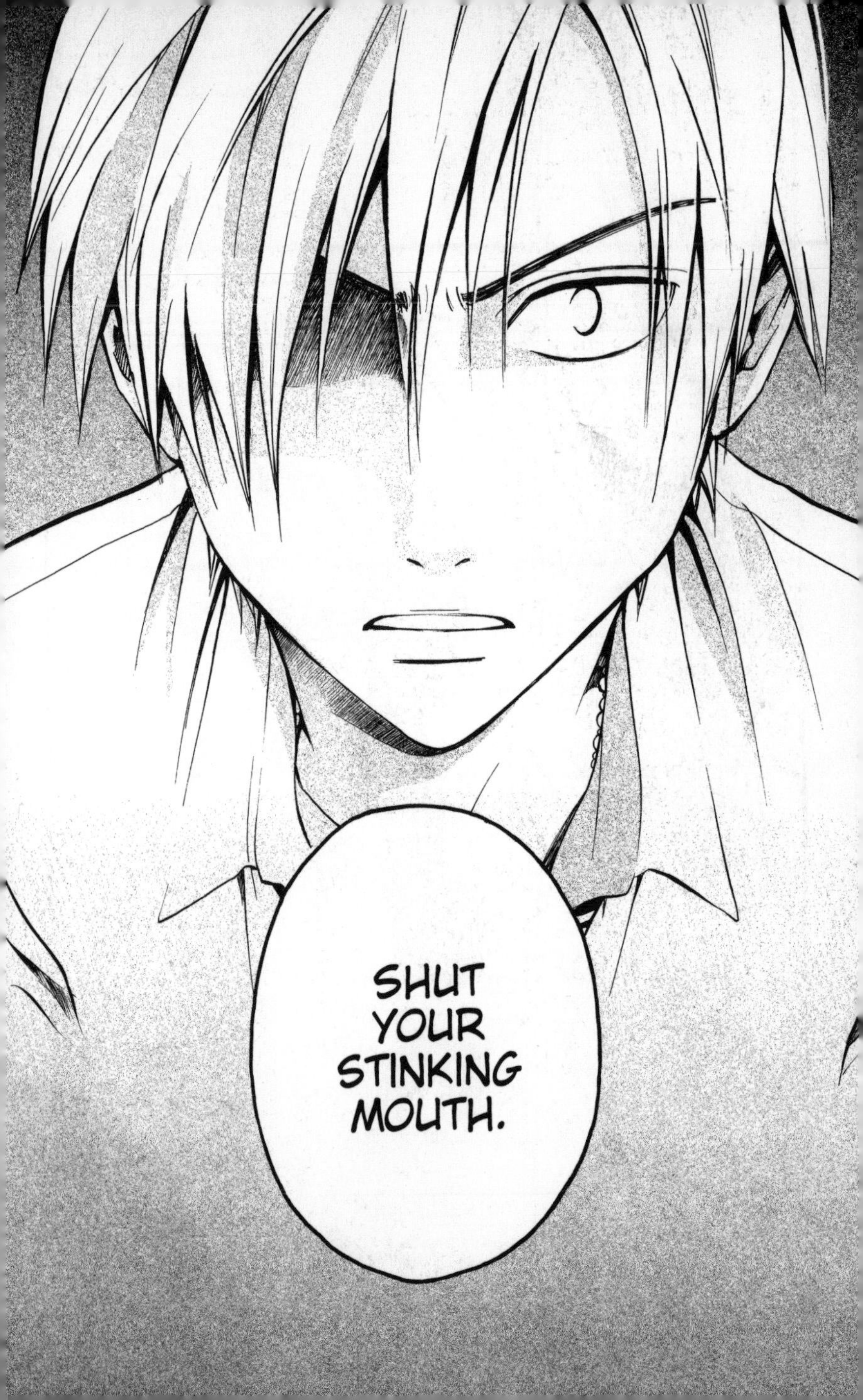
SHUT YOUR STINKING MOUTH.

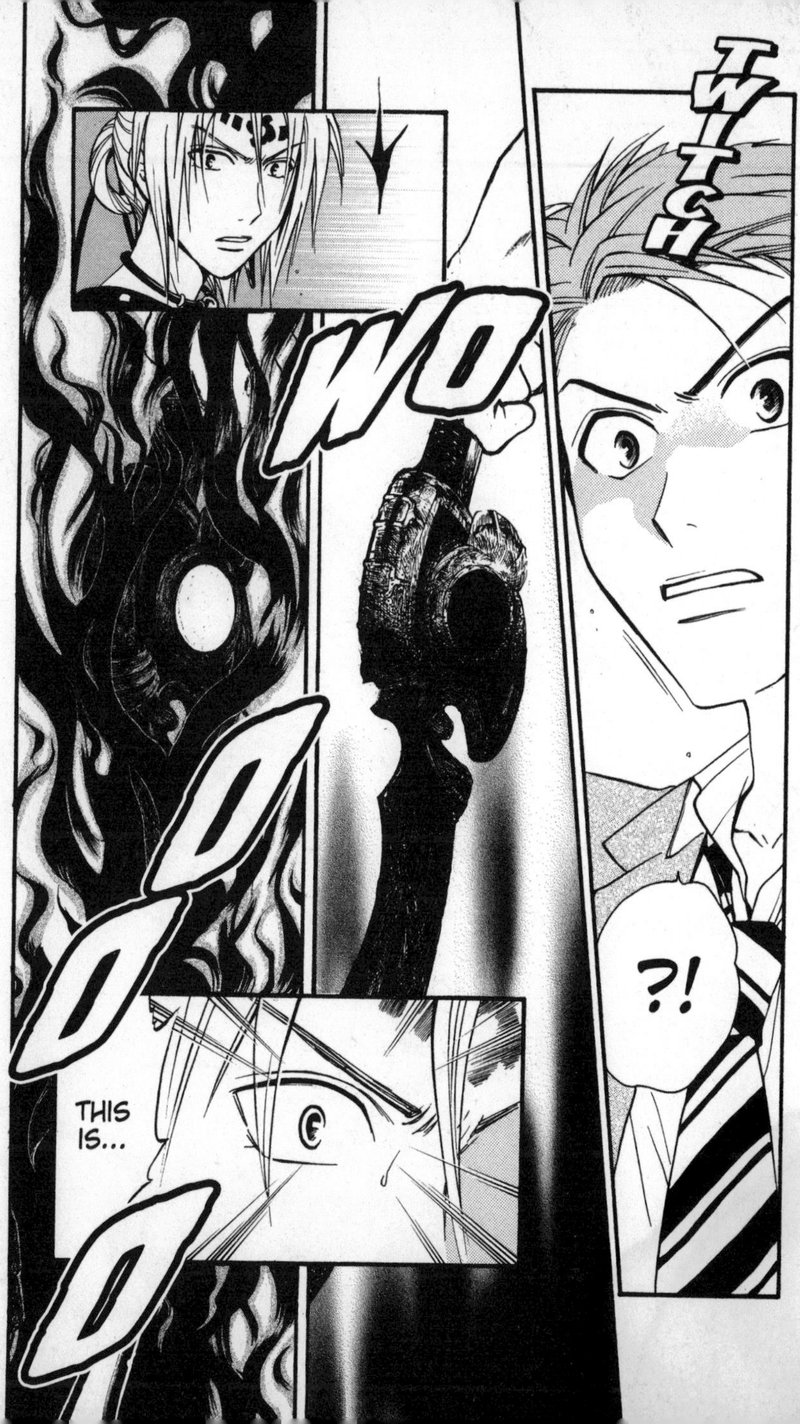
TWITCH
?!
WOOOO
THIS IS...

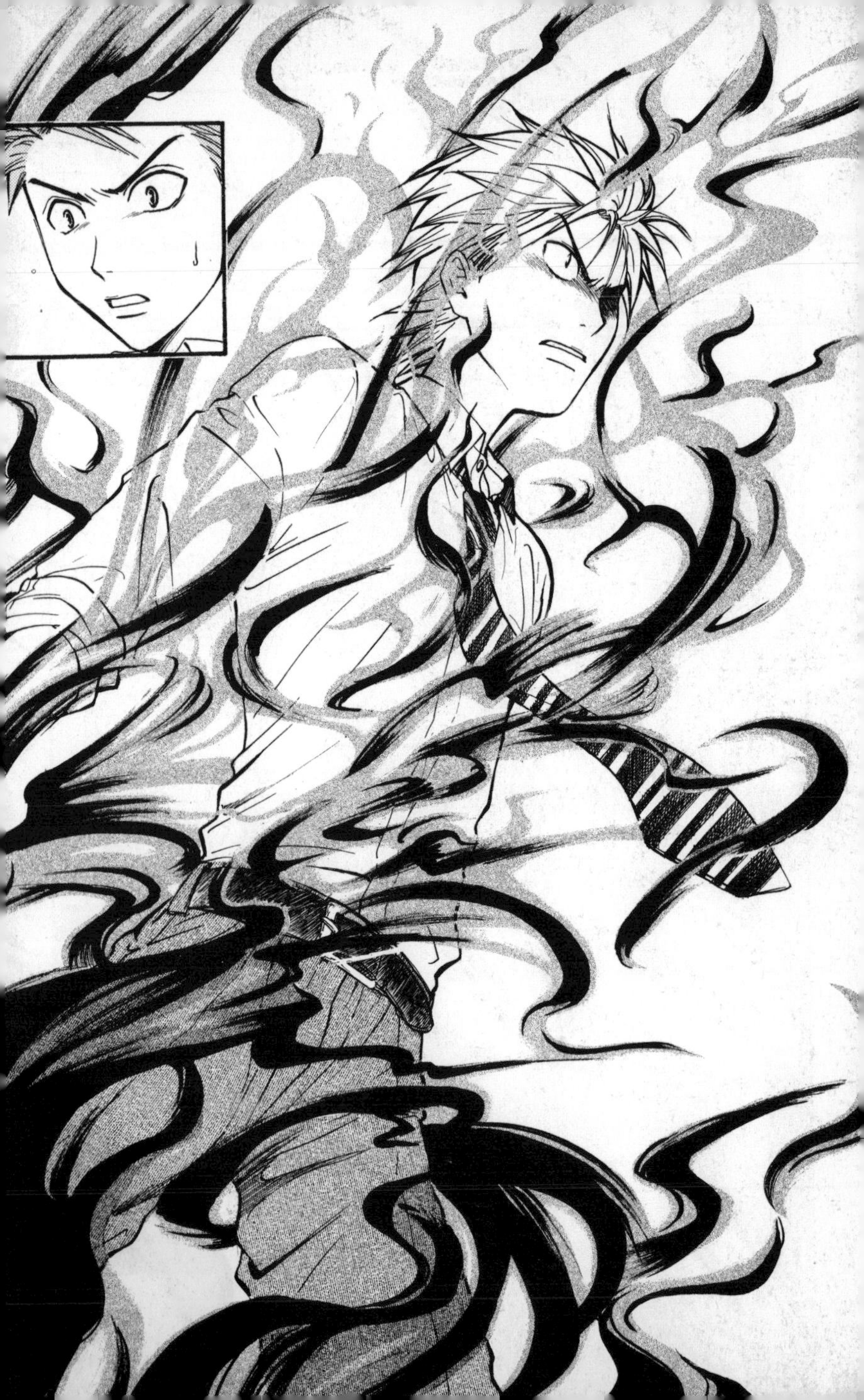

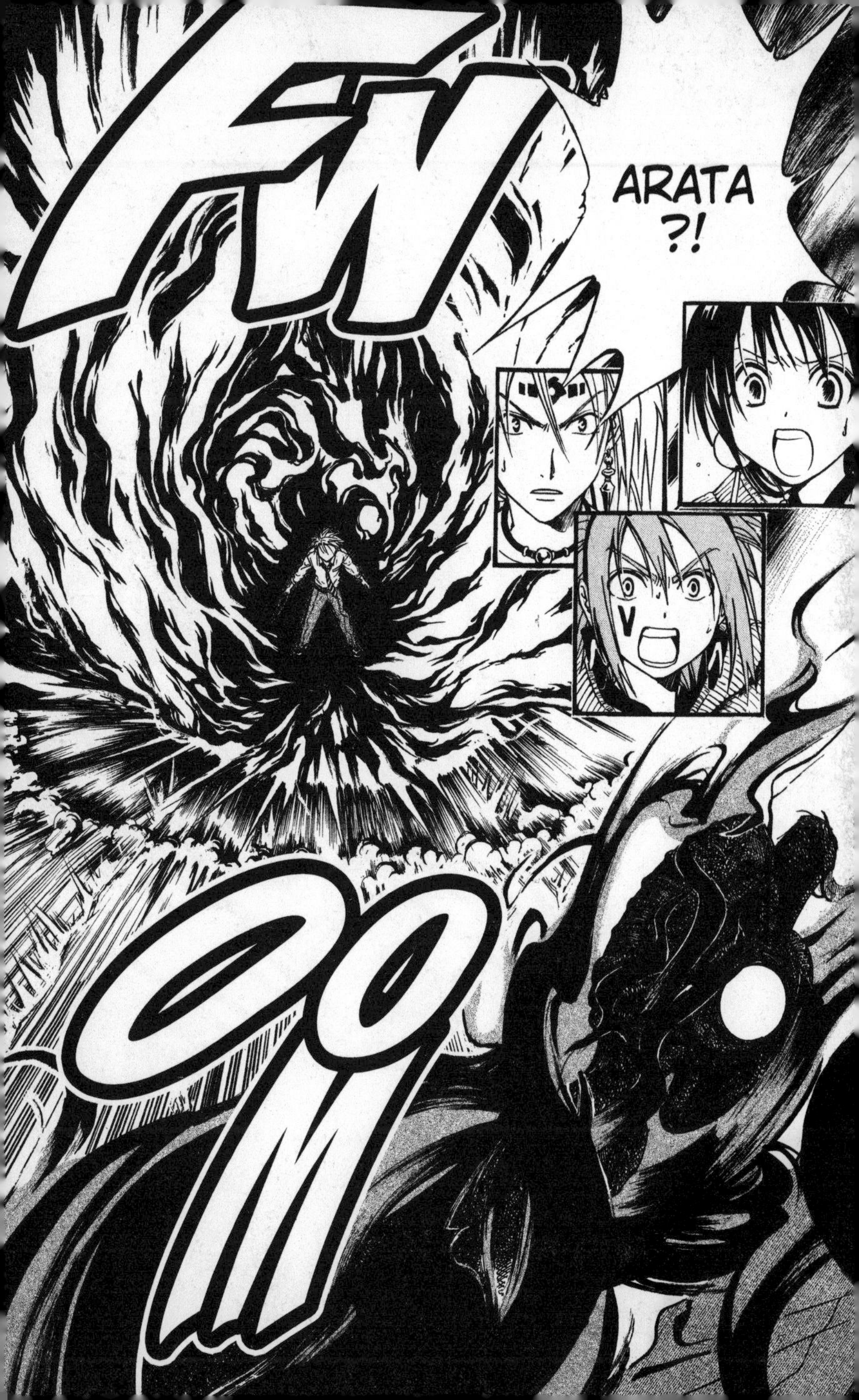
ARATA ?!

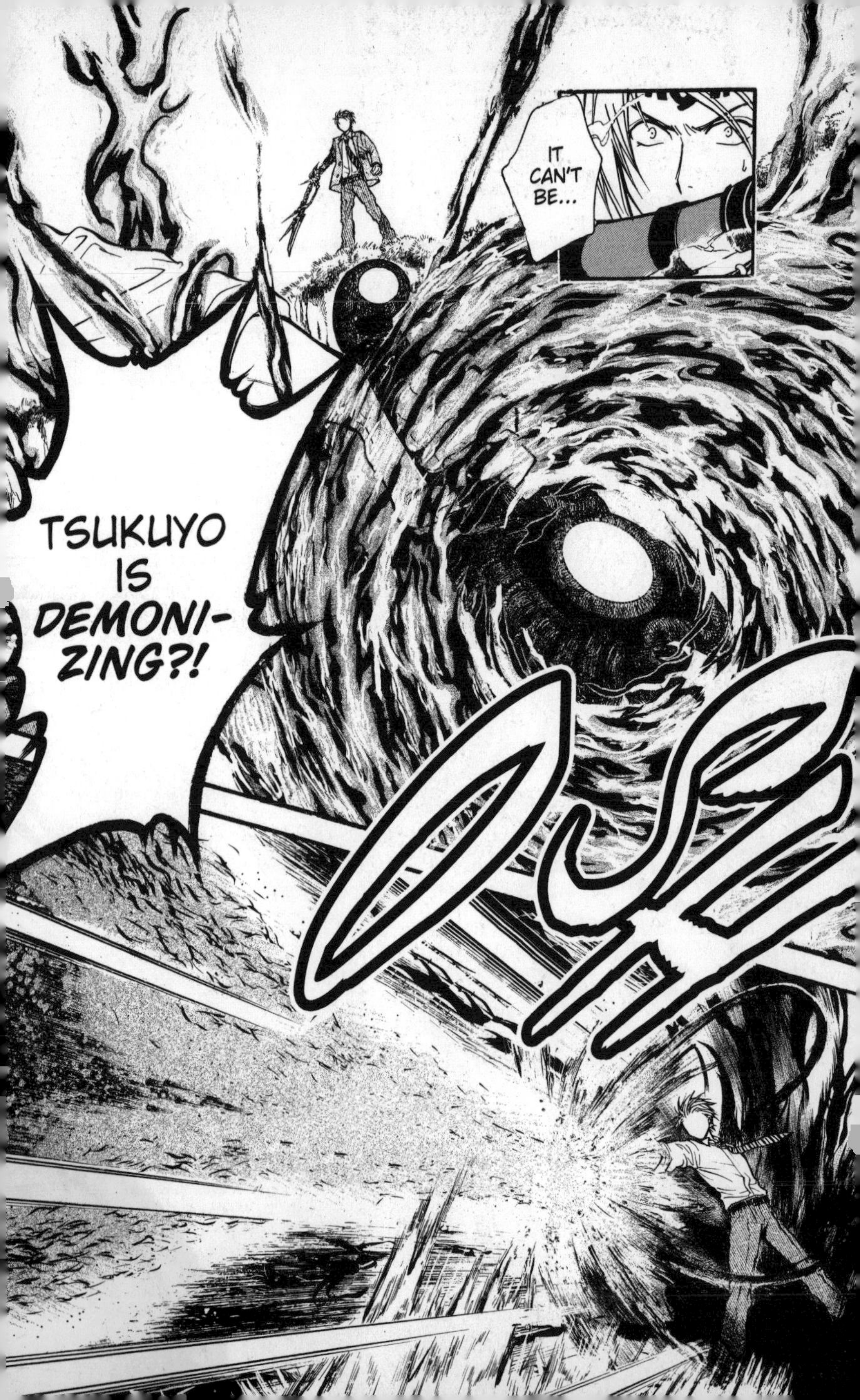
IT CAN'T BE...
TSUKUYO IS DEMONI-ZING?!

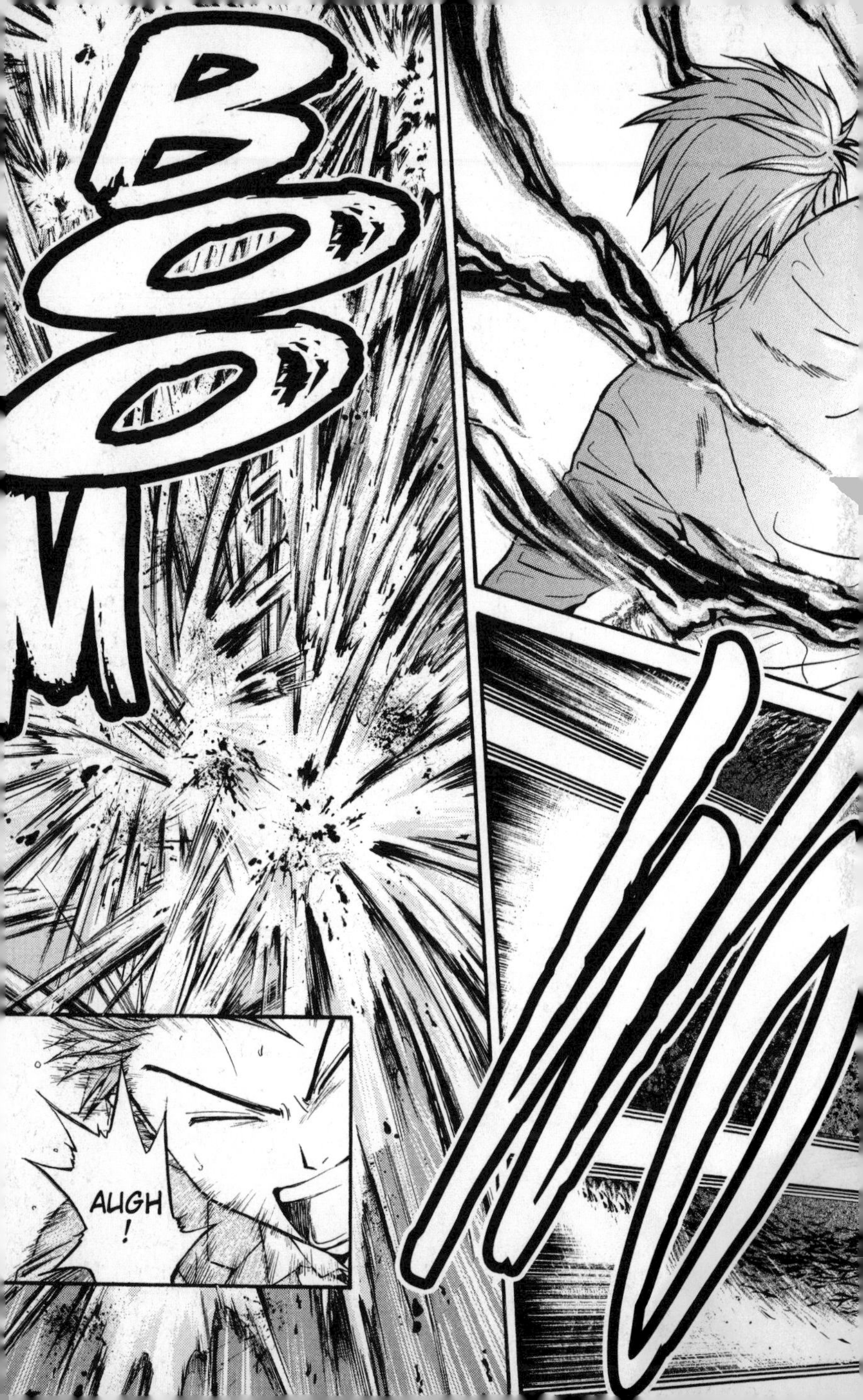
BOOM
AUGH!

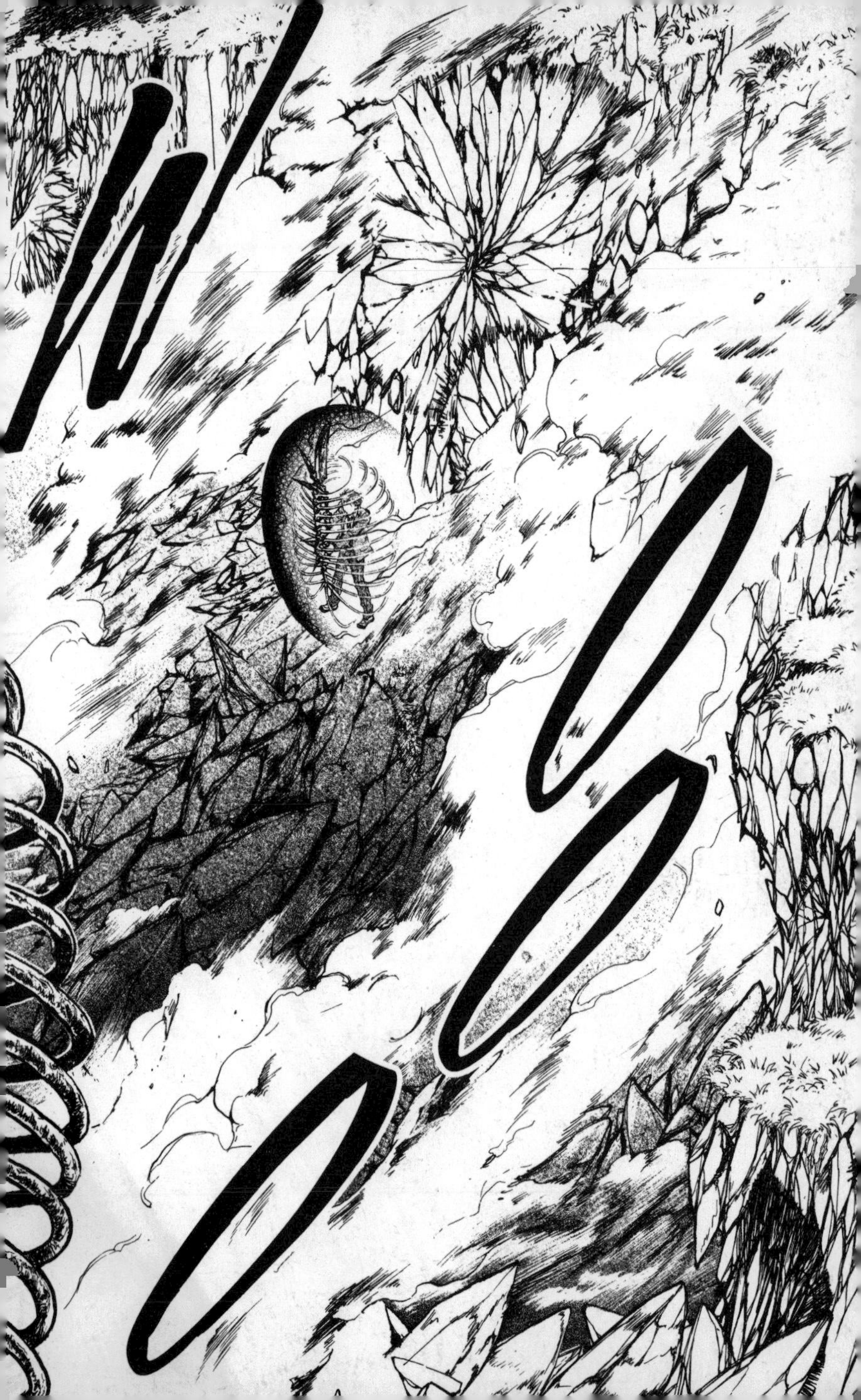

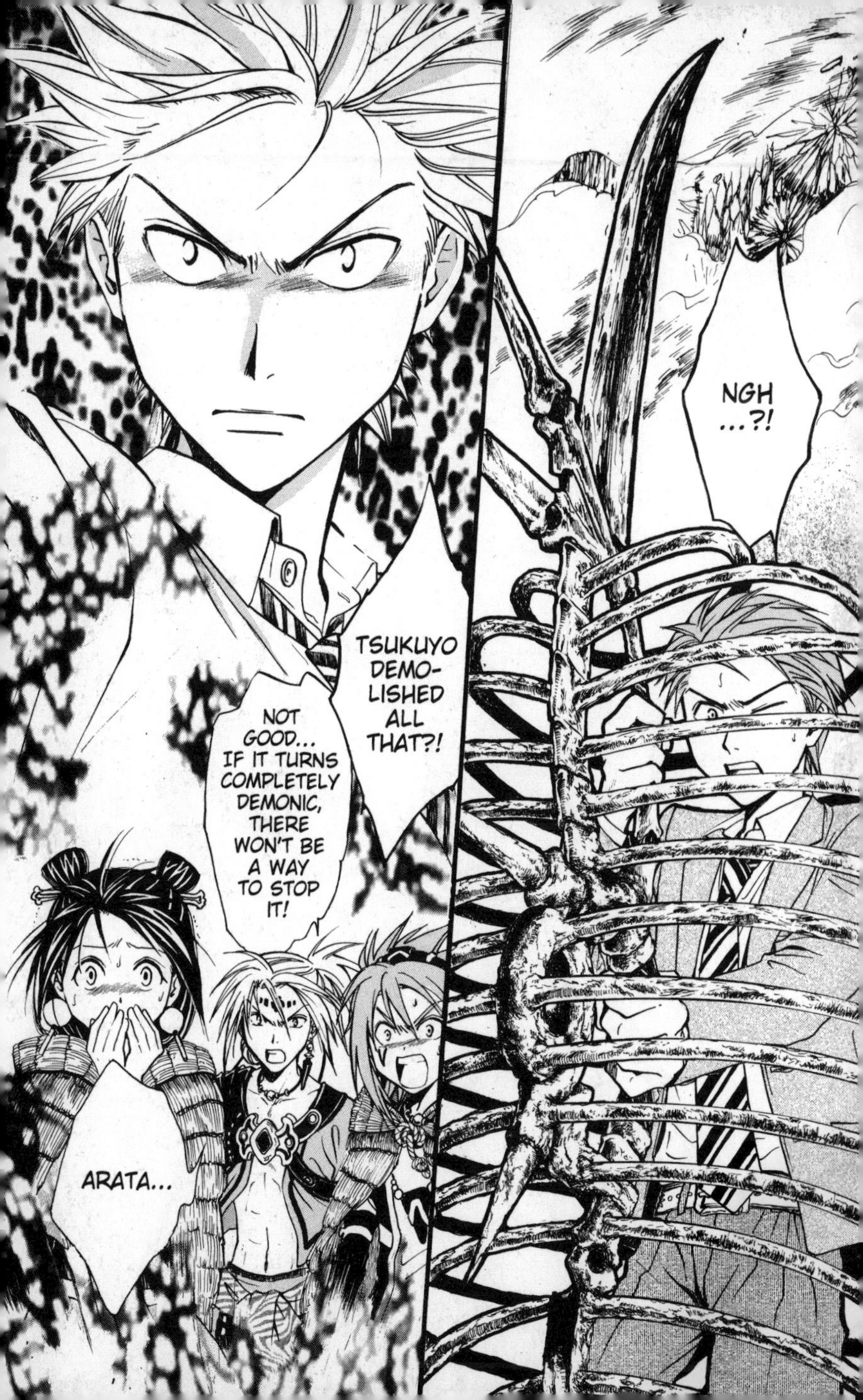
NGH ...?!
TSUKUYO DEMOLISHED ALL THAT?!
NOT GOOD... IF IT TURNS COMPLETELY DEMONIC, THERE WON'T BE A WAY TO STOP IT!
ARATA...

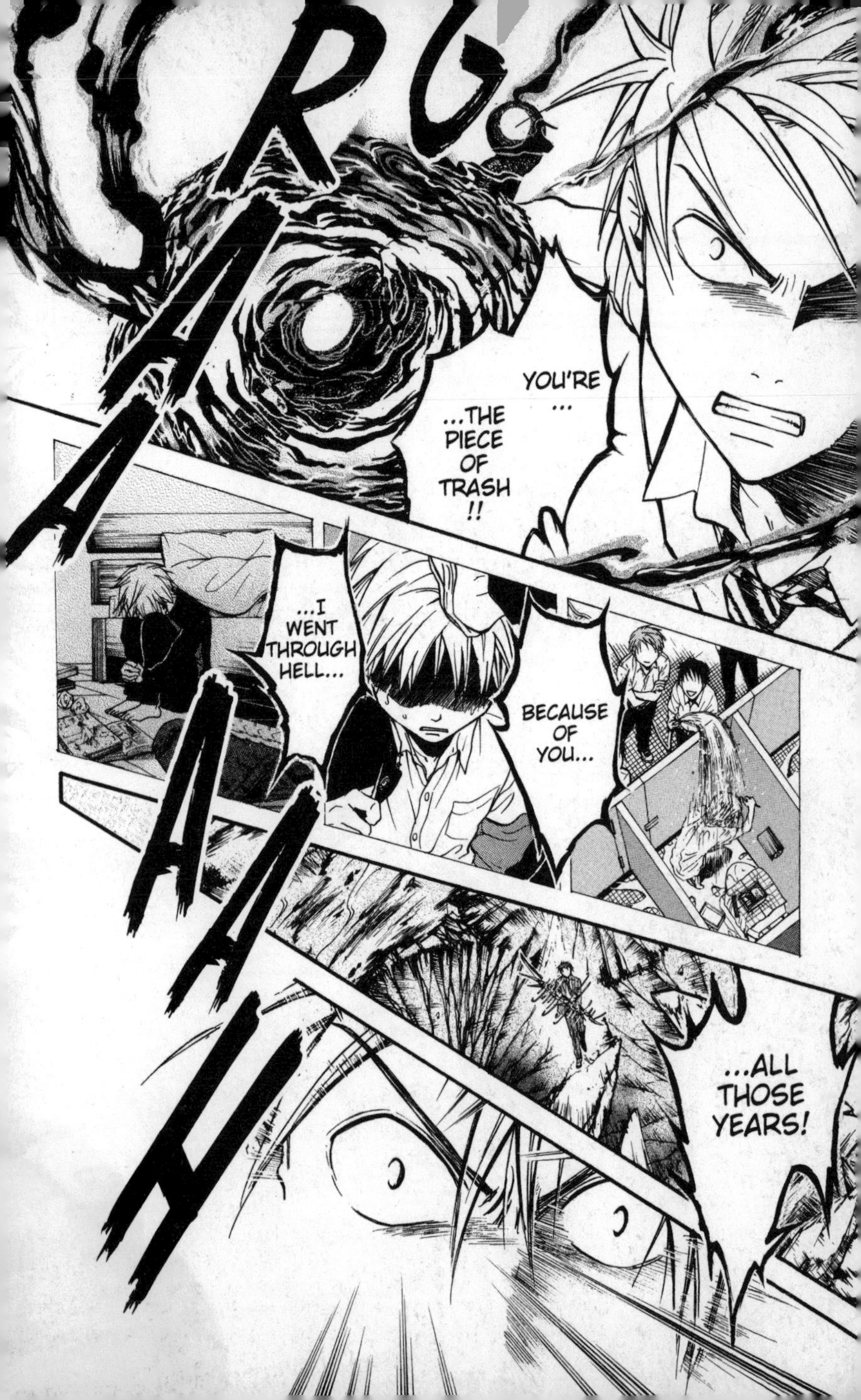
YOU'RE ...
...THE PIECE OF TRASH !!
BECAUSE OF YOU...
...I WENT THROUGH HELL...
...ALL THOSE YEARS!

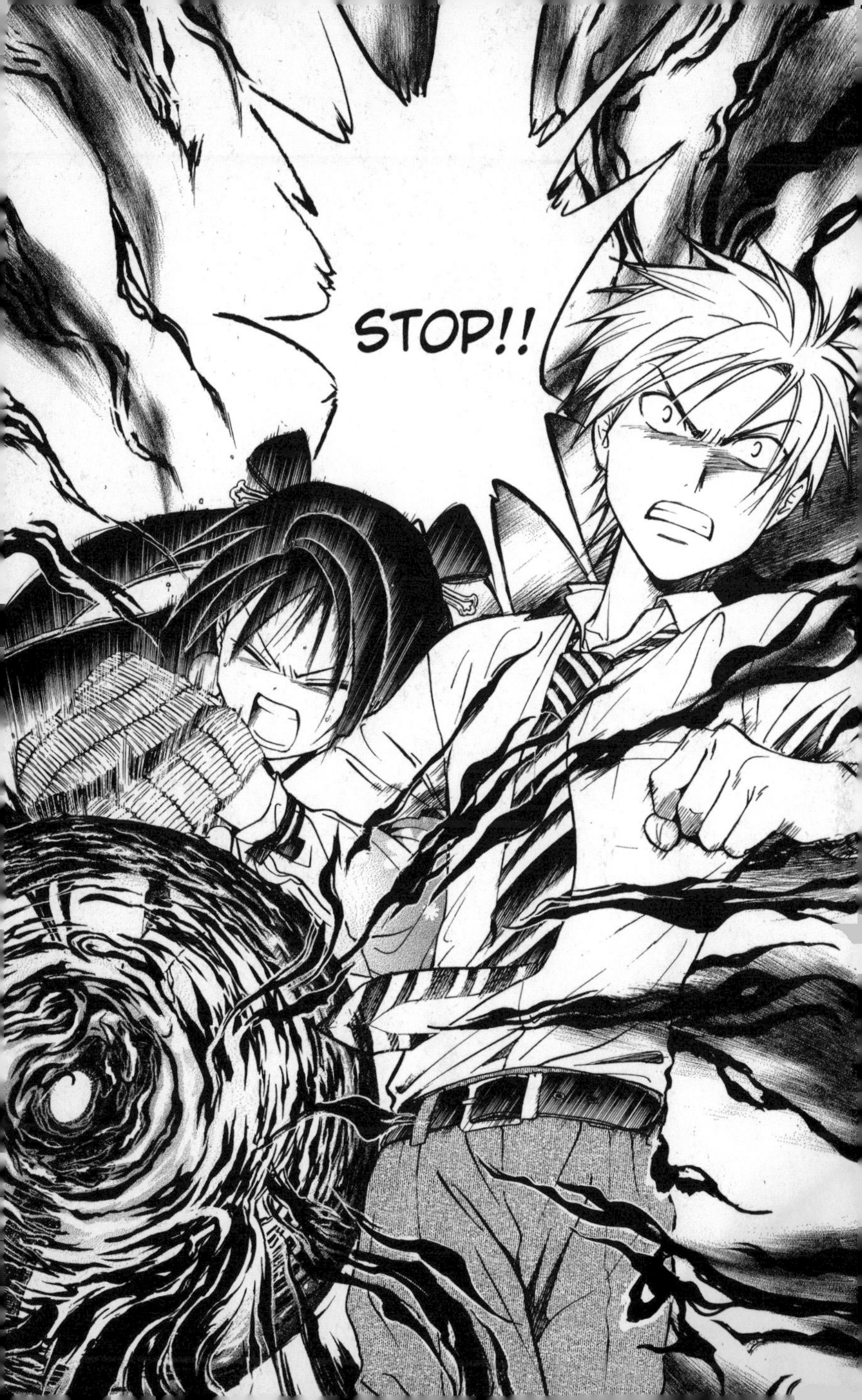
STOP!!

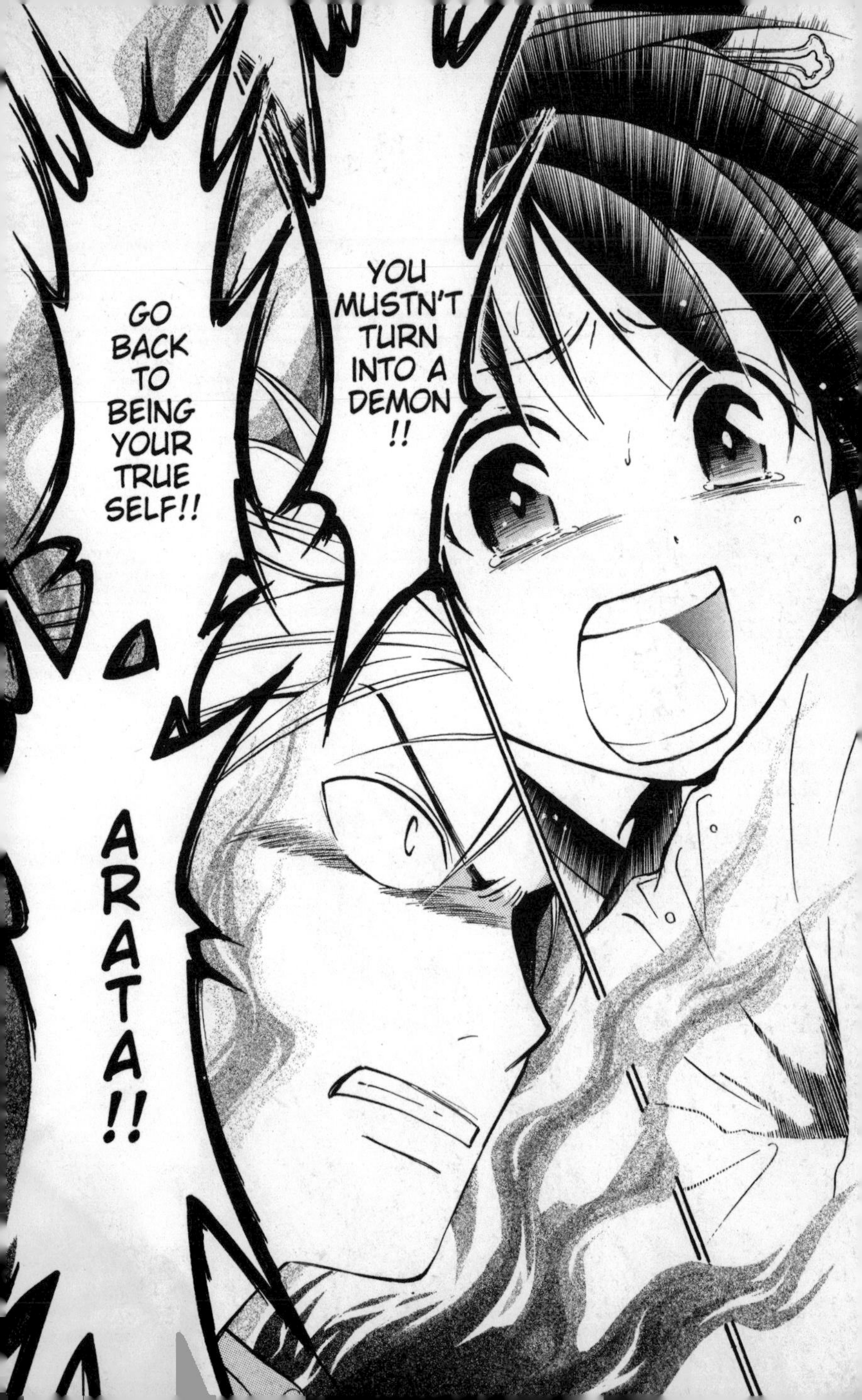
YOU MUSTN'T TURN INTO A DEMON !!
GO BACK TO BEING YOUR TRUE SELF!!
ARATA!!

CHAPTER 49
DEMON

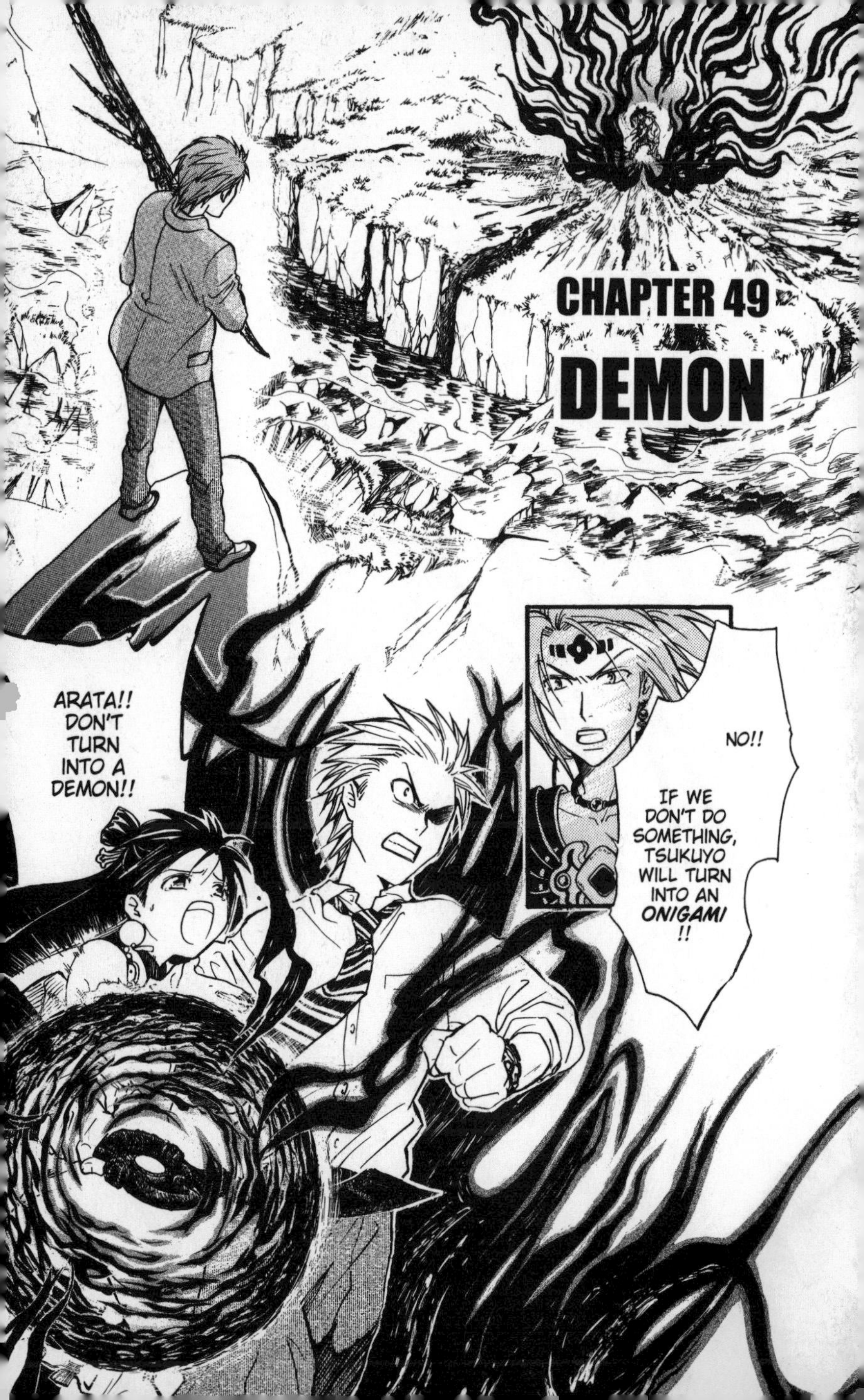
NO!!
IF WE DON'T DO SOMETHING, TSUKUYO WILL TURN INTO AN *ONIGAMI* !!
ARATA!! DON'T TURN INTO A DEMON!!

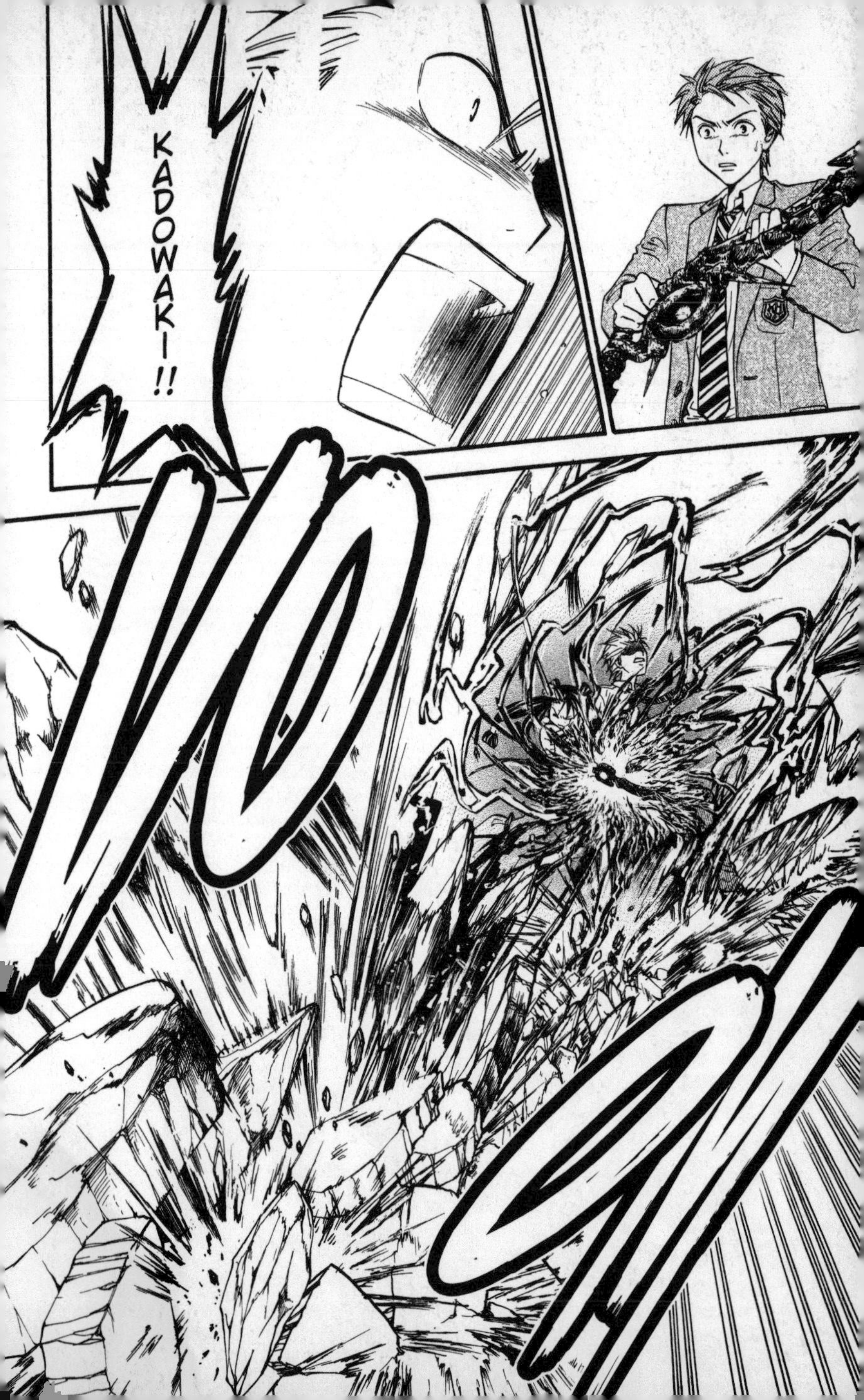
KADOWAKI!!

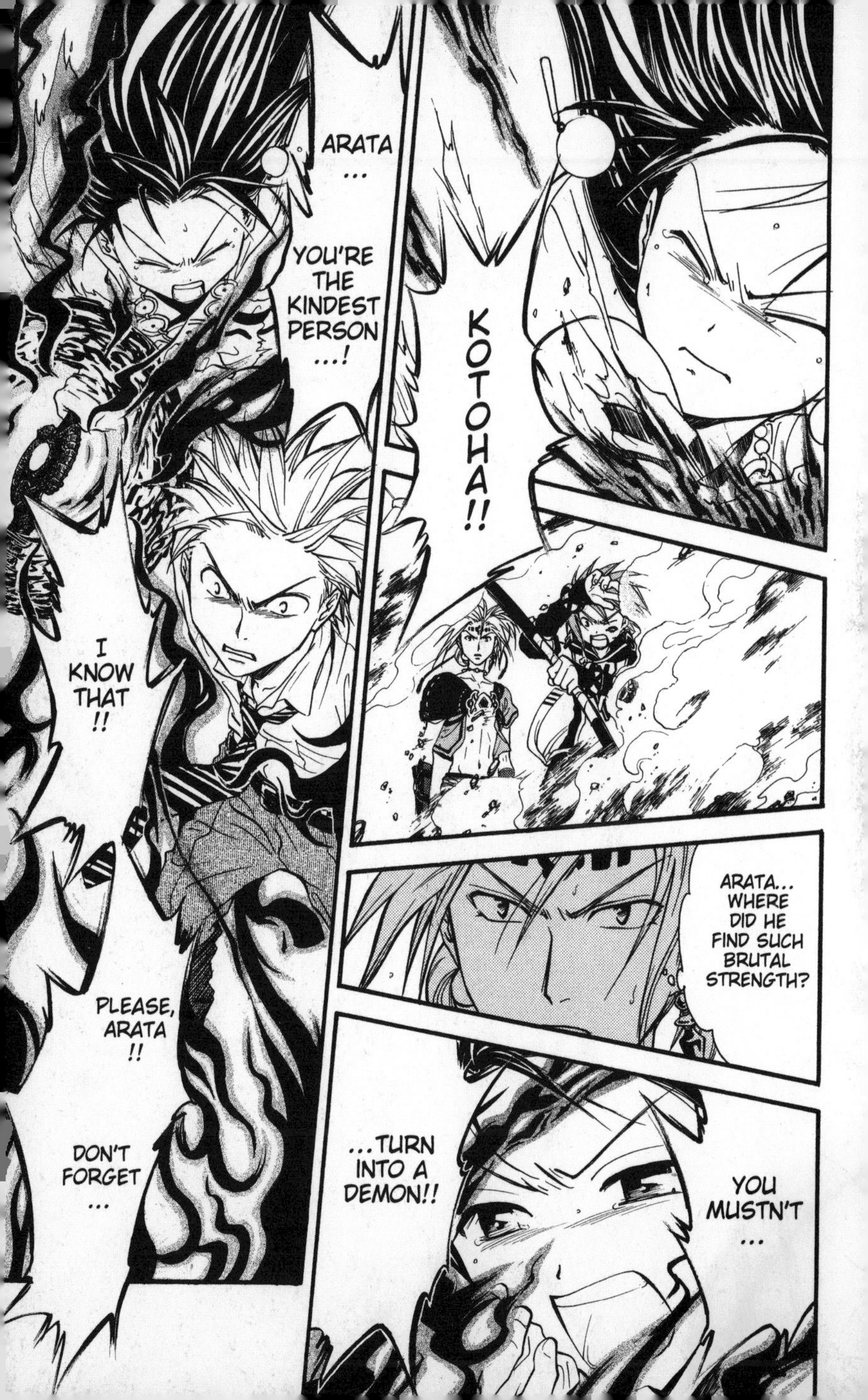
KOTOHA!!
ARATA...
YOU'RE THE KINDEST PERSON...!
I KNOW THAT!!
PLEASE, ARATA!!
DON'T FORGET...
ARATA... WHERE DID HE FIND SUCH BRUTAL STRENGTH?
YOU MUSTN'T...
...TURN INTO A DEMON!!

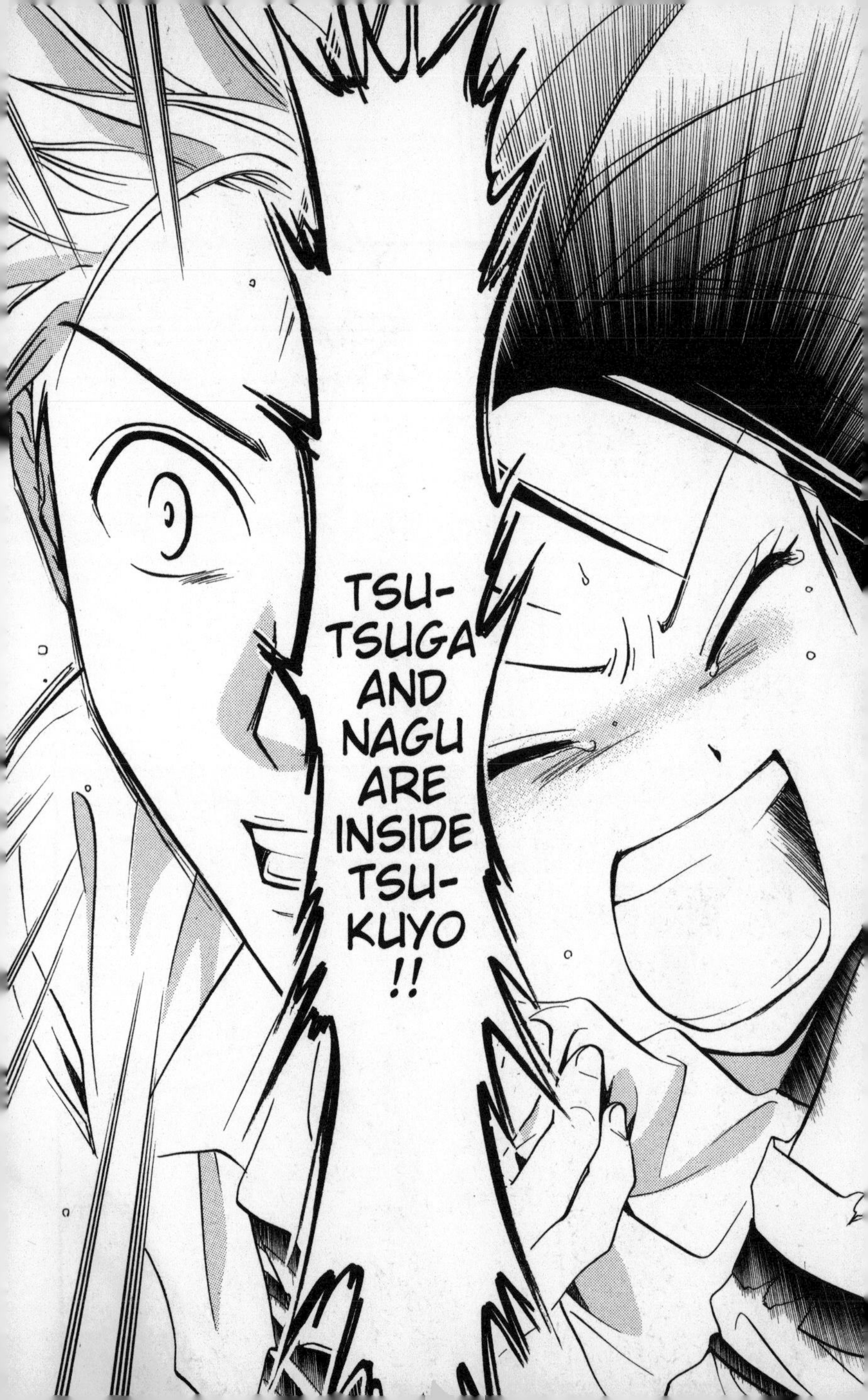
TSU-TSUGA AND NAGU ARE INSIDE TSU-KUYO!!

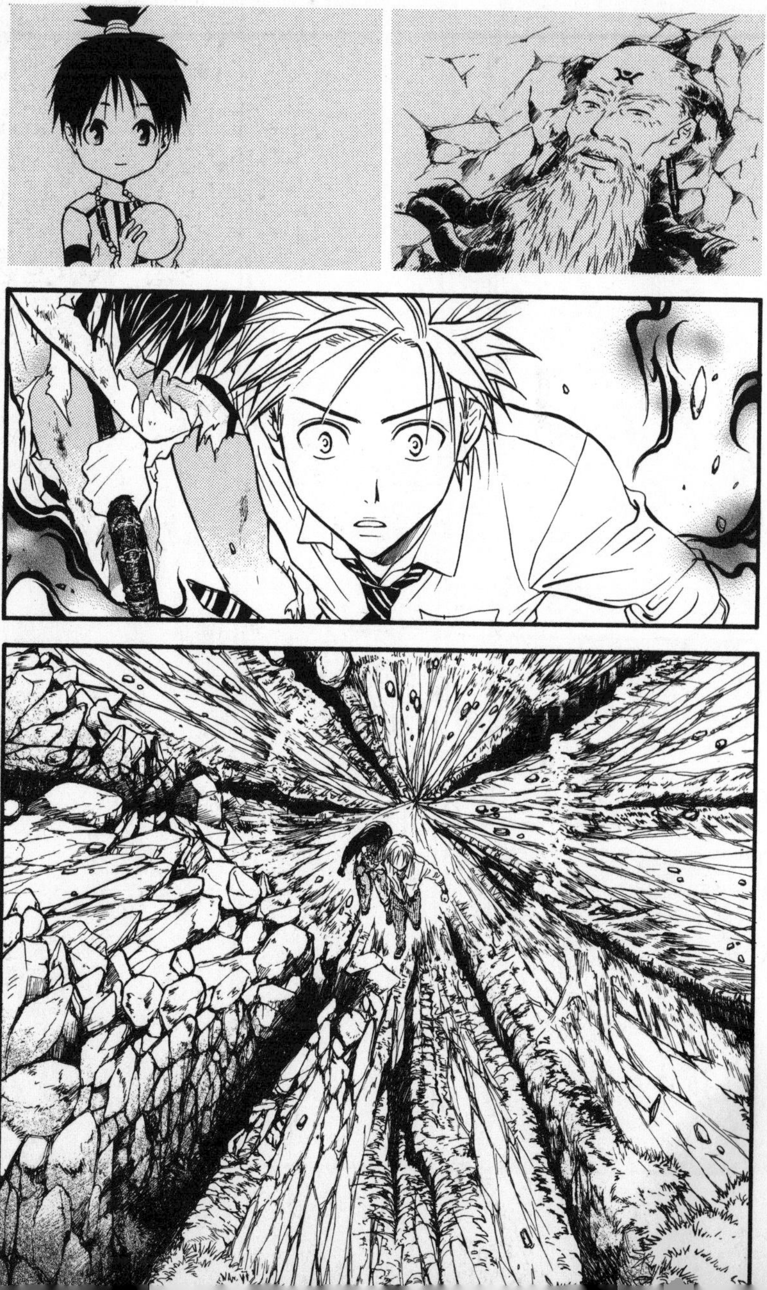

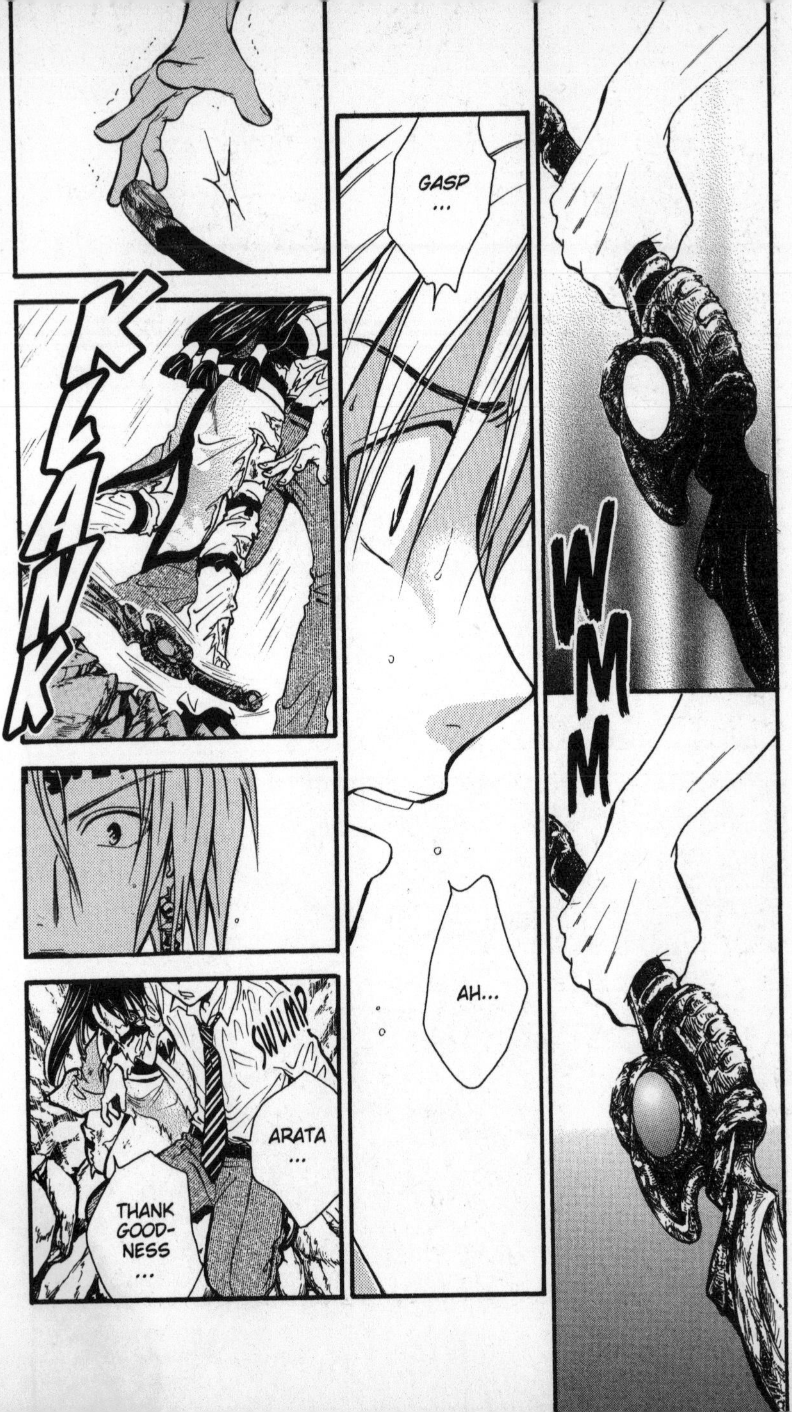
WMMM
GASP ...
AH...
KLANK
SWUMP
ARATA ...
THANK GOODNESS ...

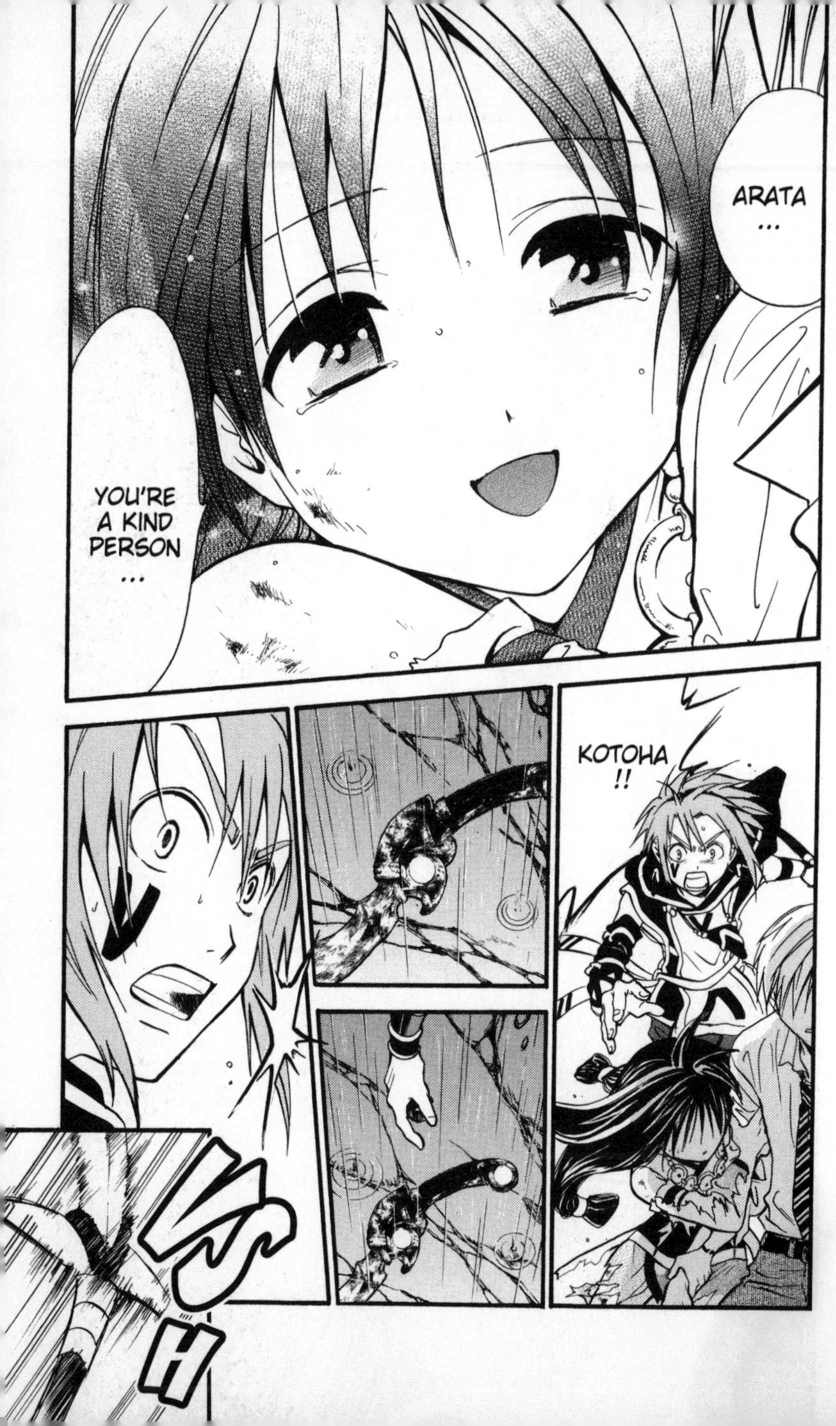
ARATA ...
YOU'RE A KIND PERSON ...
KOTOHA !!

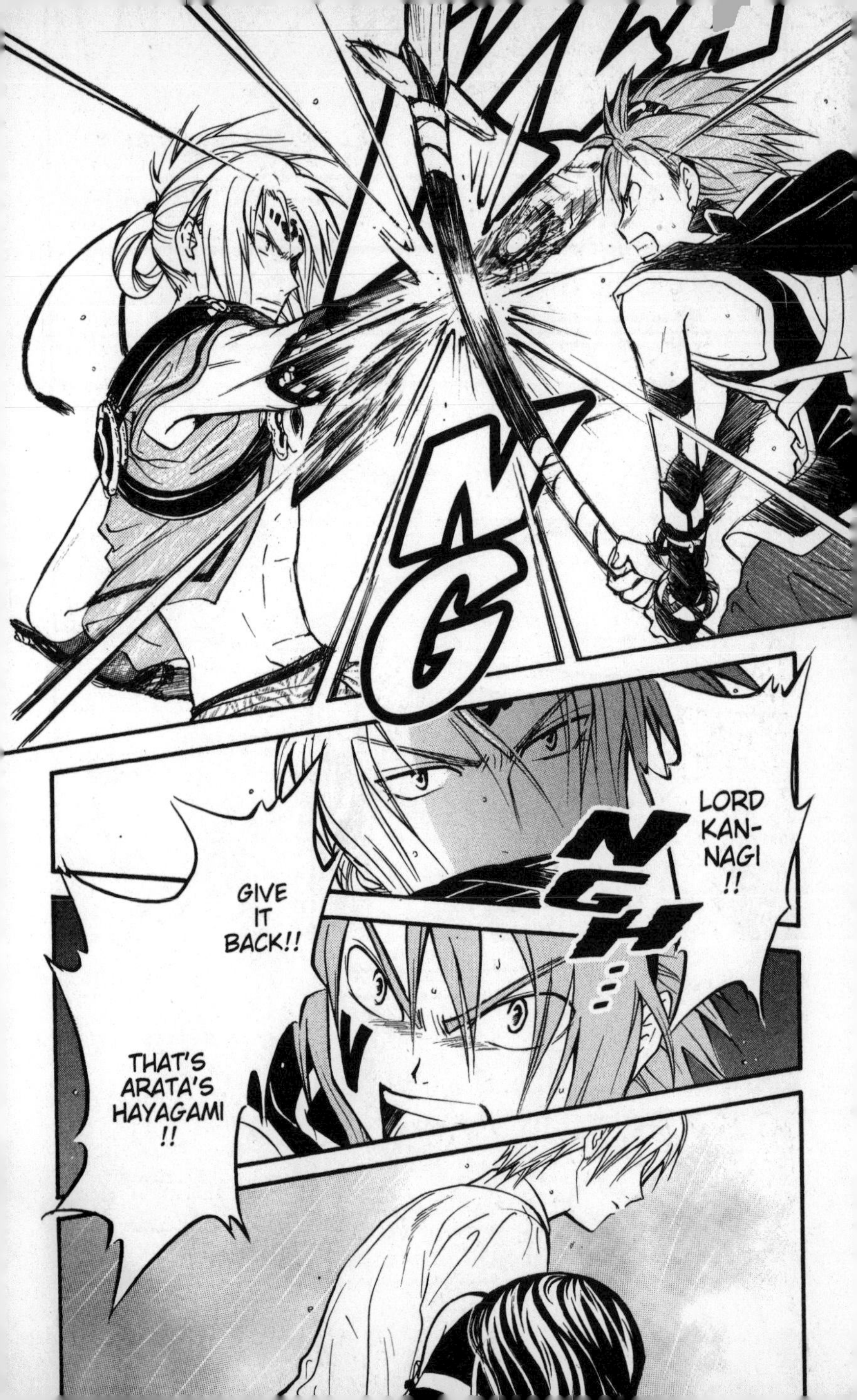
NG
LORD KAN-NAGI!!
NGH...
GIVE IT BACK!!
THAT'S ARATA'S HAYAGAMI!!

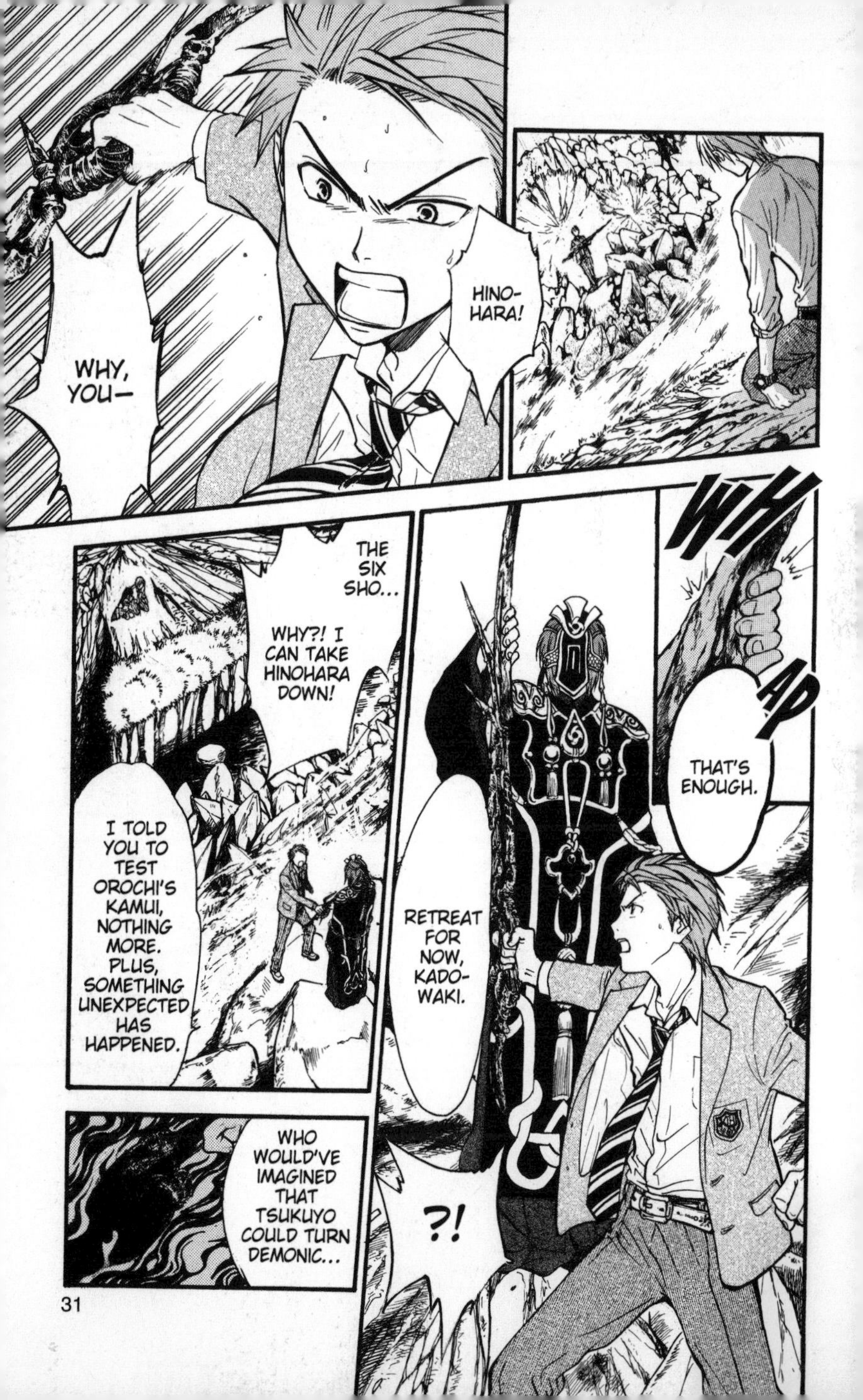
HINO-HARA!
WHY, YOU—
WHAP
THAT'S ENOUGH.
?!
RETREAT FOR NOW, KADO-WAKI.
THE SIX SHO...
WHY?! I CAN TAKE HINOHARA DOWN!
I TOLD YOU TO TEST OROCHI'S KAMUI, NOTHING MORE. PLUS, SOMETHING UNEXPECTED HAS HAPPENED.
WHO WOULD'VE IMAGINED THAT TSUKUYO COULD TURN DEMONIC...

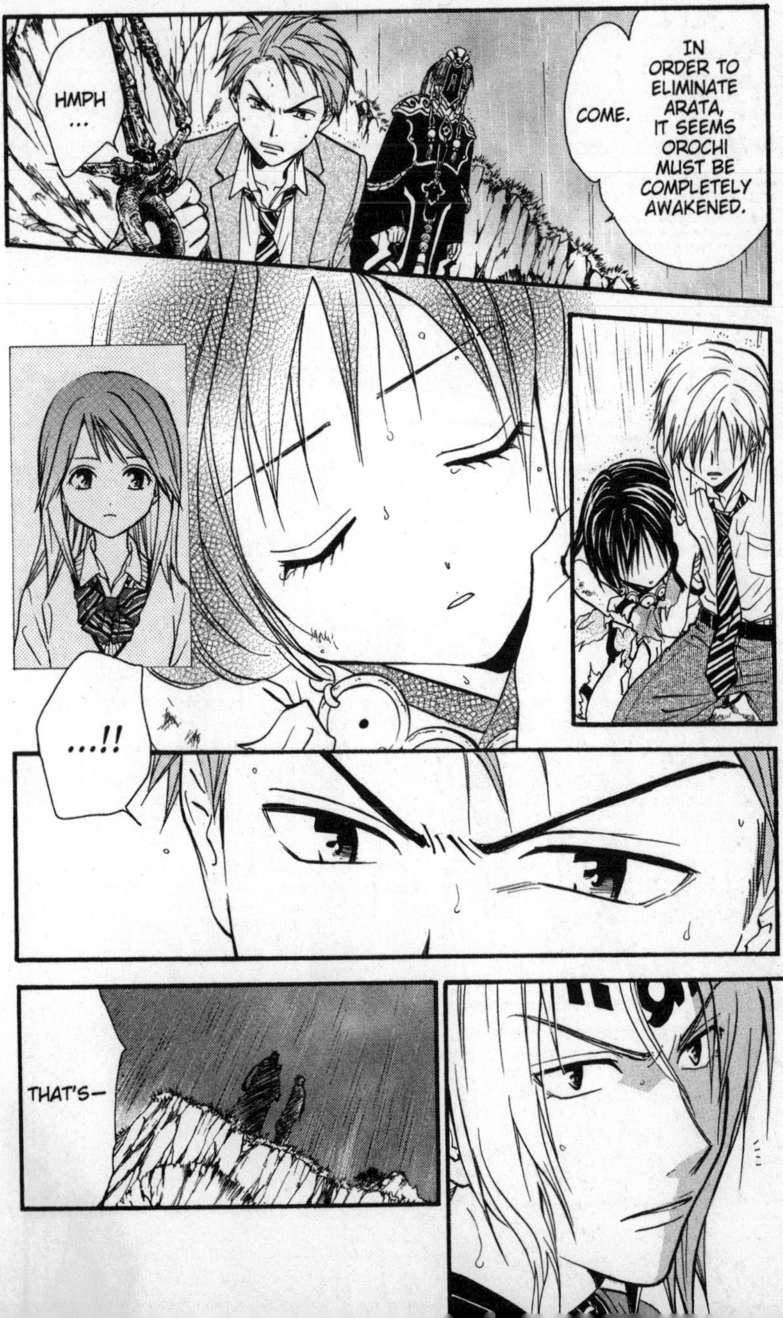
IN ORDER TO ELIMINATE ARATA, IT SEEMS OROCHI MUST BE COMPLETELY AWAKENED.
COME.
HMPH ...
...!!
THAT'S—

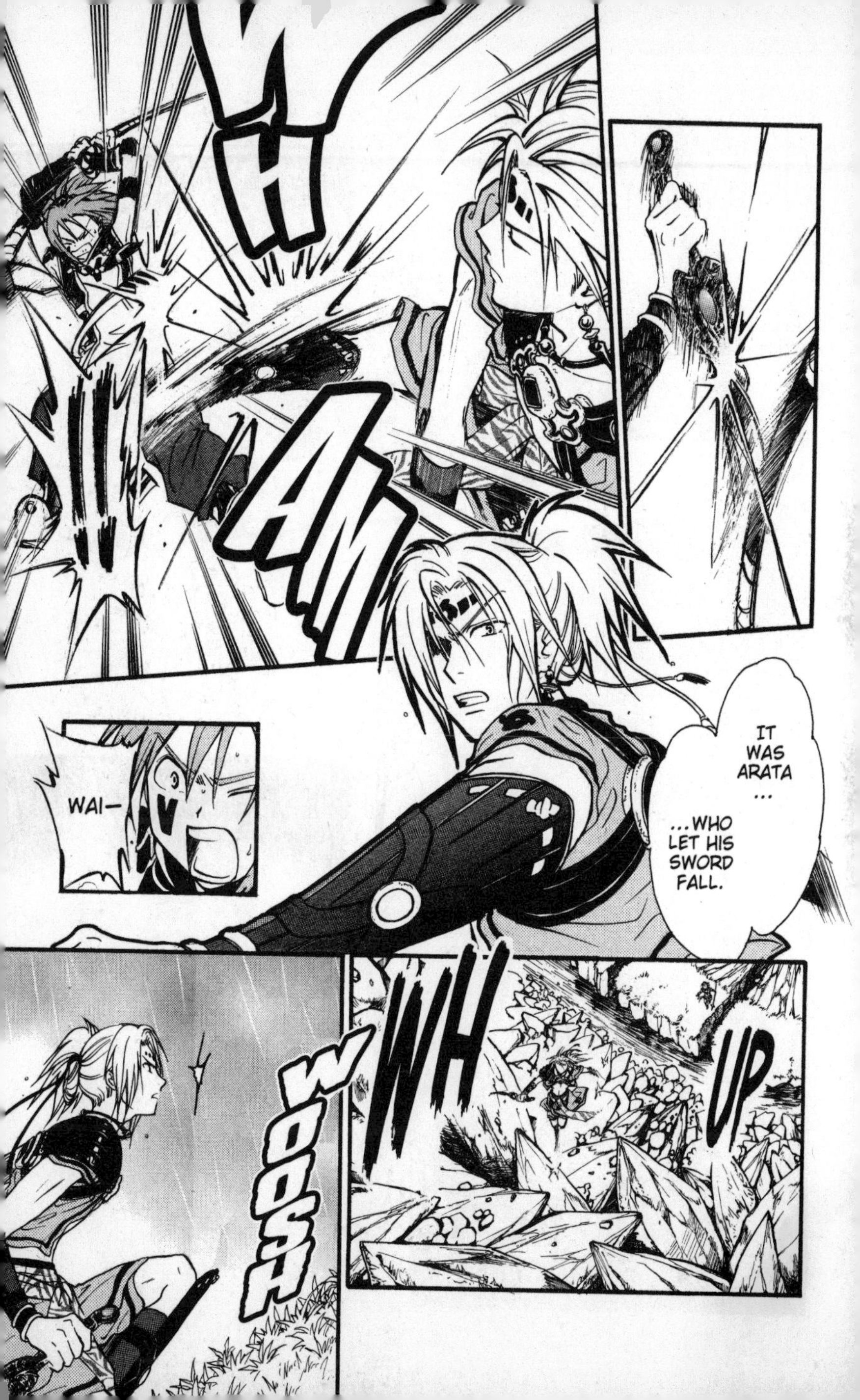
H
AM
IT WAS ARATA ...
...WHO LET HIS SWORD FALL.
WAI—
WH
UP
WOOSH

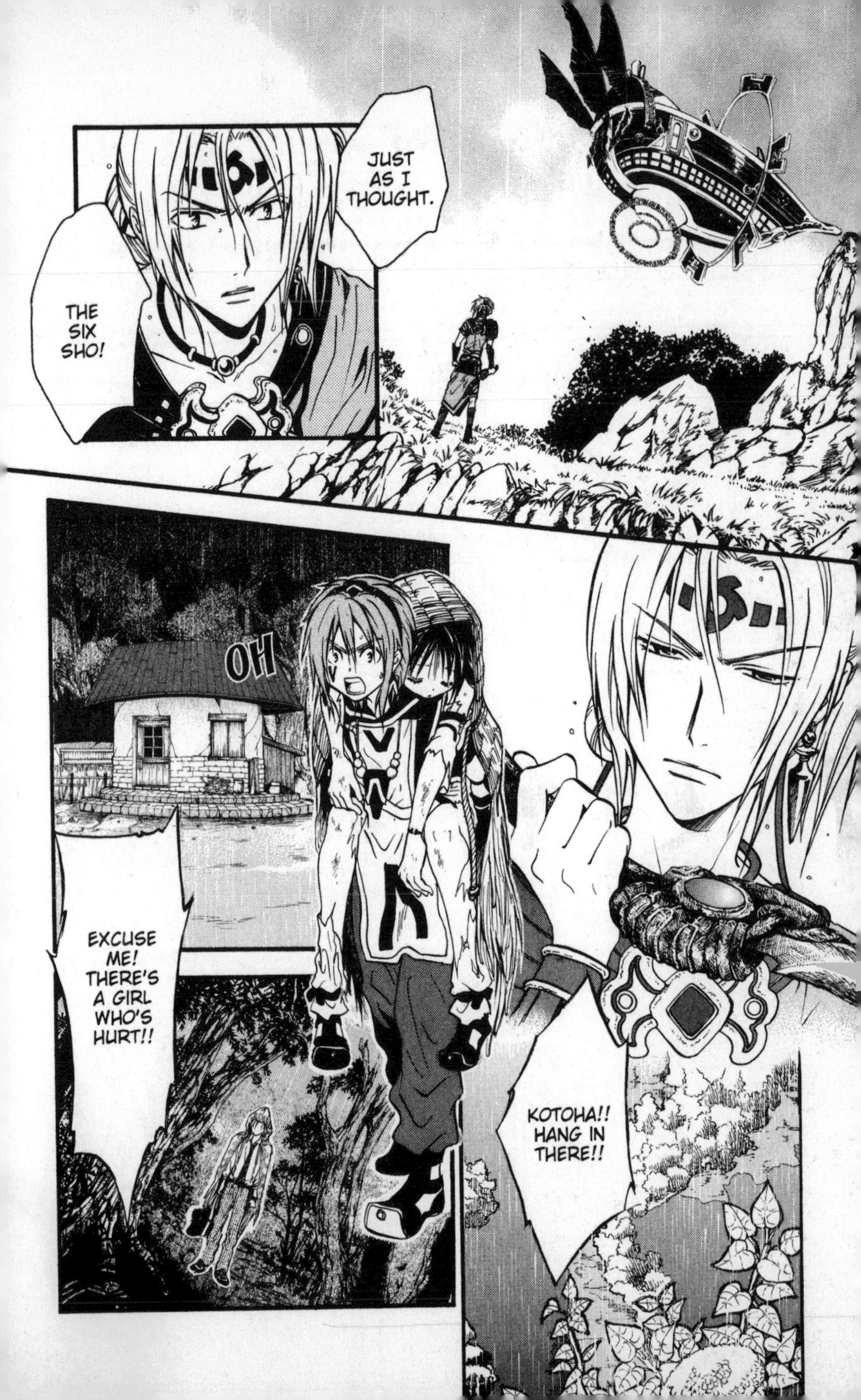
JUST AS I THOUGHT.
THE SIX SHO!
KOTOHA!! HANG IN THERE!!
OH
EXCUSE ME! THERE'S A GIRL WHO'S HURT!!

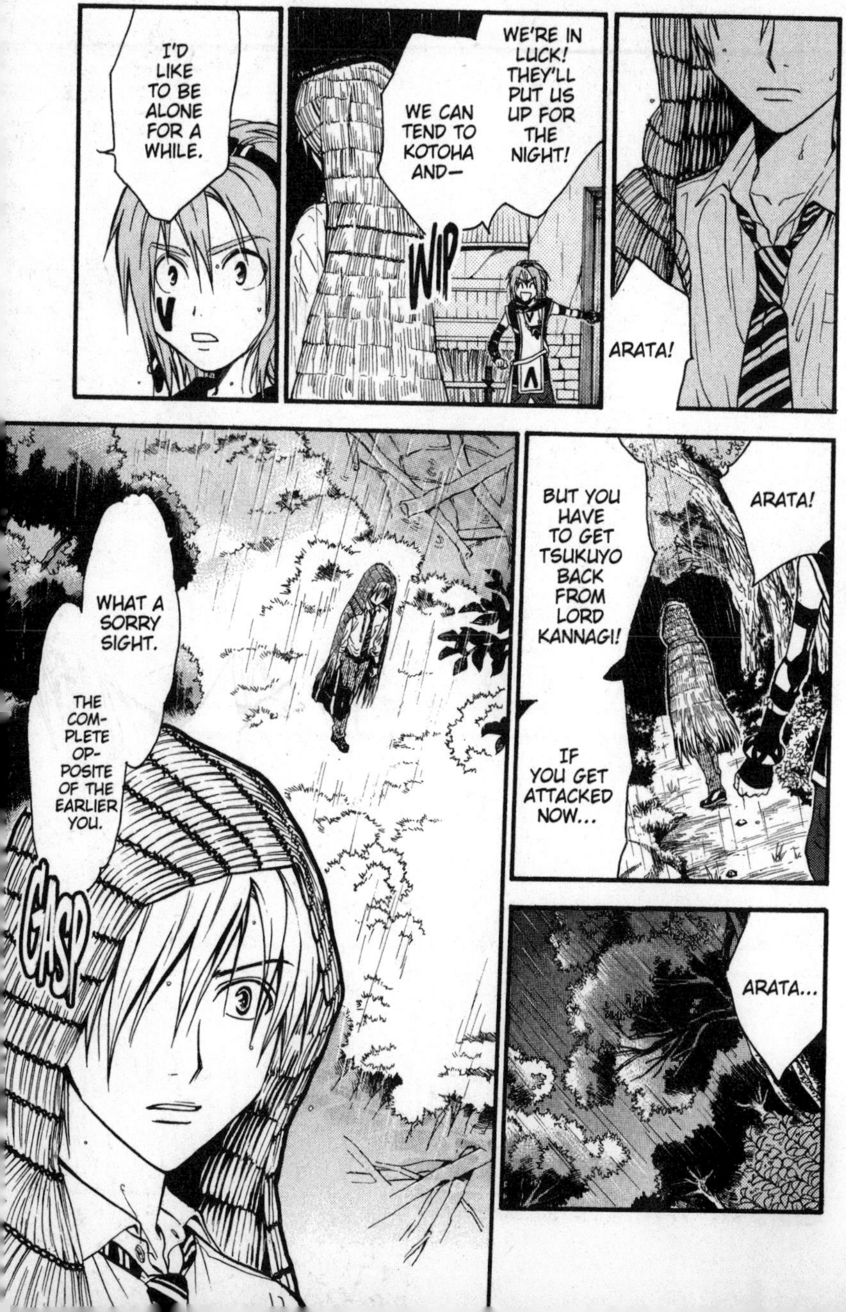
ARATA!
WE'RE IN LUCK! THEY'LL PUT US UP FOR THE NIGHT!
WE CAN TEND TO KOTOHA AND—
WIP
I'D LIKE TO BE ALONE FOR A WHILE.
ARATA!
BUT YOU HAVE TO GET TSUKUYO BACK FROM LORD KANNAGI!
IF YOU GET ATTACKED NOW...
ARATA...
WHAT A SORRY SIGHT.
THE COMPLETE OPPOSITE OF THE EARLIER YOU.
GASP

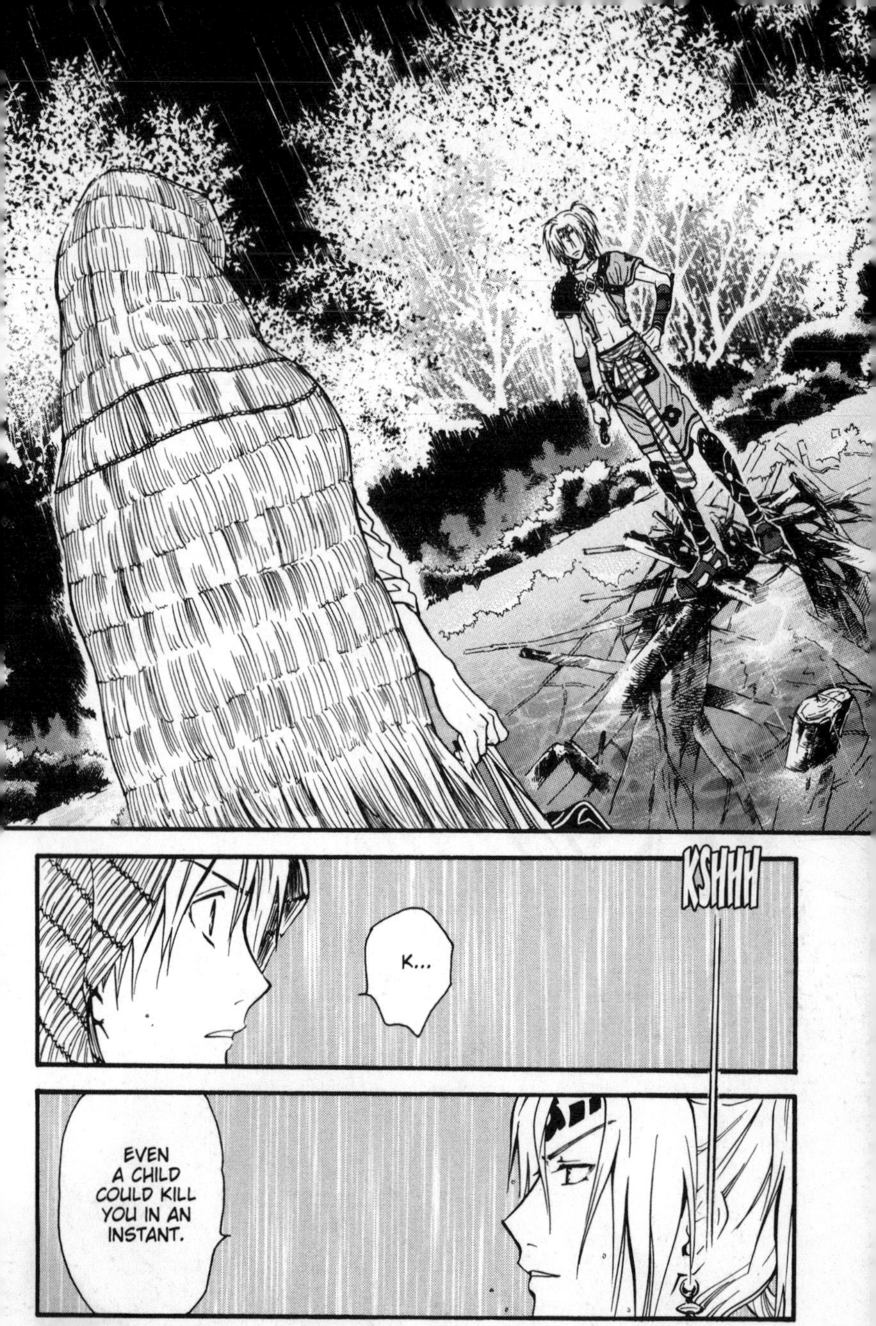
KSHHH
K...
EVEN A CHILD COULD KILL YOU IN AN INSTANT.

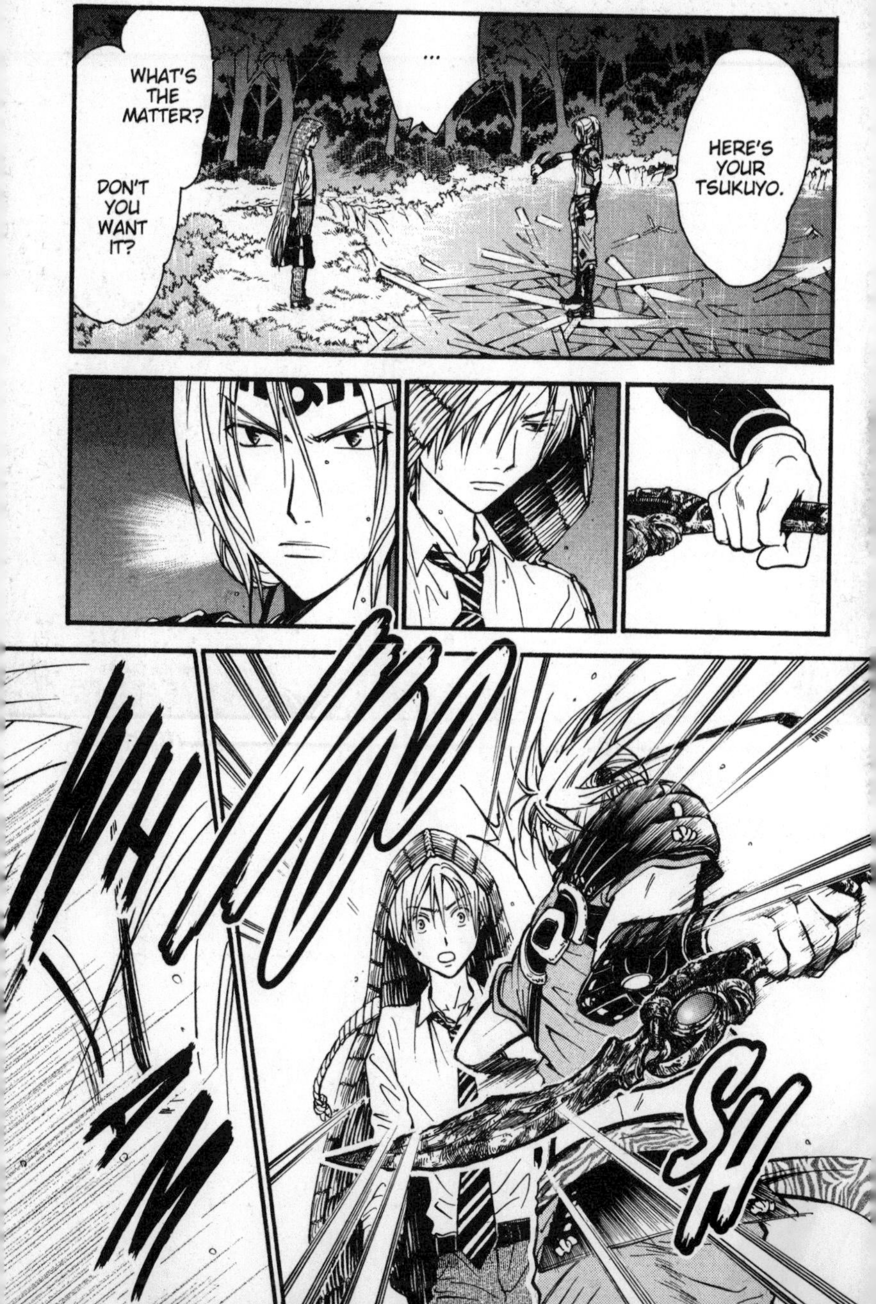
HERE'S YOUR TSUKUYO.
...
WHAT'S THE MATTER?
DON'T YOU WANT IT?
SH

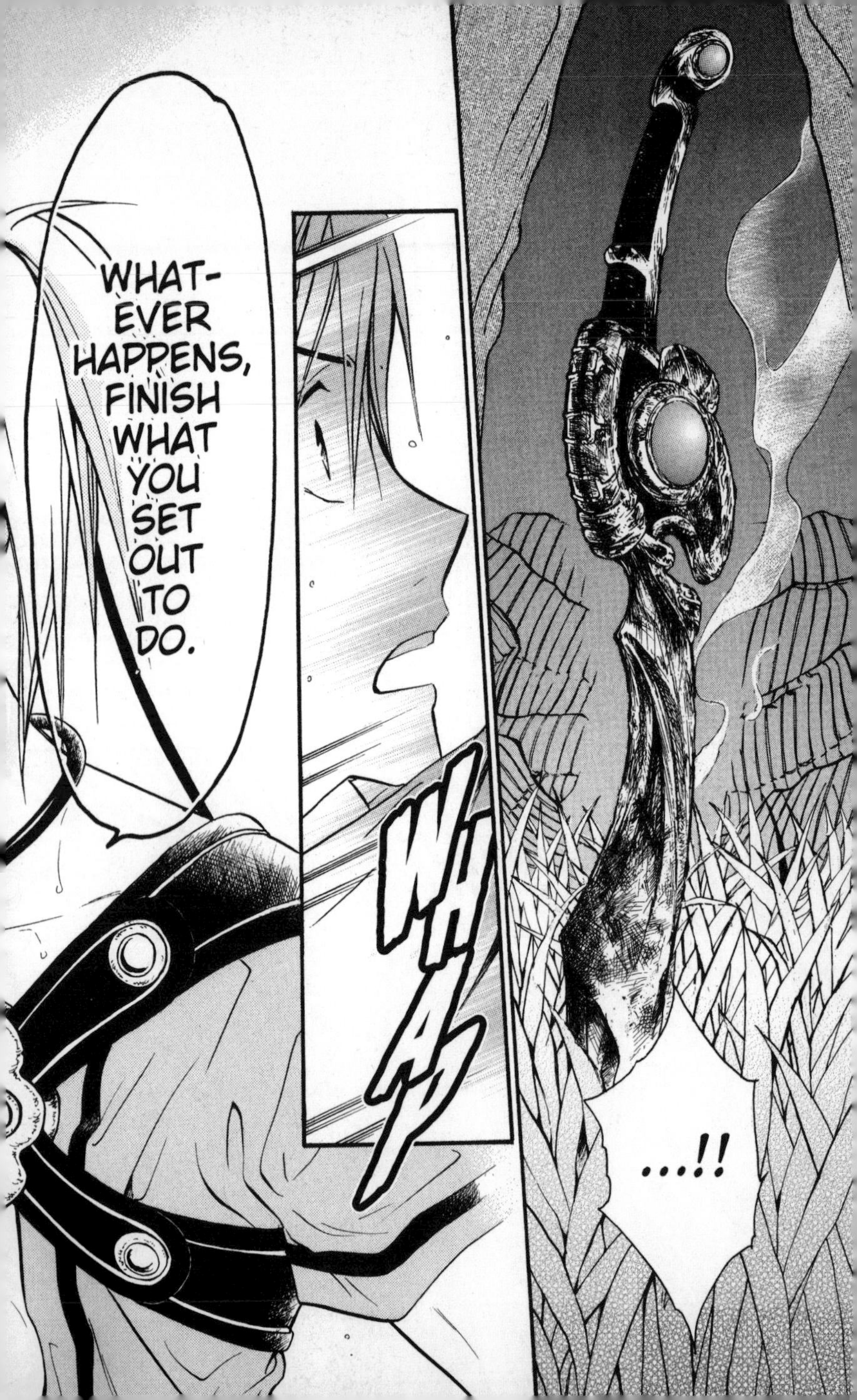
...!!
WHAP
WHATEVER HAPPENS, FINISH WHAT YOU SET OUT TO DO.

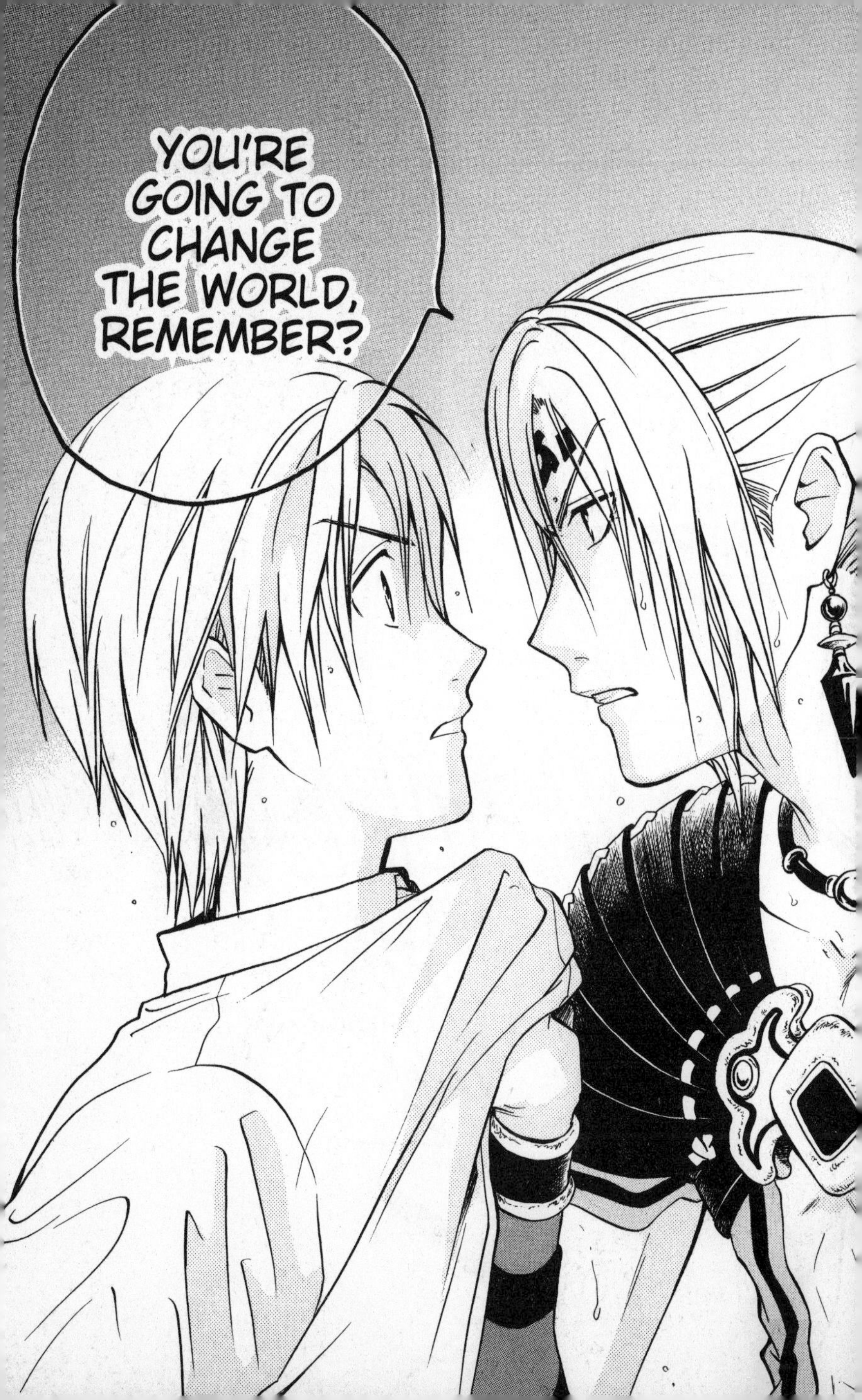
YOU'RE GOING TO CHANGE THE WORLD, REMEMBER?

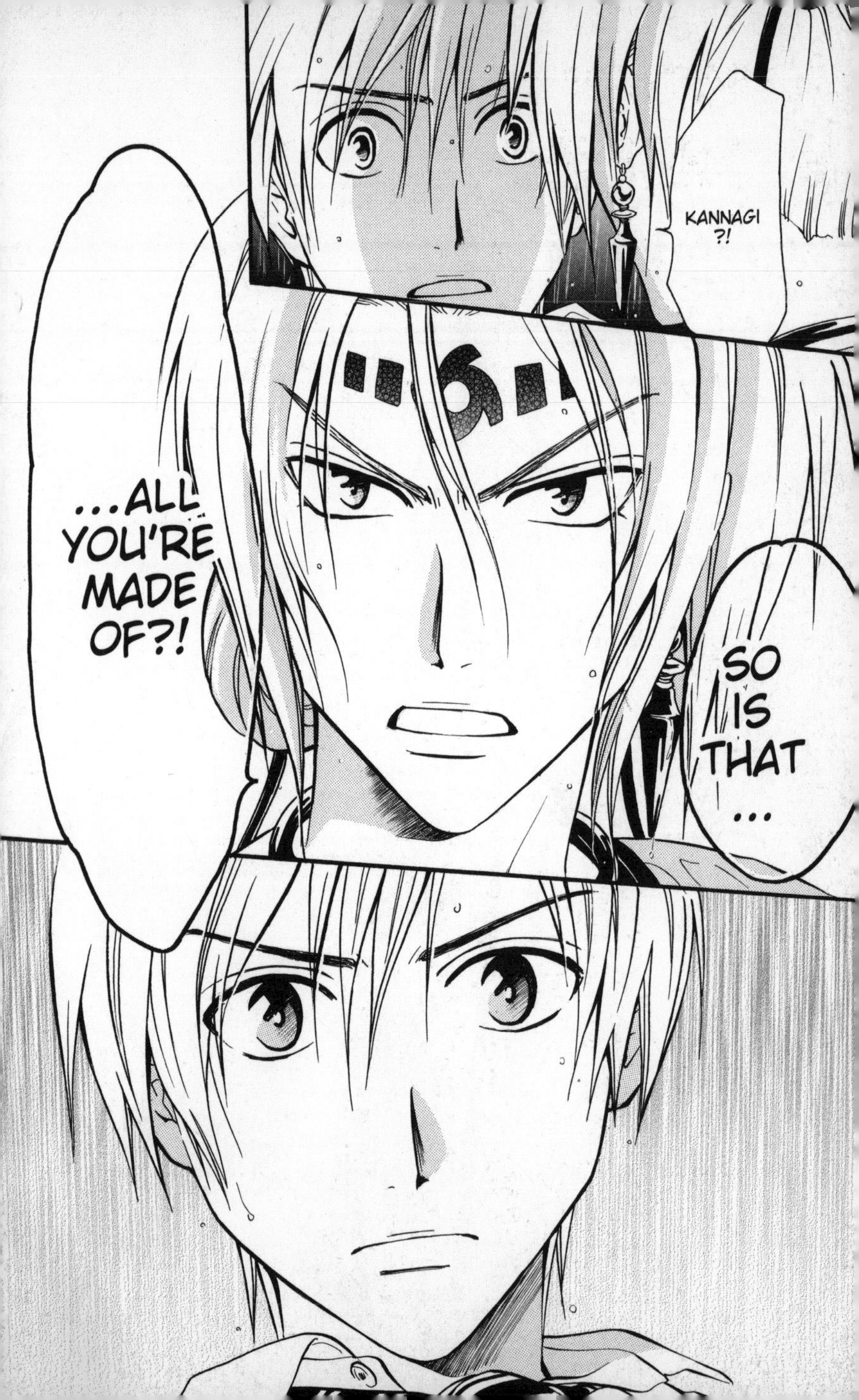
KANNAGI ?!
SO IS THAT ...
...ALL YOU'RE MADE OF?!

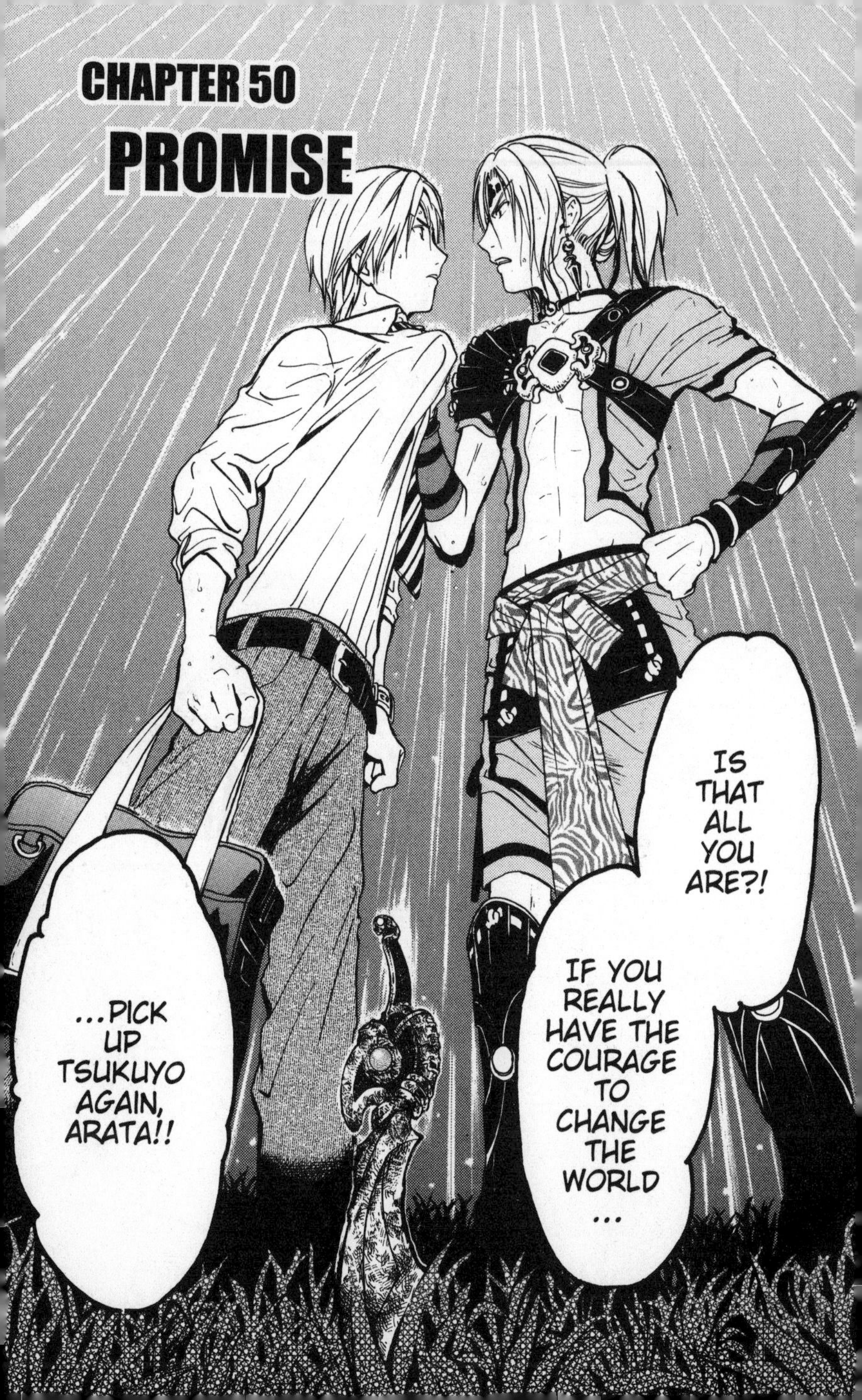
CHAPTER 50
PROMISE
IS THAT ALL YOU ARE?!
IF YOU REALLY HAVE THE COURAGE TO CHANGE THE WORLD ...
...PICK UP TSUKUYO AGAIN, ARATA!!

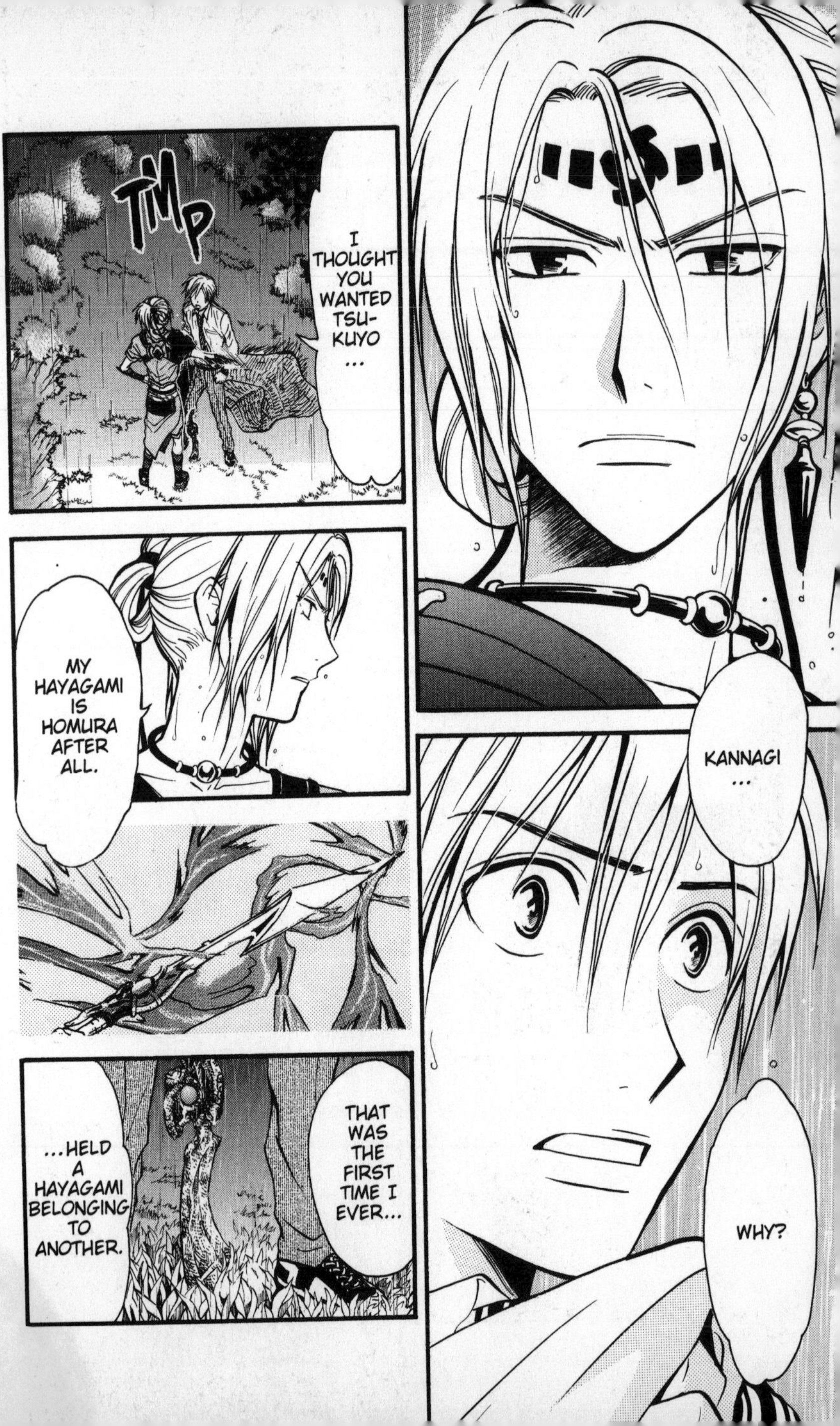
KANNAGI
...
TMP
I THOUGHT YOU WANTED TSU-KUYO
...
MY HAYAGAMI IS HOMURA AFTER ALL.
THAT WAS THE FIRST TIME I EVER...
...HELD A HAYAGAMI BELONGING TO ANOTHER.
WHY?

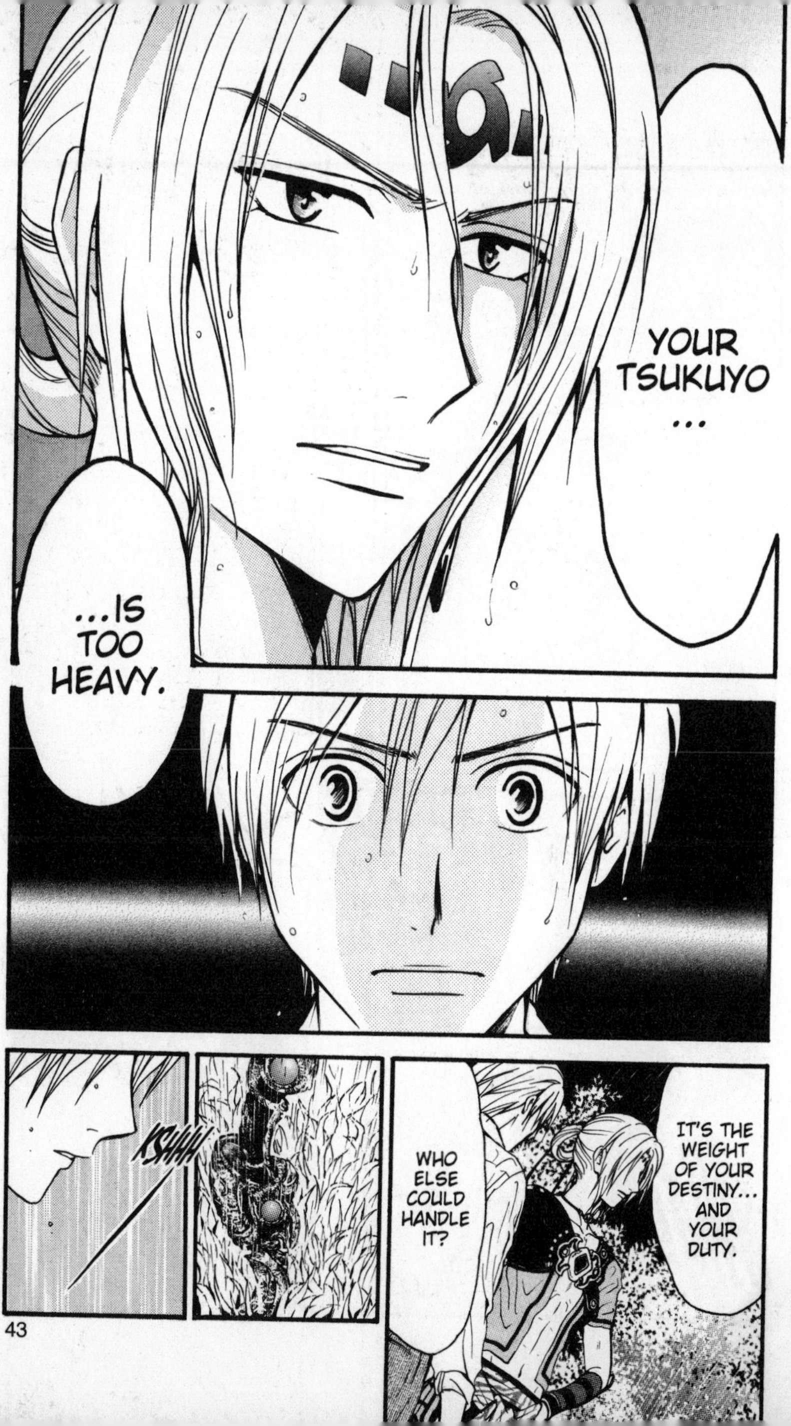
YOUR TSUKUYO ...
...IS TOO HEAVY.
IT'S THE WEIGHT OF YOUR DESTINY... AND YOUR DUTY.
WHO ELSE COULD HANDLE IT?
KSHHH

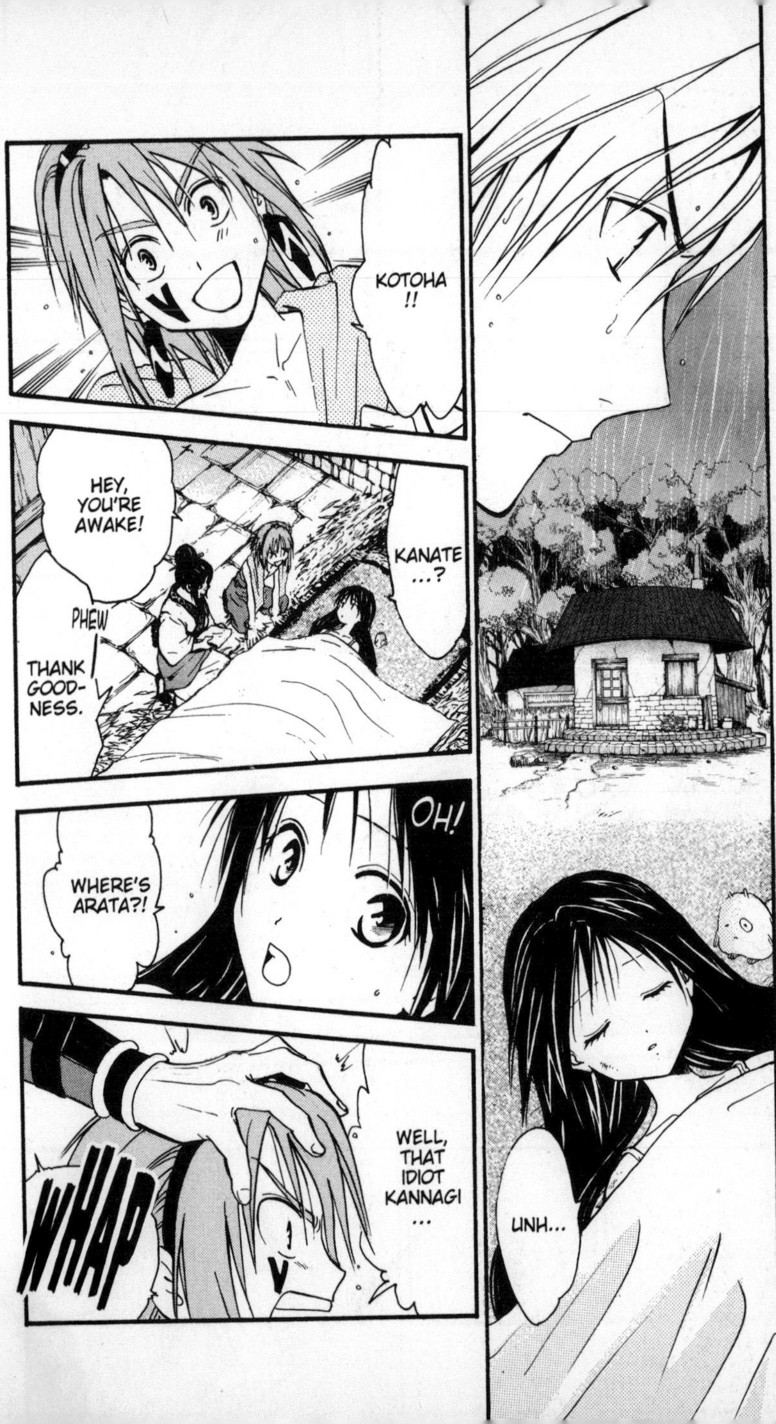
UNH...
KOTOHA !!
KANATE ...?
HEY, YOU'RE AWAKE!
PHEW
THANK GOODNESS.
OH!
WHERE'S ARATA?!
WELL, THAT IDIOT KANNAGI ...
WHAP

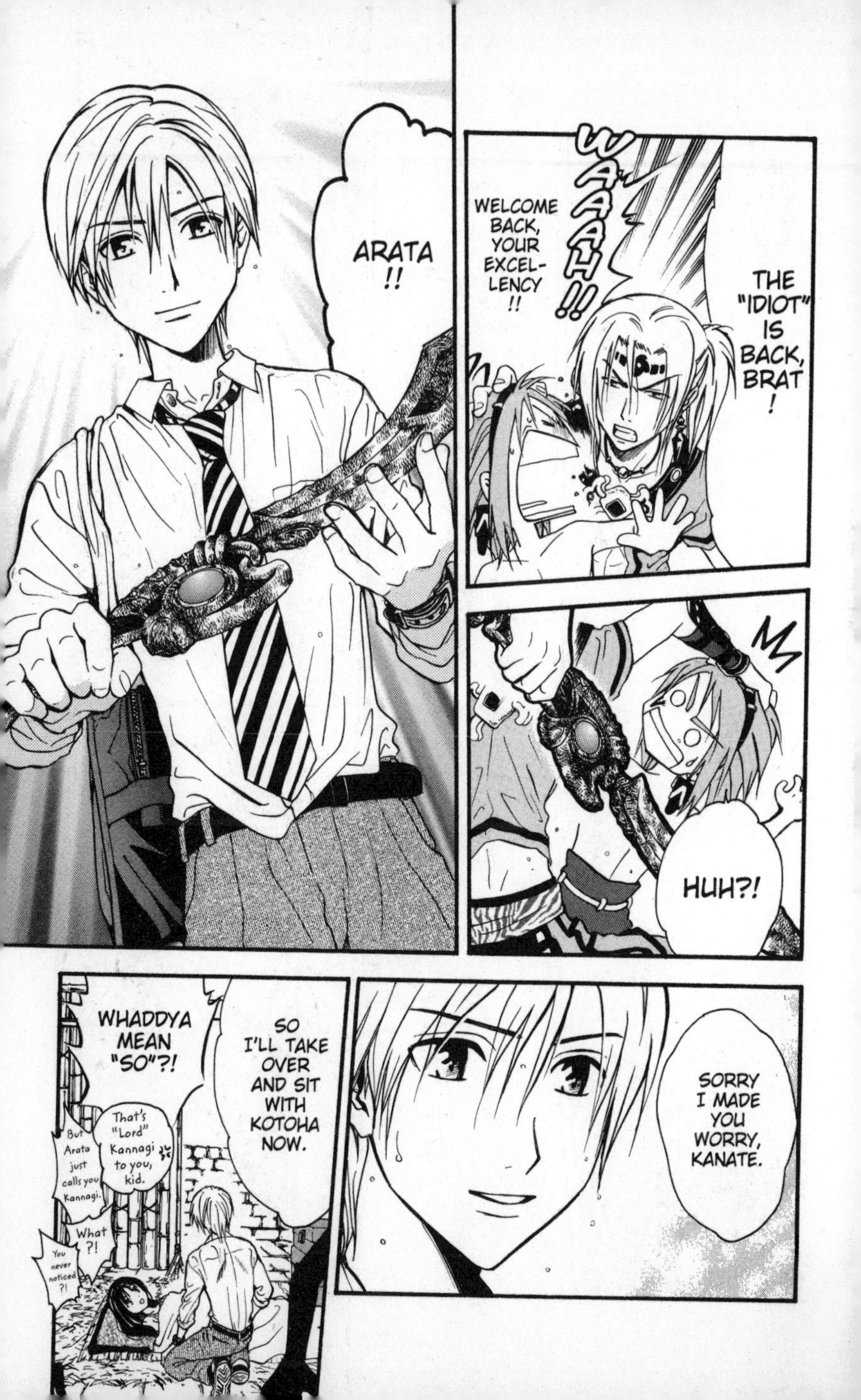
WAAAAH!!
WELCOME BACK, YOUR EXCEL-LENCY!!
THE "IDIOT" IS BACK, BRAT!
M
HUH?!
ARATA!!
SORRY I MADE YOU WORRY, KANATE.
SO I'LL TAKE OVER AND SIT WITH KOTOHA NOW.
WHADDYA MEAN "SO"?!
That's "Lord" Kannagi to you, kid.
But Arata just calls you Kannagi.
What?!
You never noticed?!

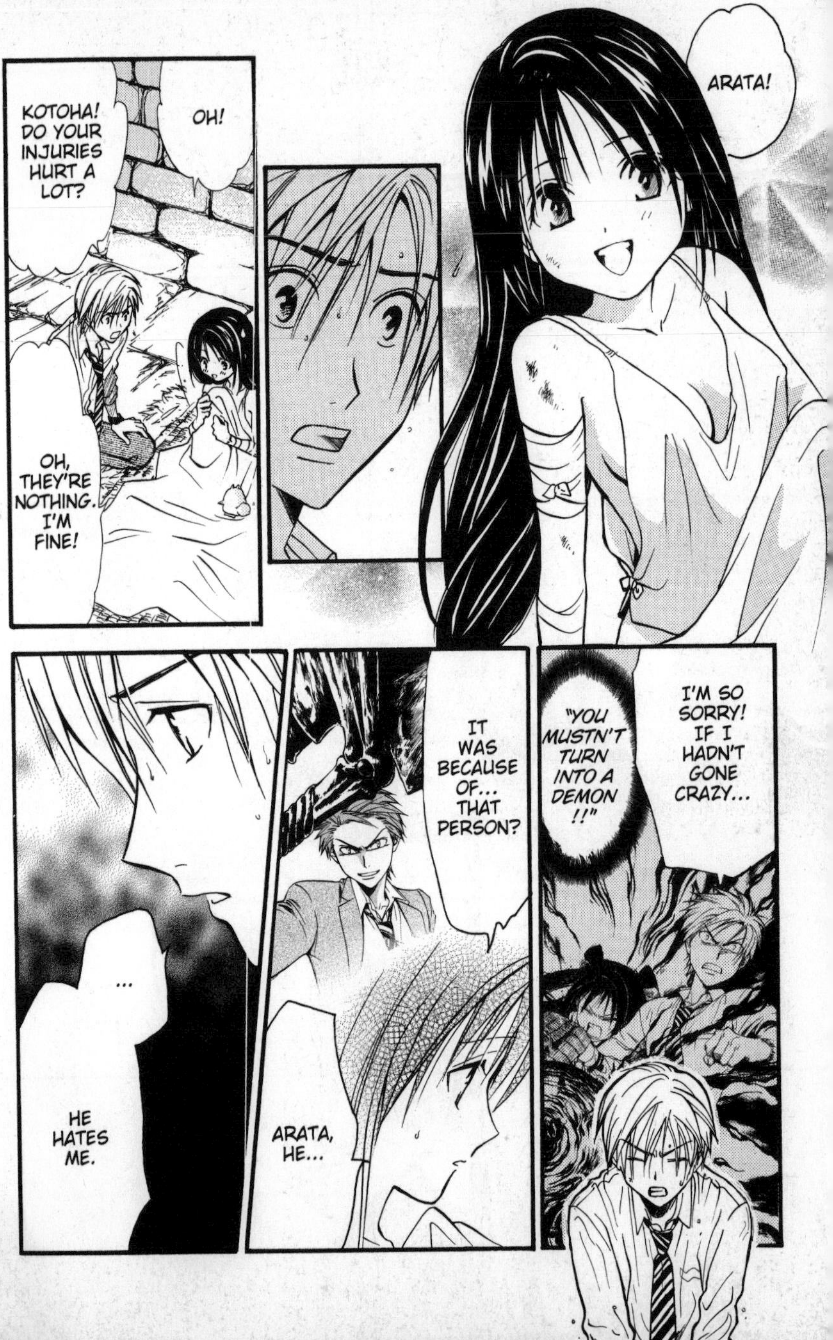
ARATA!
OH!
KOTOHA! DO YOUR INJURIES HURT A LOT?
OH, THEY'RE NOTHING. I'M FINE!
I'M SO SORRY! IF I HADN'T GONE CRAZY...
"YOU MUSTN'T TURN INTO A DEMON !!"
IT WAS BECAUSE OF... THAT PERSON?
ARATA, HE...
...
HE HATES ME.

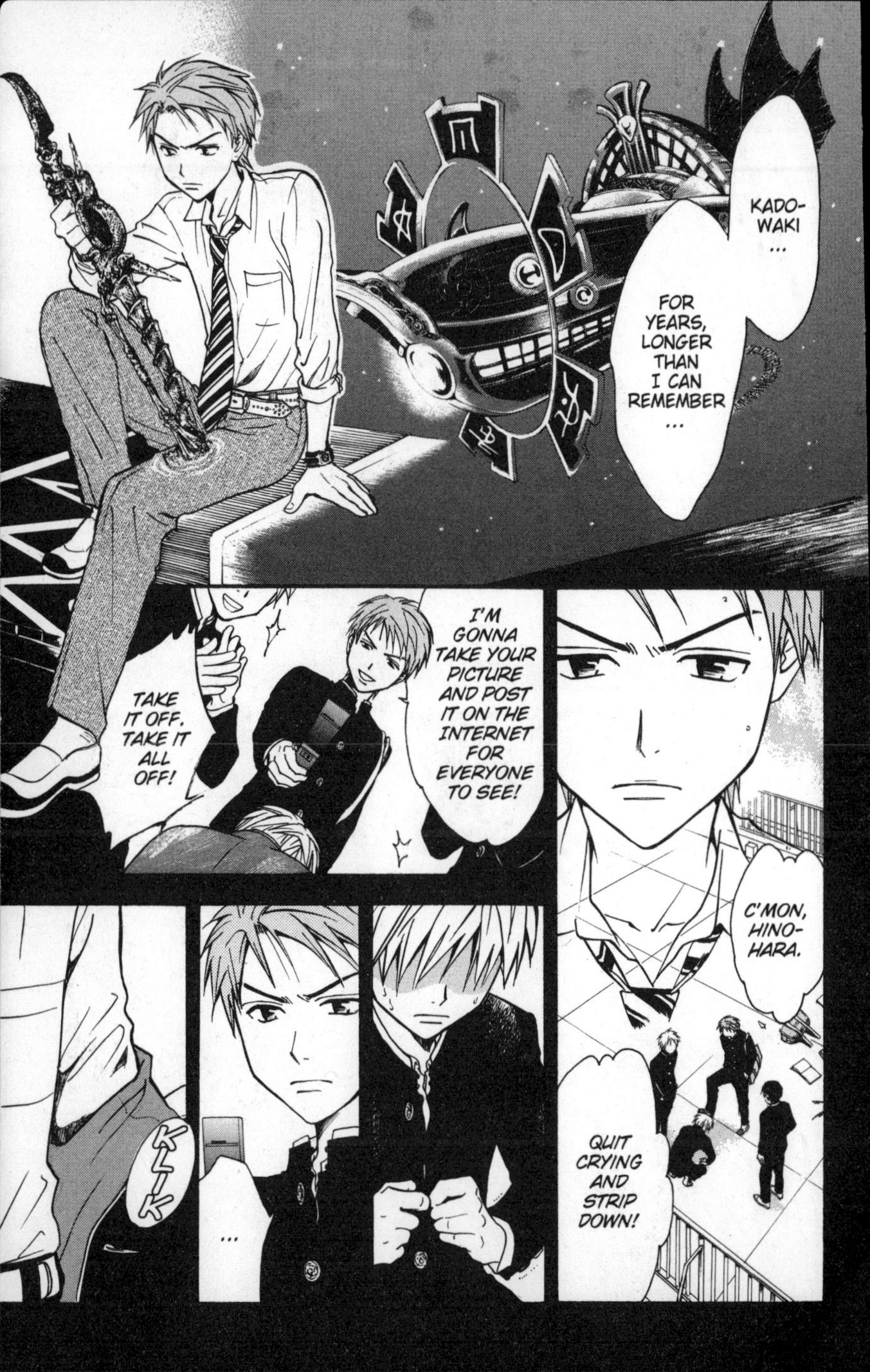
KADO-WAKI ...
FOR YEARS, LONGER THAN I CAN REMEMBER ...
C'MON, HINO-HARA.
QUIT CRYING AND STRIP DOWN!
I'M GONNA TAKE YOUR PICTURE AND POST IT ON THE INTERNET FOR EVERYONE TO SEE!
TAKE IT OFF. TAKE IT ALL OFF!
...
KLIK

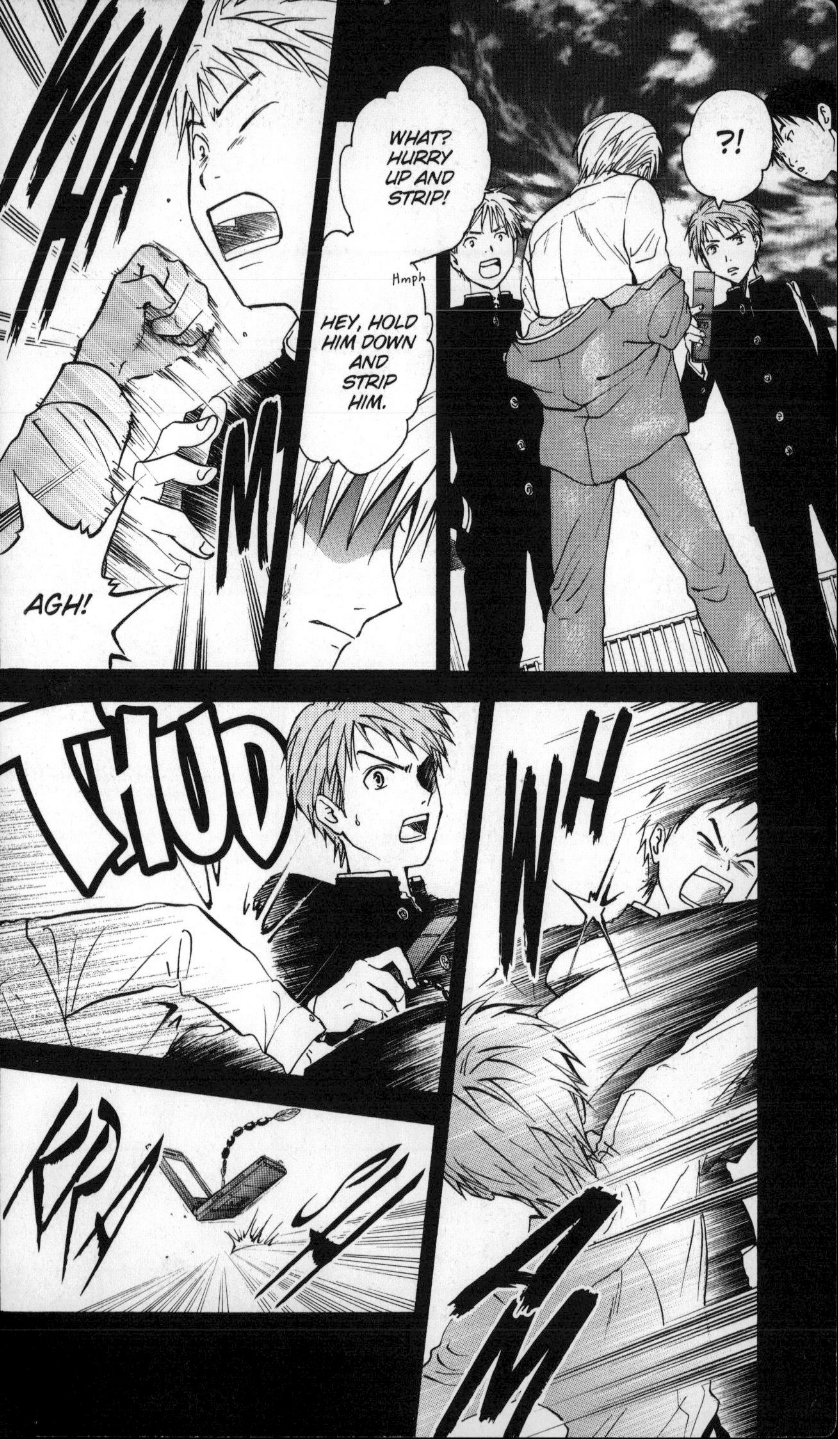
?!
WHAT? HURRY UP AND STRIP!
Hmph
HEY, HOLD HIM DOWN AND STRIP HIM.
WHAM
AGH!
WHAM
THUD
KRASH

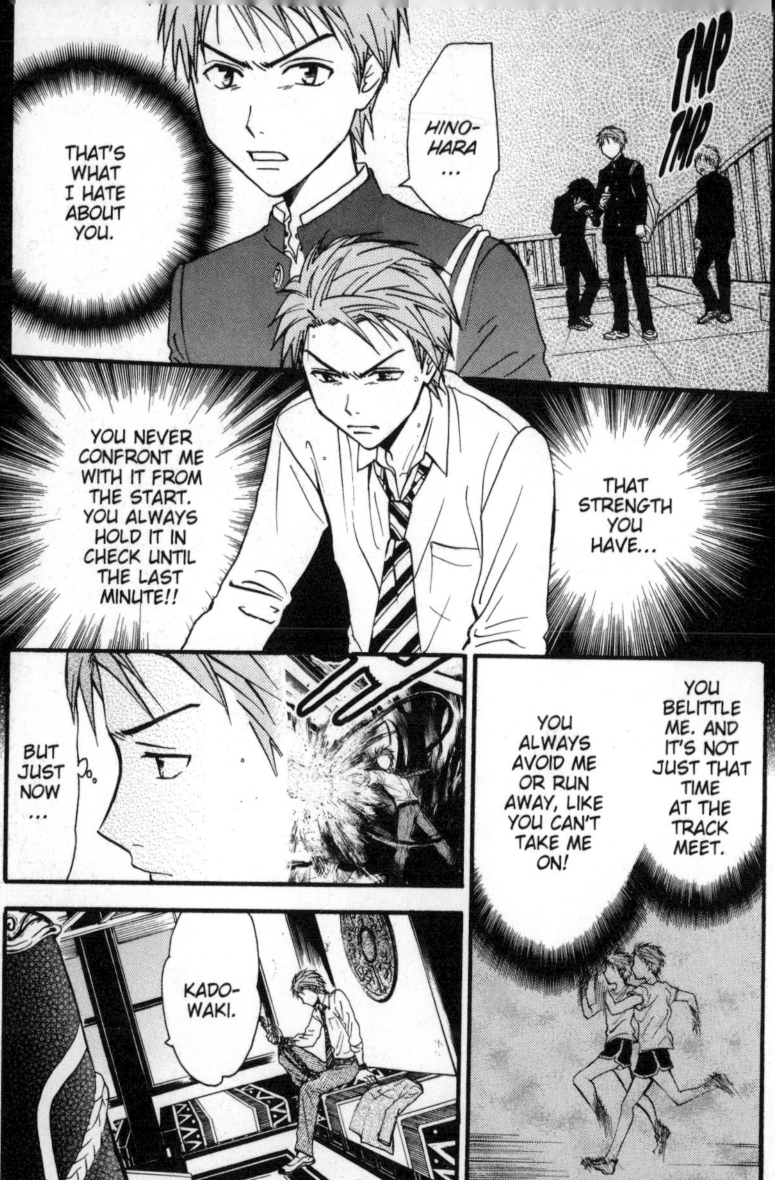
TMP TMP
HINO-HARA...
THAT'S WHAT I HATE ABOUT YOU.
THAT STRENGTH YOU HAVE...
YOU NEVER CONFRONT ME WITH IT FROM THE START. YOU ALWAYS HOLD IT IN CHECK UNTIL THE LAST MINUTE!!
YOU BELITTLE ME. AND IT'S NOT JUST THAT TIME AT THE TRACK MEET.
YOU ALWAYS AVOID ME OR RUN AWAY, LIKE YOU CAN'T TAKE ME ON!
BUT JUST NOW...
KADO-WAKI.

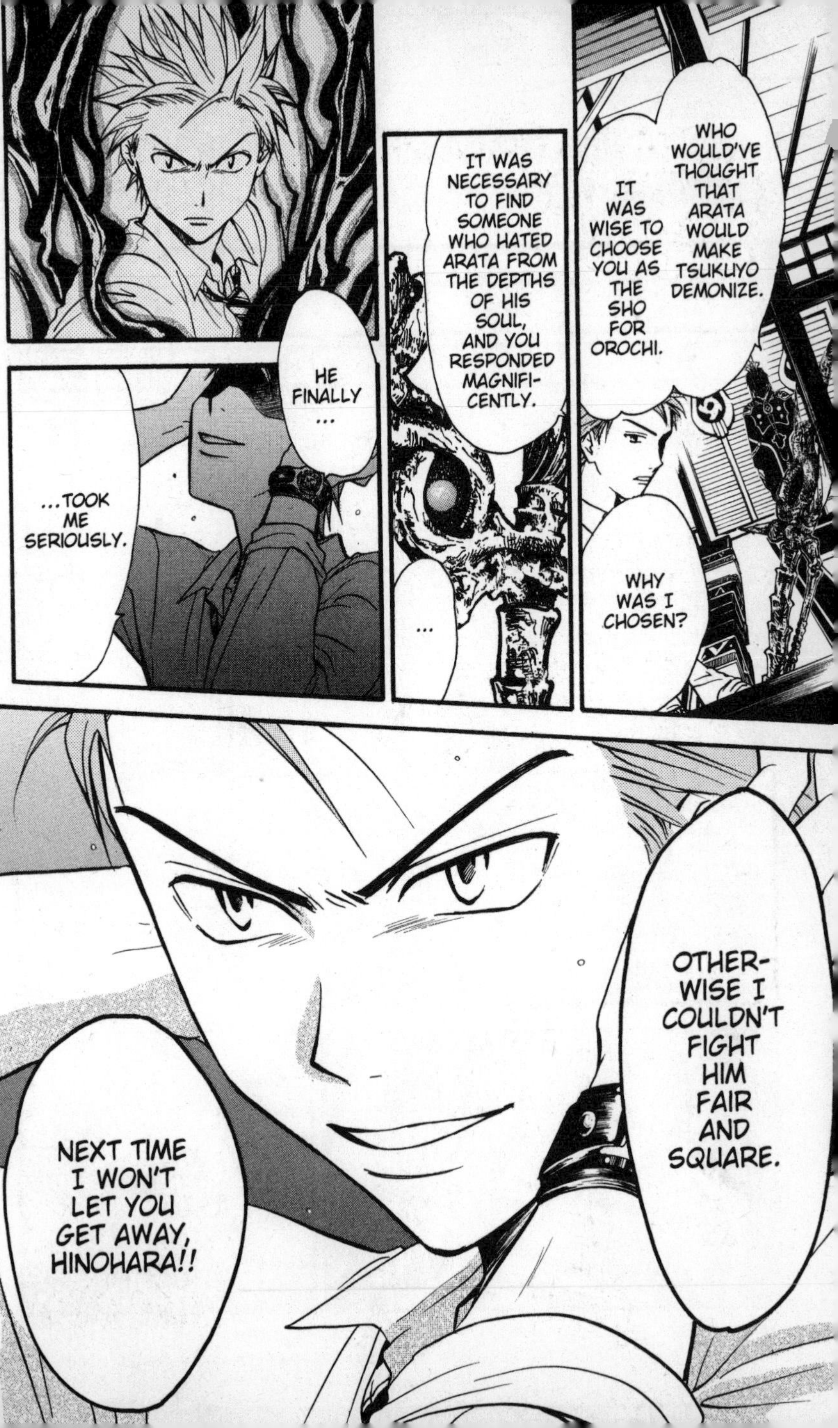
WHO WOULD'VE THOUGHT THAT ARATA WOULD MAKE TSUKUYO DEMONIZE.
IT WAS WISE TO CHOOSE YOU AS THE SHO FOR OROCHI.
WHY WAS I CHOSEN?
IT WAS NECESSARY TO FIND SOMEONE WHO HATED ARATA FROM THE DEPTHS OF HIS SOUL, AND YOU RESPONDED MAGNIFI- CENTLY.
...
HE FINALLY ...
...TOOK ME SERIOUSLY.
OTHER- WISE I COULDN'T FIGHT HIM FAIR AND SQUARE.
NEXT TIME I WON'T LET YOU GET AWAY, HINOHARA!!

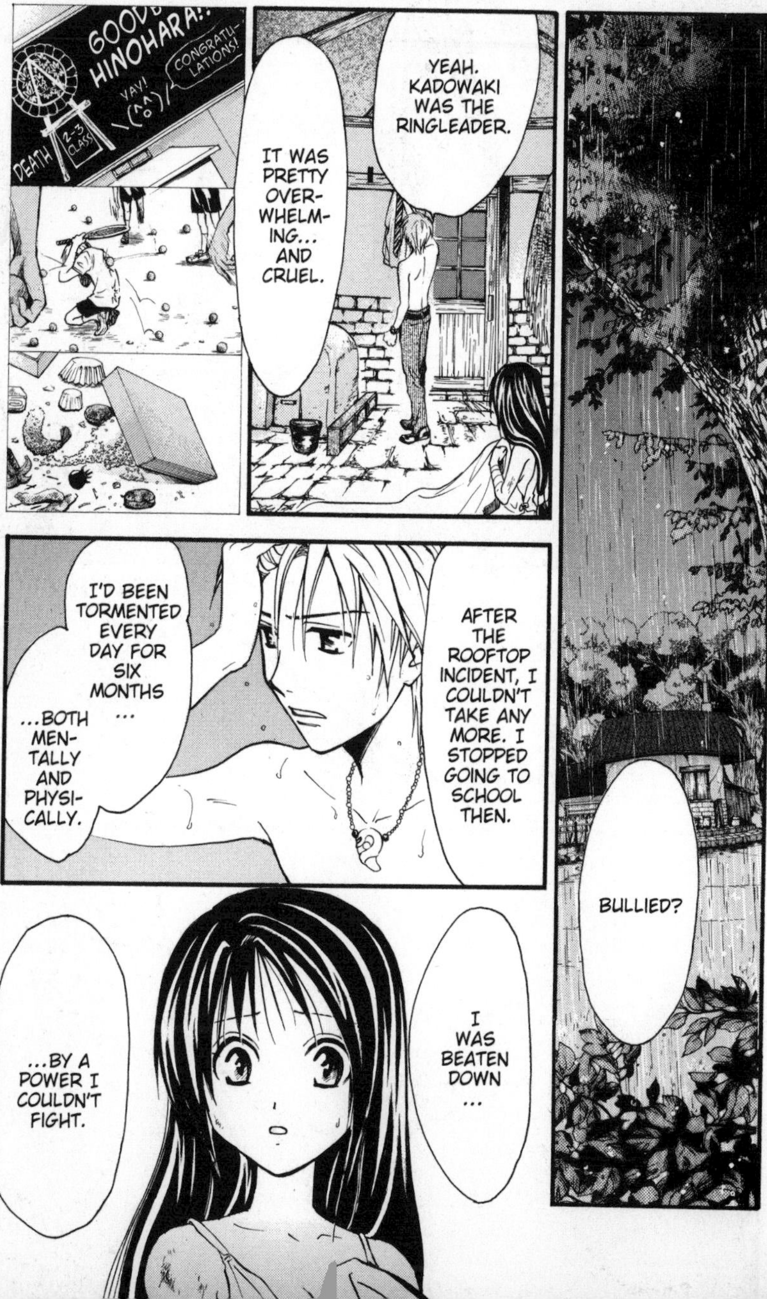
BULLIED?
YEAH. KADOWAKI WAS THE RINGLEADER.
IT WAS PRETTY OVER-WHELM-ING... AND CRUEL.
GOOD
HINOHARA!!
CONGRATU-LATIONS!
YAY!
\(^o^)/
DEATH
2-3 CLASS
AFTER THE ROOFTOP INCIDENT, I COULDN'T TAKE ANY MORE. I STOPPED GOING TO SCHOOL THEN.
I'D BEEN TORMENTED EVERY DAY FOR SIX MONTHS...
...BOTH MEN-TALLY AND PHYSI-CALLY.
I WAS BEATEN DOWN...
...BY A POWER I COULDN'T FIGHT.

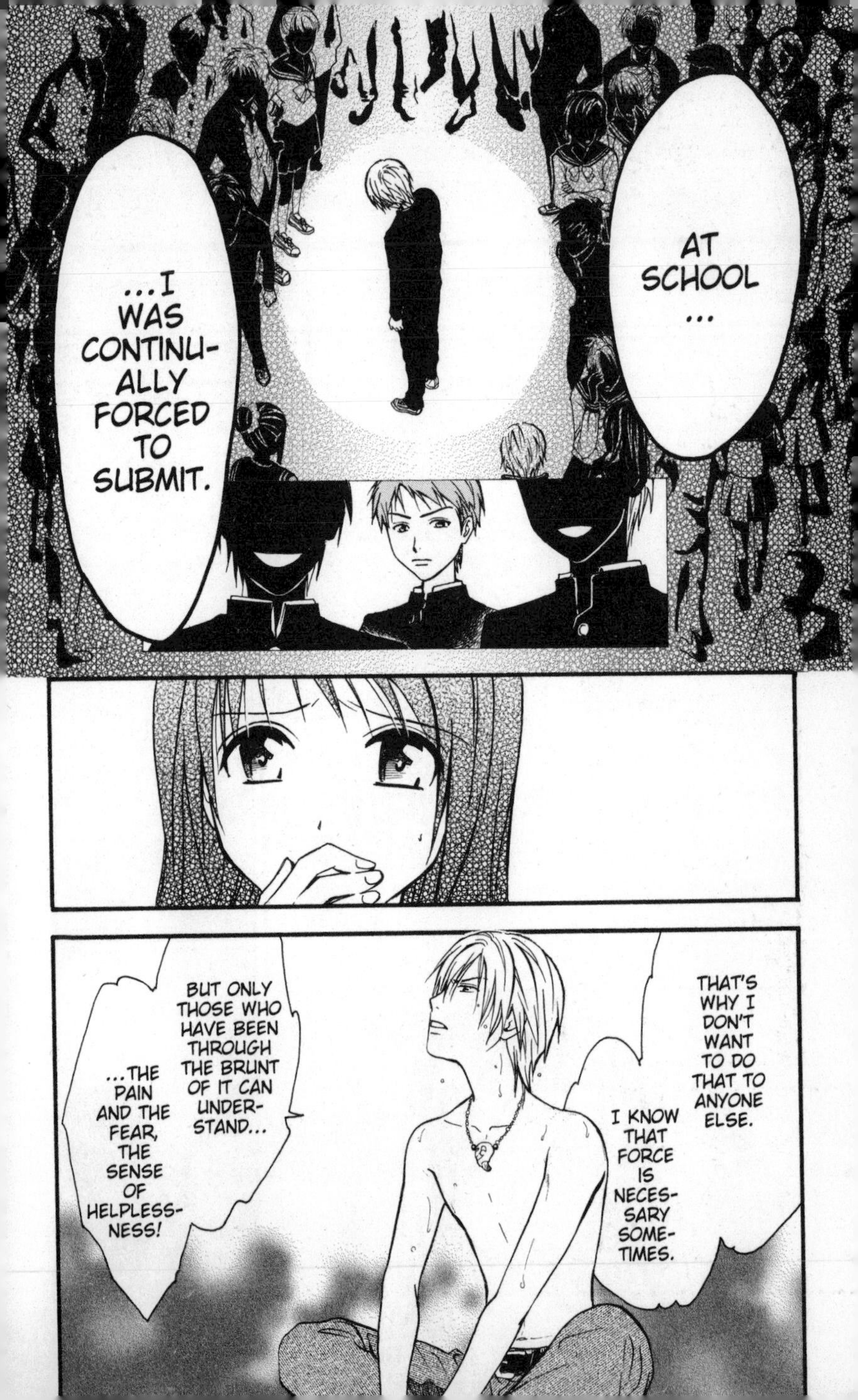
AT SCHOOL ...
...I WAS CONTINU-ALLY FORCED TO SUBMIT.
I KNOW THAT FORCE IS NECES-SARY SOME-TIMES.
BUT ONLY THOSE WHO HAVE BEEN THROUGH THE BRUNT OF IT CAN UNDER-STAND...
...THE PAIN AND THE FEAR, THE SENSE OF HELPLESS-NESS!
THAT'S WHY I DON'T WANT TO DO THAT TO ANYONE ELSE.

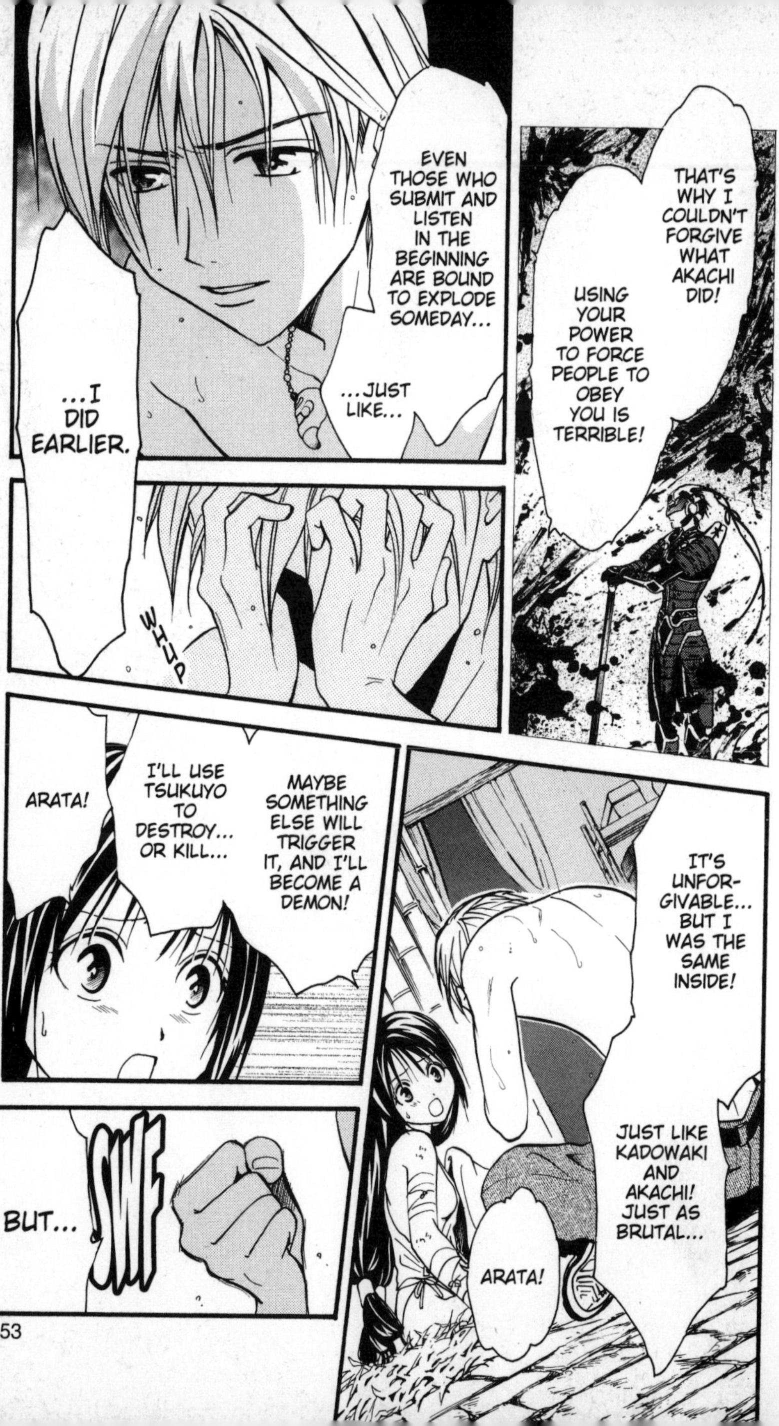
THAT'S WHY I COULDN'T FORGIVE WHAT AKACHI DID!
USING YOUR POWER TO FORCE PEOPLE TO OBEY YOU IS TERRIBLE!
EVEN THOSE WHO SUBMIT AND LISTEN IN THE BEGINNING ARE BOUND TO EXPLODE SOMEDAY...
...JUST LIKE...
...I DID EARLIER.
WHUP
IT'S UNFORGIVABLE... BUT I WAS THE SAME INSIDE!
JUST LIKE KADOWAKI AND AKACHI! JUST AS BRUTAL...
ARATA!
MAYBE SOMETHING ELSE WILL TRIGGER IT, AND I'LL BECOME A DEMON!
I'LL USE TSUKUYO TO DESTROY... OR KILL...
ARATA!
SWF
BUT...

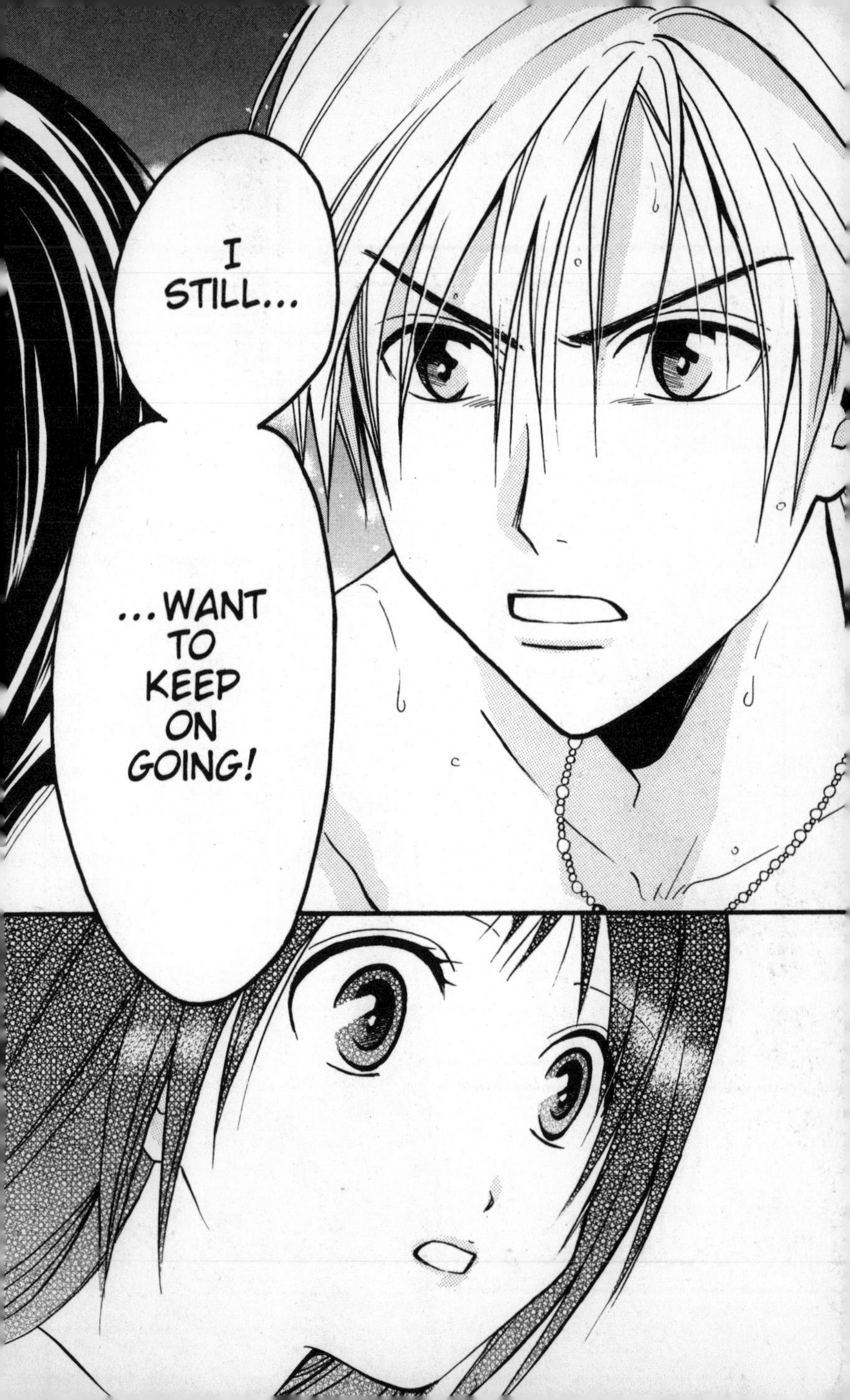
I STILL...
...WANT TO KEEP ON GOING!

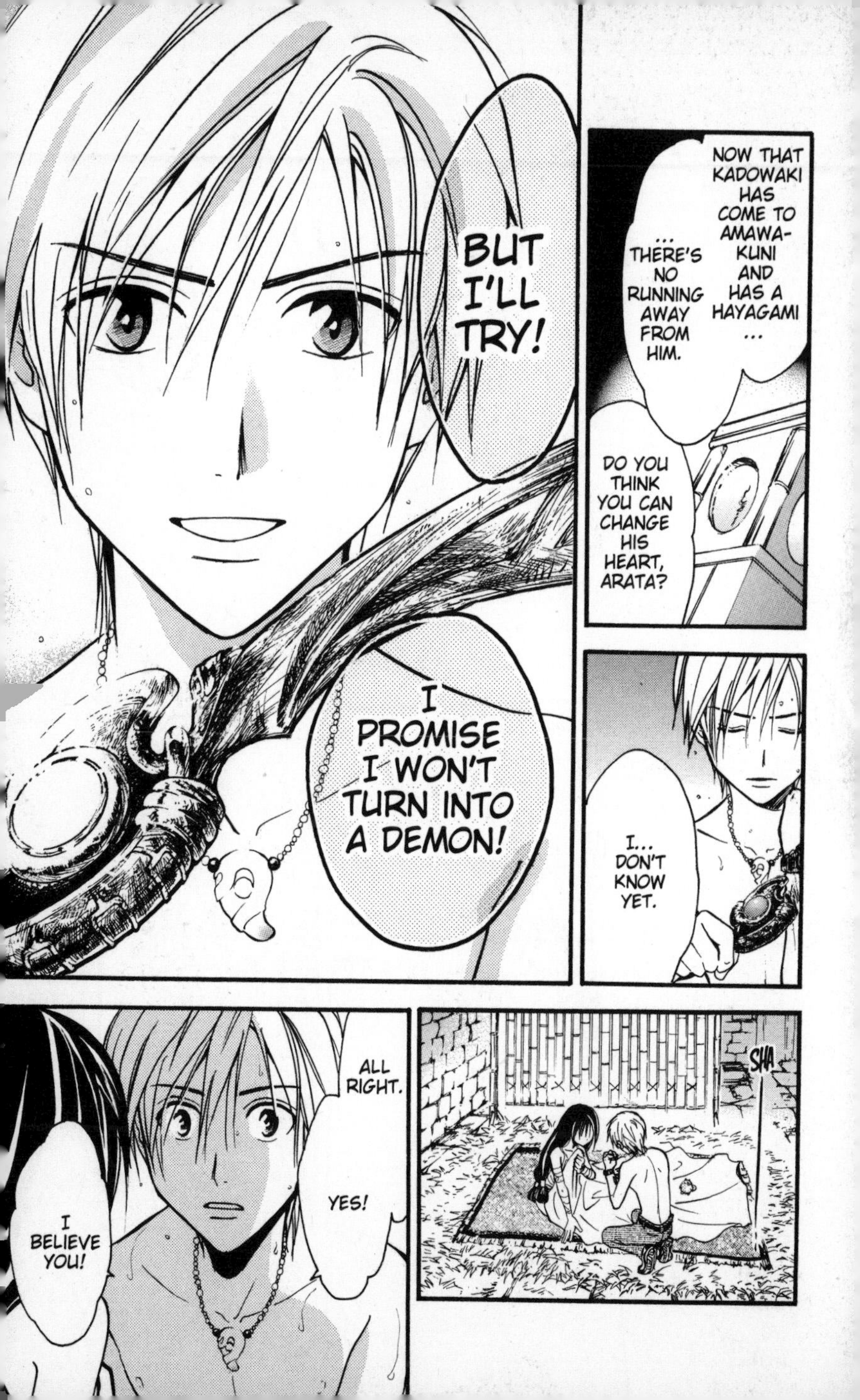
NOW THAT KADOWAKI HAS COME TO AMAWA-KUNI AND HAS A HAYAGAMI...
...THERE'S NO RUNNING AWAY FROM HIM.
DO YOU THINK YOU CAN CHANGE HIS HEART, ARATA?
I... DON'T KNOW YET.
BUT I'LL TRY!
I PROMISE I WON'T TURN INTO A DEMON!
SHA
ALL RIGHT.
YES!
I BELIEVE YOU!

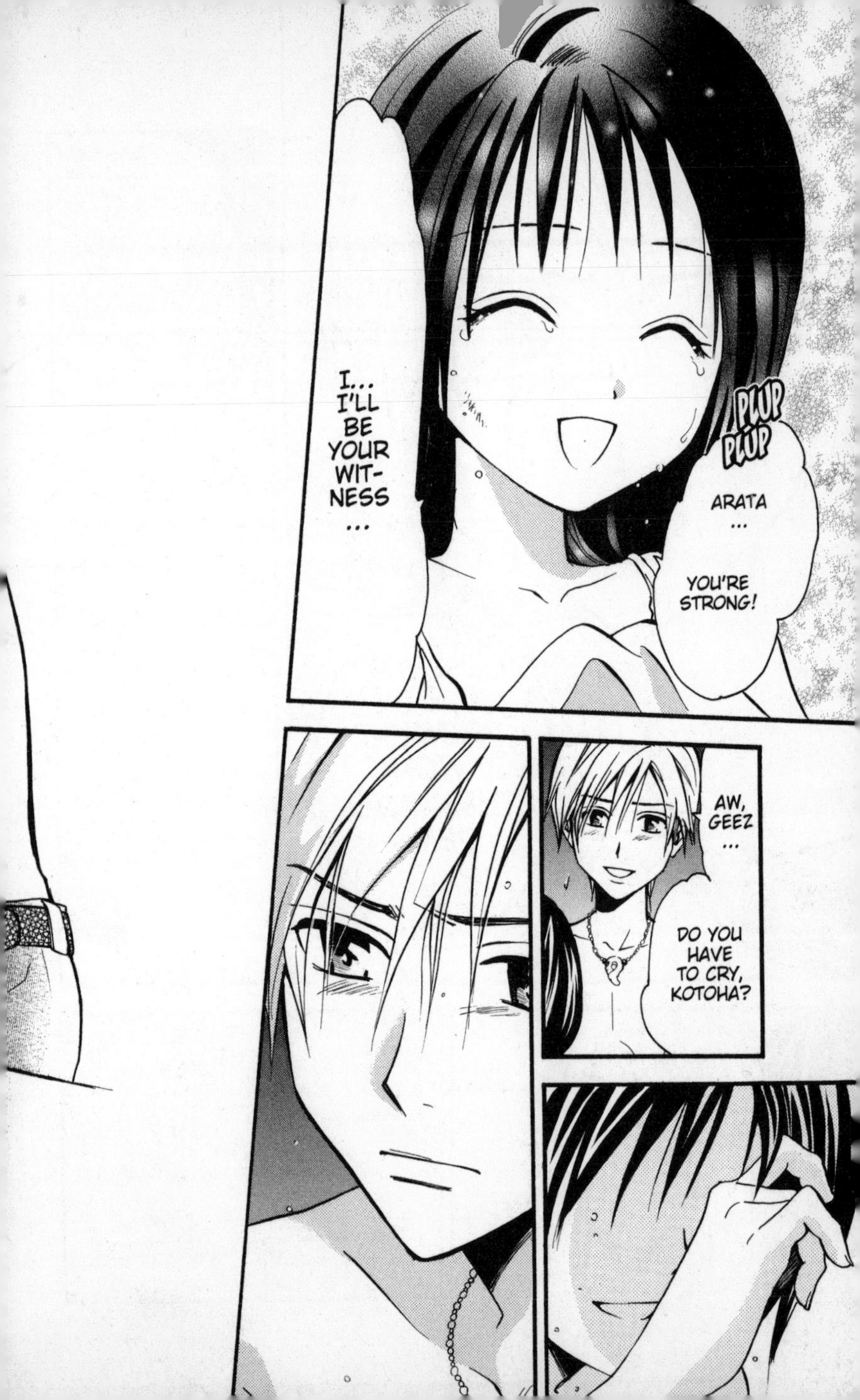
PLUP PLUP
ARATA ...
YOU'RE STRONG!
I... I'LL BE YOUR WIT-NESS ...
AW, GEEZ ...
DO YOU HAVE TO CRY, KOTOHA?

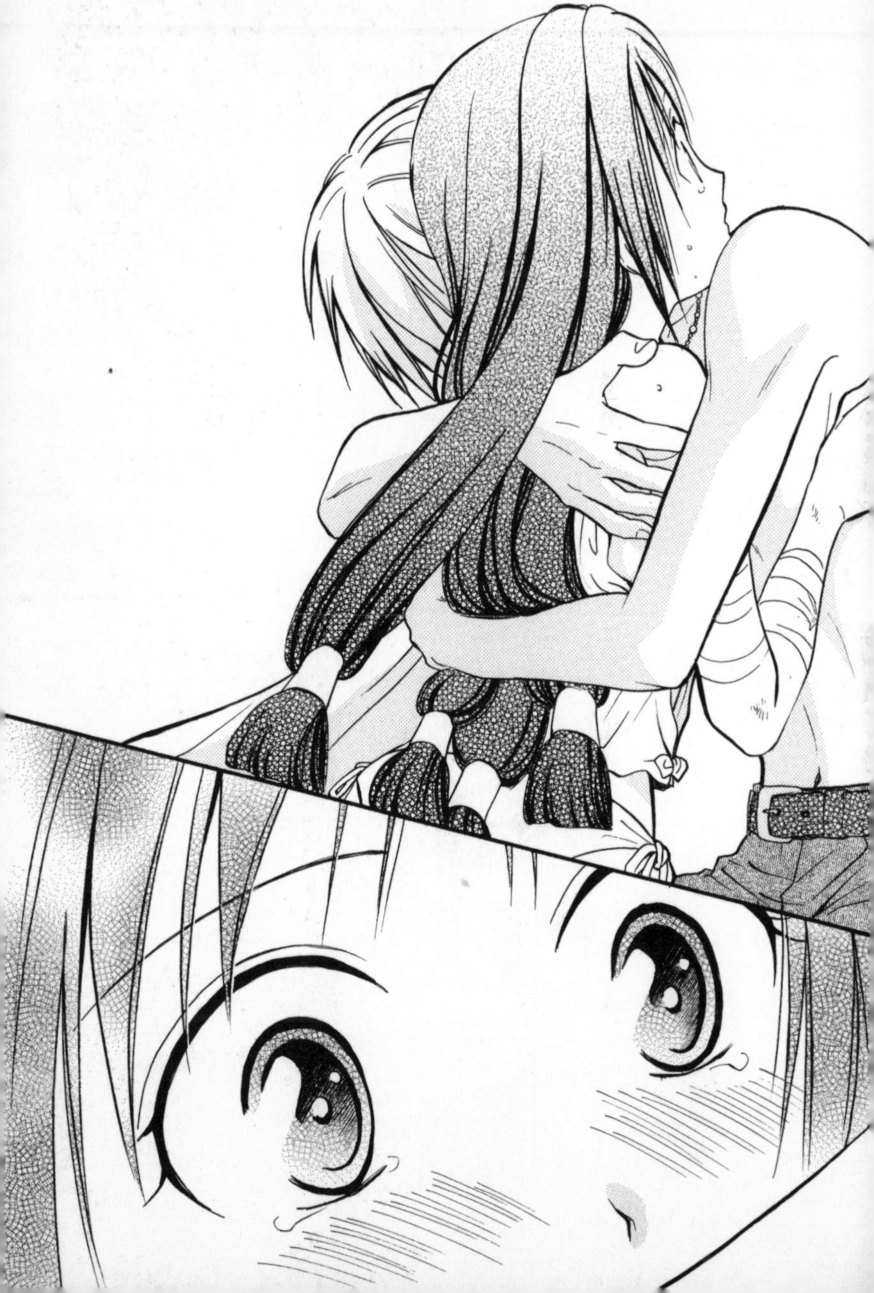

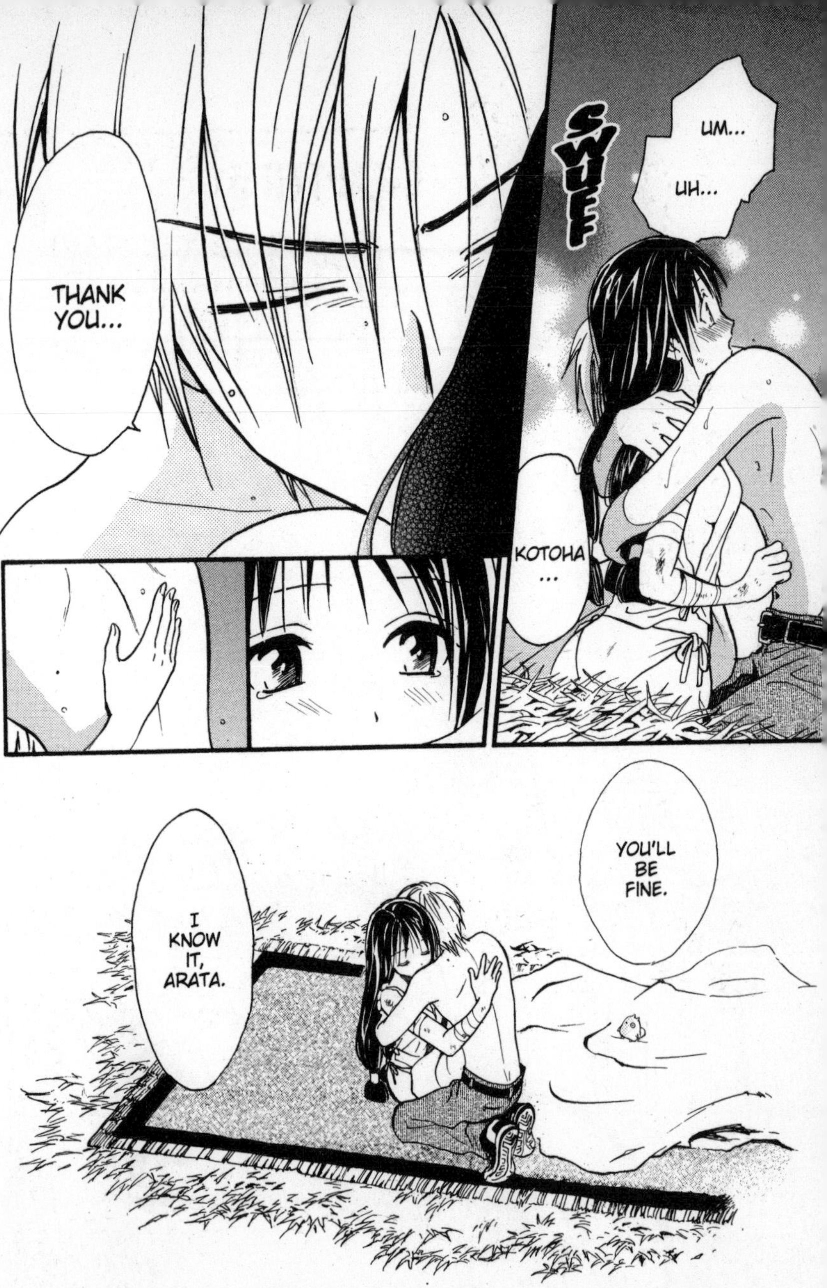
SWUFF
UM...
UH...
KOTOHA...
THANK YOU...
YOU'LL BE FINE.
I KNOW IT, ARATA.

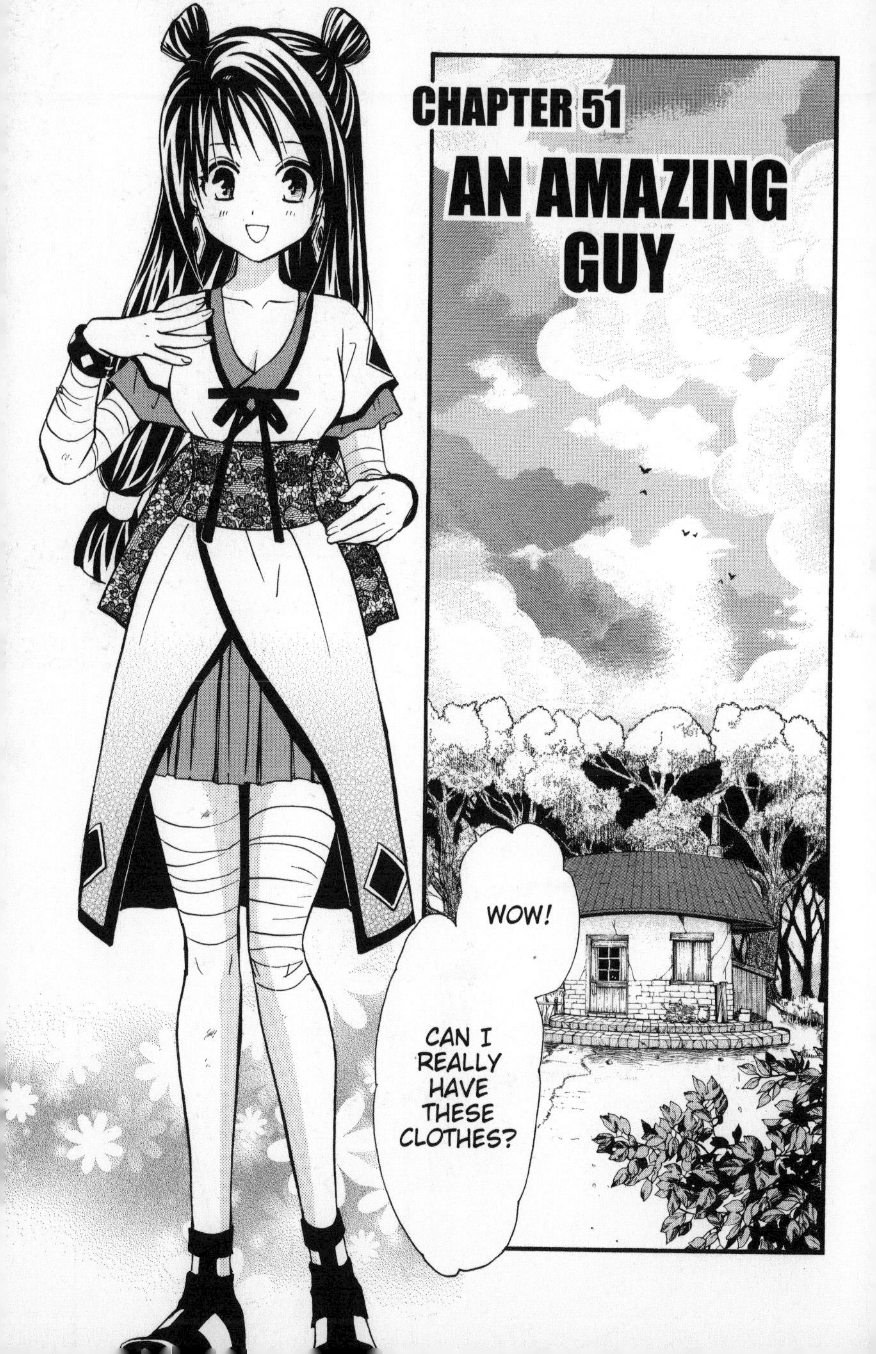
CHAPTER 51
AN AMAZING GUY
WOW!
CAN I REALLY HAVE THESE CLOTHES?

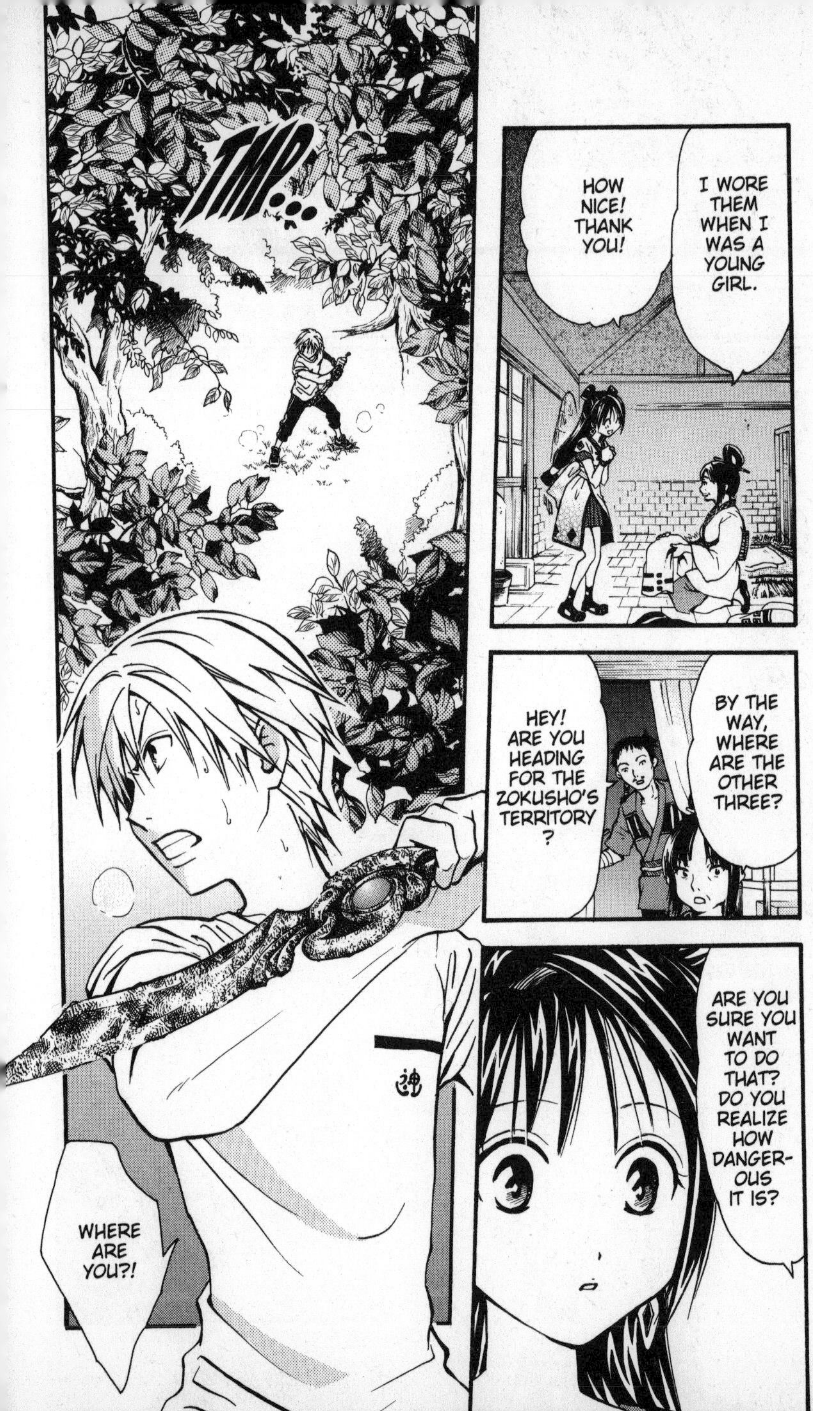
I WORE THEM WHEN I WAS A YOUNG GIRL.
HOW NICE! THANK YOU!
BY THE WAY, WHERE ARE THE OTHER THREE?
HEY! ARE YOU HEADING FOR THE ZOKUSHO'S TERRITORY?
ARE YOU SURE YOU WANT TO DO THAT? DO YOU REALIZE HOW DANGER-OUS IT IS?
TMP...
WHERE ARE YOU?!

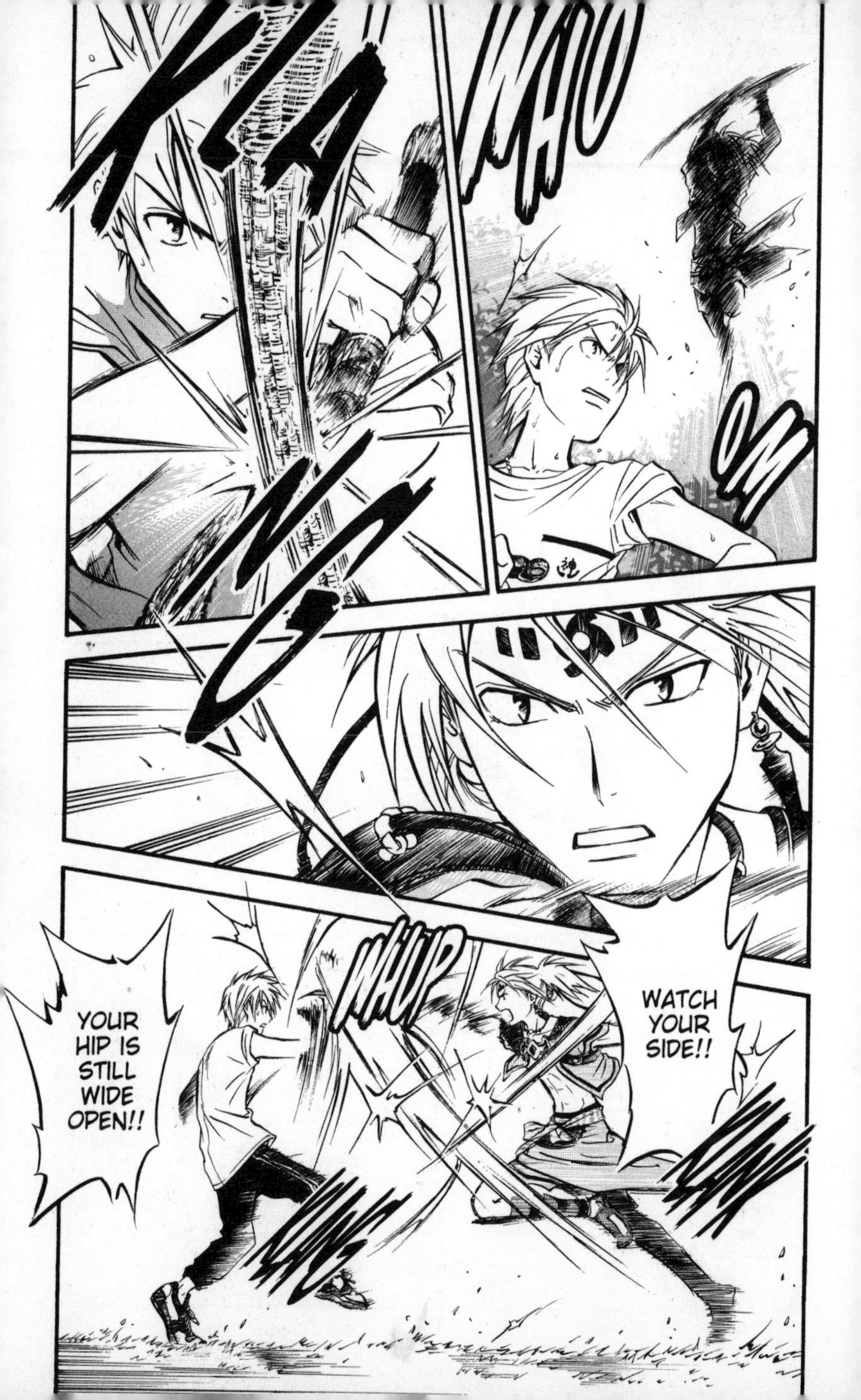
WHUP
WATCH YOUR SIDE!!
YOUR HIP IS STILL WIDE OPEN!!

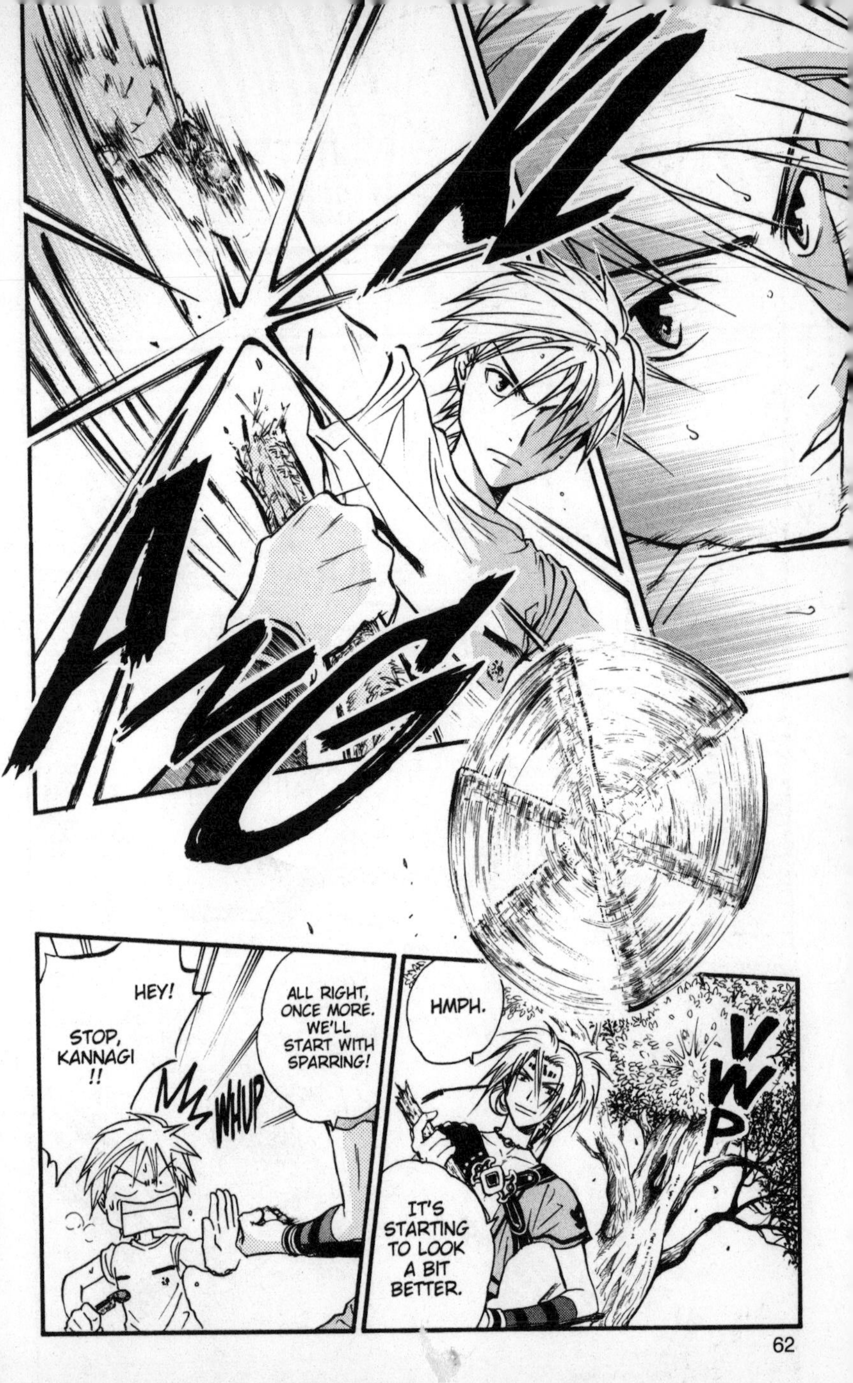
KANG
HMPH.
VWP
IT'S STARTING TO LOOK A BIT BETTER.
ALL RIGHT, ONCE MORE. WE'LL START WITH SPARRING!
HEY!
STOP, KANNAGI !!
WHUP

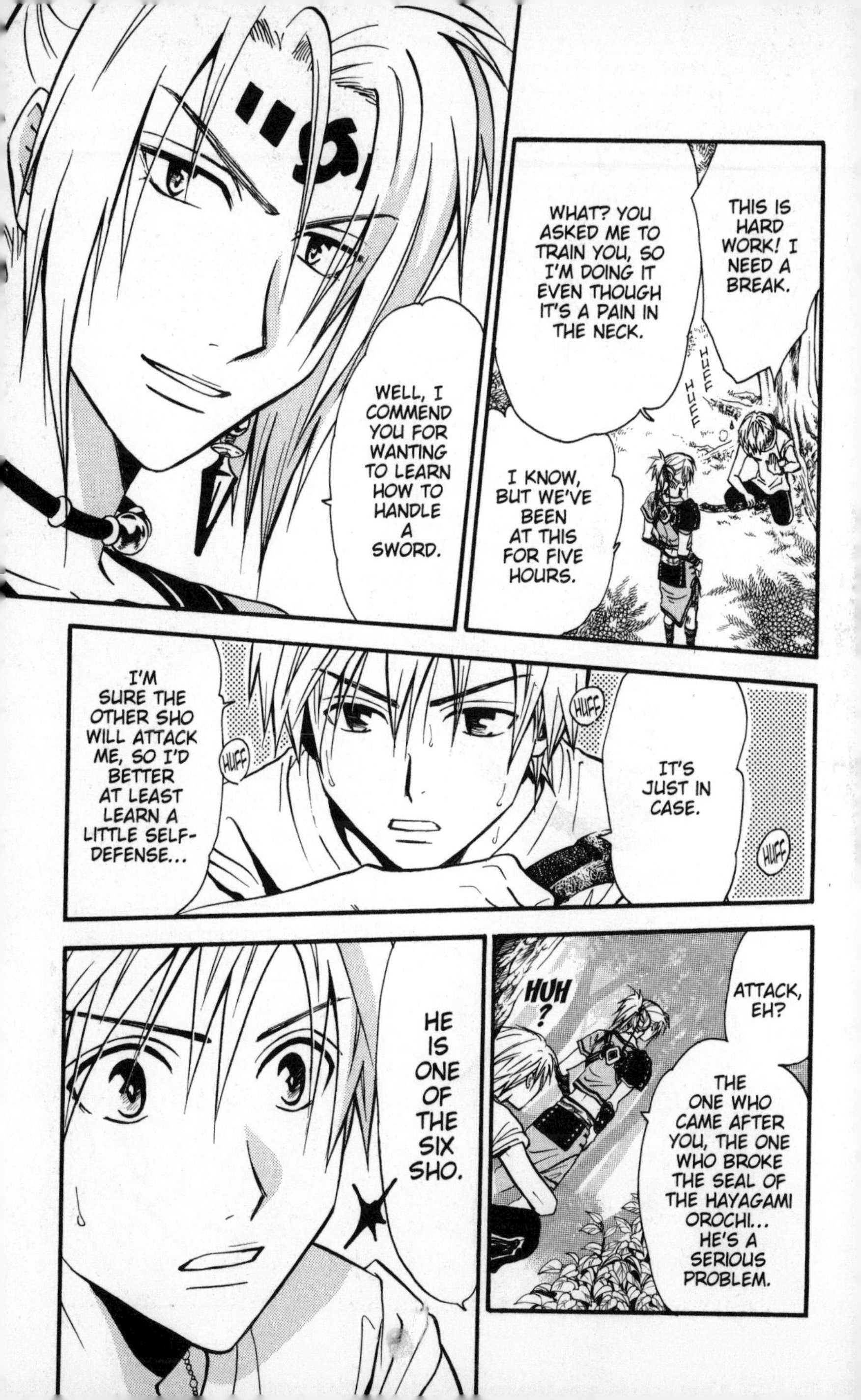
THIS IS HARD WORK! I NEED A BREAK.
WHAT? YOU ASKED ME TO TRAIN YOU, SO I'M DOING IT EVEN THOUGH IT'S A PAIN IN THE NECK.
HUFF HUFF
I KNOW, BUT WE'VE BEEN AT THIS FOR FIVE HOURS.
WELL, I COMMEND YOU FOR WANTING TO LEARN HOW TO HANDLE A SWORD.
HUFF
IT'S JUST IN CASE.
HUFF
I'M SURE THE OTHER SHO WILL ATTACK ME, SO I'D BETTER AT LEAST LEARN A LITTLE SELF-DEFENSE...
HUFF
ATTACK, EH?
HUH?
THE ONE WHO CAME AFTER YOU, THE ONE WHO BROKE THE SEAL OF THE HAYAGAMI OROCHI... HE'S A SERIOUS PROBLEM.
HE IS ONE OF THE SIX SHO.

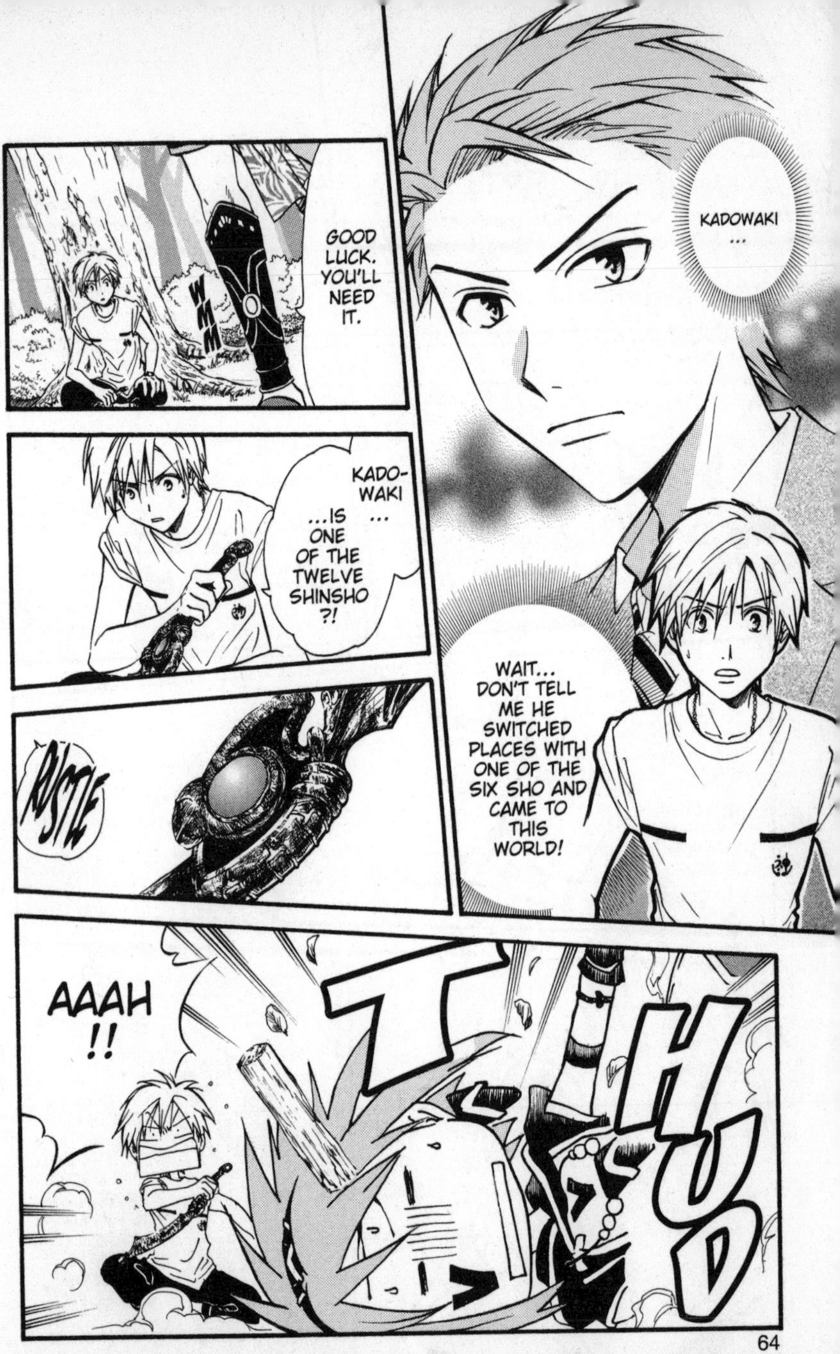
KADOWAKI ...
WAIT... DON'T TELL ME HE SWITCHED PLACES WITH ONE OF THE SIX SHO AND CAME TO THIS WORLD!
GOOD LUCK. YOU'LL NEED IT.
WMM
KADO-WAKI ...
...IS ONE OF THE TWELVE SHINSHO ?!
RUSTLE
THUD
AAAH !!

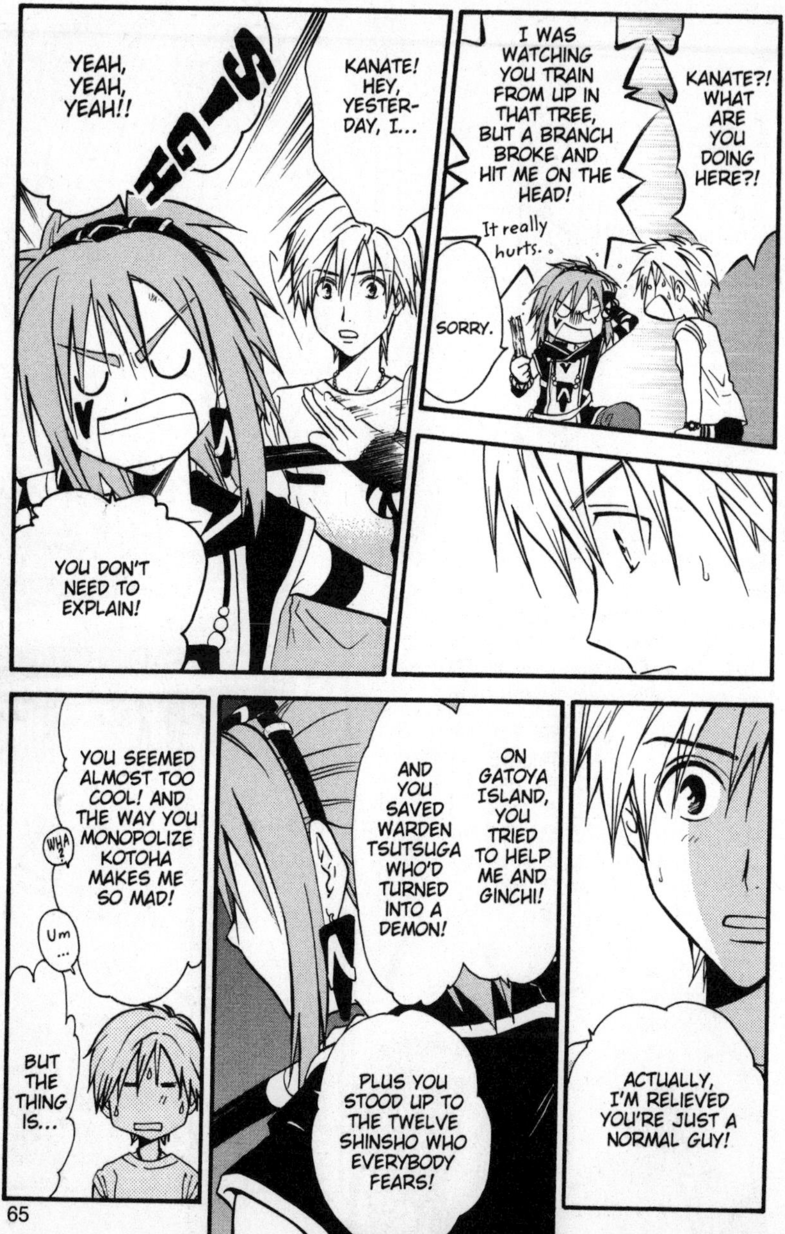
KANATE?! WHAT ARE YOU DOING HERE?!
I WAS WATCHING YOU TRAIN FROM UP IN THAT TREE, BUT A BRANCH BROKE AND HIT ME ON THE HEAD!
It really hurts..
SORRY.
KANATE! HEY, YESTER-DAY, I...
YEAH, YEAH, YEAH!!
YOU DON'T NEED TO EXPLAIN!
ACTUALLY, I'M RELIEVED YOU'RE JUST A NORMAL GUY!
ON GATOYA ISLAND, YOU TRIED TO HELP ME AND GINCHI!
AND YOU SAVED WARDEN TSUTSUGA WHO'D TURNED INTO A DEMON!
PLUS YOU STOOD UP TO THE TWELVE SHINSHO WHO EVERYBODY FEARS!
YOU SEEMED ALMOST TOO COOL! AND THE WAY YOU MONOPOLIZE KOTOHA MAKES ME SO MAD!
WHA?
Um...
BUT THE THING IS...

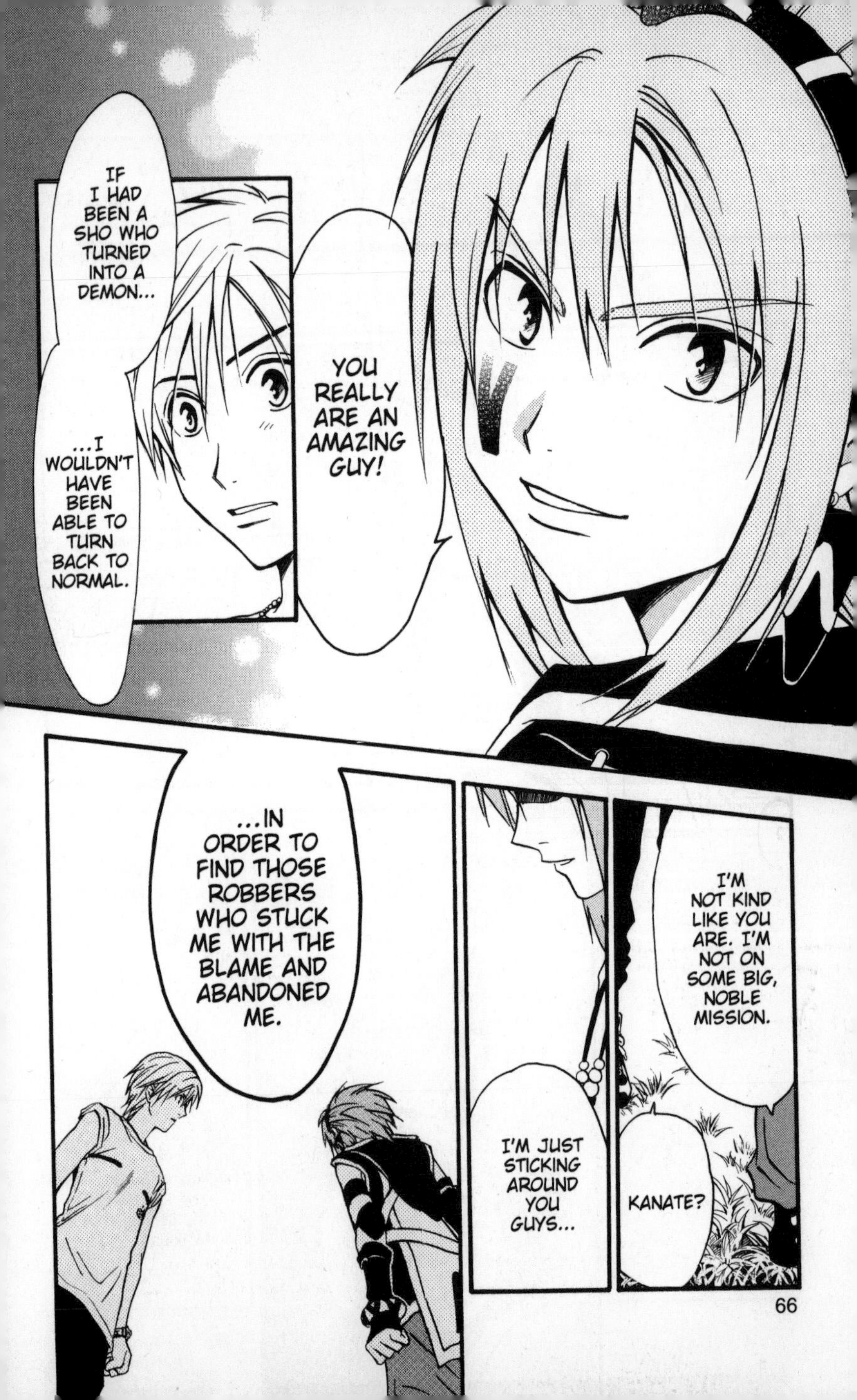
YOU REALLY ARE AN AMAZING GUY!
IF I HAD BEEN A SHO WHO TURNED INTO A DEMON...
...I WOULDN'T HAVE BEEN ABLE TO TURN BACK TO NORMAL.
I'M NOT KIND LIKE YOU ARE. I'M NOT ON SOME BIG, NOBLE MISSION.
KANATE?
I'M JUST STICKING AROUND YOU GUYS...
...IN ORDER TO FIND THOSE ROBBERS WHO STUCK ME WITH THE BLAME AND ABANDONED ME.

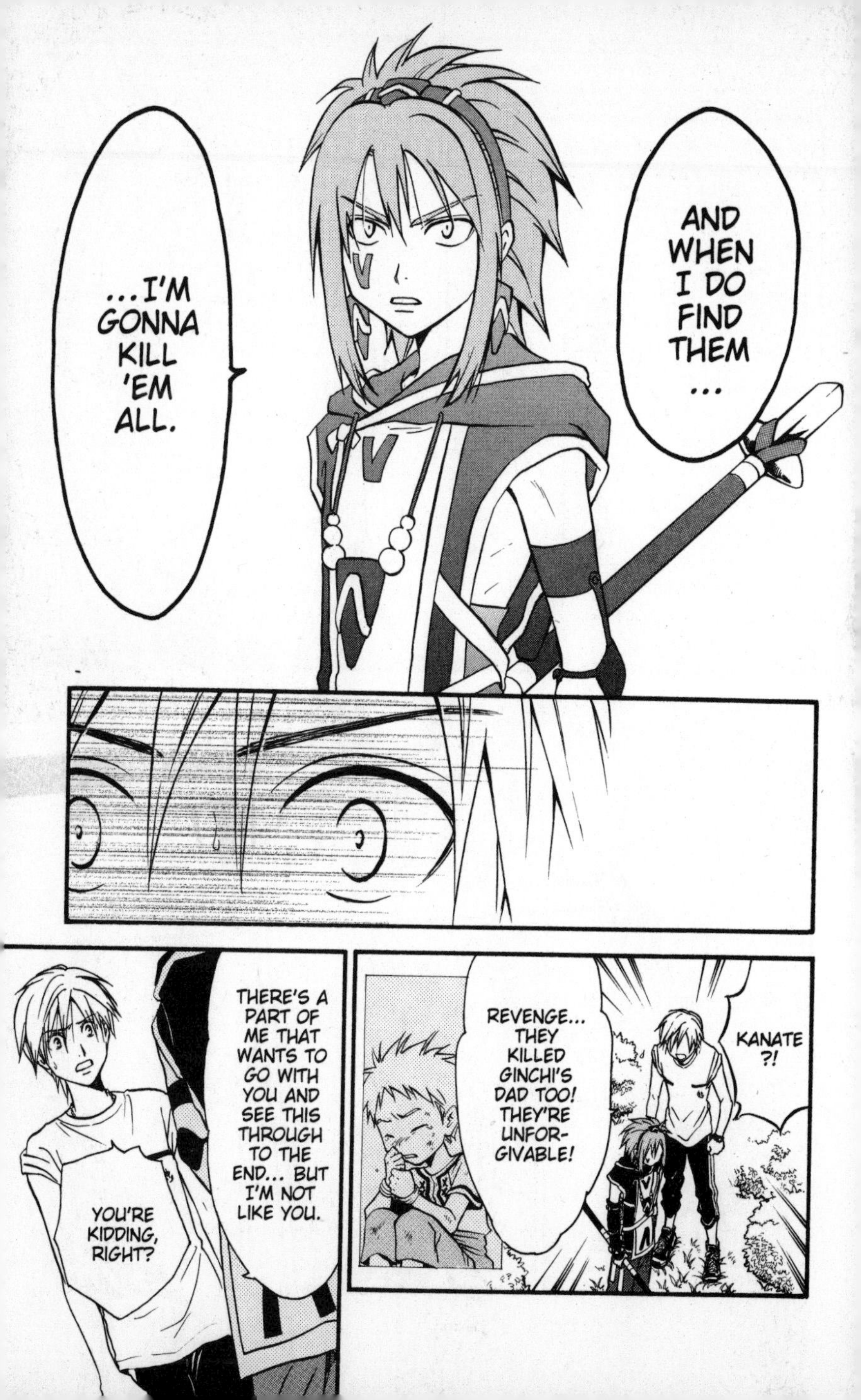
AND WHEN I DO FIND THEM...
...I'M GONNA KILL 'EM ALL.
KANATE?!
REVENGE... THEY KILLED GINCHI'S DAD TOO! THEY'RE UNFORGIVABLE!
THERE'S A PART OF ME THAT WANTS TO GO WITH YOU AND SEE THIS THROUGH TO THE END... BUT I'M NOT LIKE YOU.
YOU'RE KIDDING, RIGHT?

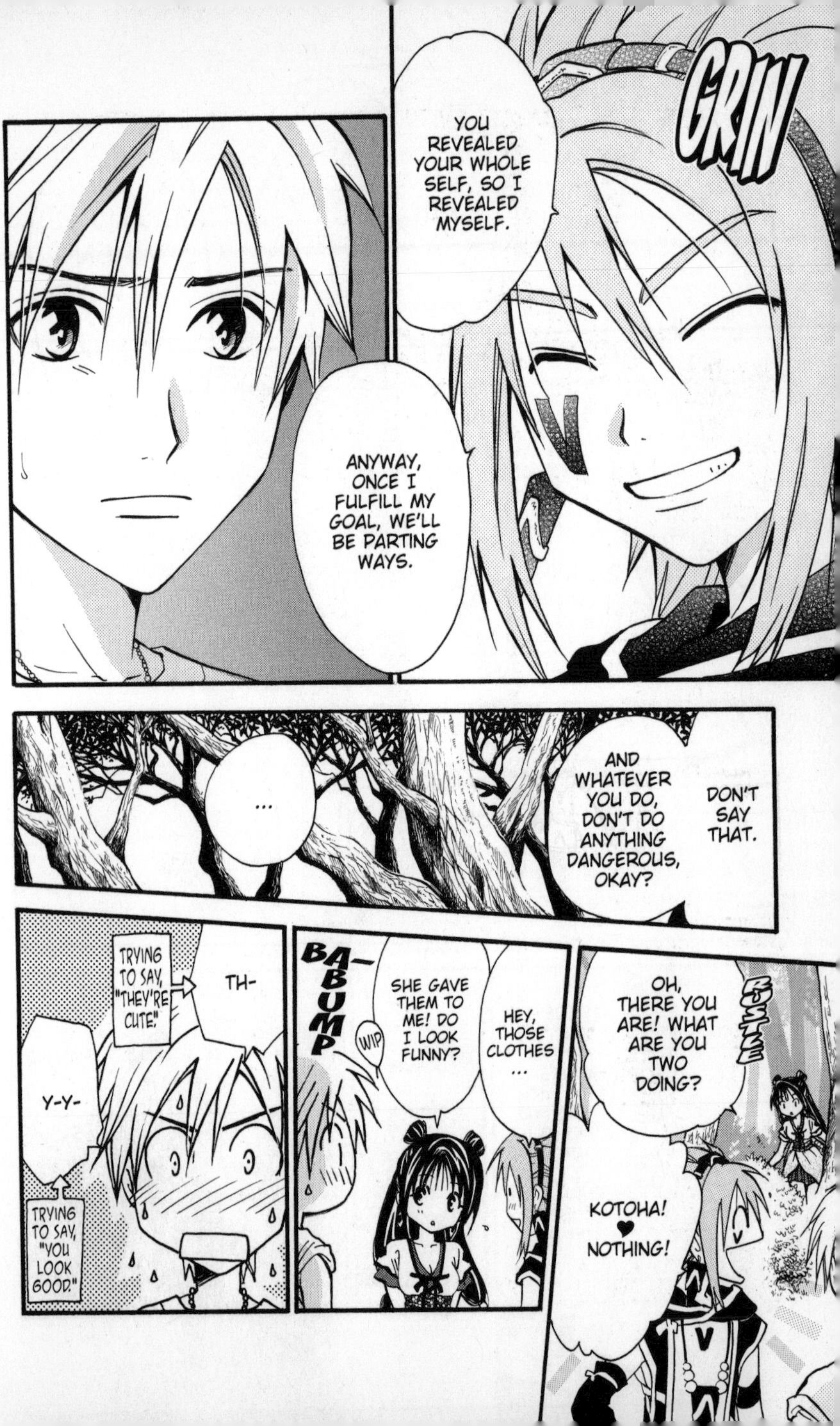
GRIN
YOU REVEALED YOUR WHOLE SELF, SO I REVEALED MYSELF.
ANYWAY, ONCE I FULFILL MY GOAL, WE'LL BE PARTING WAYS.
DON'T SAY THAT.
AND WHATEVER YOU DO, DON'T DO ANYTHING DANGEROUS, OKAY?
...
RUSTLE
OH, THERE YOU ARE! WHAT ARE YOU TWO DOING?
KOTOHA! ♥ NOTHING!
HEY, THOSE CLOTHES...
SHE GAVE THEM TO ME! DO I LOOK FUNNY?
WIP
BA-BUMP
TH-
TRYING TO SAY, "THEY'RE CUTE."
Y-Y-
TRYING TO SAY, "YOU LOOK GOOD."

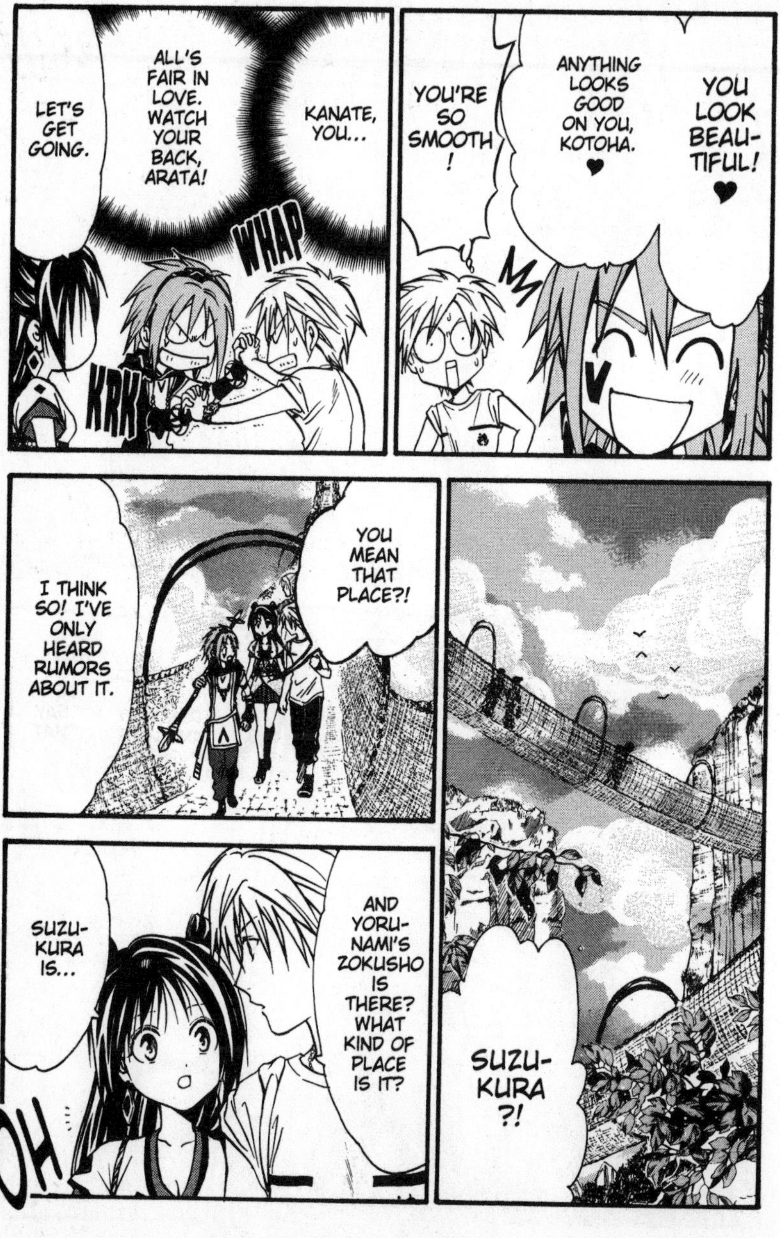
YOU LOOK BEAU-TIFUL! ♥
ANYTHING LOOKS GOOD ON YOU, KOTOHA. ♥
YOU'RE SO SMOOTH!
KANATE, YOU...
ALL'S FAIR IN LOVE. WATCH YOUR BACK, ARATA!
WHAP
KRK
LET'S GET GOING.
SUZU-KURA?!
YOU MEAN THAT PLACE?!
I THINK SO! I'VE ONLY HEARD RUMORS ABOUT IT.
AND YORU-NAMI'S ZOKUSHO IS THERE? WHAT KIND OF PLACE IS IT?
SUZU-KURA IS...
OH...

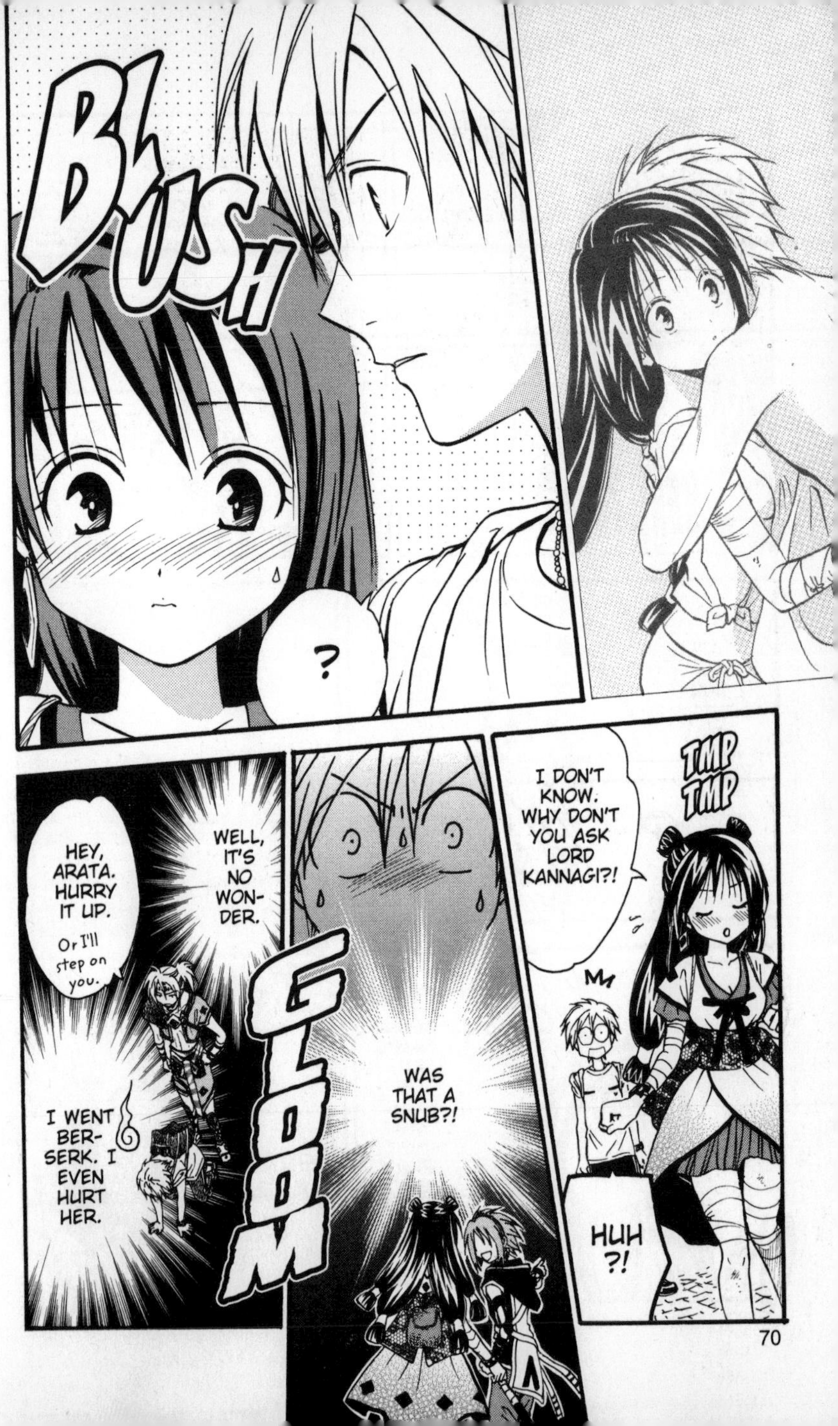
BLUSH
?
TMP TMP
I DON'T KNOW. WHY DON'T YOU ASK LORD KANNAGI?!
HUH?!
WAS THAT A SNUB?!
GLOOM
WELL, IT'S NO WON-DER.
HEY, ARATA. HURRY IT UP.
Or I'll step on you.
I WENT BER-SERK. I EVEN HURT HER.

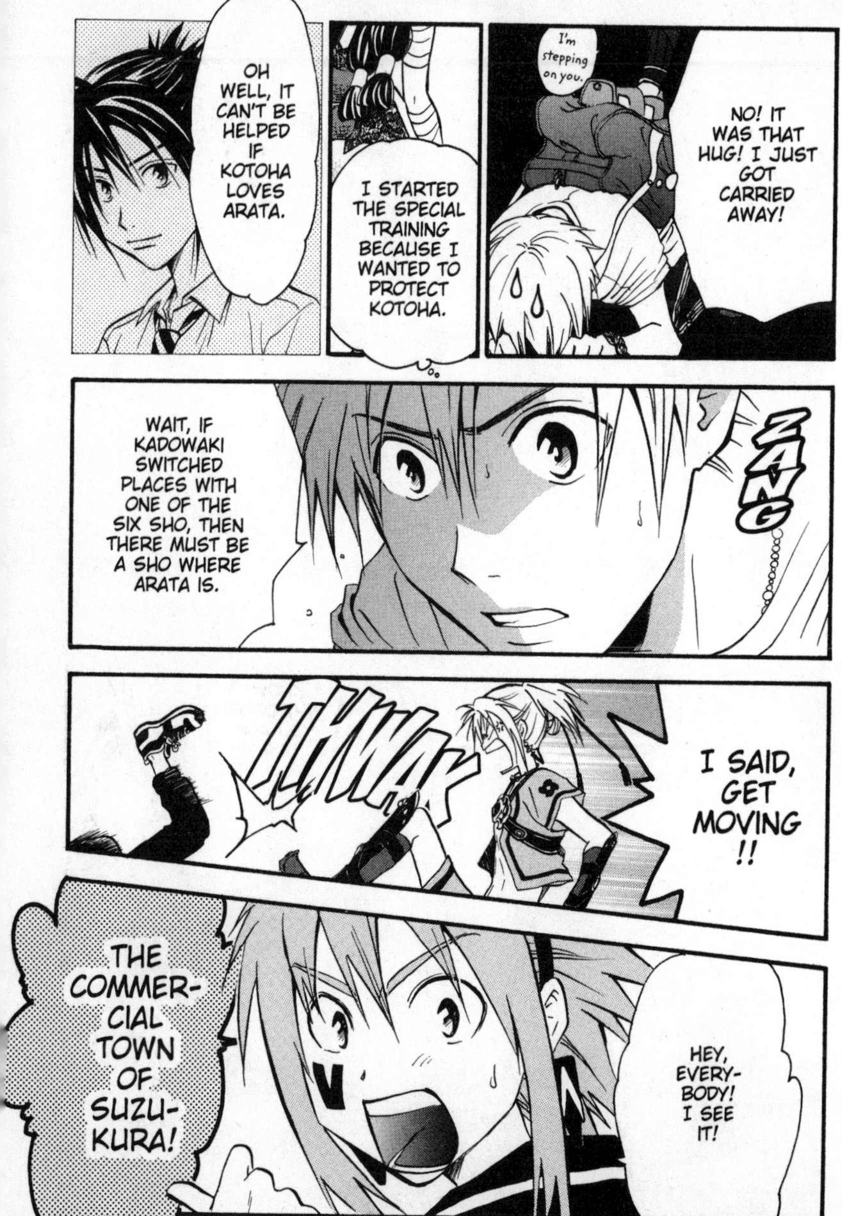
NO! IT WAS THAT HUG! I JUST GOT CARRIED AWAY!
I'm stepping on you.
I STARTED THE SPECIAL TRAINING BECAUSE I WANTED TO PROTECT KOTOHA.
OH WELL, IT CAN'T BE HELPED IF KOTOHA LOVES ARATA.
ZANG
WAIT, IF KADOWAKI SWITCHED PLACES WITH ONE OF THE SIX SHO, THEN THERE MUST BE A SHO WHERE ARATA IS.
I SAID, GET MOVING!!
THWAK
HEY, EVERY-BODY! I SEE IT!
THE COMMER-CIAL TOWN OF SUZU-KURA!

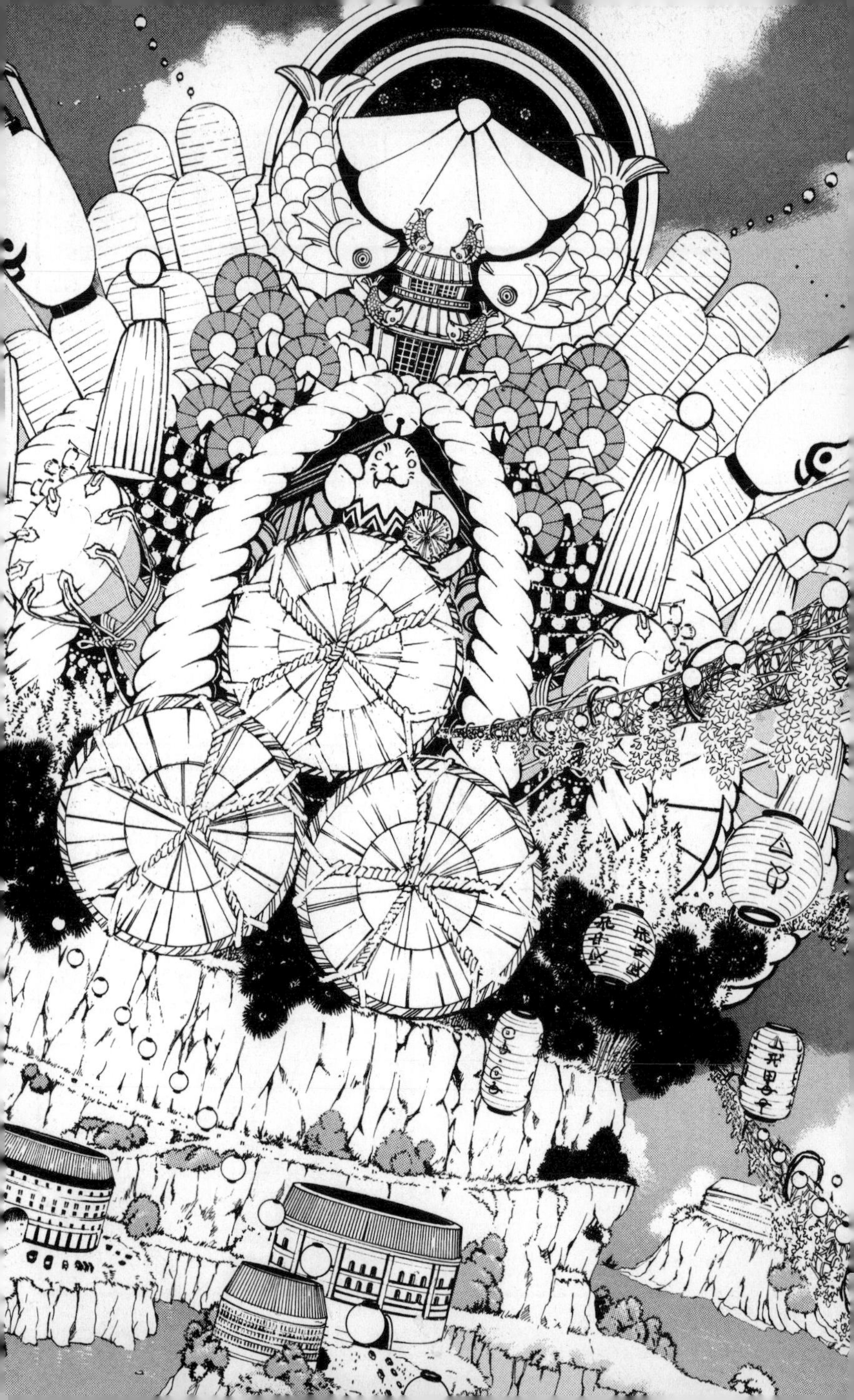

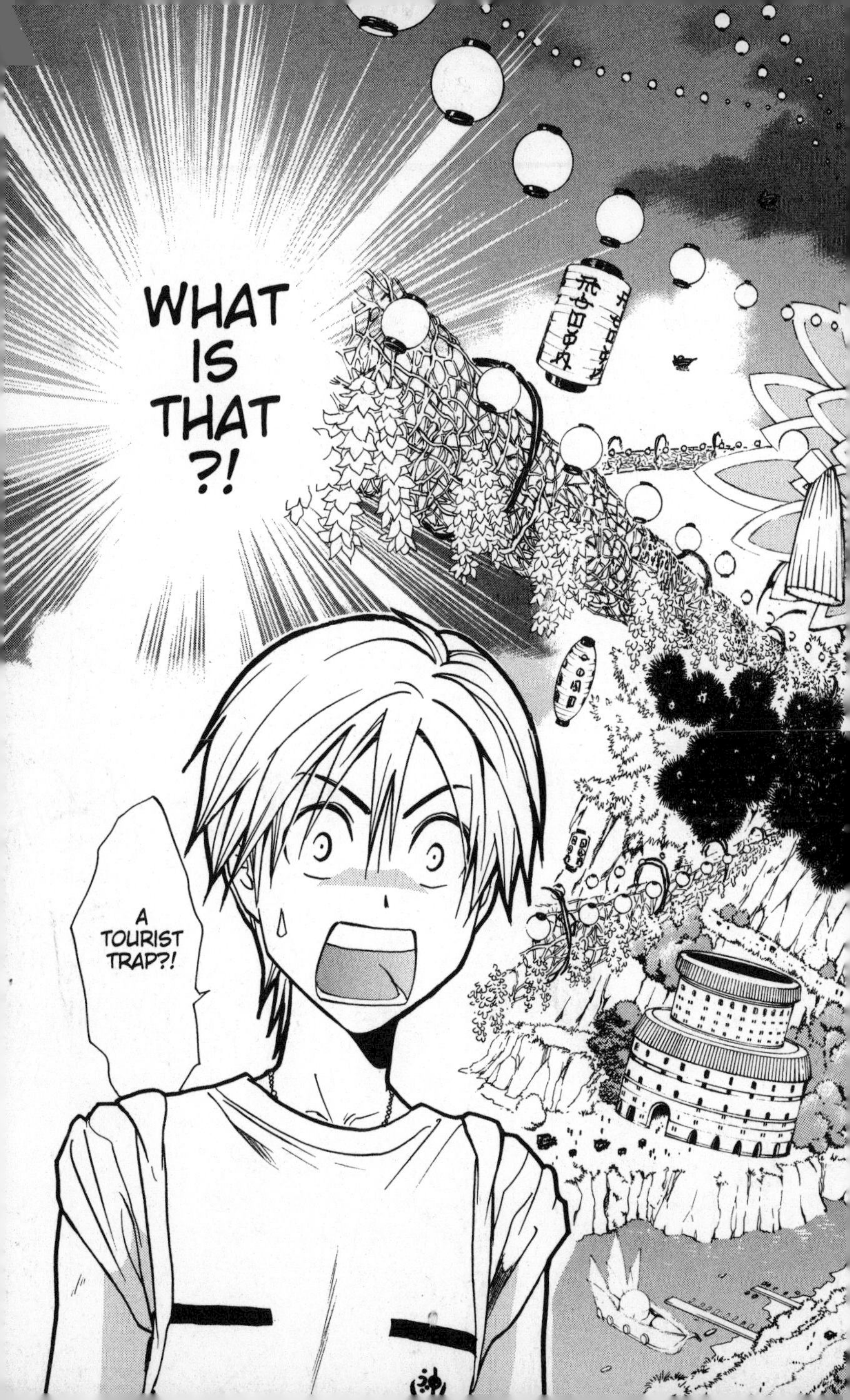
WHAT IS THAT?!
A TOURIST TRAP?!

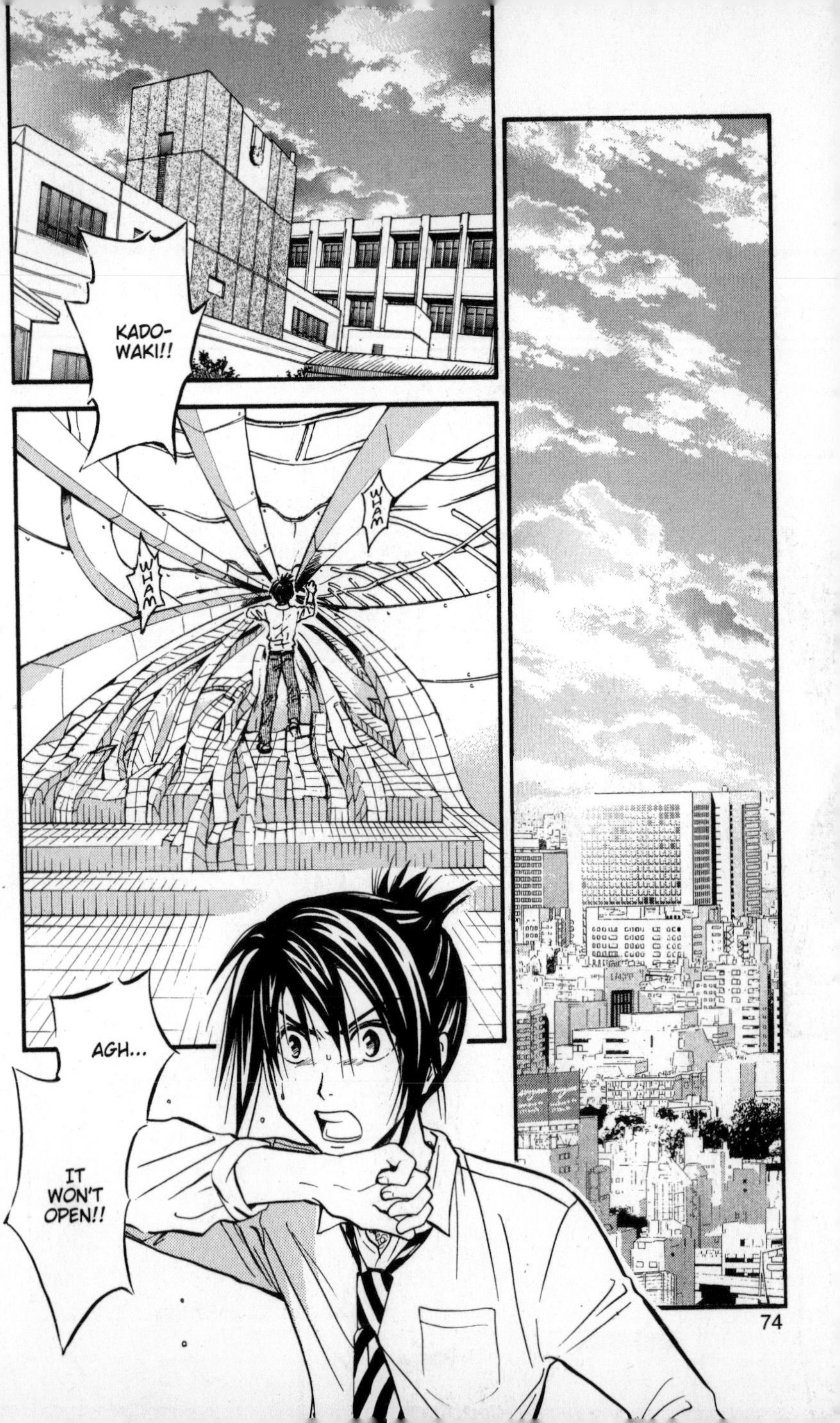
KADO-WAKI!!
WHAM
WHAM
AGH...
IT WON'T OPEN!!

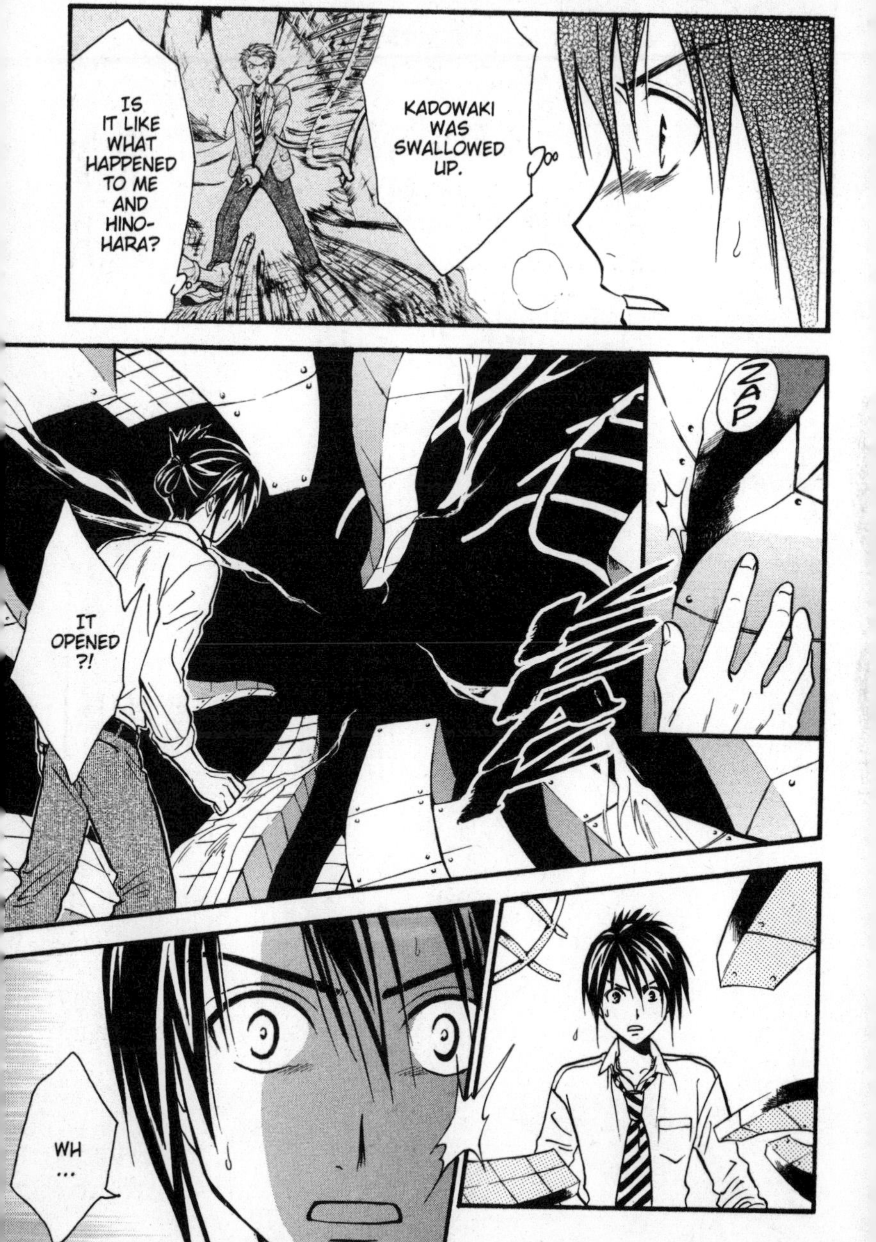
KADOWAKI WAS SWALLOWED UP.
IS IT LIKE WHAT HAPPENED TO ME AND HINO-HARA?
ZAP
IT OPENED ?!
WH ...

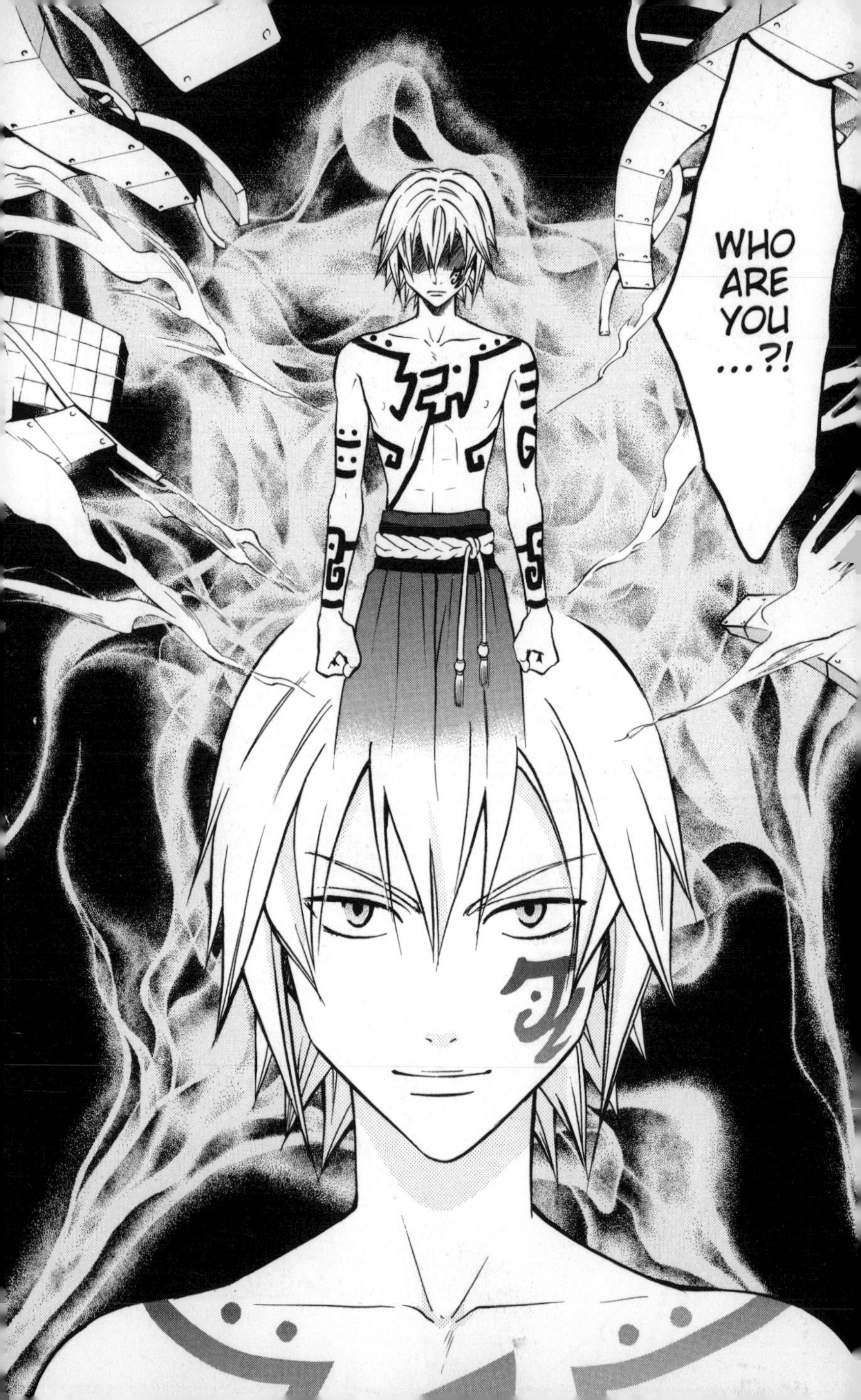
WHO ARE YOU ...?!

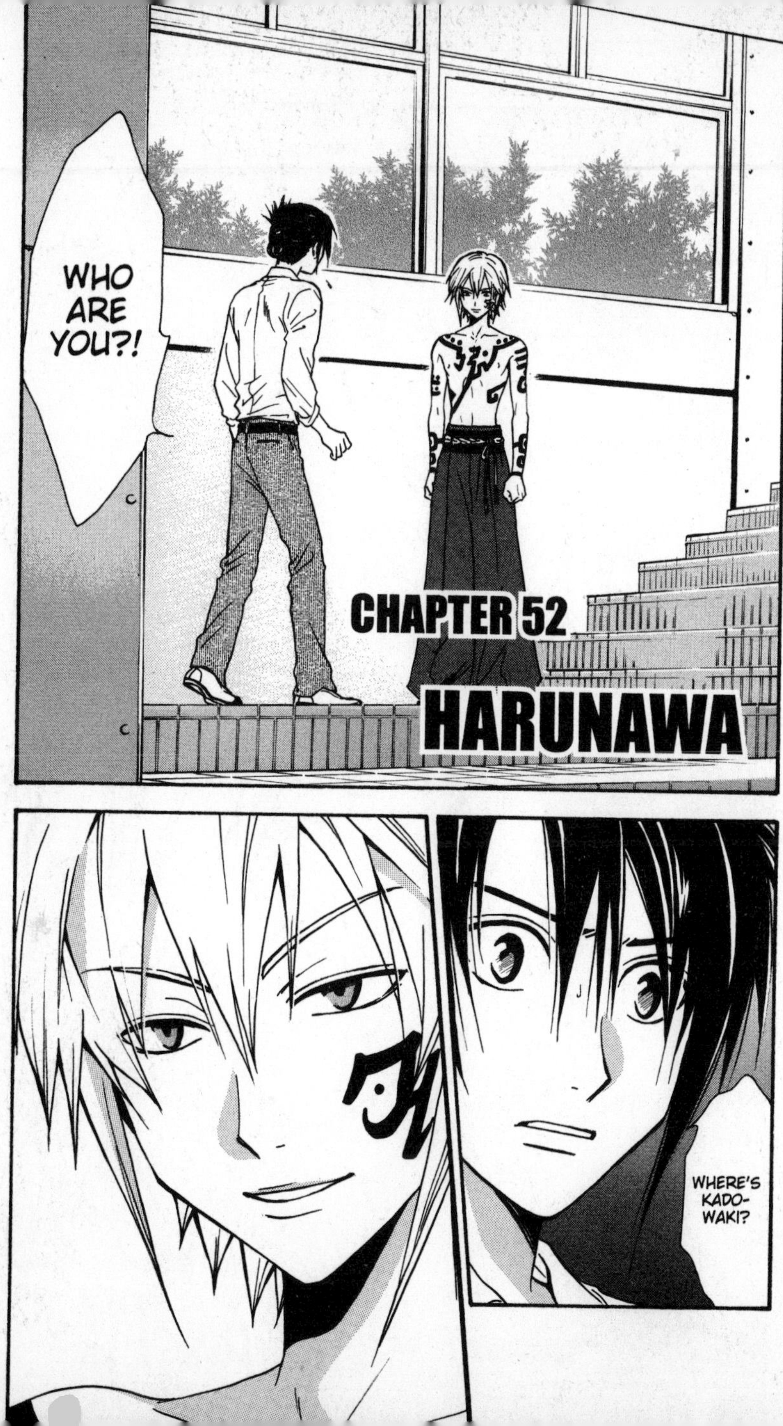
WHO ARE YOU?!
CHAPTER 52
HARUNAWA
WHERE'S KADO-WAKI?

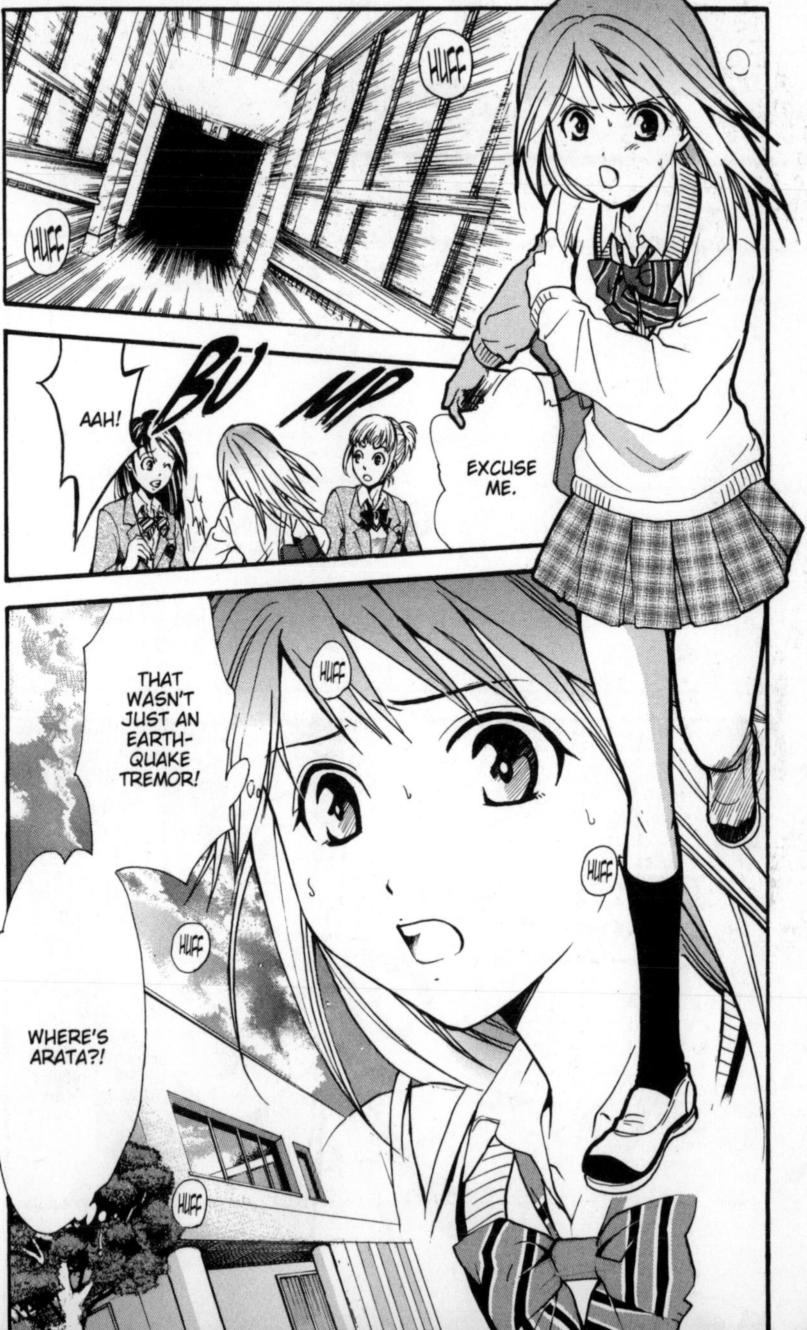
HUFF
HUFF
EXCUSE ME.
BUMP
AAH!
HUFF
THAT WASN'T JUST AN EARTH-QUAKE TREMOR!
HUFF
HUFF
WHERE'S ARATA?!
HUFF

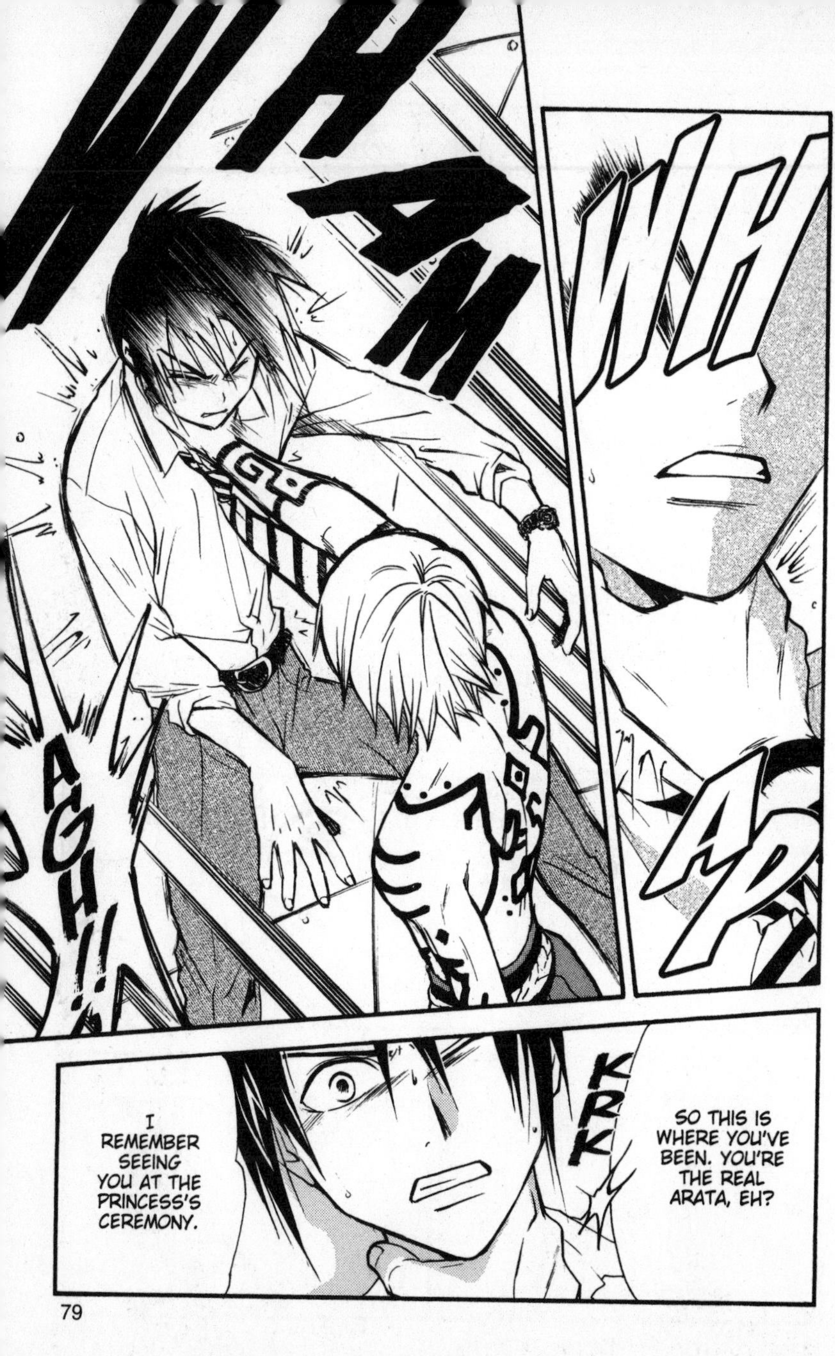
WHAP
WHAM
AGH!!
SO THIS IS WHERE YOU'VE BEEN. YOU'RE THE REAL ARATA, EH?
KRK
I REMEMBER SEEING YOU AT THE PRINCESS'S CEREMONY.

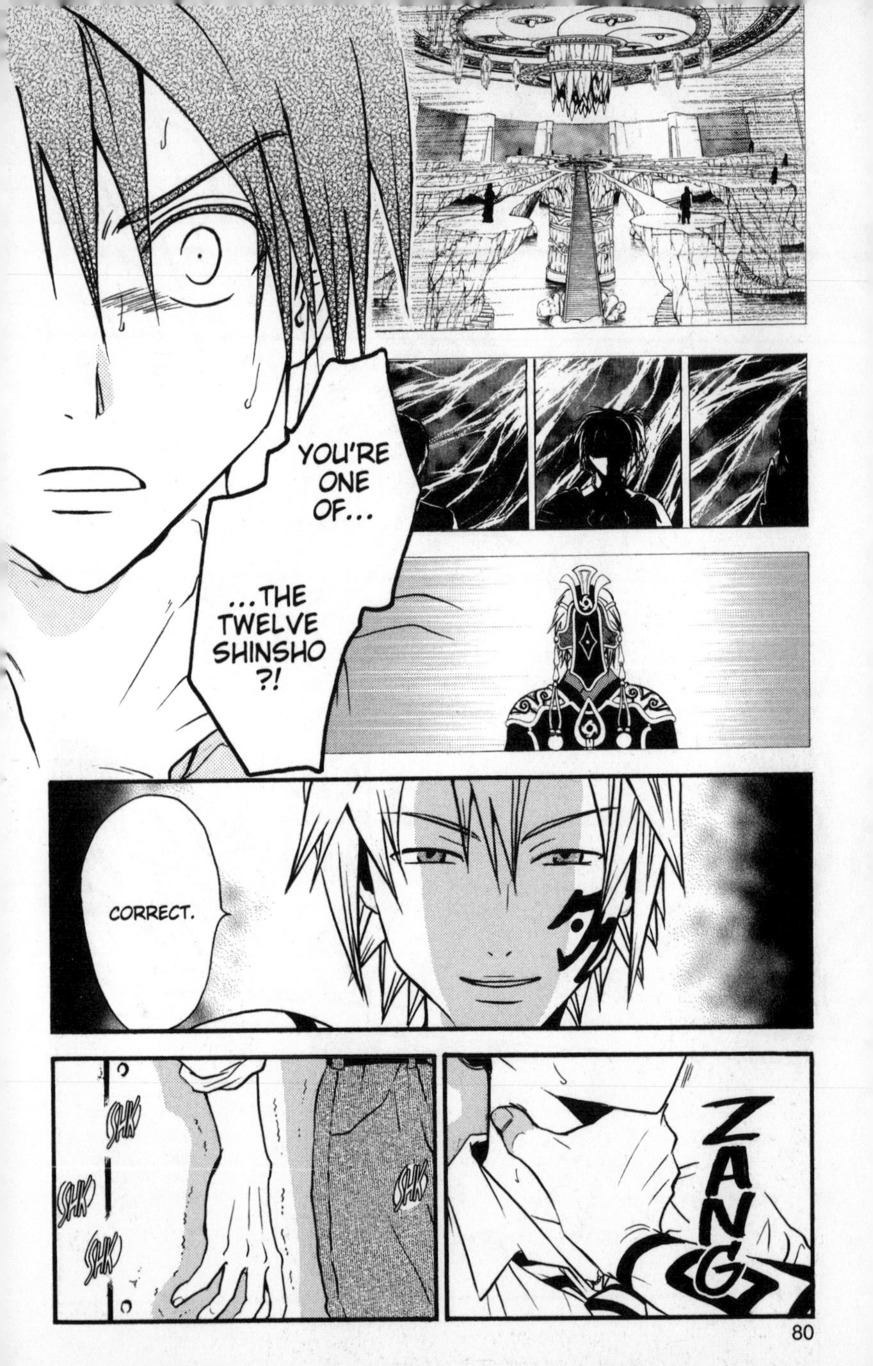
YOU'RE ONE OF...
...THE TWELVE SHINSHO ?!
CORRECT.
ZANG
SHK SHK SHK SHK

SCARED
...

...OF THIS GUY?!

WHAT ?!

AM I SCARED ...?!

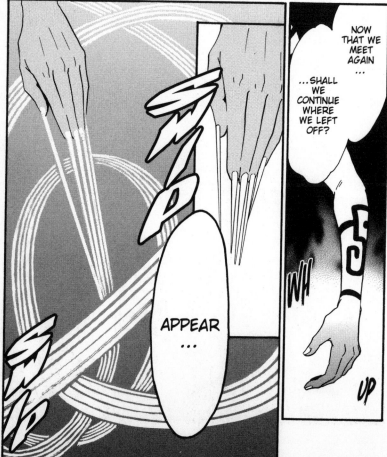

NOW THAT WE MEET AGAIN ...

...SHALL WE CONTINUE WHERE WE LEFT OFF?

APPEAR ...

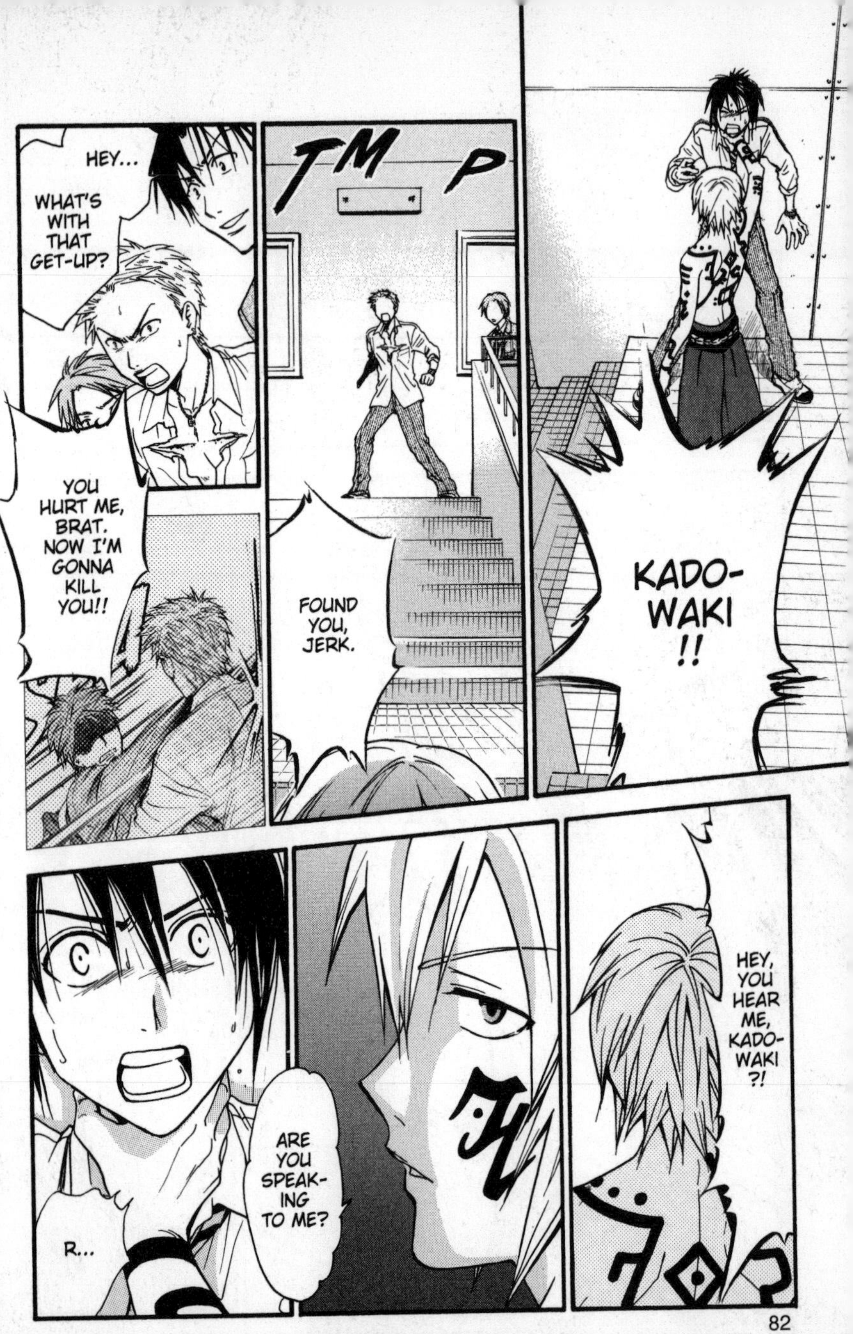
KADO-WAKI!!
TMP
FOUND YOU, JERK.
HEY...
WHAT'S WITH THAT GET-UP?
YOU HURT ME, BRAT. NOW I'M GONNA KILL YOU!!
HEY, YOU HEAR ME, KADO-WAKI?!
ARE YOU SPEAK-ING TO ME?
R...

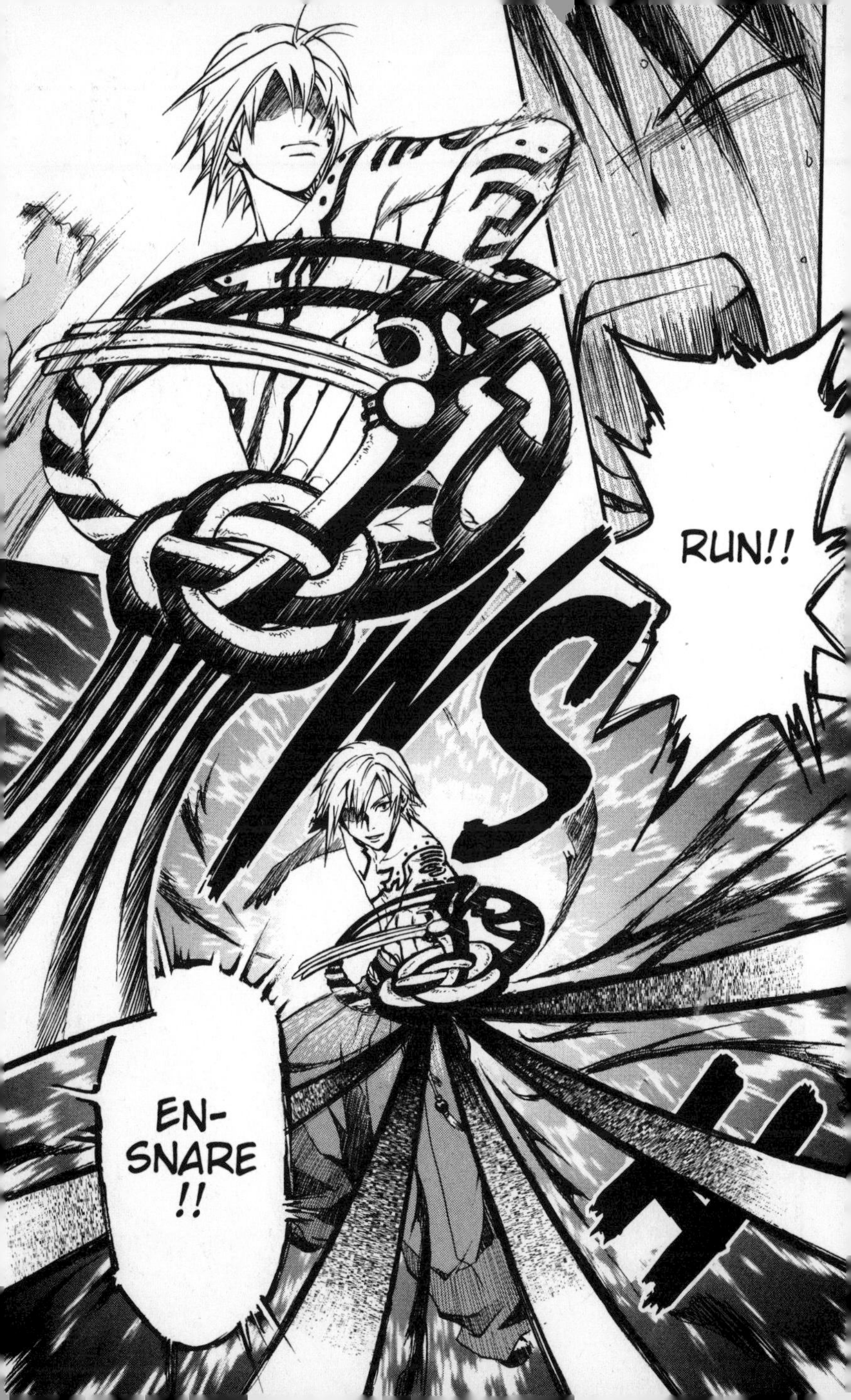
RUN!!
EN-
SNARE
!!

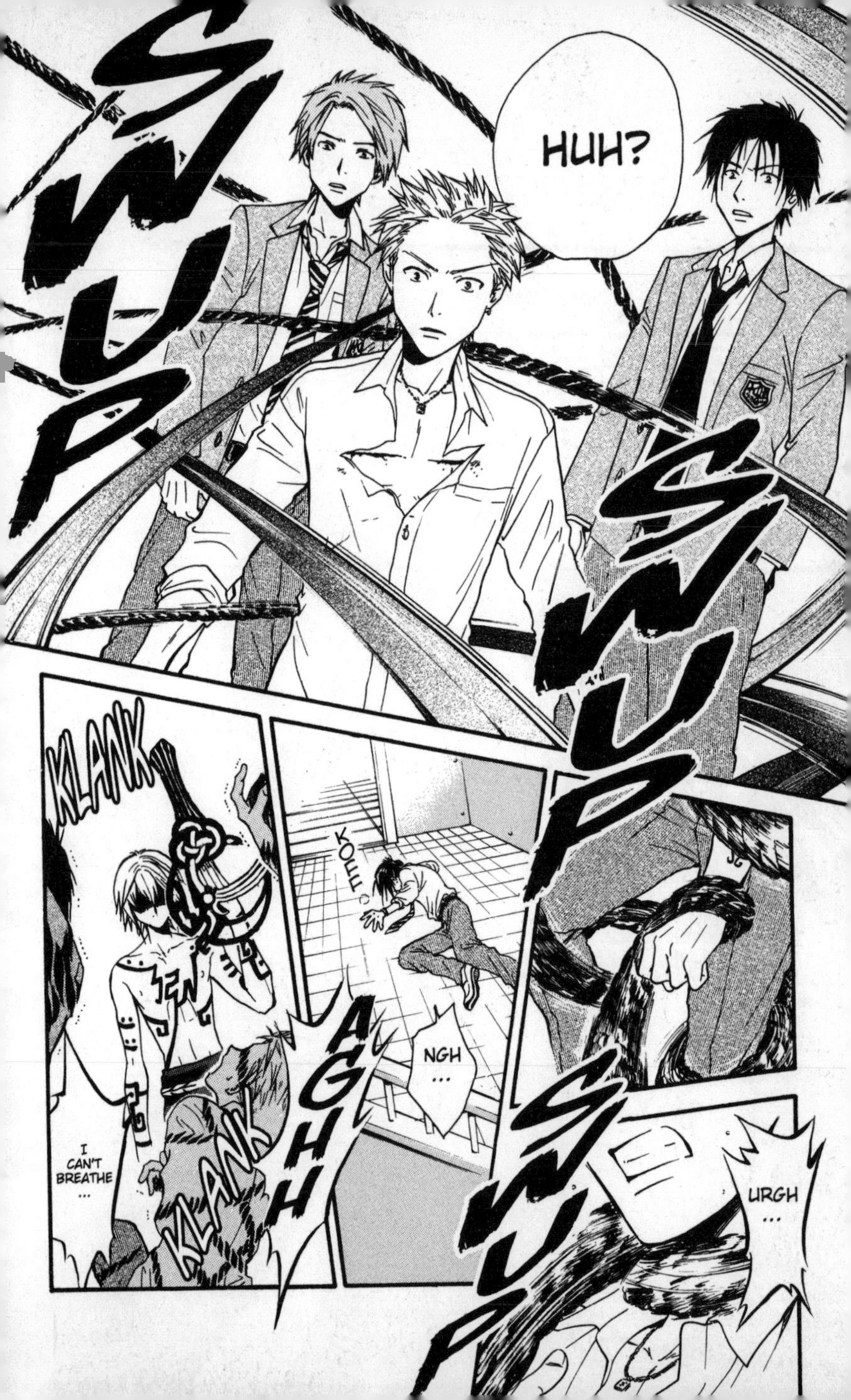
HUH?
SWUP
SWUP
URGH ...
SWUP
KOFF
NGH ...
AGHHH
KLANK
I CAN'T BREATHE ...
KLANK

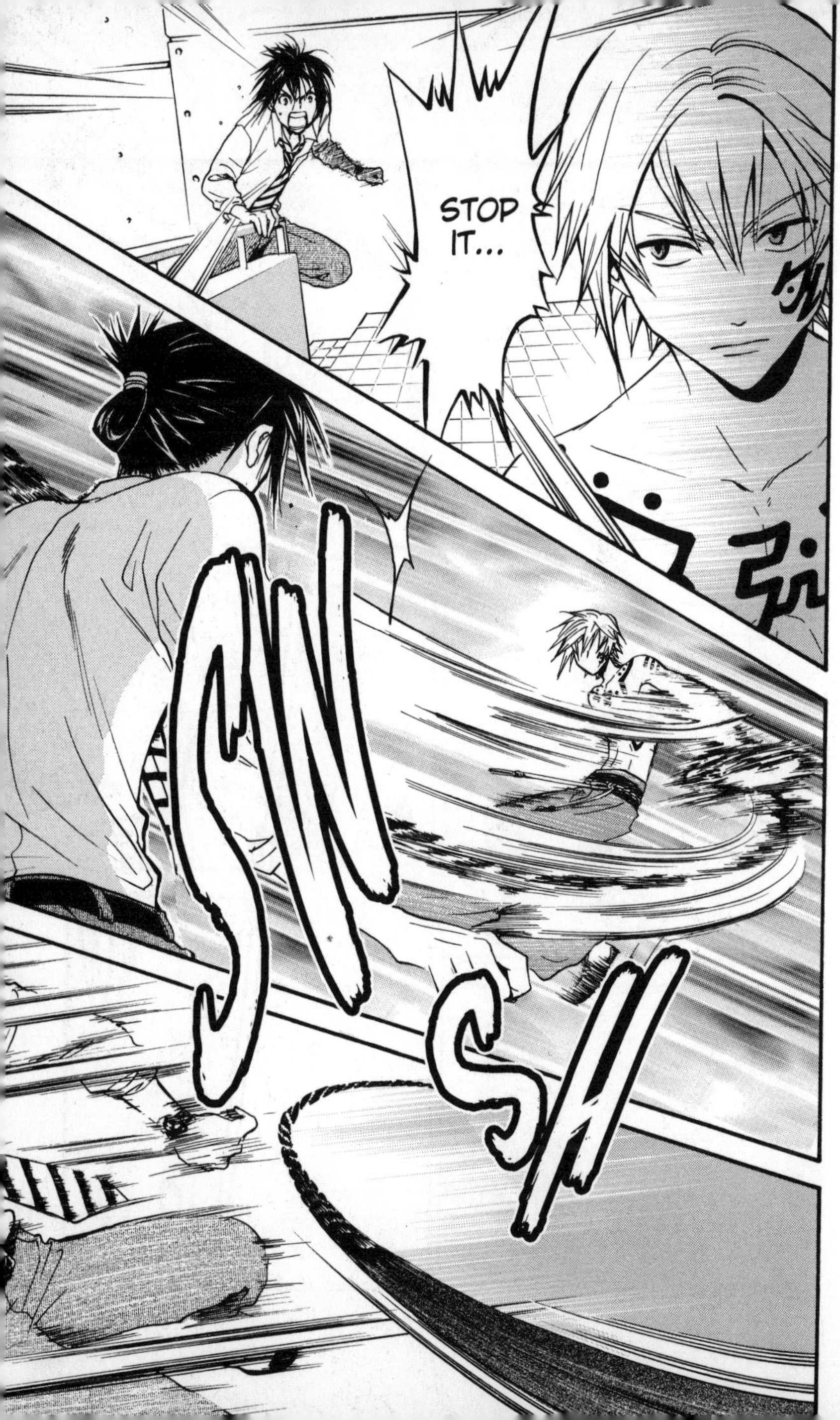
STOP IT...
SWSH

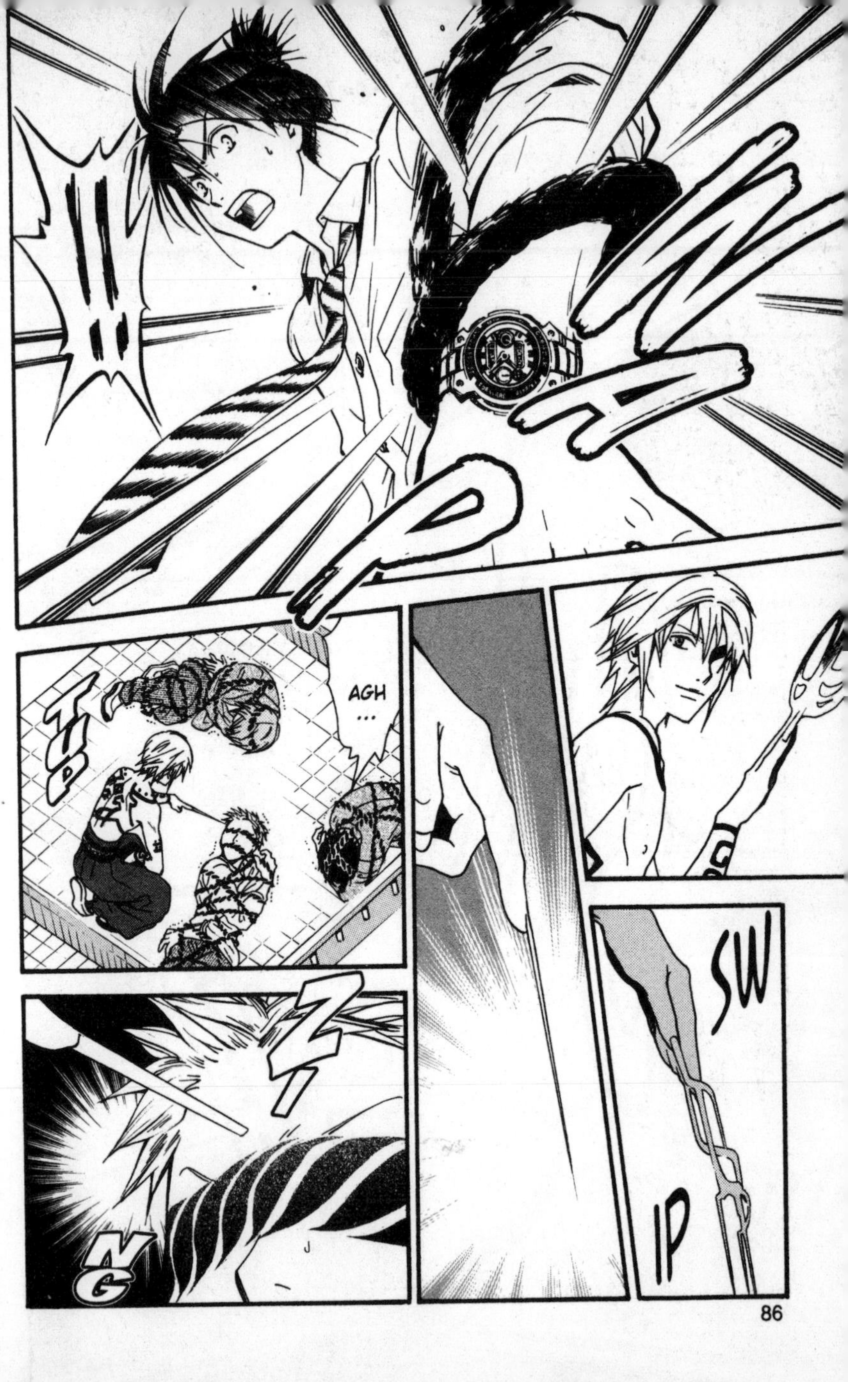
!!
NAP
SW
IP
AGH ...
TUD
Z
I
NG

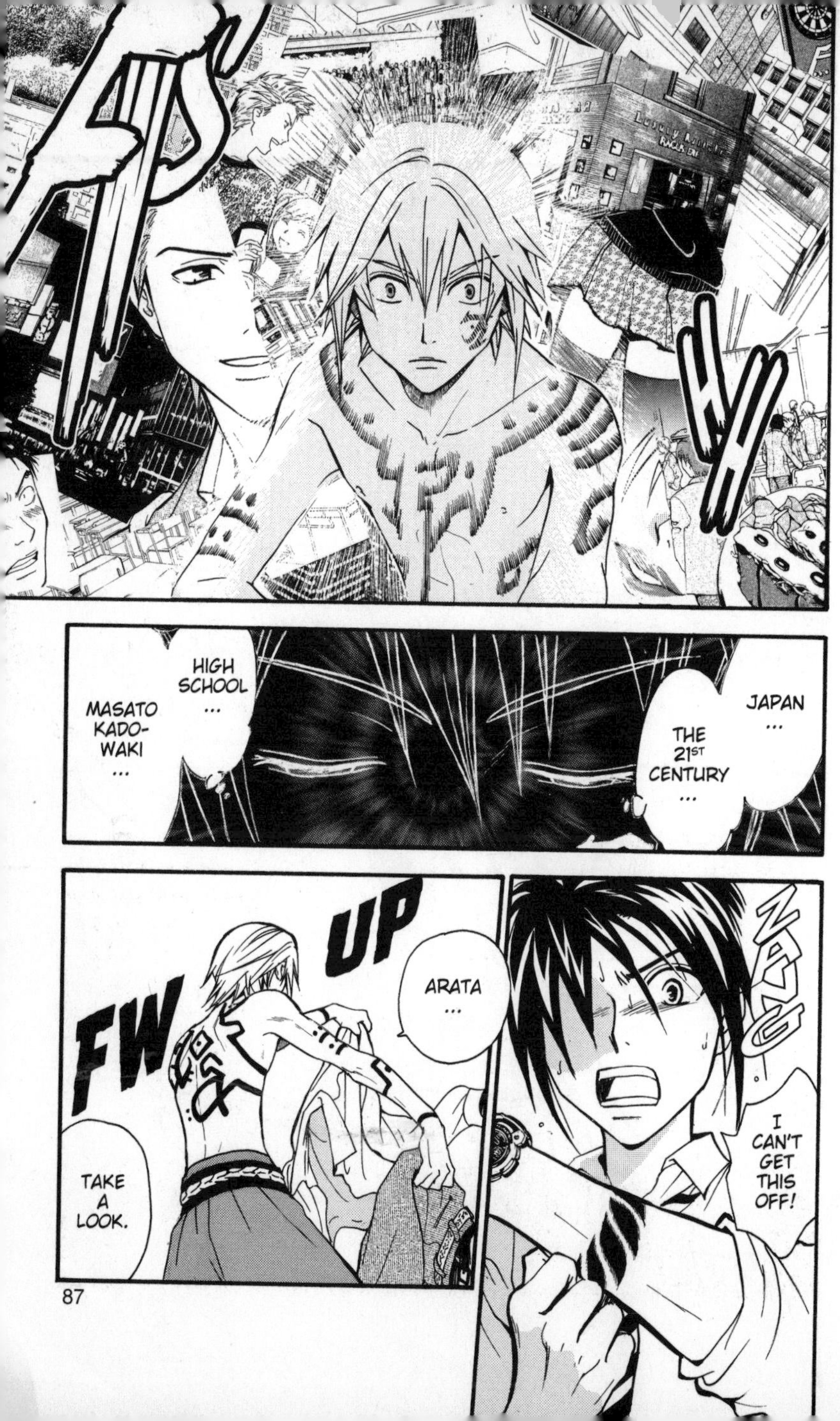

HH
FLAP
JAPAN ...
THE 21ST CENTURY ...
HIGH SCHOOL ...
MASATO KADO-WAKI ...
NNGH
I CAN'T GET THIS OFF!
ARATA ...
FWUP
TAKE A LOOK.

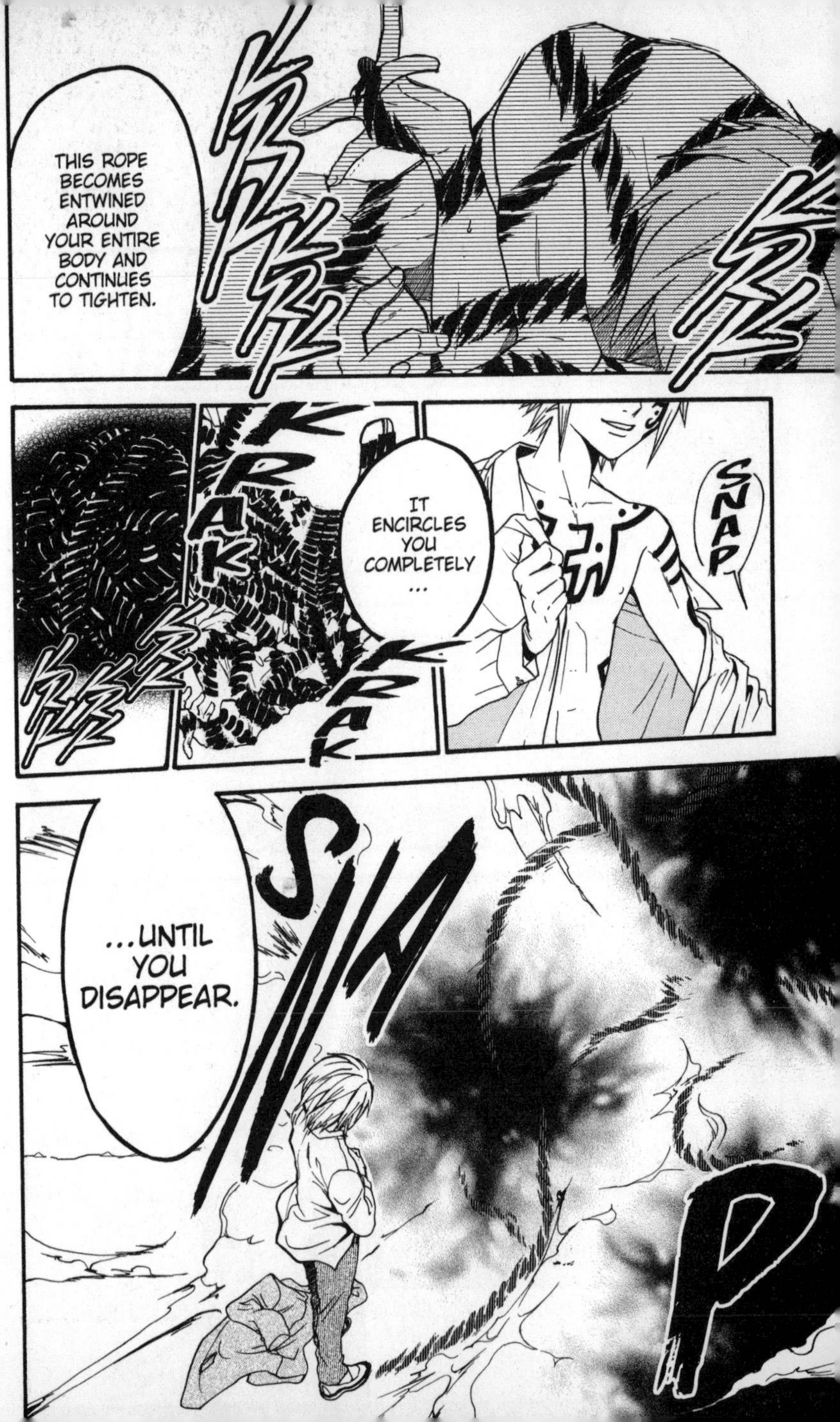
THIS ROPE BECOMES ENTWINED AROUND YOUR ENTIRE BODY AND CONTINUES TO TIGHTEN.
SNAP
IT ENCIRCLES YOU COMPLETELY ...
FRAK
FRAK
...UNTIL YOU DISAPPEAR.

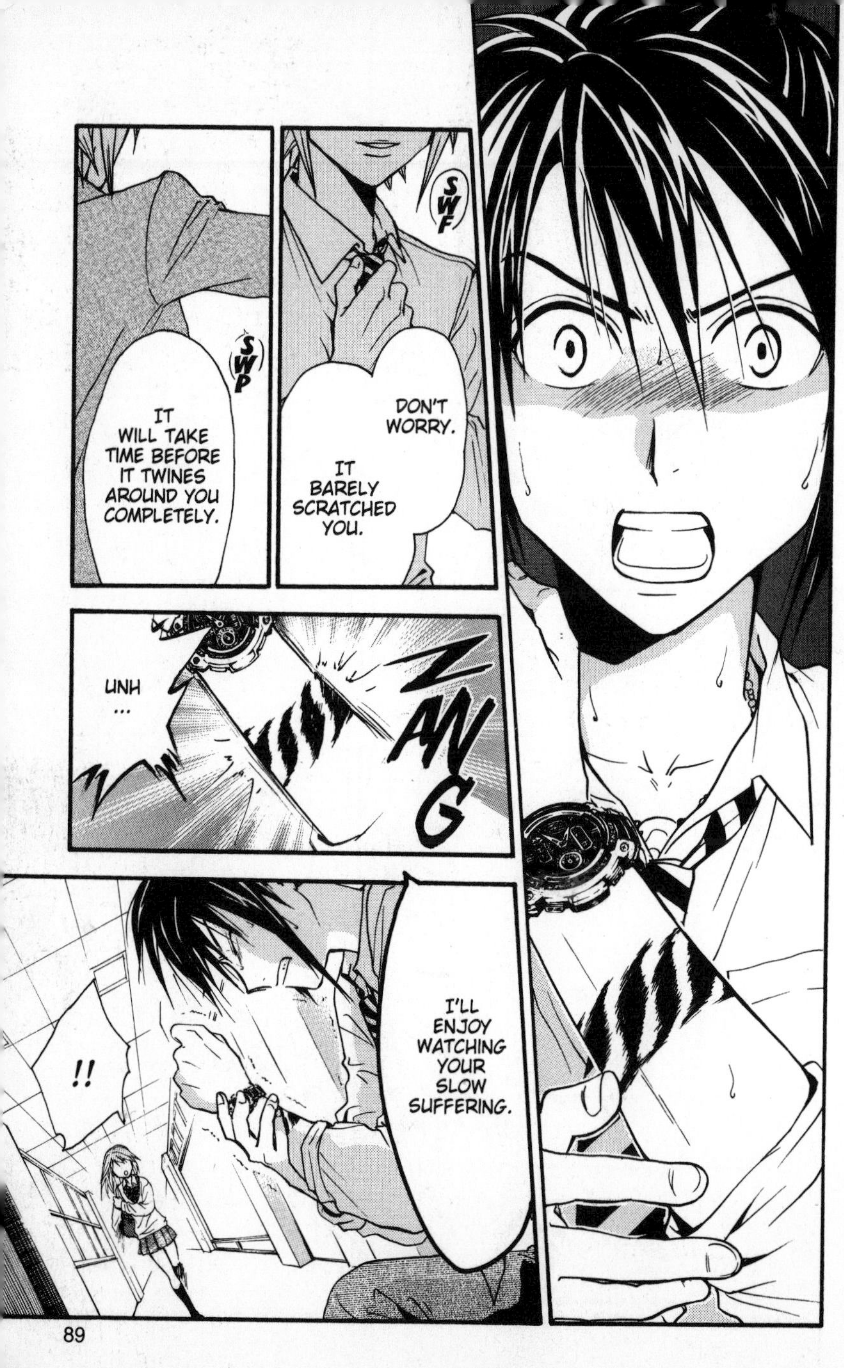
SWF
DON'T WORRY.
IT BARELY SCRATCHED YOU.
SWP
IT WILL TAKE TIME BEFORE IT TWINES AROUND YOU COMPLETELY.
ZANG
UNH ...
I'LL ENJOY WATCHING YOUR SLOW SUFFERING.
!!

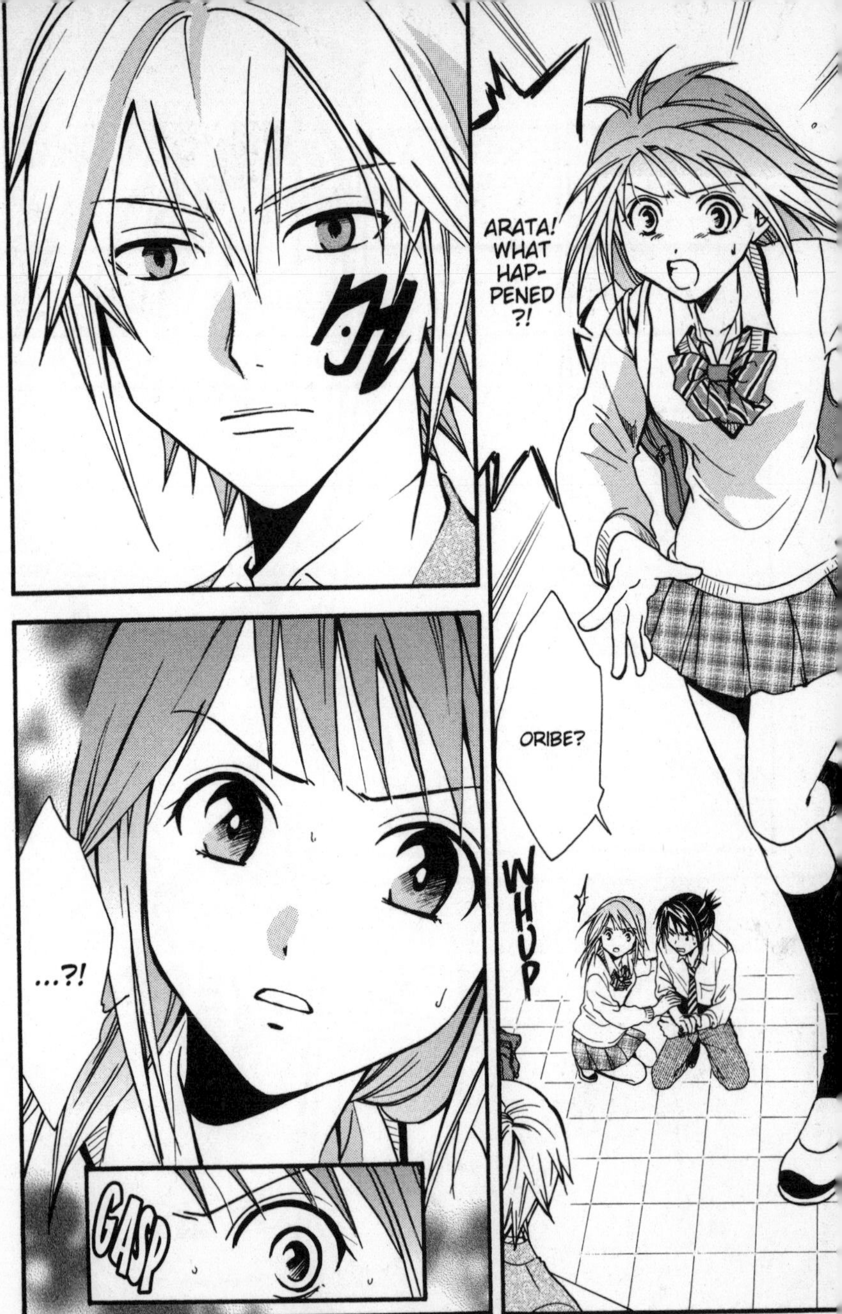
ARATA! WHAT HAP-PENED ?!
ORIBE?
WHUP
...?!
GASP

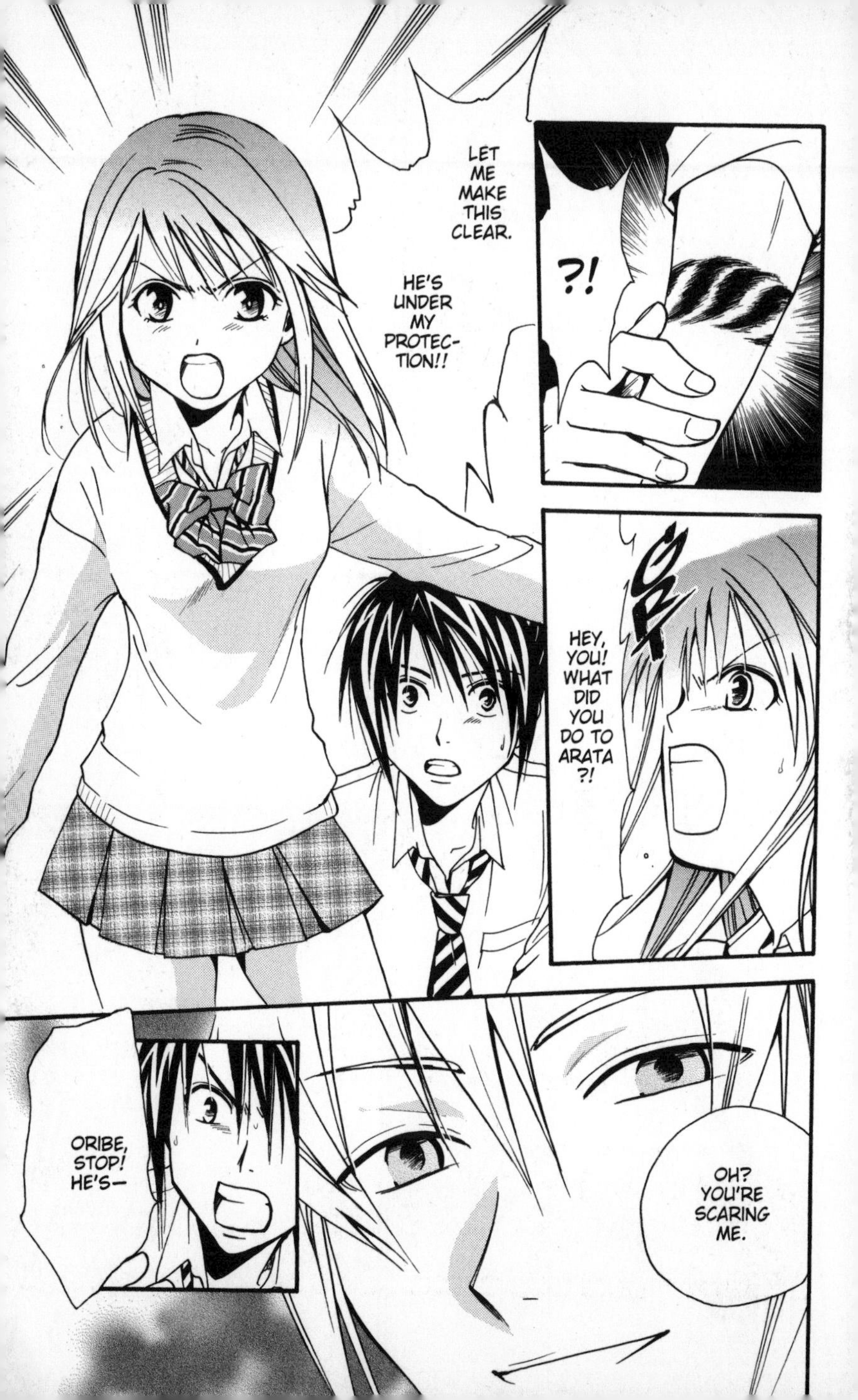
?!
HEY, YOU! WHAT DID YOU DO TO ARATA?!
LET ME MAKE THIS CLEAR.
HE'S UNDER MY PROTECTION!!
OH? YOU'RE SCARING ME.
ORIBE, STOP! HE'S—

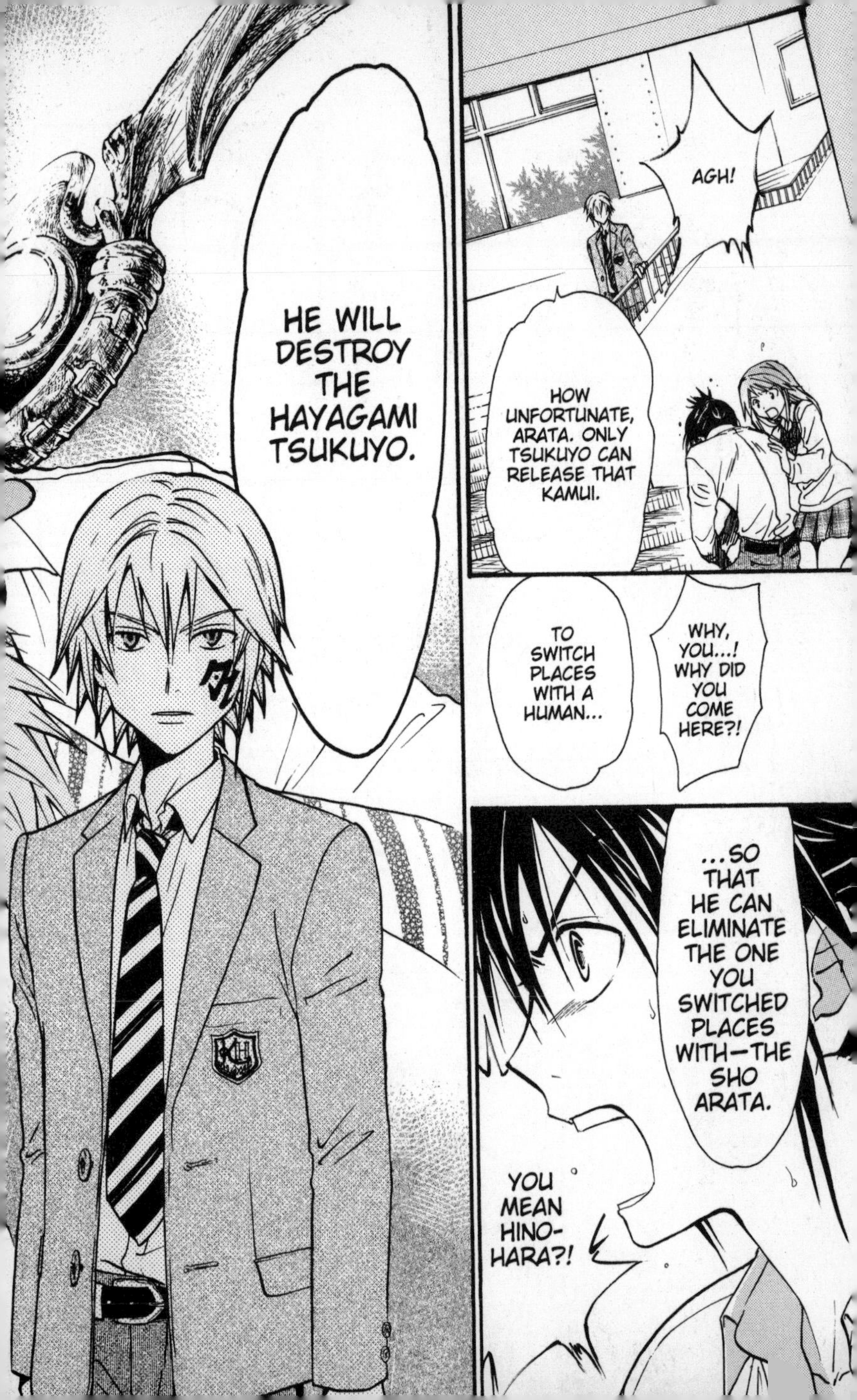
AGH!
HOW UNFORTUNATE, ARATA. ONLY TSUKUYO CAN RELEASE THAT KAMUI.
WHY, YOU...! WHY DID YOU COME HERE?!
TO SWITCH PLACES WITH A HUMAN...
...SO THAT HE CAN ELIMINATE THE ONE YOU SWITCHED PLACES WITH—THE SHO ARATA.
YOU MEAN HINO-HARA?!
HE WILL DESTROY THE HAYAGAMI TSUKUYO.

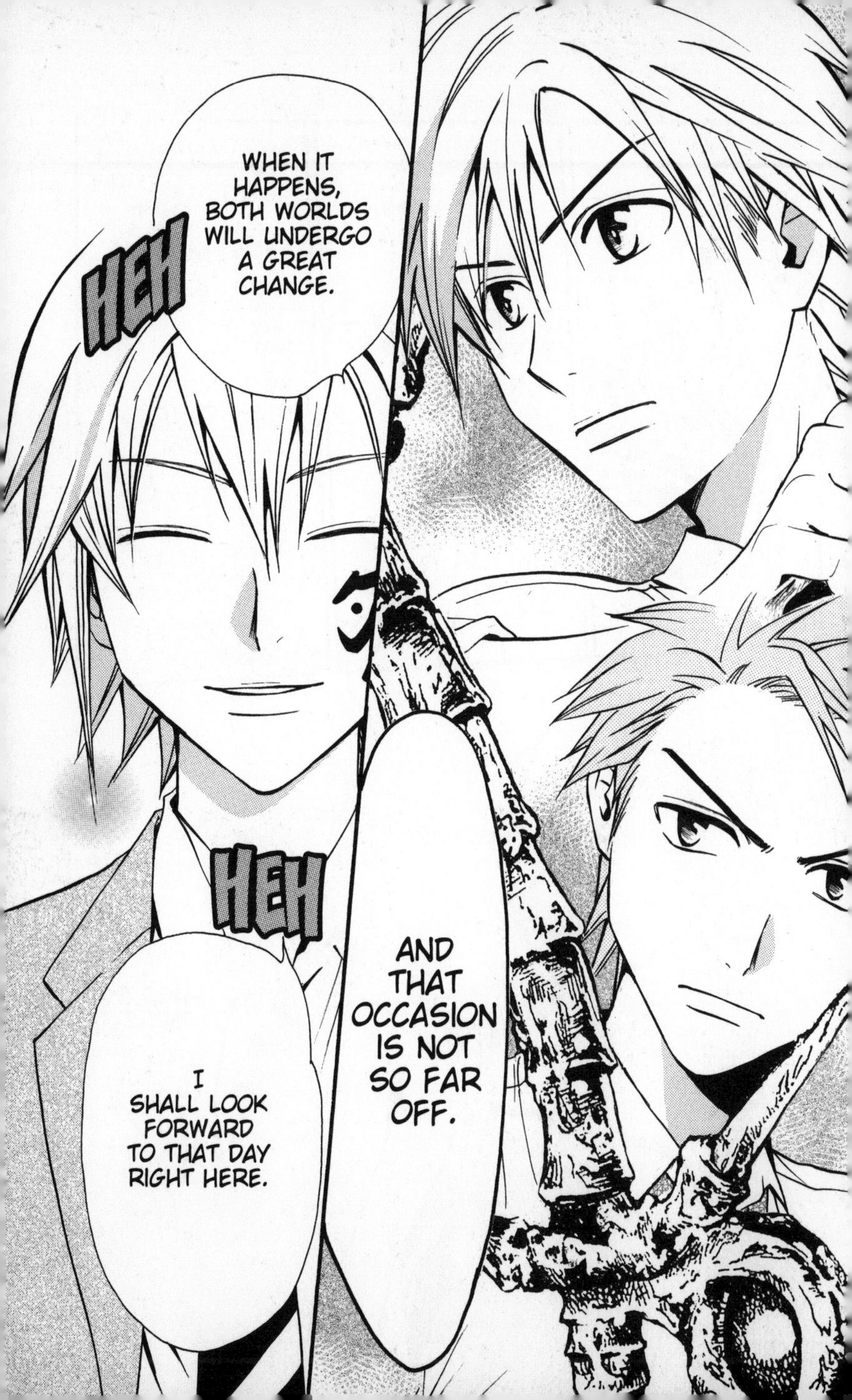
WHEN IT HAPPENS, BOTH WORLDS WILL UNDERGO A GREAT CHANGE.
HEH
HEH
AND THAT OCCASION IS NOT SO FAR OFF.
I SHALL LOOK FORWARD TO THAT DAY RIGHT HERE.

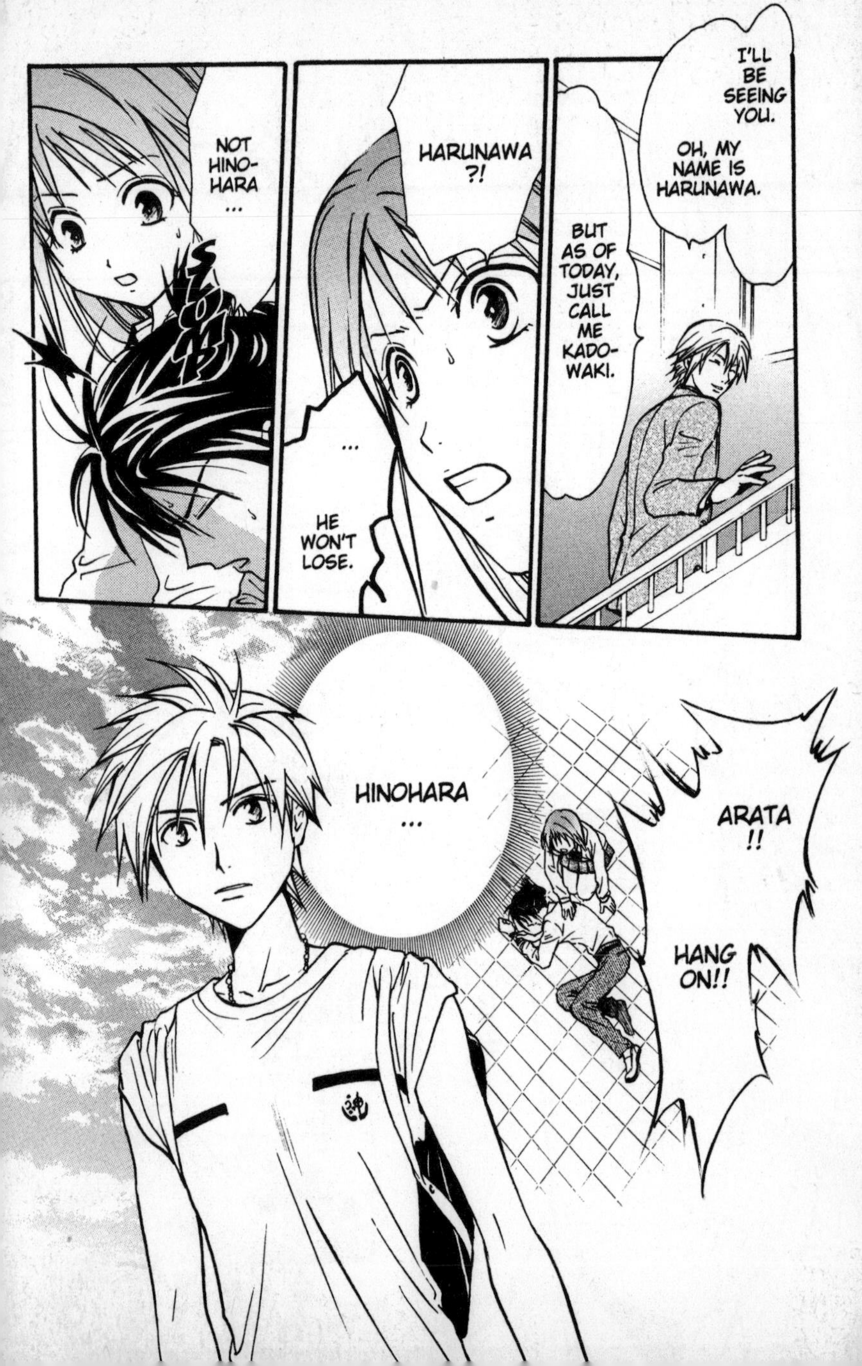
I'LL BE SEEING YOU.
OH, MY NAME IS HARUNAWA.
BUT AS OF TODAY, JUST CALL ME KADOWAKI.
HARUNAWA?!
...
HE WON'T LOSE.
NOT HINOHARA...
ARATA!!
HANG ON!!
HINOHARA...

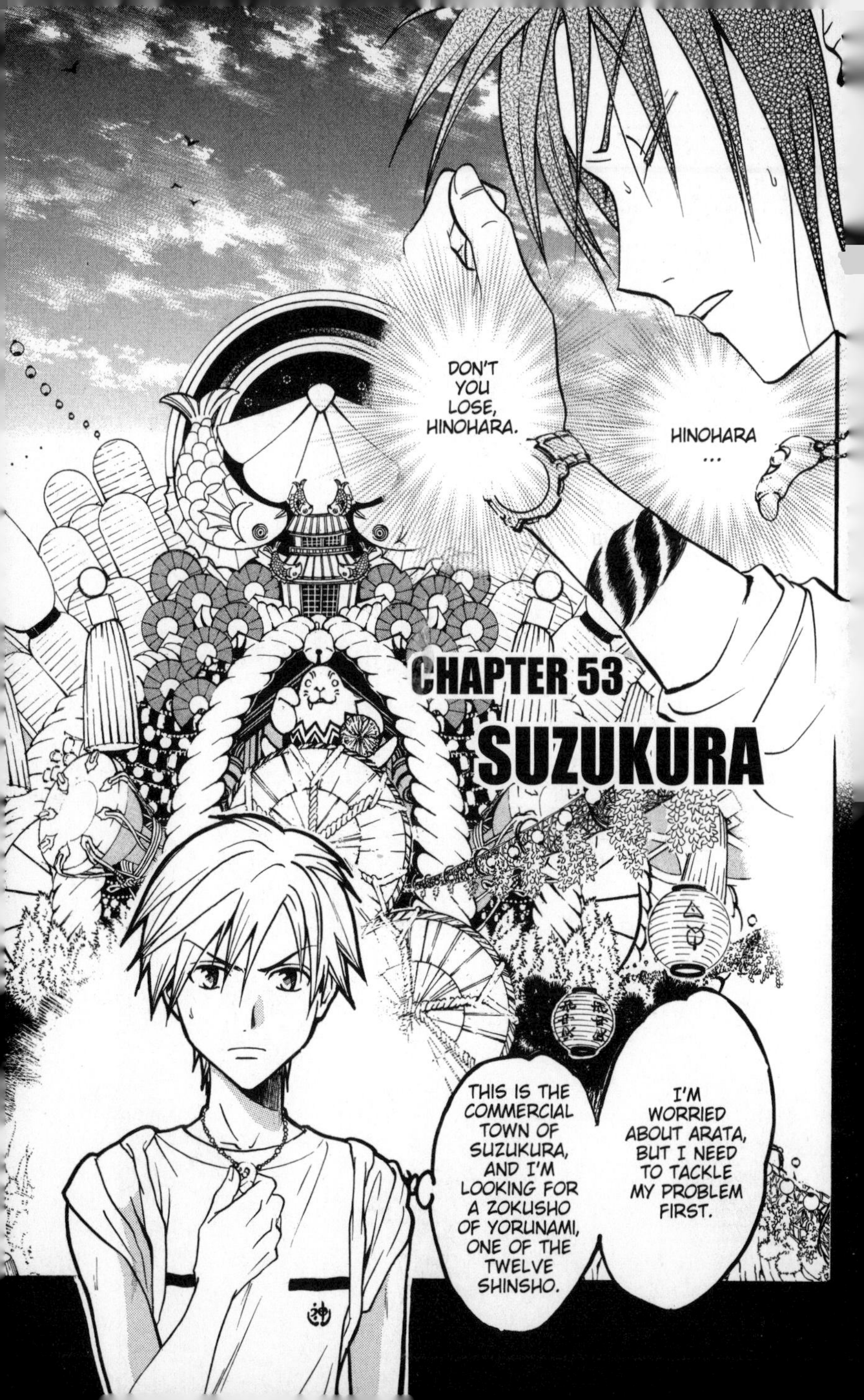
HINOHARA ...
DON'T YOU LOSE, HINOHARA.
CHAPTER 53
SUZUKURA
I'M WORRIED ABOUT ARATA, BUT I NEED TO TACKLE MY PROBLEM FIRST.
THIS IS THE COMMERCIAL TOWN OF SUZUKURA, AND I'M LOOKING FOR A ZOKUSHO OF YORUNAMI, ONE OF THE TWELVE SHINSHO.

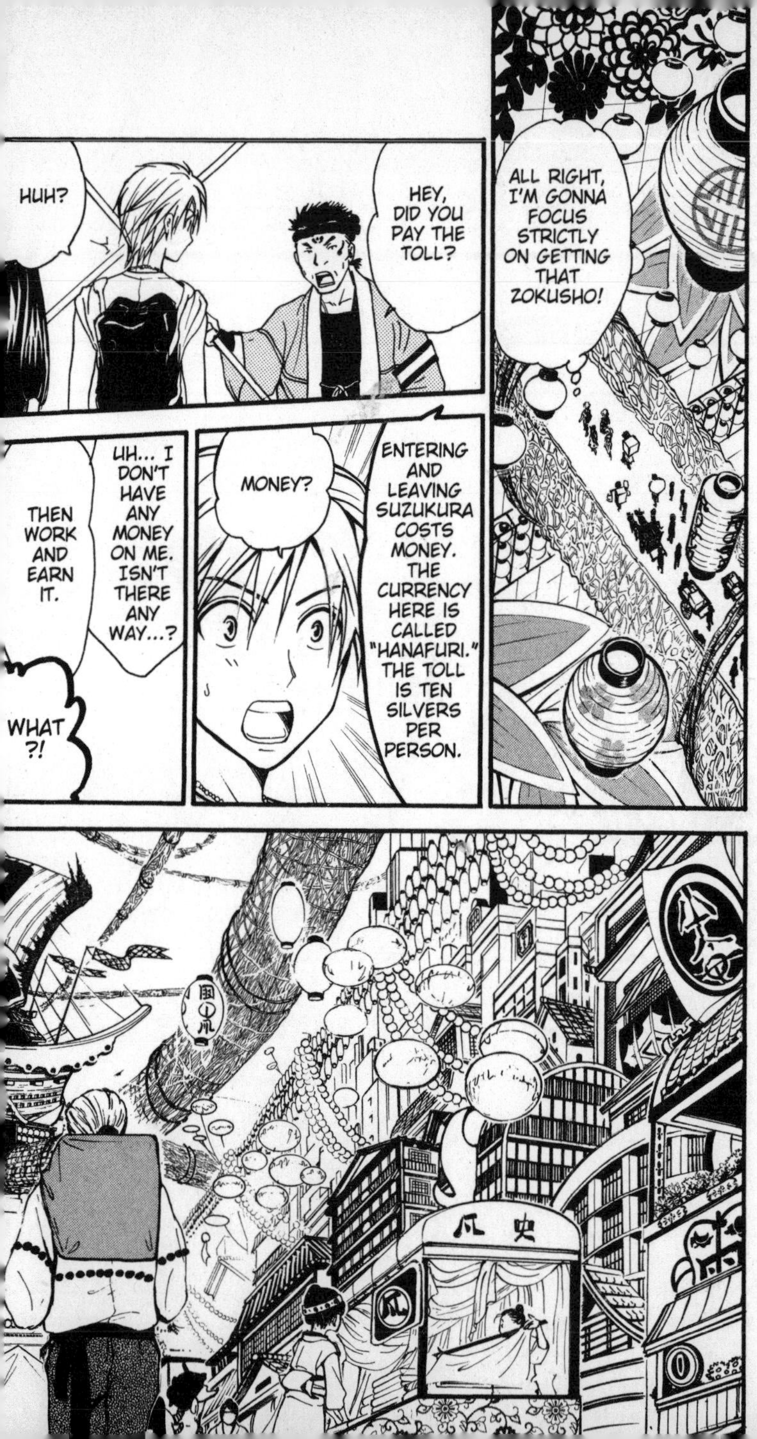
ALL RIGHT, I'M GONNA FOCUS STRICTLY ON GETTING THAT ZOKUSHO!
HEY, DID YOU PAY THE TOLL?
HUH?
ENTERING AND LEAVING SUZUKURA COSTS MONEY. THE CURRENCY HERE IS CALLED "HANAFURI." THE TOLL IS TEN SILVERS PER PERSON.
MONEY?
UH... I DON'T HAVE ANY MONEY ON ME. ISN'T THERE ANY WAY...?
THEN WORK AND EARN IT.
WHAT?!

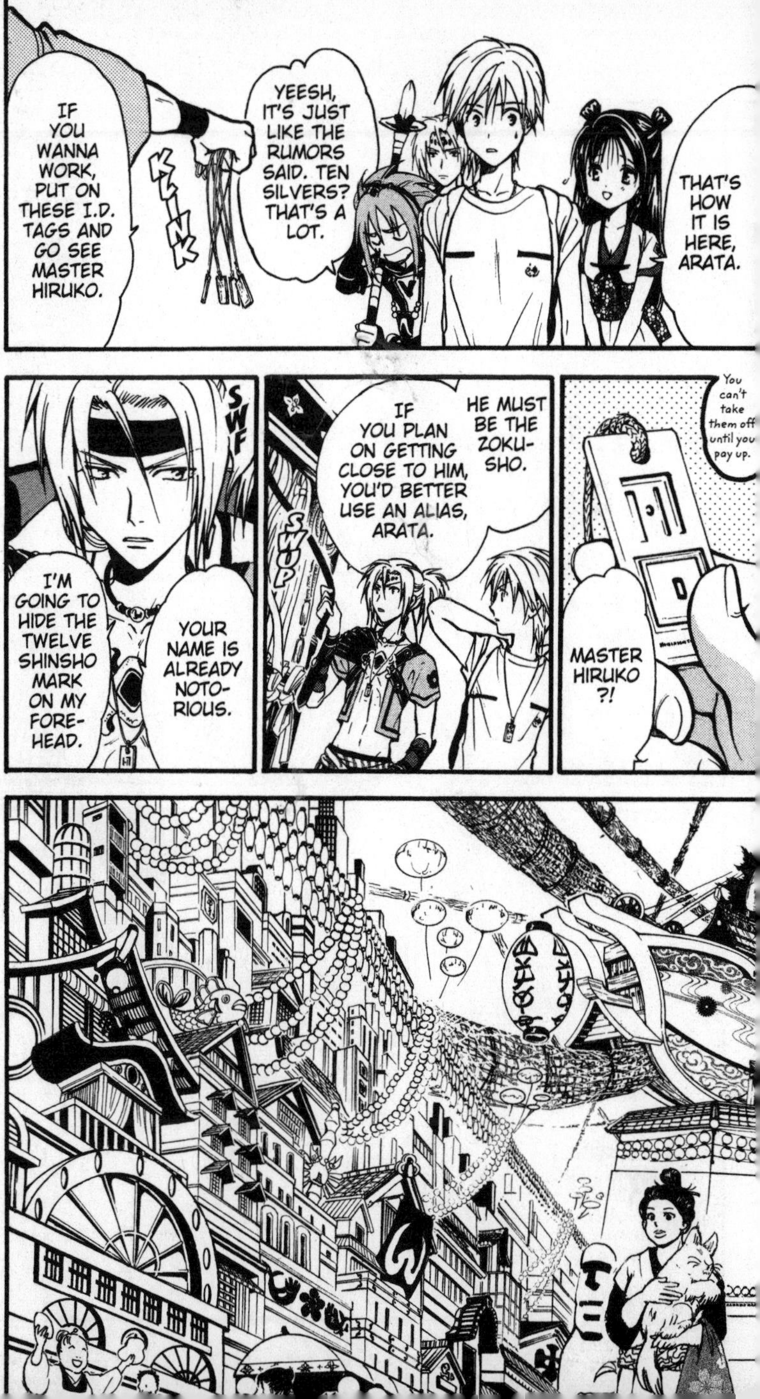
THAT'S HOW IT IS HERE, ARATA.
YEESH, IT'S JUST LIKE THE RUMORS SAID. TEN SILVERS? THAT'S A LOT.
KLINK
IF YOU WANNA WORK, PUT ON THESE I.D. TAGS AND GO SEE MASTER HIRUKO.
You can't take them off until you pay up.
MASTER HIRUKO?!
HE MUST BE THE ZOKU-SHO.
IF YOU PLAN ON GETTING CLOSE TO HIM, YOU'D BETTER USE AN ALIAS, ARATA.
SWUP
SWF
YOUR NAME IS ALREADY NOTORIOUS.
I'M GOING TO HIDE THE TWELVE SHINSHO MARK ON MY FORE-HEAD.

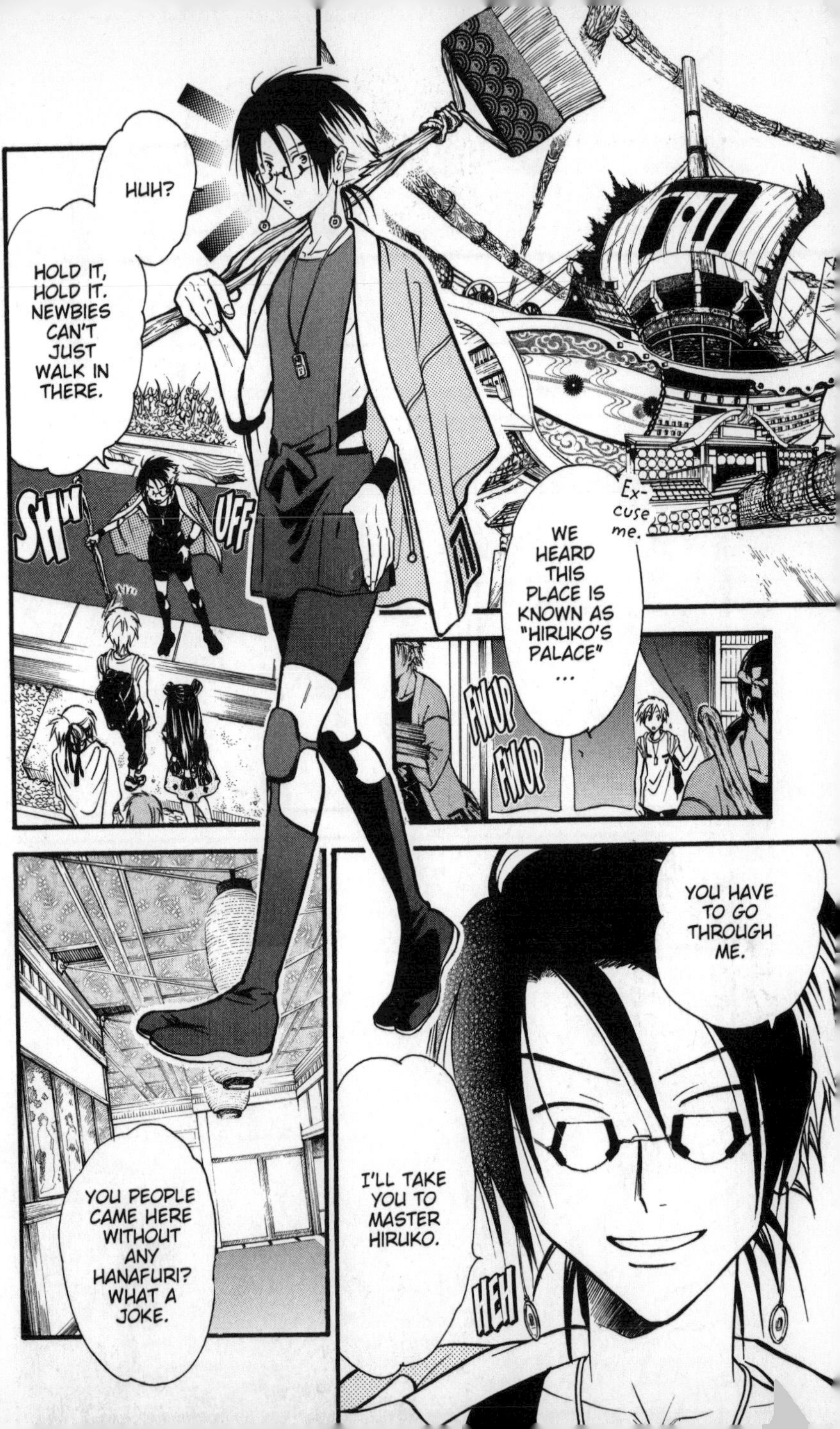
Ex-cuse me.
WE HEARD THIS PLACE IS KNOWN AS "HIRUKO'S PALACE"...
FWUP
FWUP
HUH?
HOLD IT, HOLD IT. NEWBIES CAN'T JUST WALK IN THERE.
SHWUFF
YOU HAVE TO GO THROUGH ME.
YOU PEOPLE CAME HERE WITHOUT ANY HANAFURI? WHAT A JOKE.
I'LL TAKE YOU TO MASTER HIRUKO.
HEH

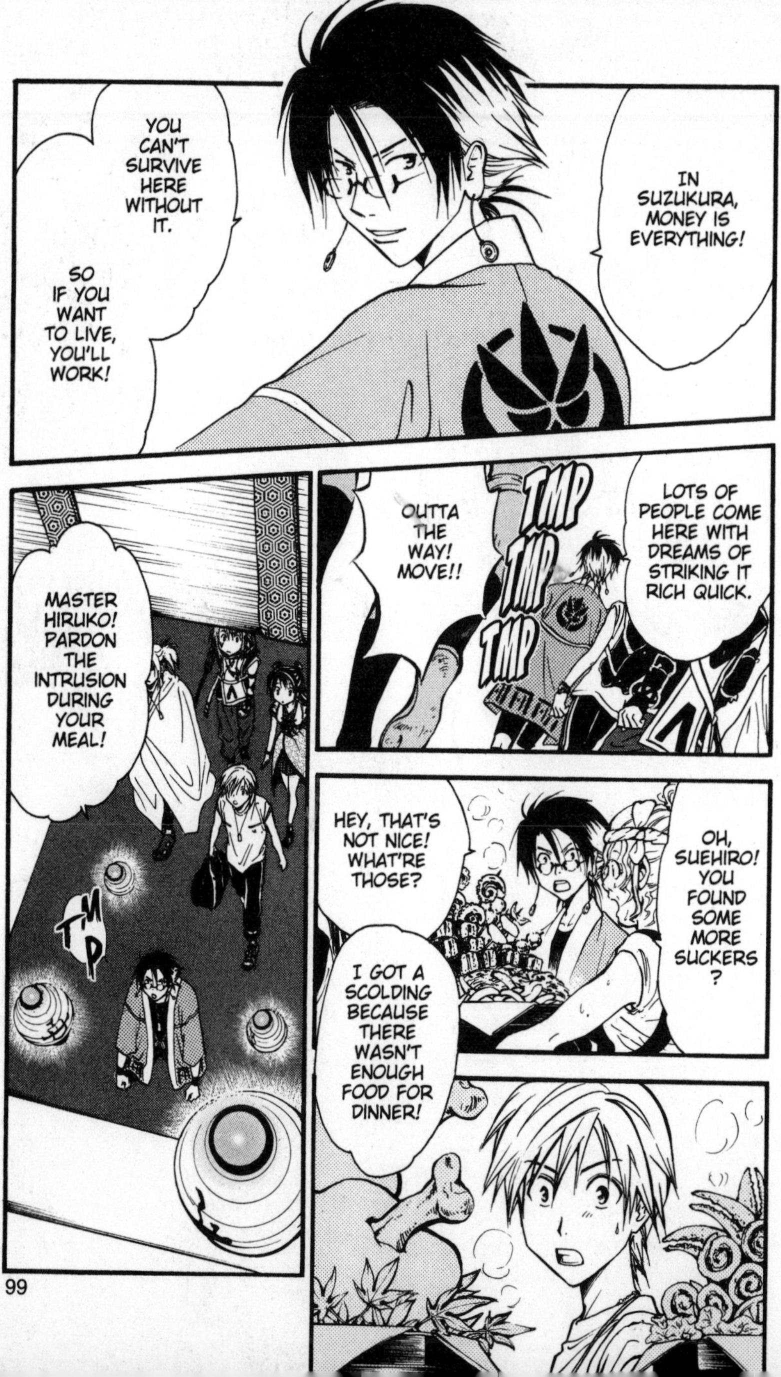
IN SUZUKURA, MONEY IS EVERYTHING!
YOU CAN'T SURVIVE HERE WITHOUT IT.
SO IF YOU WANT TO LIVE, YOU'LL WORK!
LOTS OF PEOPLE COME HERE WITH DREAMS OF STRIKING IT RICH QUICK.
TMP TMP TMP TMP
OUTTA THE WAY! MOVE!!
OH, SUEHIRO! YOU FOUND SOME MORE SUCKERS?
HEY, THAT'S NOT NICE! WHAT'RE THOSE?
I GOT A SCOLDING BECAUSE THERE WASN'T ENOUGH FOOD FOR DINNER!
MASTER HIRUKO! PARDON THE INTRUSION DURING YOUR MEAL!
TMP

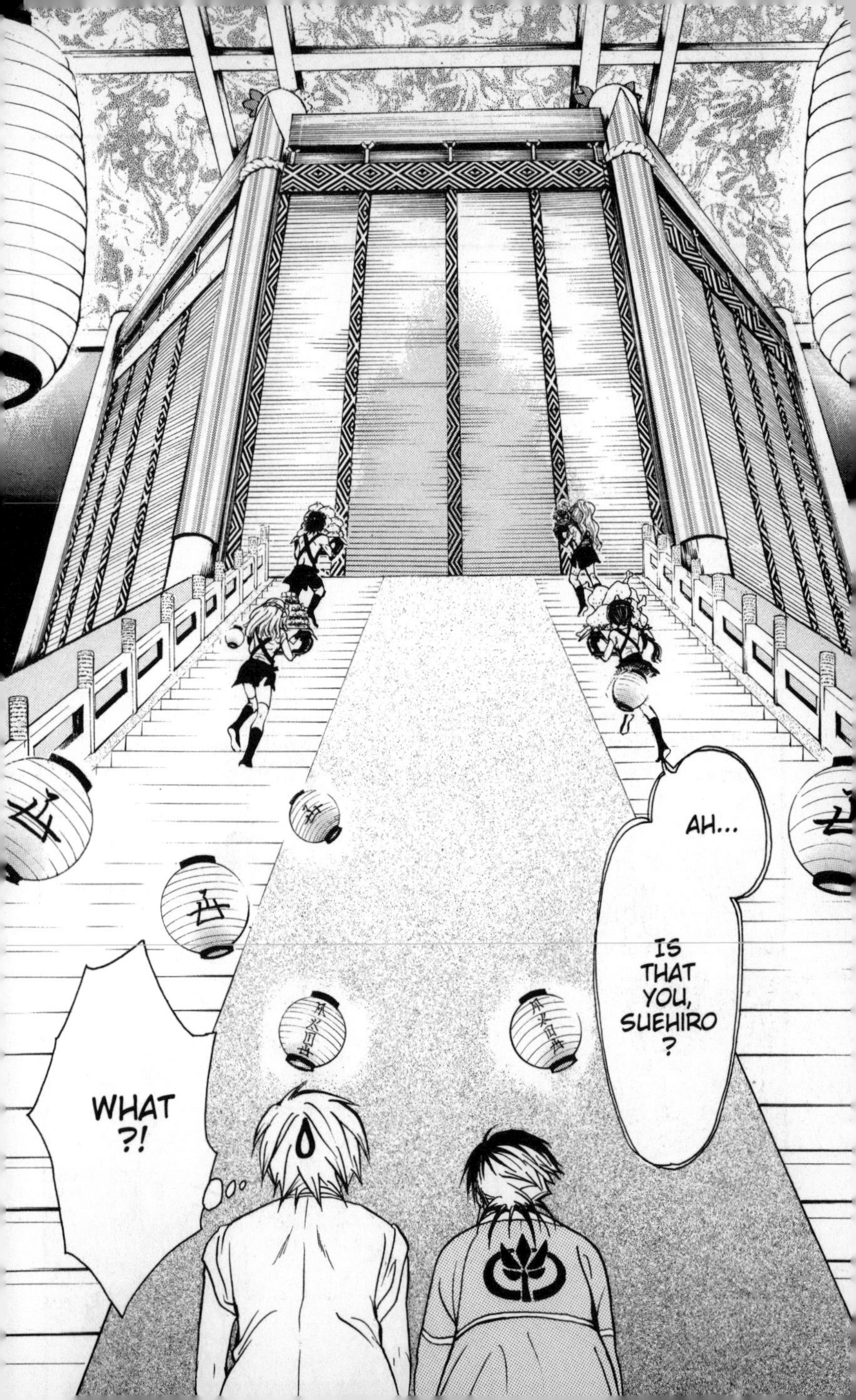
AH...
IS THAT YOU, SUEHIRO?
WHAT ?!

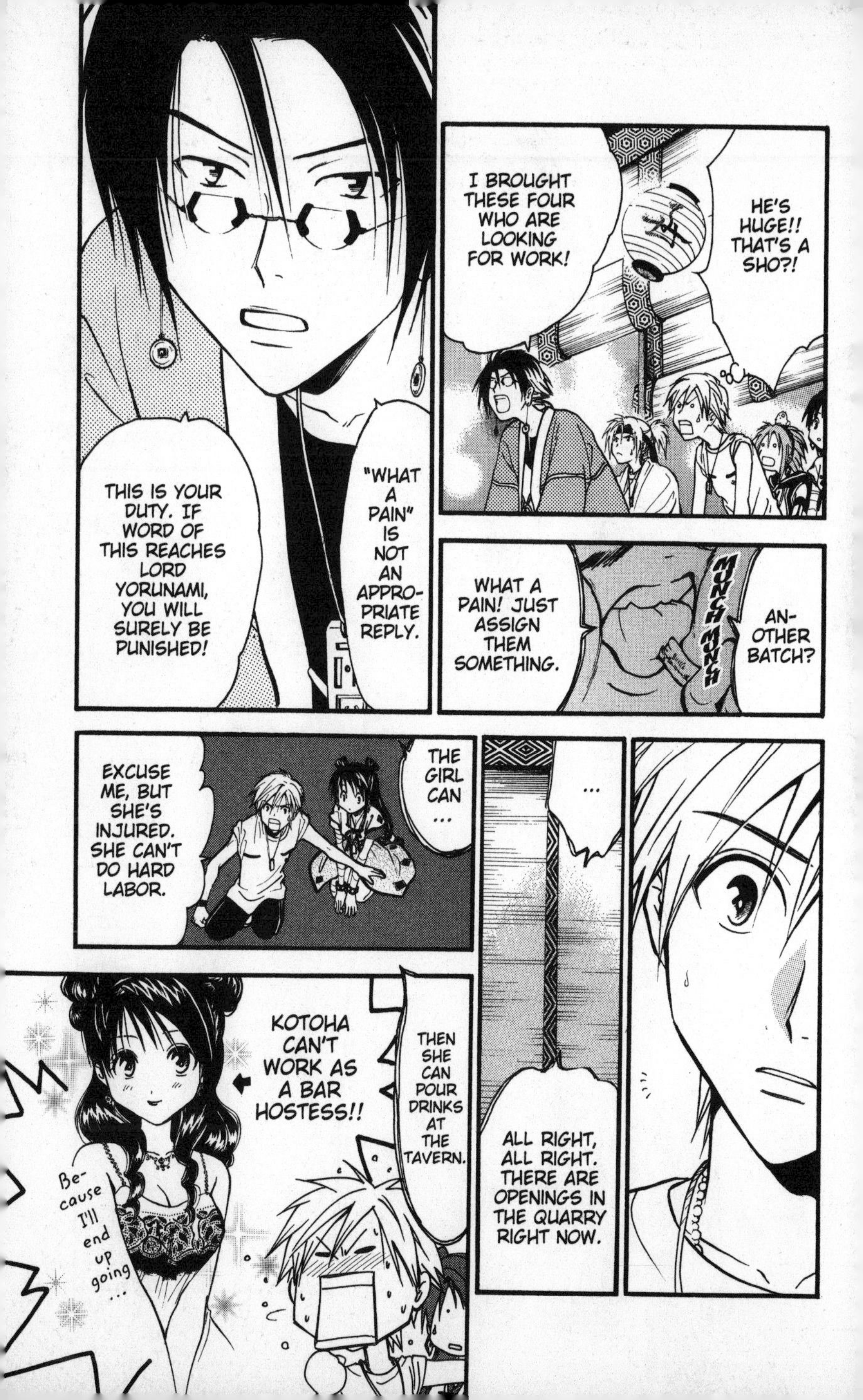
I BROUGHT THESE FOUR WHO ARE LOOKING FOR WORK!
HE'S HUGE!! THAT'S A SHO?!
AN-OTHER BATCH?
MUNCH MUNCH
WHAT A PAIN! JUST ASSIGN THEM SOMETHING.
"WHAT A PAIN" IS NOT AN APPROPRIATE REPLY.
THIS IS YOUR DUTY. IF WORD OF THIS REACHES LORD YORUNAMI, YOU WILL SURELY BE PUNISHED!
...
ALL RIGHT, ALL RIGHT. THERE ARE OPENINGS IN THE QUARRY RIGHT NOW.
THE GIRL CAN ...
EXCUSE ME, BUT SHE'S INJURED. SHE CAN'T DO HARD LABOR.
THEN SHE CAN POUR DRINKS AT THE TAVERN.
KOTOHA CAN'T WORK AS A BAR HOSTESS!!
Because I'll end up going ...

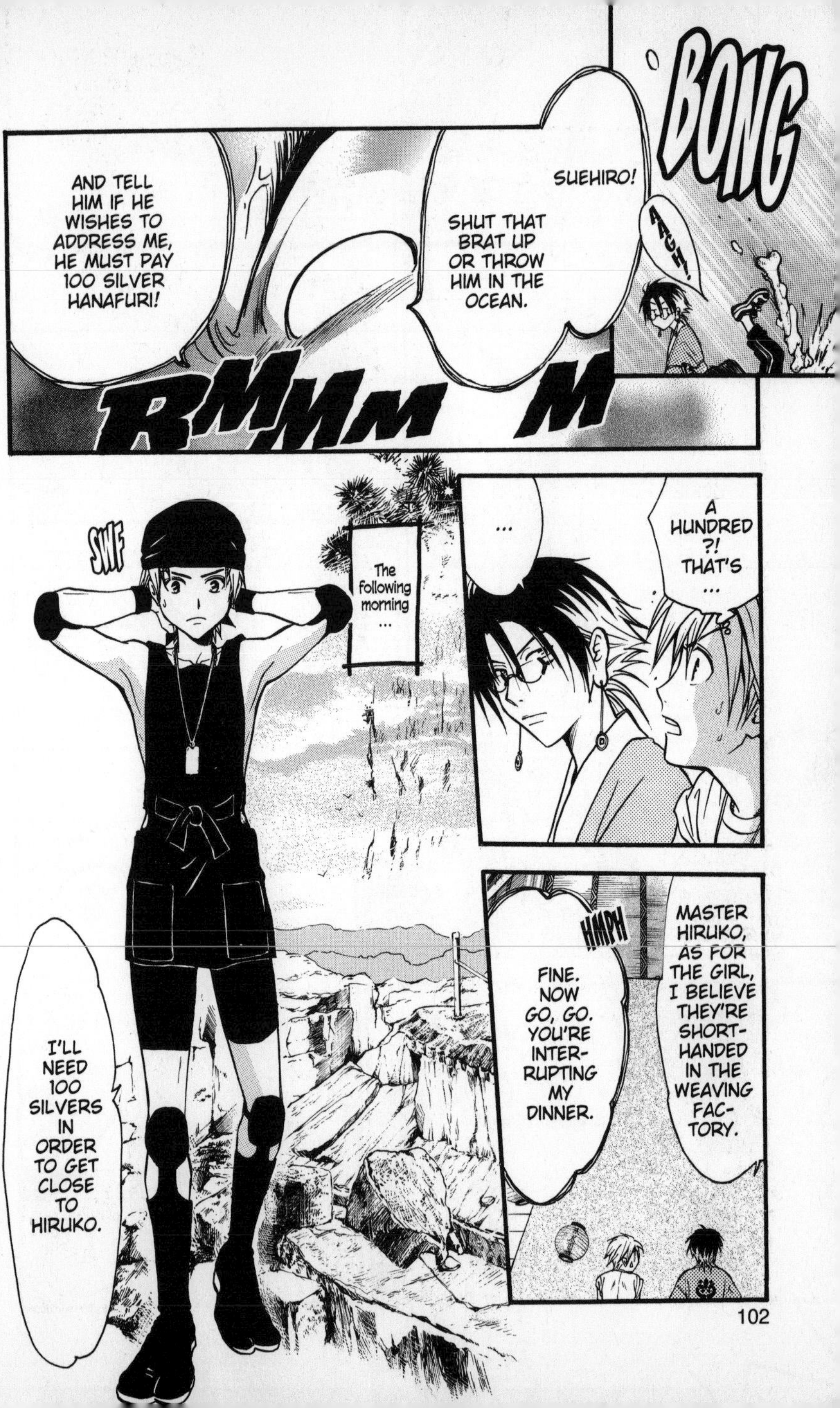
BONG
AAGH!
SUEHIRO!
SHUT THAT BRAT UP OR THROW HIM IN THE OCEAN.
AND TELL HIM IF HE WISHES TO ADDRESS ME, HE MUST PAY 100 SILVER HANAFURI!
RMMMM M
A HUNDRED?! THAT'S ...
...
MASTER HIRUKO, AS FOR THE GIRL, I BELIEVE THEY'RE SHORT-HANDED IN THE WEAVING FACTORY.
HMPH
FINE. NOW GO, GO. YOU'RE INTER-RUPTING MY DINNER.
The following morning ...
SWF
I'LL NEED 100 SILVERS IN ORDER TO GET CLOSE TO HIRUKO.

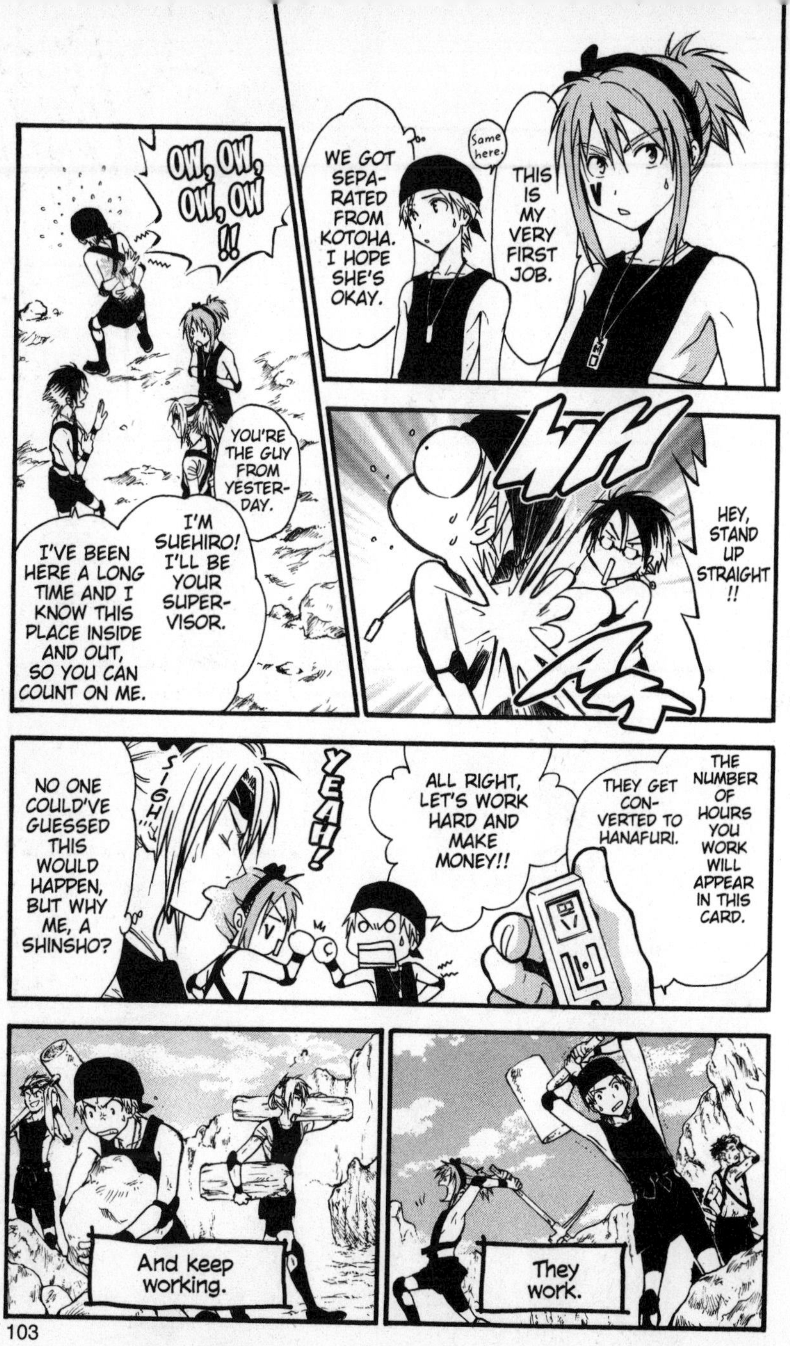
THIS IS MY VERY FIRST JOB.
Same here.
WE GOT SEPARATED FROM KOTOHA. I HOPE SHE'S OKAY.
HEY, STAND UP STRAIGHT!!
WHAM
OW, OW, OW, OW!!
YOU'RE THE GUY FROM YESTERDAY.
I'M SUEHIRO! I'LL BE YOUR SUPERVISOR.
I'VE BEEN HERE A LONG TIME AND I KNOW THIS PLACE INSIDE AND OUT, SO YOU CAN COUNT ON ME.
THE NUMBER OF HOURS YOU WORK WILL APPEAR IN THIS CARD.
THEY GET CONVERTED TO HANAFURI.
ALL RIGHT, LET'S WORK HARD AND MAKE MONEY!!
YEAH!
SIGH...
NO ONE COULD'VE GUESSED THIS WOULD HAPPEN, BUT WHY ME, A SHINSHO?
They work.
And keep working.

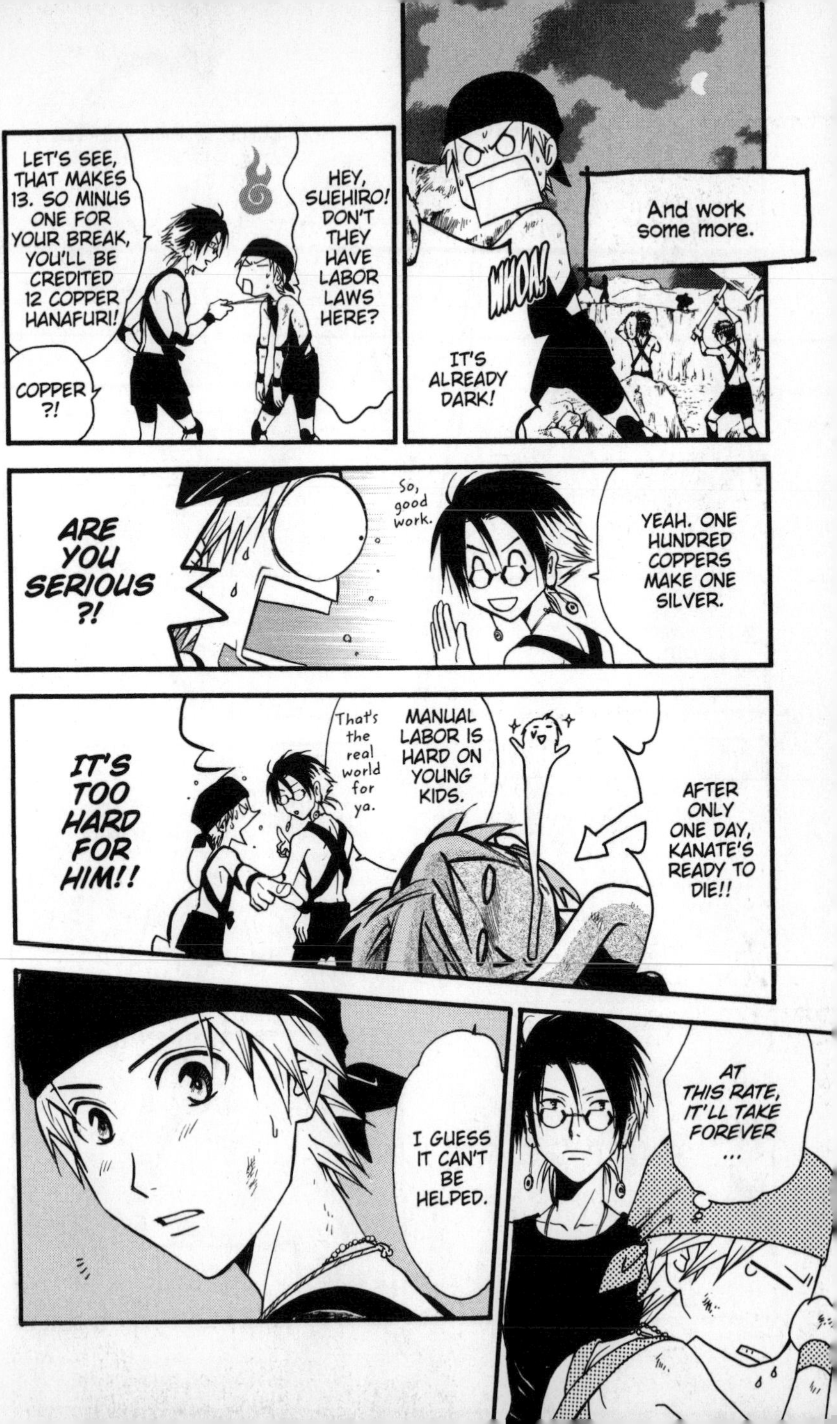
And work some more.
WHOA!
IT'S ALREADY DARK!
HEY, SUEHIRO! DON'T THEY HAVE LABOR LAWS HERE?
LET'S SEE, THAT MAKES 13. SO MINUS ONE FOR YOUR BREAK, YOU'LL BE CREDITED 12 COPPER HANAFURI!
COPPER?!
YEAH. ONE HUNDRED COPPERS MAKE ONE SILVER.
So, good work.
ARE YOU SERIOUS?!
AFTER ONLY ONE DAY, KANATE'S READY TO DIE!!
MANUAL LABOR IS HARD ON YOUNG KIDS.
That's the real world for ya.
IT'S TOO HARD FOR HIM!!
AT THIS RATE, IT'LL TAKE FOREVER...
I GUESS IT CAN'T BE HELPED.

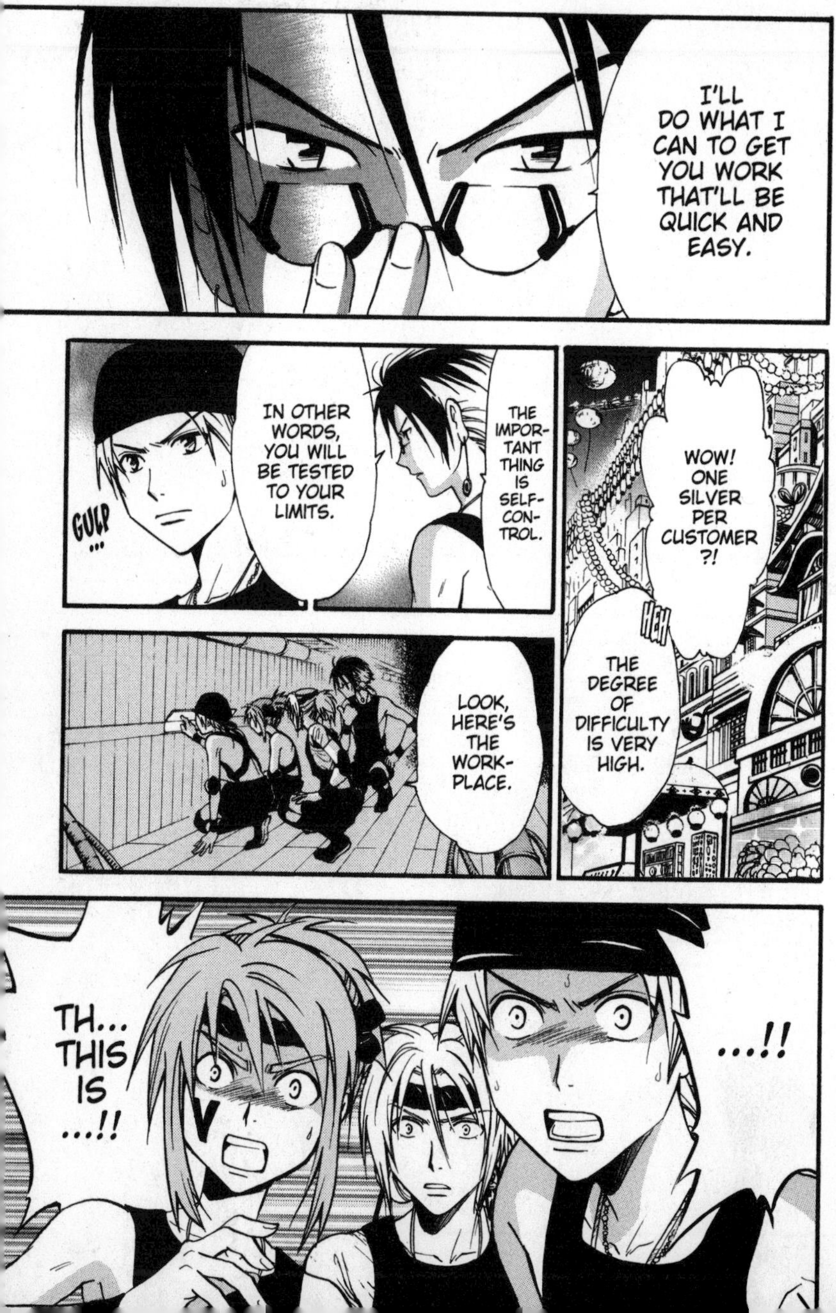
I'LL DO WHAT I CAN TO GET YOU WORK THAT'LL BE QUICK AND EASY.
WOW! ONE SILVER PER CUSTOMER?!
HEH
THE DEGREE OF DIFFICULTY IS VERY HIGH.
THE IMPORTANT THING IS SELF-CONTROL.
IN OTHER WORDS, YOU WILL BE TESTED TO YOUR LIMITS.
GULP...
LOOK, HERE'S THE WORKPLACE.
...!!
TH... THIS IS ...!!

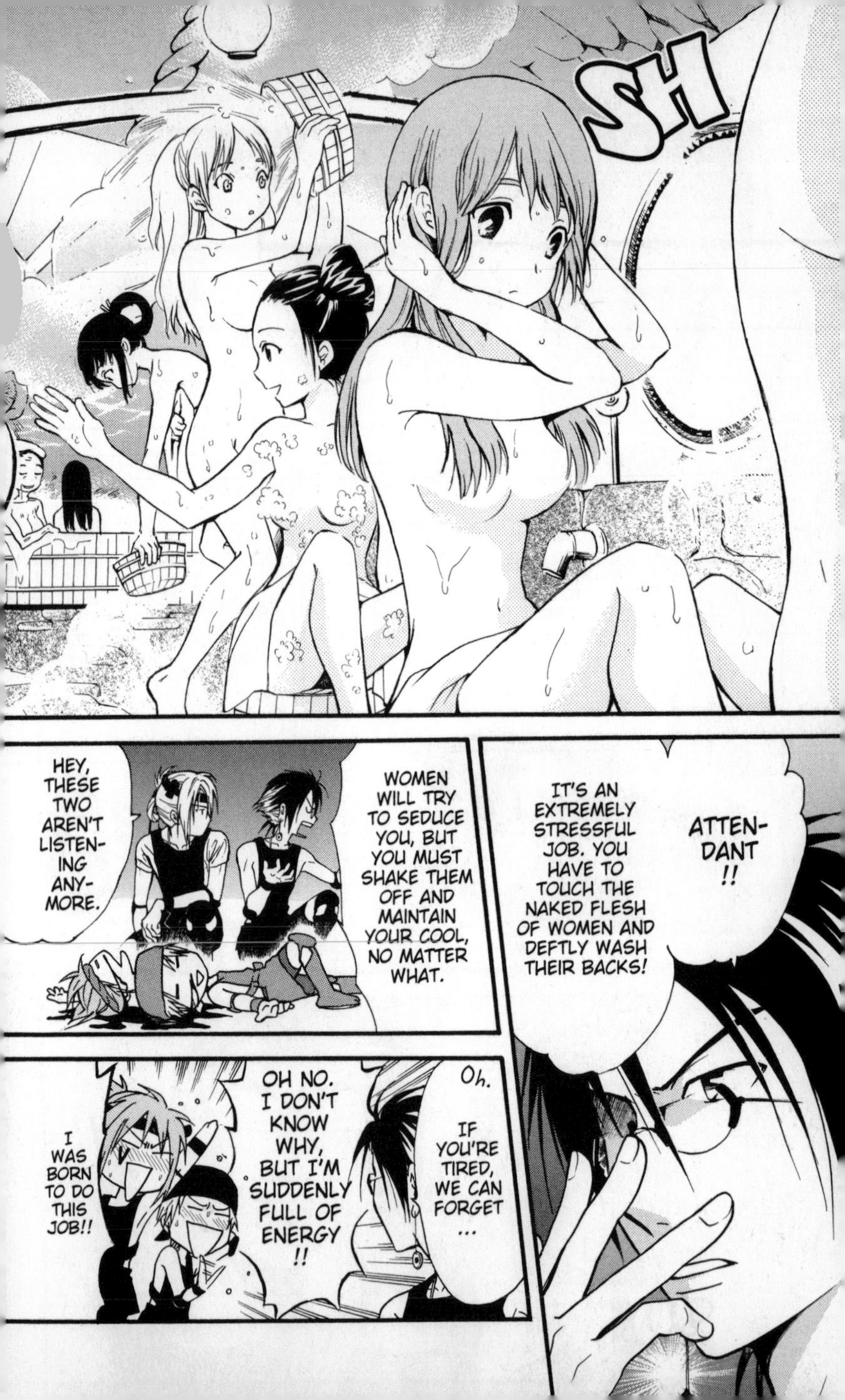
SH
ATTEN-DANT!!
IT'S AN EXTREMELY STRESSFUL JOB. YOU HAVE TO TOUCH THE NAKED FLESH OF WOMEN AND DEFTLY WASH THEIR BACKS!
WOMEN WILL TRY TO SEDUCE YOU, BUT YOU MUST SHAKE THEM OFF AND MAINTAIN YOUR COOL, NO MATTER WHAT.
HEY, THESE TWO AREN'T LISTEN-ING ANY-MORE.
Oh.
IF YOU'RE TIRED, WE CAN FORGET ...
OH NO. I DON'T KNOW WHY, BUT I'M SUDDENLY FULL OF ENERGY !!
I WAS BORN TO DO THIS JOB!!

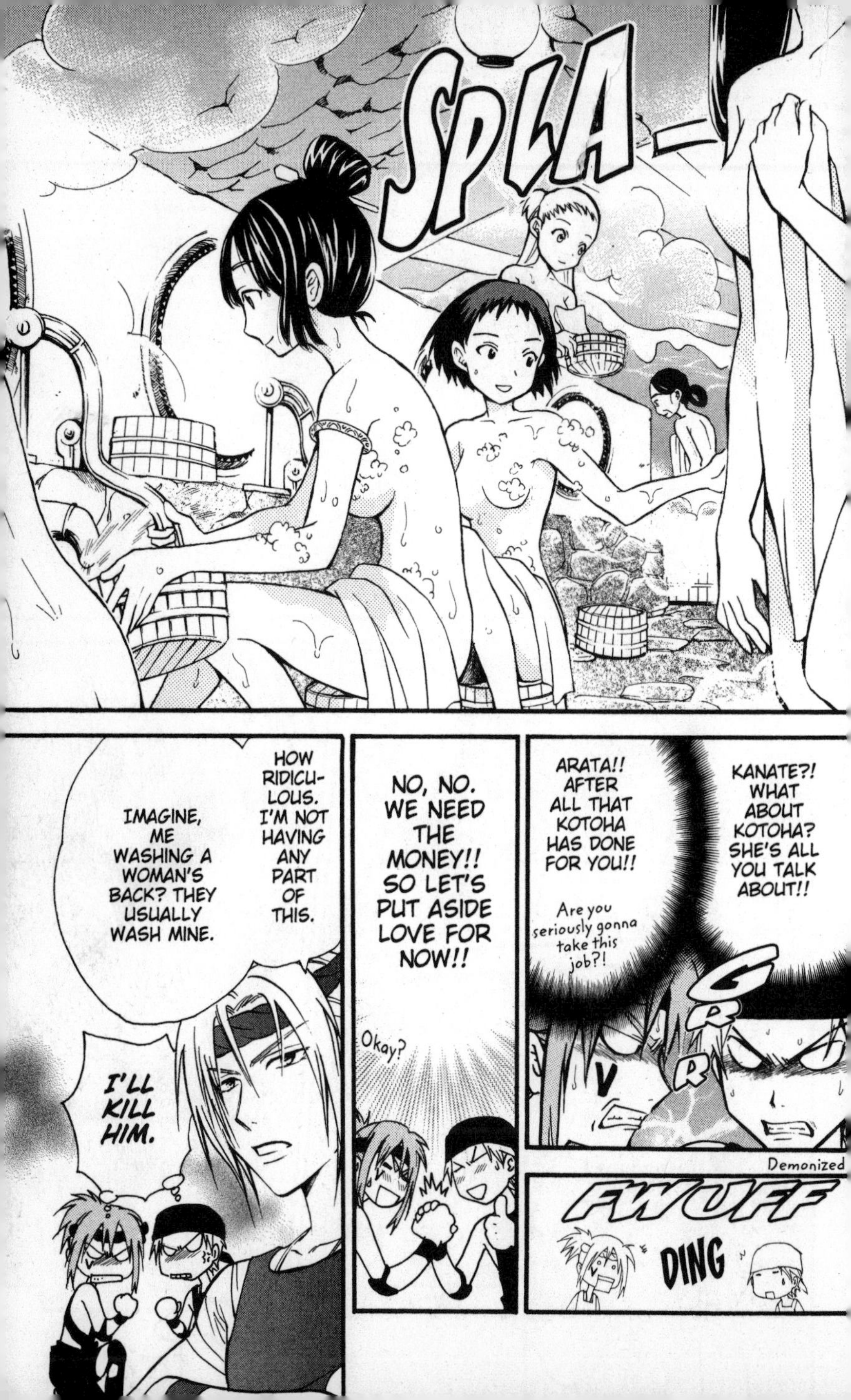
SPLA-
KANATE?! WHAT ABOUT KOTOHA? SHE'S ALL YOU TALK ABOUT!!
ARATA!! AFTER ALL THAT KOTOHA HAS DONE FOR YOU!!
Are you seriously gonna take this job?!
GRR
Demonized
FWUFF
DING
NO, NO. WE NEED THE MONEY!! SO LET'S PUT ASIDE LOVE FOR NOW!!
Okay?
HOW RIDICU-LOUS. I'M NOT HAVING ANY PART OF THIS.
IMAGINE, ME WASHING A WOMAN'S BACK? THEY USUALLY WASH MINE.
I'LL KILL HIM.

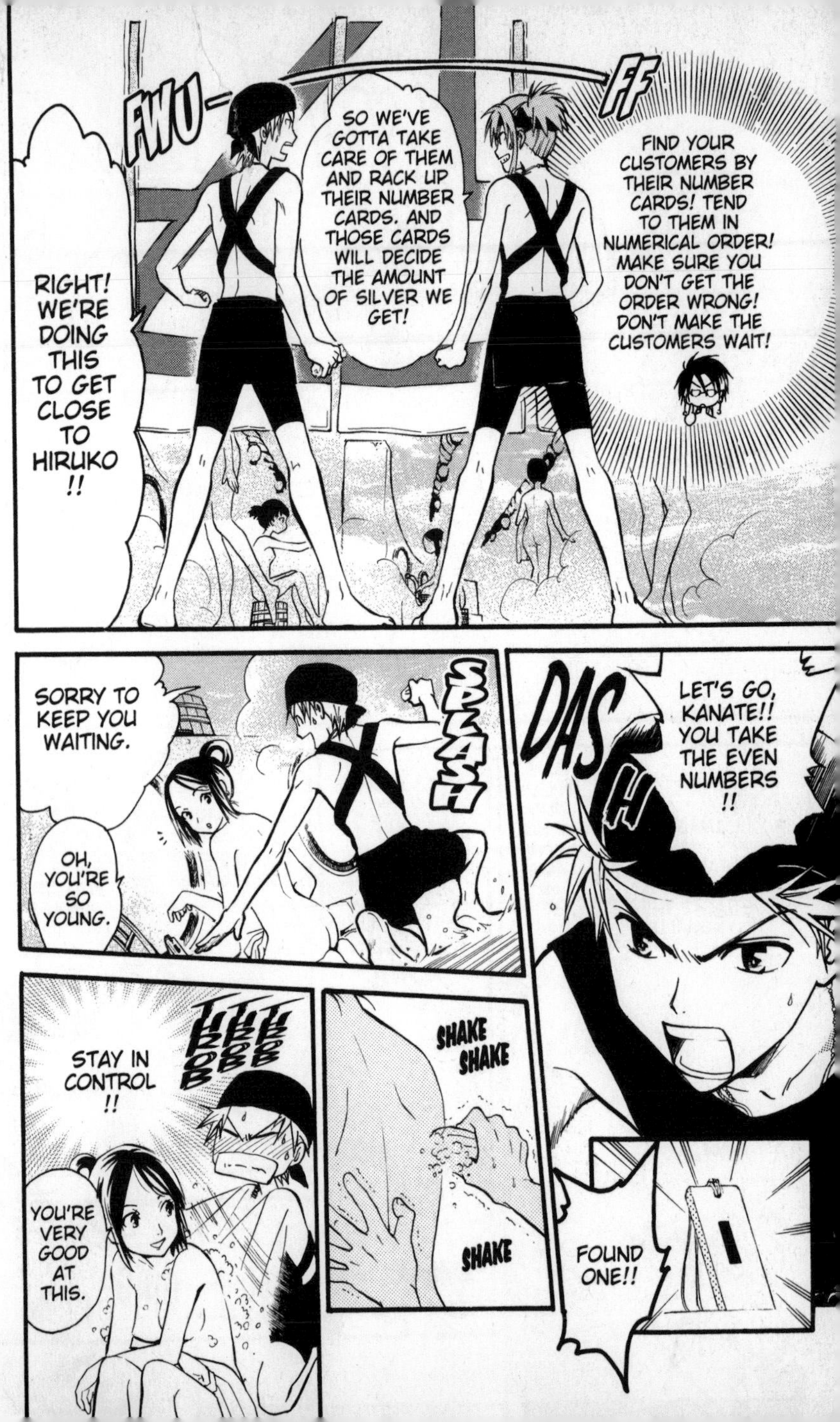
FWU-FF
FIND YOUR CUSTOMERS BY THEIR NUMBER CARDS! TEND TO THEM IN NUMERICAL ORDER! MAKE SURE YOU DON'T GET THE ORDER WRONG! DON'T MAKE THE CUSTOMERS WAIT!
SO WE'VE GOTTA TAKE CARE OF THEM AND RACK UP THEIR NUMBER CARDS. AND THOSE CARDS WILL DECIDE THE AMOUNT OF SILVER WE GET!
RIGHT! WE'RE DOING THIS TO GET CLOSE TO HIRUKO!!
LET'S GO, KANATE!! YOU TAKE THE EVEN NUMBERS!!
DASH
FOUND ONE!!
SPLASH
SORRY TO KEEP YOU WAITING.
OH, YOU'RE SO YOUNG.
SHAKE SHAKE
SHAKE
THROB THROB THROB
STAY IN CONTROL!!
YOU'RE VERY GOOD AT THIS.

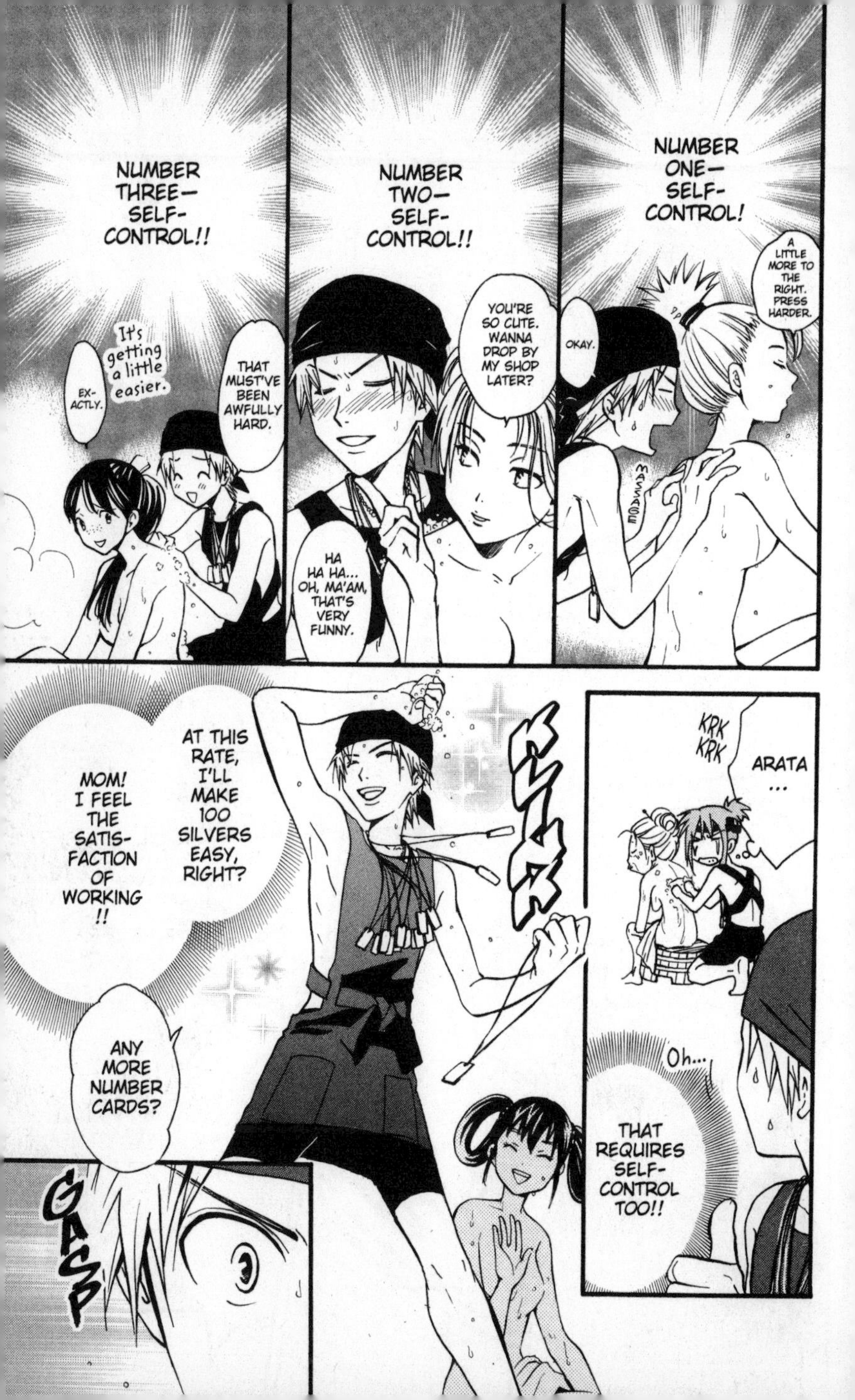
NUMBER ONE—SELF-CONTROL!
A LITTLE MORE TO THE RIGHT. PRESS HARDER.
OKAY.
MASSAGE
NUMBER TWO—SELF-CONTROL!!
YOU'RE SO CUTE. WANNA DROP BY MY SHOP LATER?
HA HA HA... OH, MA'AM, THAT'S VERY FUNNY.
NUMBER THREE—SELF-CONTROL!!
THAT MUST'VE BEEN AWFULLY HARD.
It's getting a little easier.
EXACTLY.
KRK KRK
ARATA ...
Oh...
THAT REQUIRES SELF-CONTROL TOO!!
AT THIS RATE, I'LL MAKE 100 SILVERS EASY, RIGHT?
MOM! I FEEL THE SATIS-FACTION OF WORKING!!
ANY MORE NUMBER CARDS?
GASP

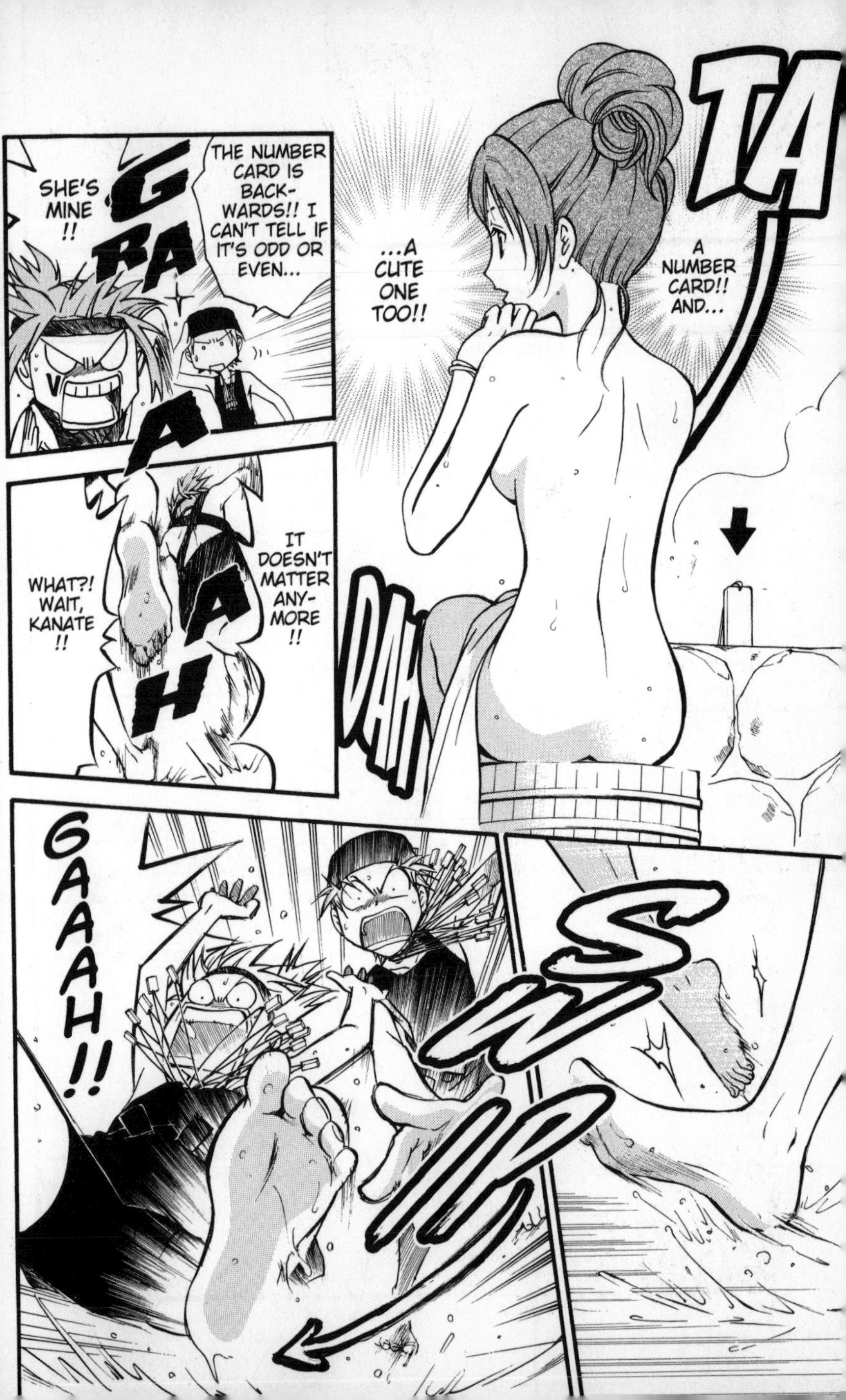
TA
A NUMBER CARD!! AND...
...A CUTE ONE TOO!!
DAH
GRAAAH
THE NUMBER CARD IS BACK-WARDS!! I CAN'T TELL IF IT'S ODD OR EVEN...
SHE'S MINE!!
IT DOESN'T MATTER ANY-MORE!!
WHAT?! WAIT, KANATE!!
SWISH
GAAAAH!!

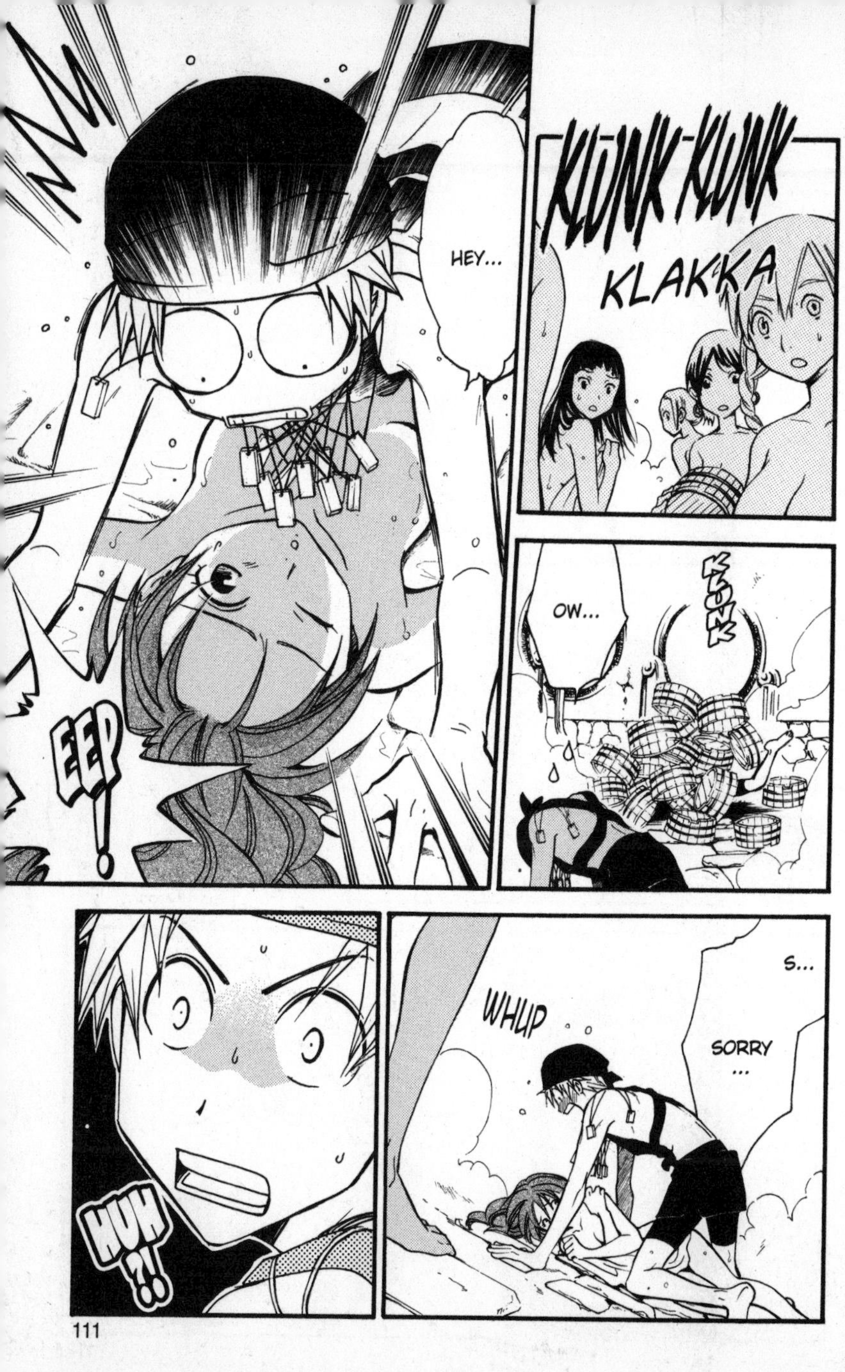
KLUNK KLUNK
KLAKKA
KLUNK
OW...
HEY...
EEP!
S...
SORRY...
WHUP
HUH?!

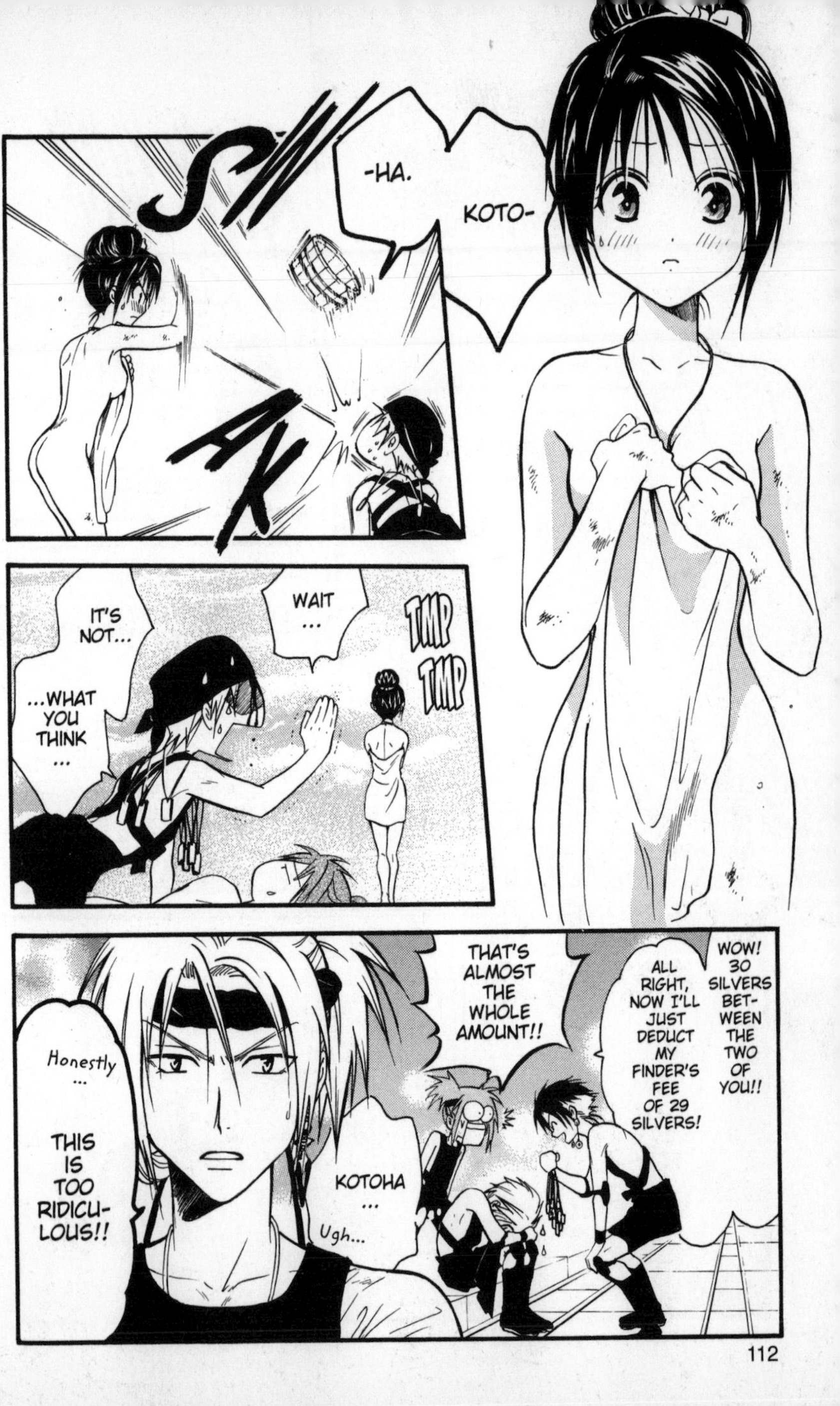
KOTO-
-HA.
TMP TMP
WAIT ...
IT'S NOT...
...WHAT YOU THINK ...
WOW! 30 SILVERS BET-WEEN THE TWO OF YOU!!
ALL RIGHT, NOW I'LL JUST DEDUCT MY FINDER'S FEE OF 29 SILVERS!
THAT'S ALMOST THE WHOLE AMOUNT!!
KOTOHA ...
Ugh...
Honestly ...
THIS IS TOO RIDICU-LOUS!!

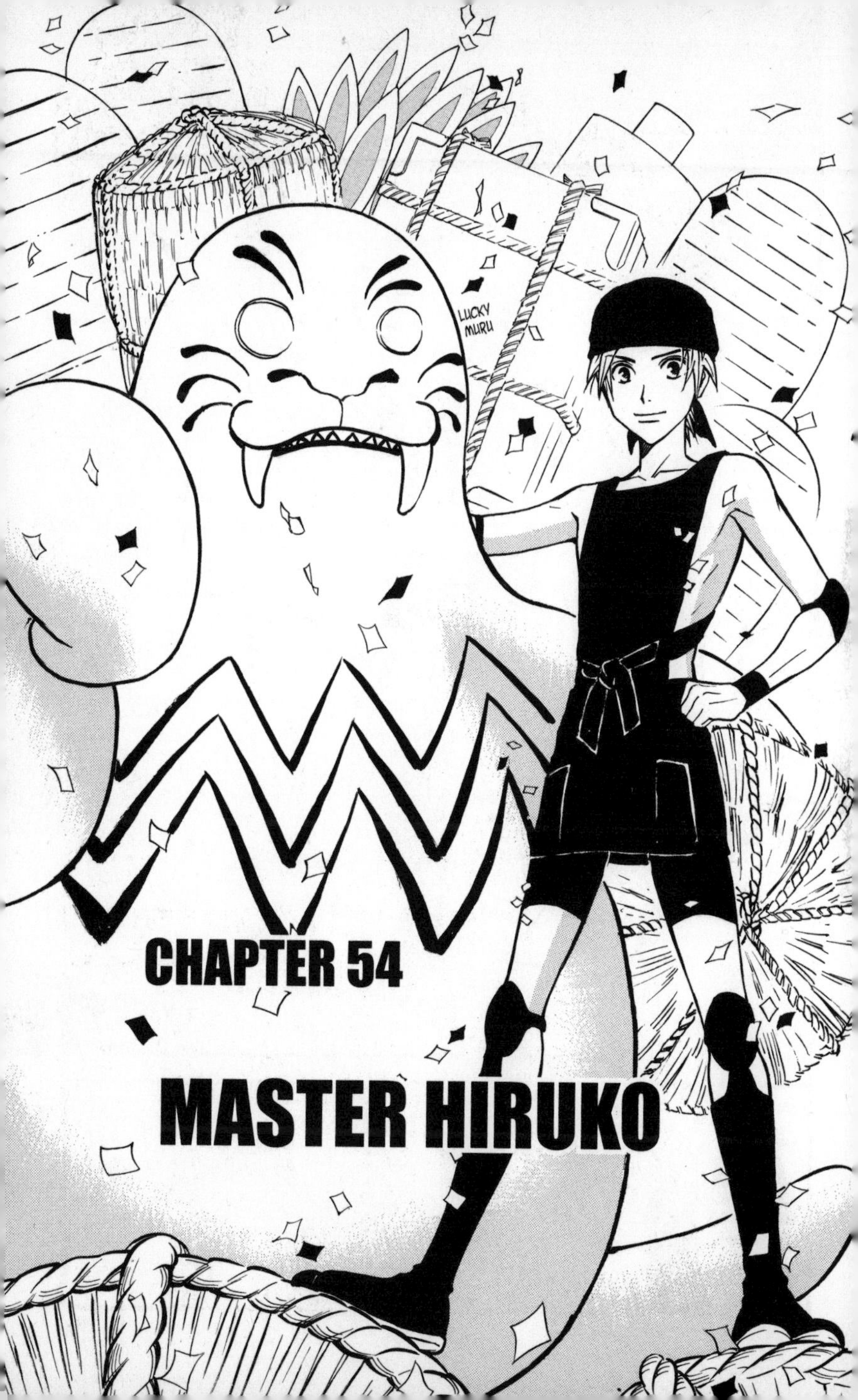
LUCKY MURU
CHAPTER 54
MASTER HIRUKO

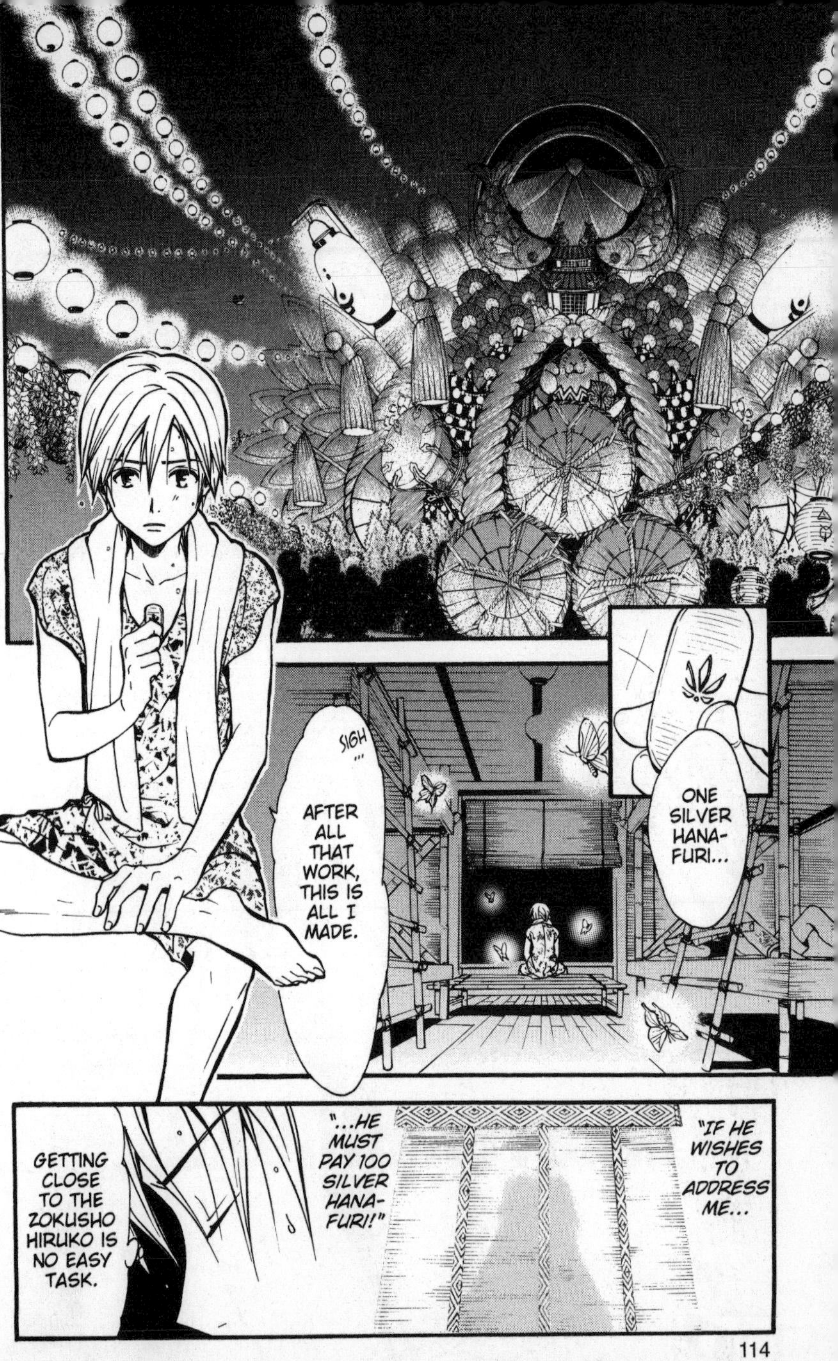
ONE SILVER HANA-FURI...
SIGH...
AFTER ALL THAT WORK, THIS IS ALL I MADE.
"IF HE WISHES TO ADDRESS ME...
"...HE MUST PAY 100 SILVER HANA-FURI!"
GETTING CLOSE TO THE ZOKUSHO HIRUKO IS NO EASY TASK.

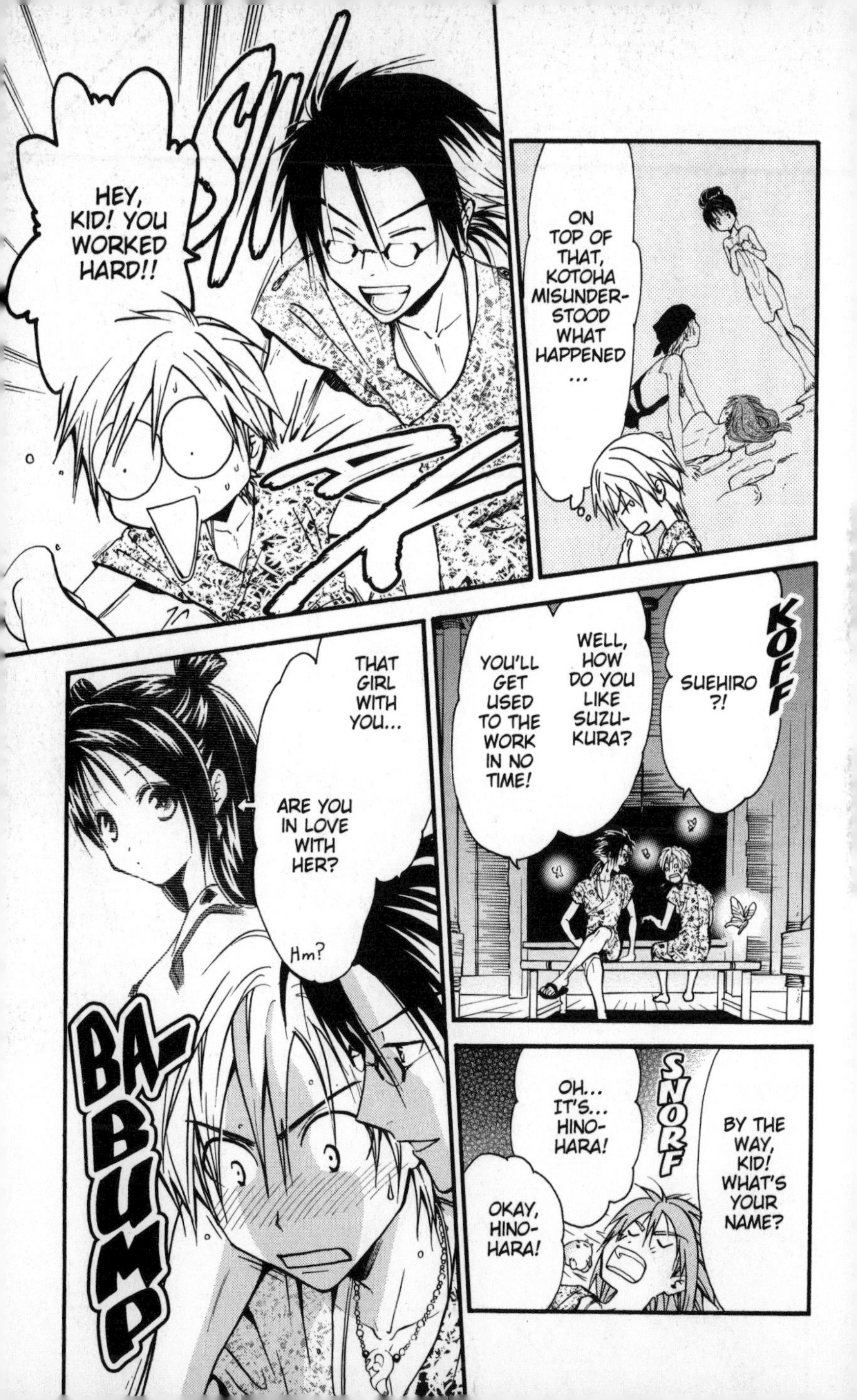
ON TOP OF THAT, KOTOHA MISUNDER-STOOD WHAT HAPPENED...
HEY, KID! YOU WORKED HARD!!
KOFF
SUEHIRO?!
WELL, HOW DO YOU LIKE SUZU-KURA?
YOU'LL GET USED TO THE WORK IN NO TIME!
SNORF
BY THE WAY, KID! WHAT'S YOUR NAME?
OH... IT'S... HINO-HARA!
OKAY, HINO-HARA!
THAT GIRL WITH YOU...
ARE YOU IN LOVE WITH HER?
Hm?
BA-BUMP

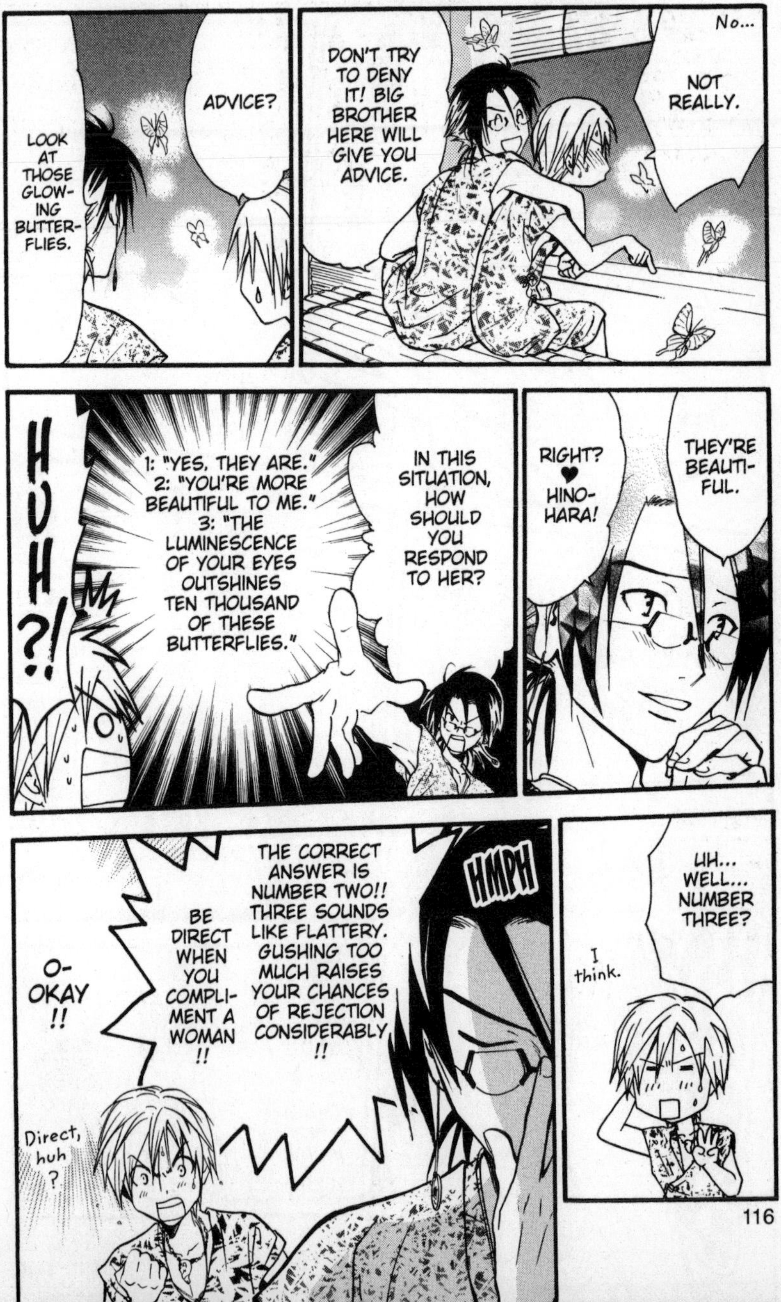
No...
NOT REALLY.
DON'T TRY TO DENY IT! BIG BROTHER HERE WILL GIVE YOU ADVICE.
ADVICE?
LOOK AT THOSE GLOWING BUTTERFLIES.
THEY'RE BEAUTIFUL.
RIGHT? ♥ HINOHARA!
IN THIS SITUATION, HOW SHOULD YOU RESPOND TO HER?
1: "YES, THEY ARE." 2: "YOU'RE MORE BEAUTIFUL TO ME." 3: "THE LUMINESCENCE OF YOUR EYES OUTSHINES TEN THOUSAND OF THESE BUTTERFLIES."
HUH?!
UH... WELL... NUMBER THREE?
I think.
HMPH
THE CORRECT ANSWER IS NUMBER TWO!! THREE SOUNDS LIKE FLATTERY. GUSHING TOO MUCH RAISES YOUR CHANCES OF REJECTION CONSIDERABLY!!
BE DIRECT WHEN YOU COMPLIMENT A WOMAN!!
O-OKAY!!
Direct, huh?

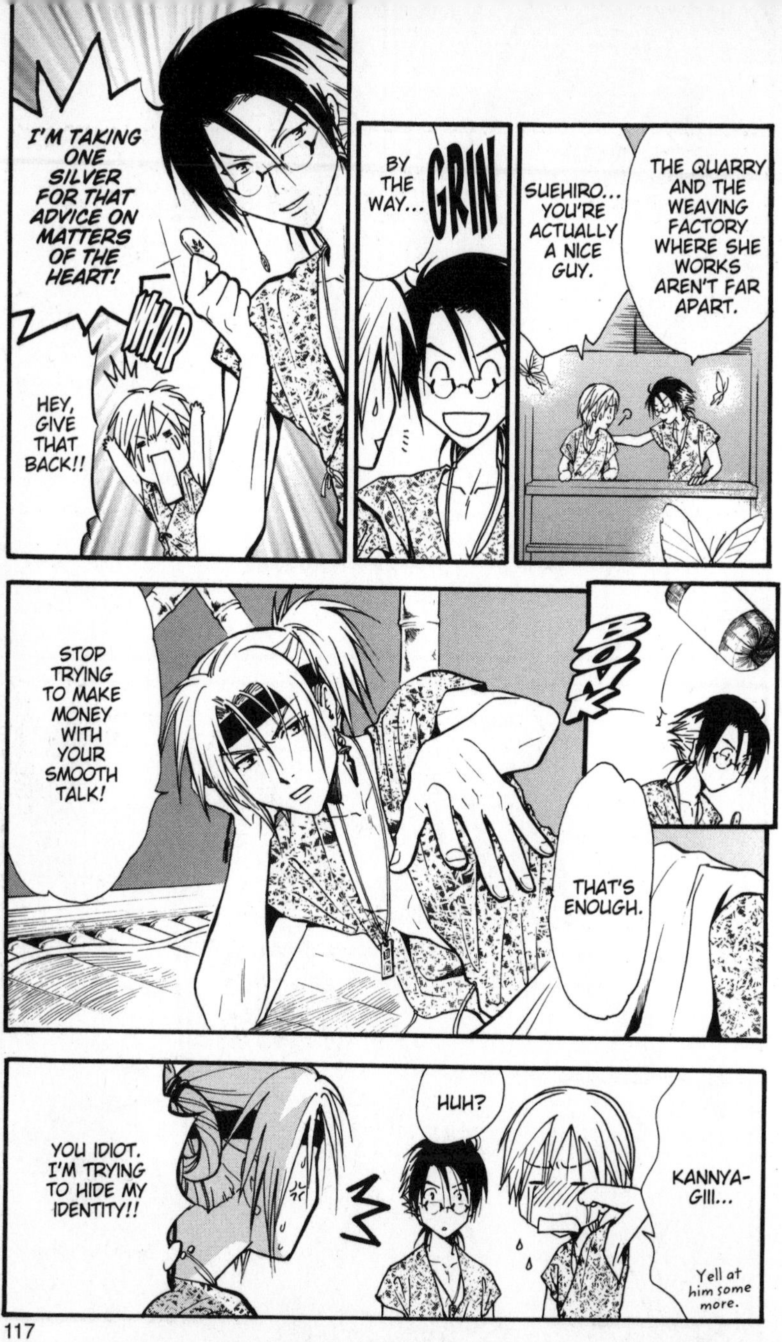
THE QUARRY AND THE WEAVING FACTORY WHERE SHE WORKS AREN'T FAR APART.
SUEHIRO... YOU'RE ACTUALLY A NICE GUY.
BY THE WAY...
GRIN
I'M TAKING ONE SILVER FOR THAT ADVICE ON MATTERS OF THE HEART!
WHAP
HEY, GIVE THAT BACK!!
BONK
THAT'S ENOUGH.
STOP TRYING TO MAKE MONEY WITH YOUR SMOOTH TALK!
KANNYA-GIII...
Yell at him some more.
HUH?
YOU IDIOT. I'M TRYING TO HIDE MY IDENTITY!!

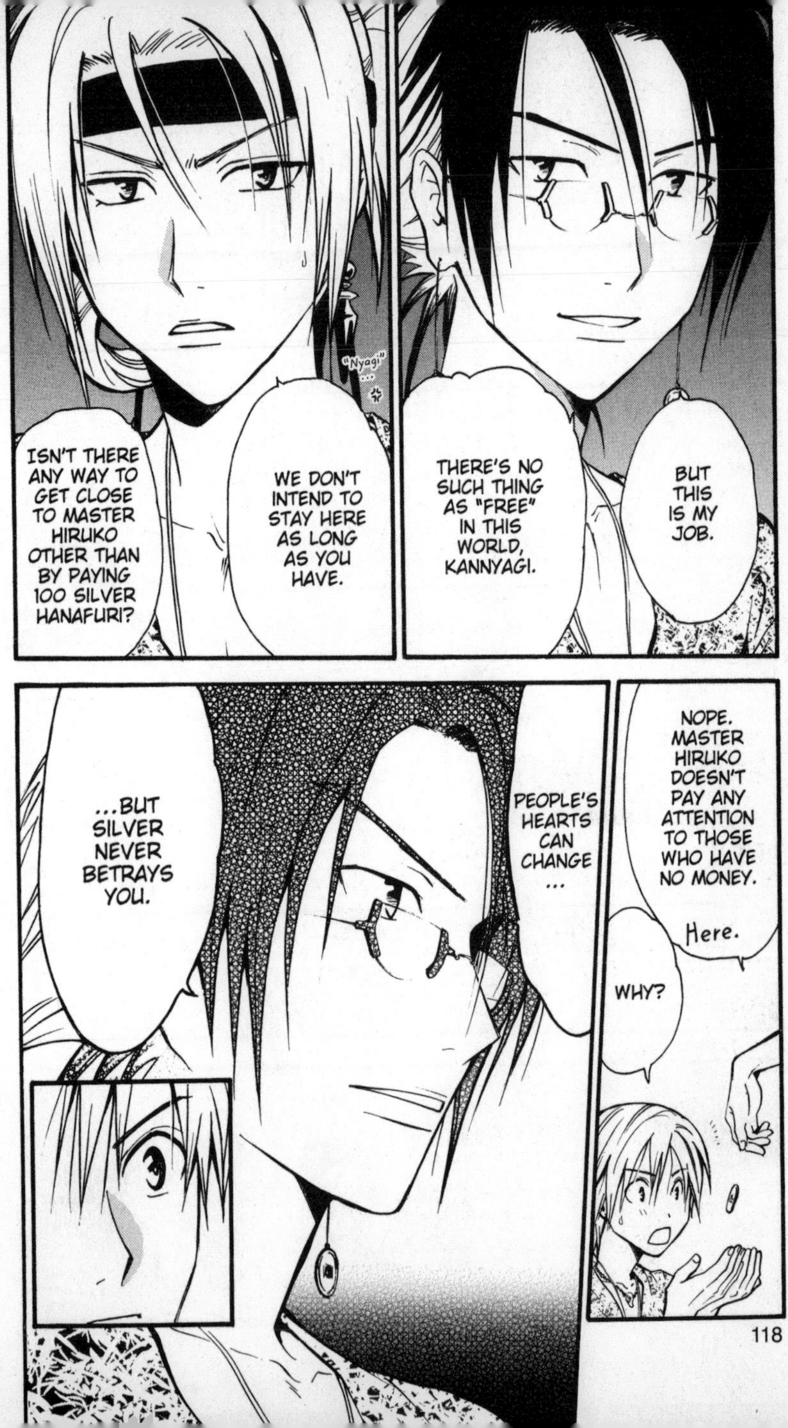

BUT THIS IS MY JOB.
THERE'S NO SUCH THING AS "FREE" IN THIS WORLD, KANNYAGI.
"Nyagi"...
WE DON'T INTEND TO STAY HERE AS LONG AS YOU HAVE.
ISN'T THERE ANY WAY TO GET CLOSE TO MASTER HIRUKO OTHER THAN BY PAYING 100 SILVER HANAFURI?
NOPE. MASTER HIRUKO DOESN'T PAY ANY ATTENTION TO THOSE WHO HAVE NO MONEY.
Here.
WHY?
PEOPLE'S HEARTS CAN CHANGE...
...BUT SILVER NEVER BETRAYS YOU.

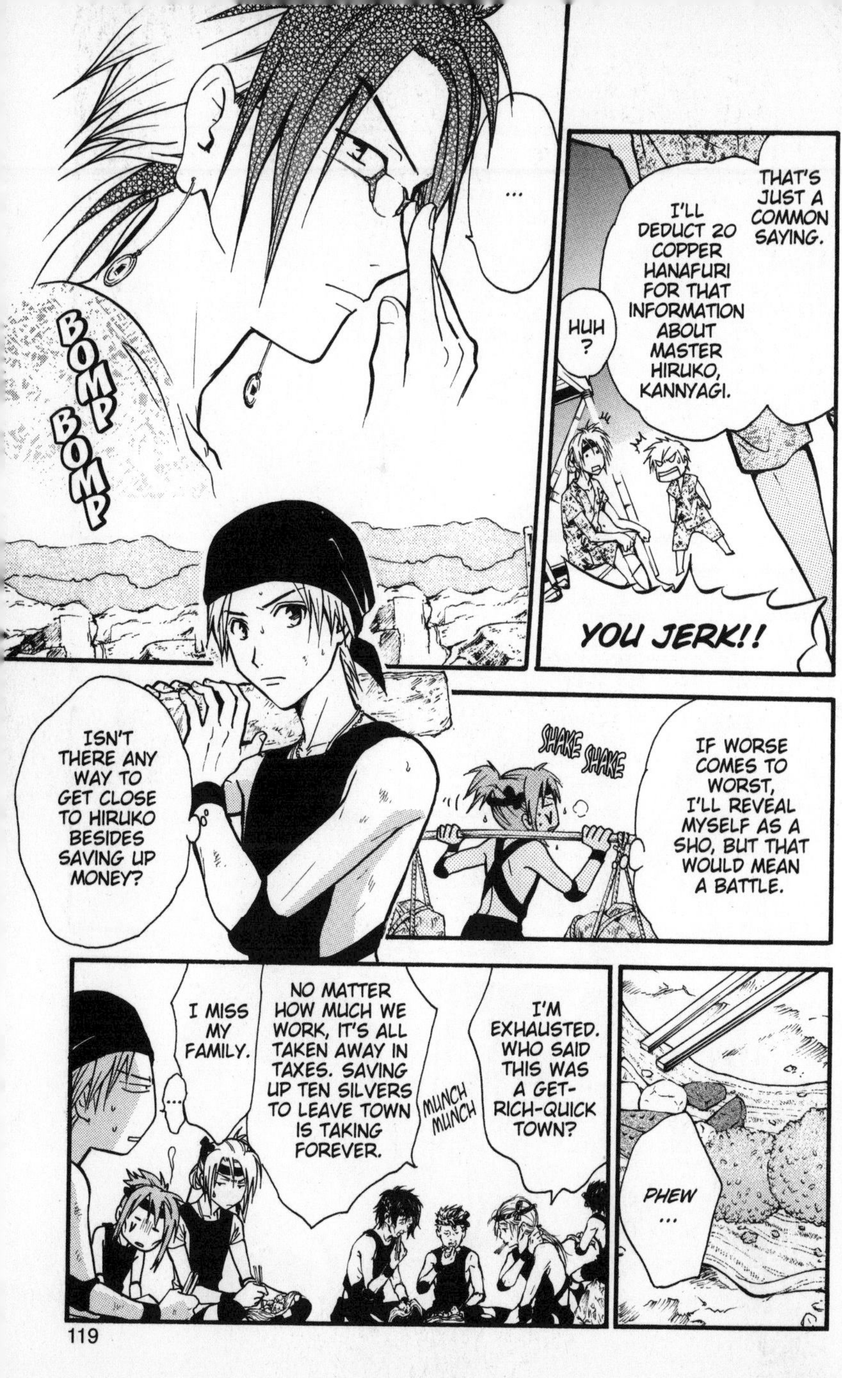
THAT'S JUST A COMMON SAYING.
I'LL DEDUCT 20 COPPER HANAFURI FOR THAT INFORMATION ABOUT MASTER HIRUKO, KANNYAGI.
HUH?
YOU JERK!!
...
BOMP BOMP
IF WORSE COMES TO WORST, I'LL REVEAL MYSELF AS A SHO, BUT THAT WOULD MEAN A BATTLE.
SHAKE SHAKE
ISN'T THERE ANY WAY TO GET CLOSE TO HIRUKO BESIDES SAVING UP MONEY?
PHEW ...
I'M EXHAUSTED. WHO SAID THIS WAS A GET-RICH-QUICK TOWN?
MUNCH MUNCH
NO MATTER HOW MUCH WE WORK, IT'S ALL TAKEN AWAY IN TAXES. SAVING UP TEN SILVERS TO LEAVE TOWN IS TAKING FOREVER.
I MISS MY FAMILY.
...

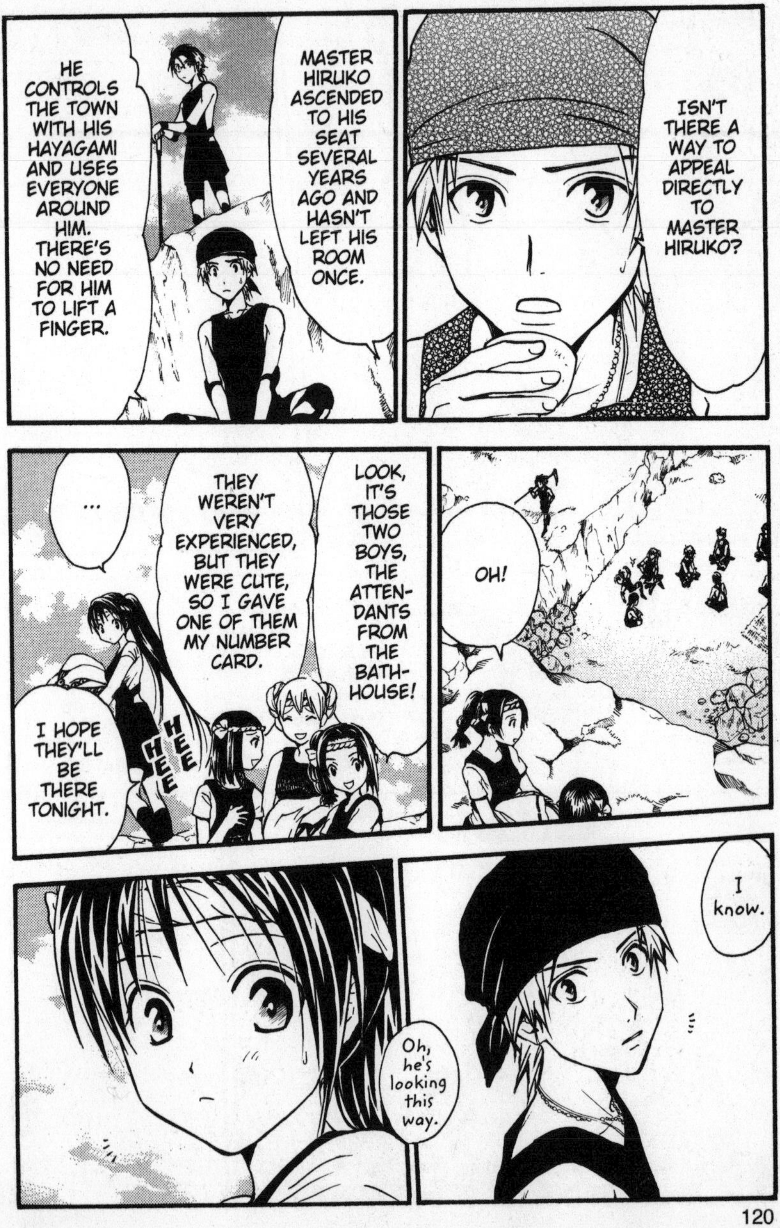
ISN'T THERE A WAY TO APPEAL DIRECTLY TO MASTER HIRUKO?
MASTER HIRUKO ASCENDED TO HIS SEAT SEVERAL YEARS AGO AND HASN'T LEFT HIS ROOM ONCE.
HE CONTROLS THE TOWN WITH HIS HAYAGAMI AND USES EVERYONE AROUND HIM. THERE'S NO NEED FOR HIM TO LIFT A FINGER.
OH!
LOOK, IT'S THOSE TWO BOYS, THE ATTENDANTS FROM THE BATH-HOUSE!
THEY WEREN'T VERY EXPERIENCED, BUT THEY WERE CUTE, SO I GAVE ONE OF THEM MY NUMBER CARD.
...
HEE HEE HEE
I HOPE THEY'LL BE THERE TONIGHT.
I know.
Oh, he's looking this way.

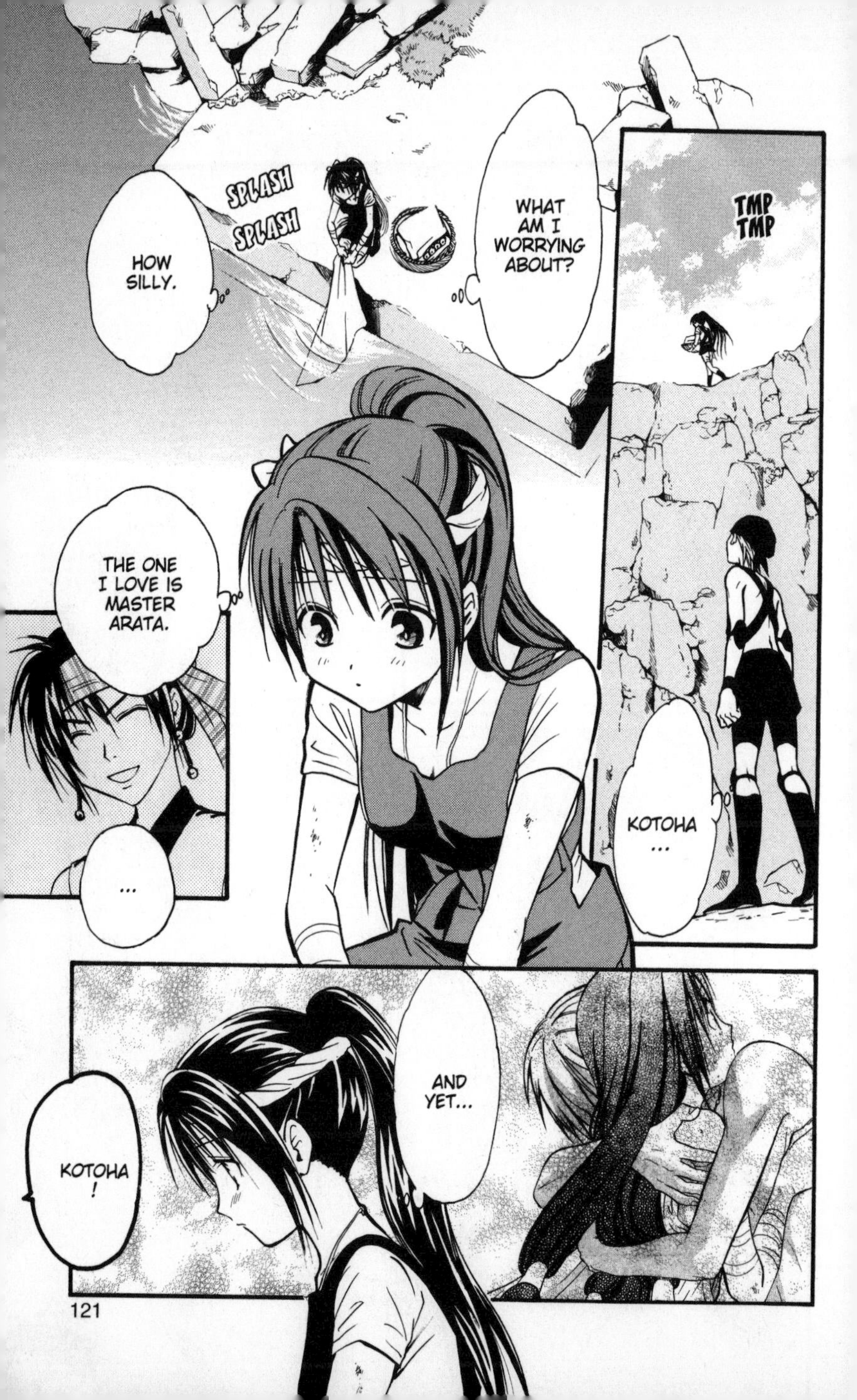
WHAT AM I WORRYING ABOUT?
SPLASH
SPLASH
HOW SILLY.
TMP TMP
KOTOHA ...
THE ONE I LOVE IS MASTER ARATA.
...
AND YET...
KOTOHA!

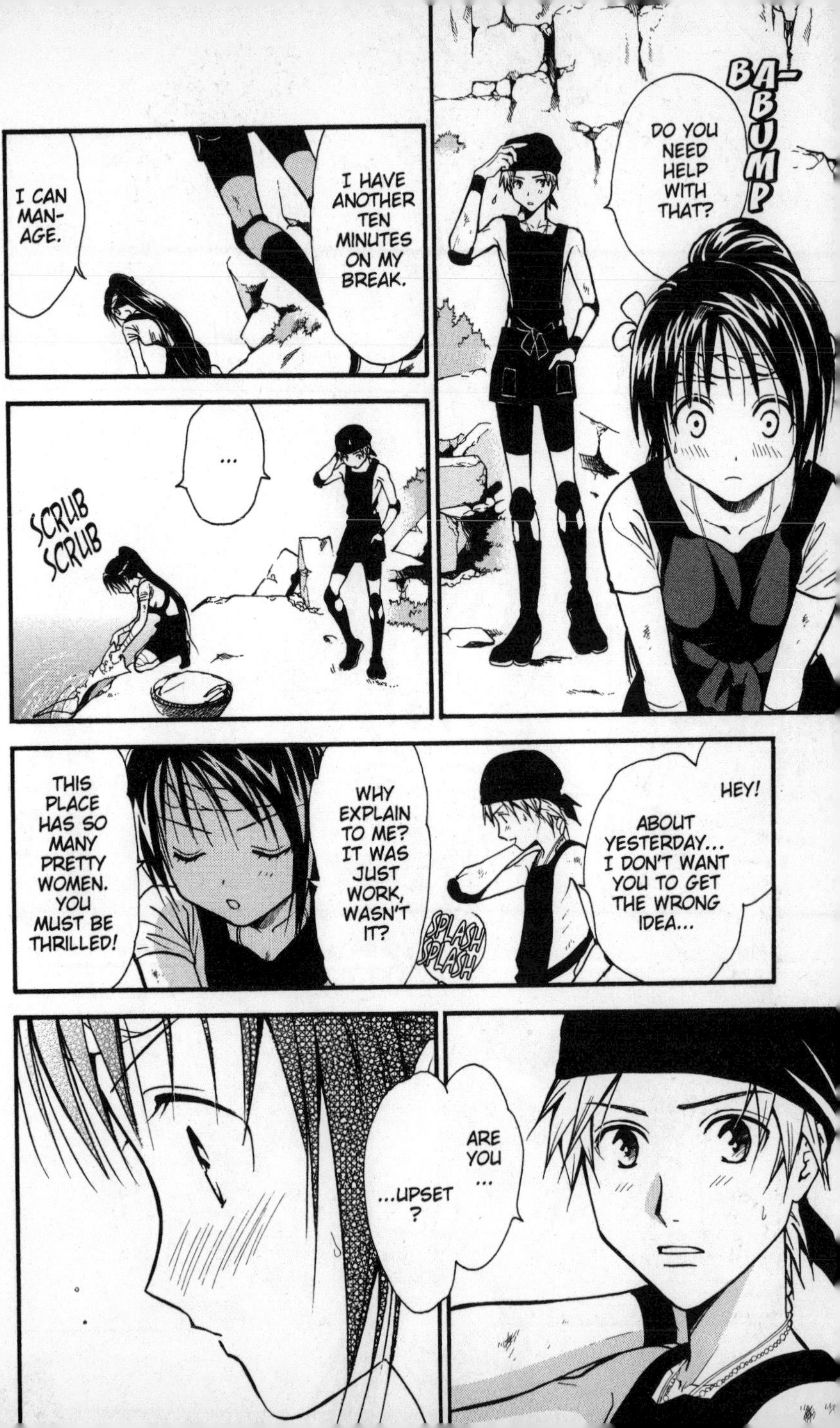
DO YOU NEED HELP WITH THAT?
BA-BUMP
I HAVE ANOTHER TEN MINUTES ON MY BREAK.
I CAN MAN-AGE.
...
SCRUB SCRUB
HEY!
ABOUT YESTERDAY... I DON'T WANT YOU TO GET THE WRONG IDEA...
SPLASH SPLASH
WHY EXPLAIN TO ME? IT WAS JUST WORK, WASN'T IT?
THIS PLACE HAS SO MANY PRETTY WOMEN. YOU MUST BE THRILLED!
ARE YOU ...
...UPSET ?

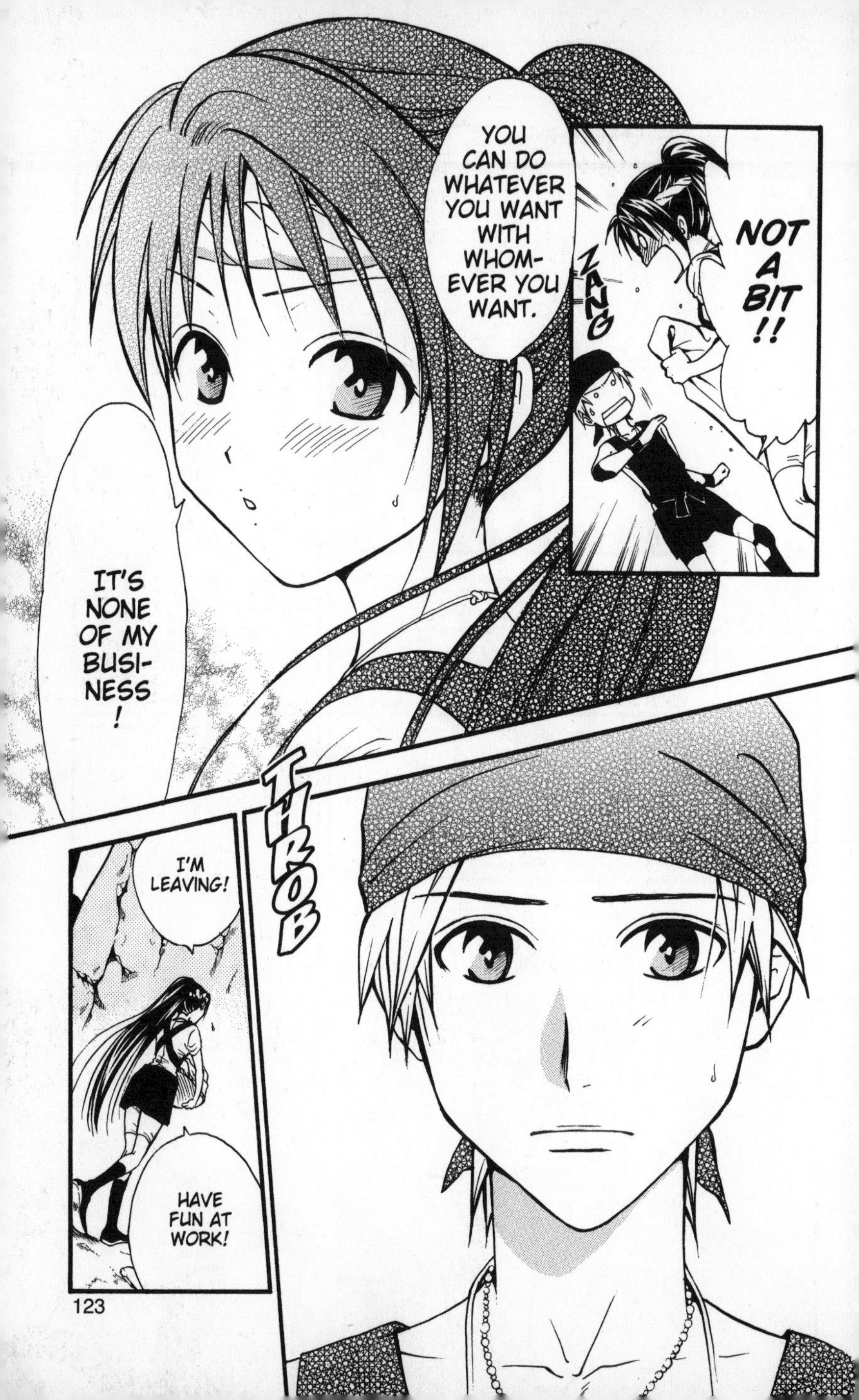
YOU CAN DO WHATEVER YOU WANT WITH WHOM-EVER YOU WANT.
NOT A BIT!!
ZANG
IT'S NONE OF MY BUSI-NESS!
THROB
I'M LEAVING!
HAVE FUN AT WORK!

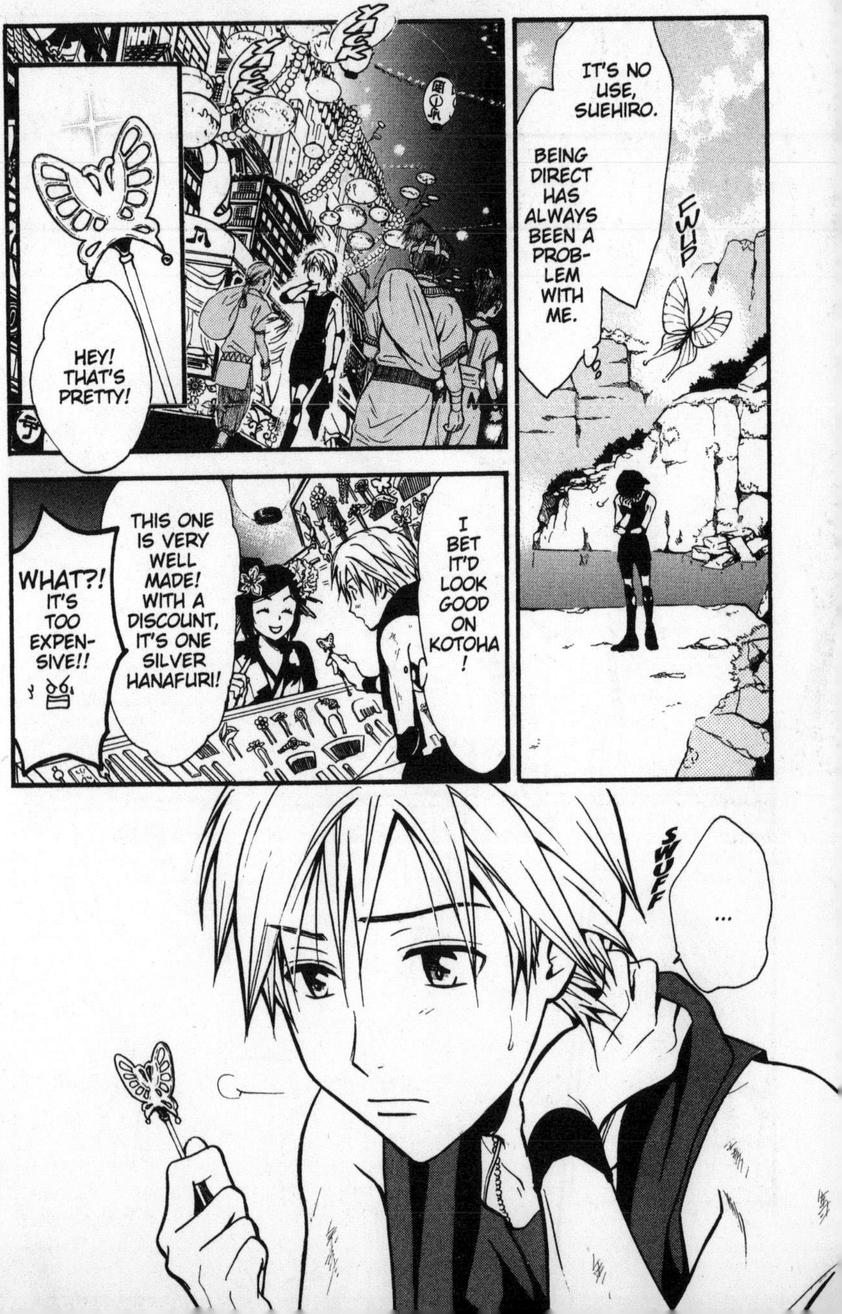
IT'S NO USE, SUEHIRO.
BEING DIRECT HAS ALWAYS BEEN A PROB-LEM WITH ME.
FWUP
YACK
YACK
HEY! THAT'S PRETTY!
I BET IT'D LOOK GOOD ON KOTOHA!
THIS ONE IS VERY WELL MADE! WITH A DISCOUNT, IT'S ONE SILVER HANAFURI!
WHAT?! IT'S TOO EXPEN-SIVE!!
SWUFF
...

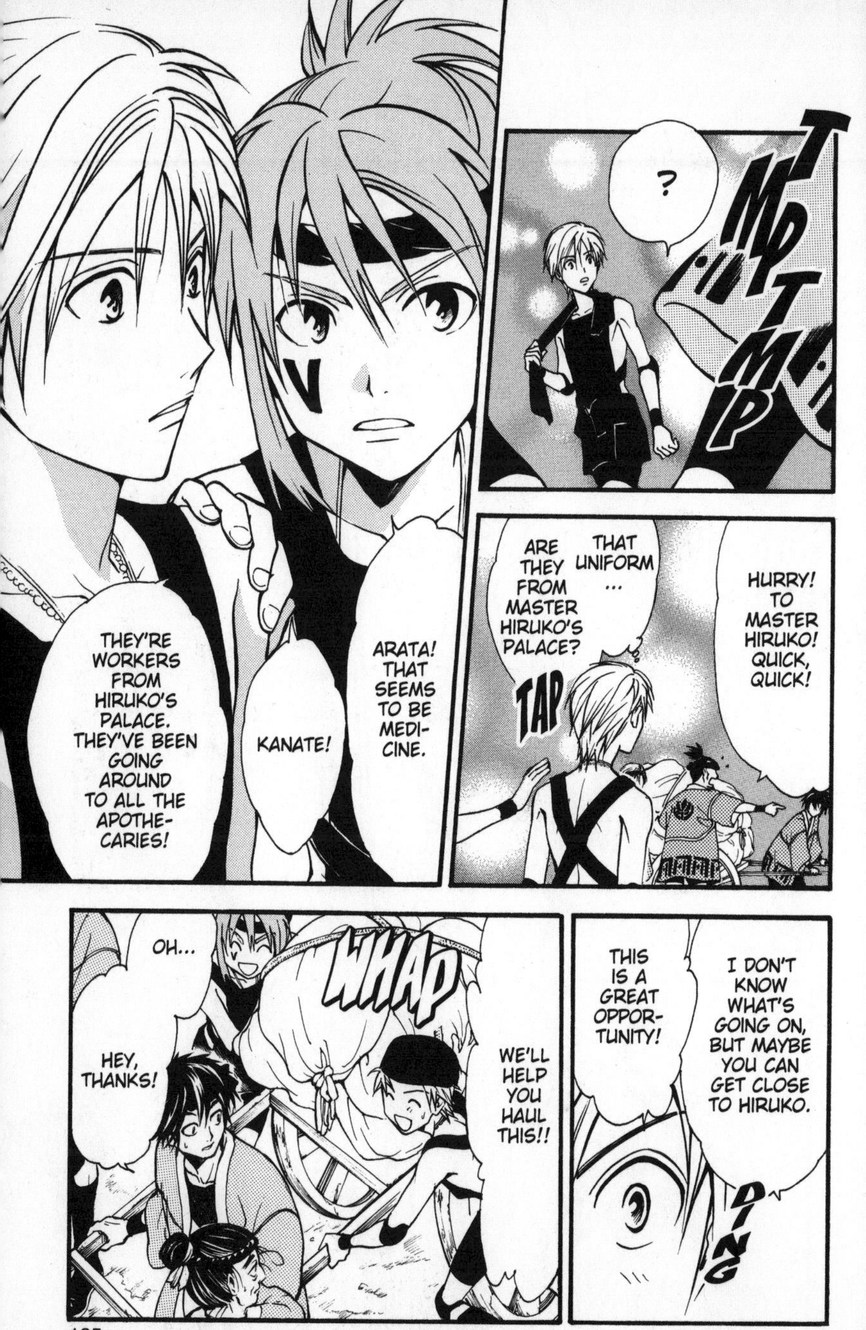
?
TMP TMP
HURRY! TO MASTER HIRUKO! QUICK, QUICK!
THAT UNIFORM ...
ARE THEY FROM MASTER HIRUKO'S PALACE?
TAP
ARATA! THAT SEEMS TO BE MEDICINE.
KANATE!
THEY'RE WORKERS FROM HIRUKO'S PALACE. THEY'VE BEEN GOING AROUND TO ALL THE APOTHECARIES!
I DON'T KNOW WHAT'S GOING ON, BUT MAYBE YOU CAN GET CLOSE TO HIRUKO.
THIS IS A GREAT OPPORTUNITY!
DING
WE'LL HELP YOU HAUL THIS!!
WHAP
OH...
HEY, THANKS!

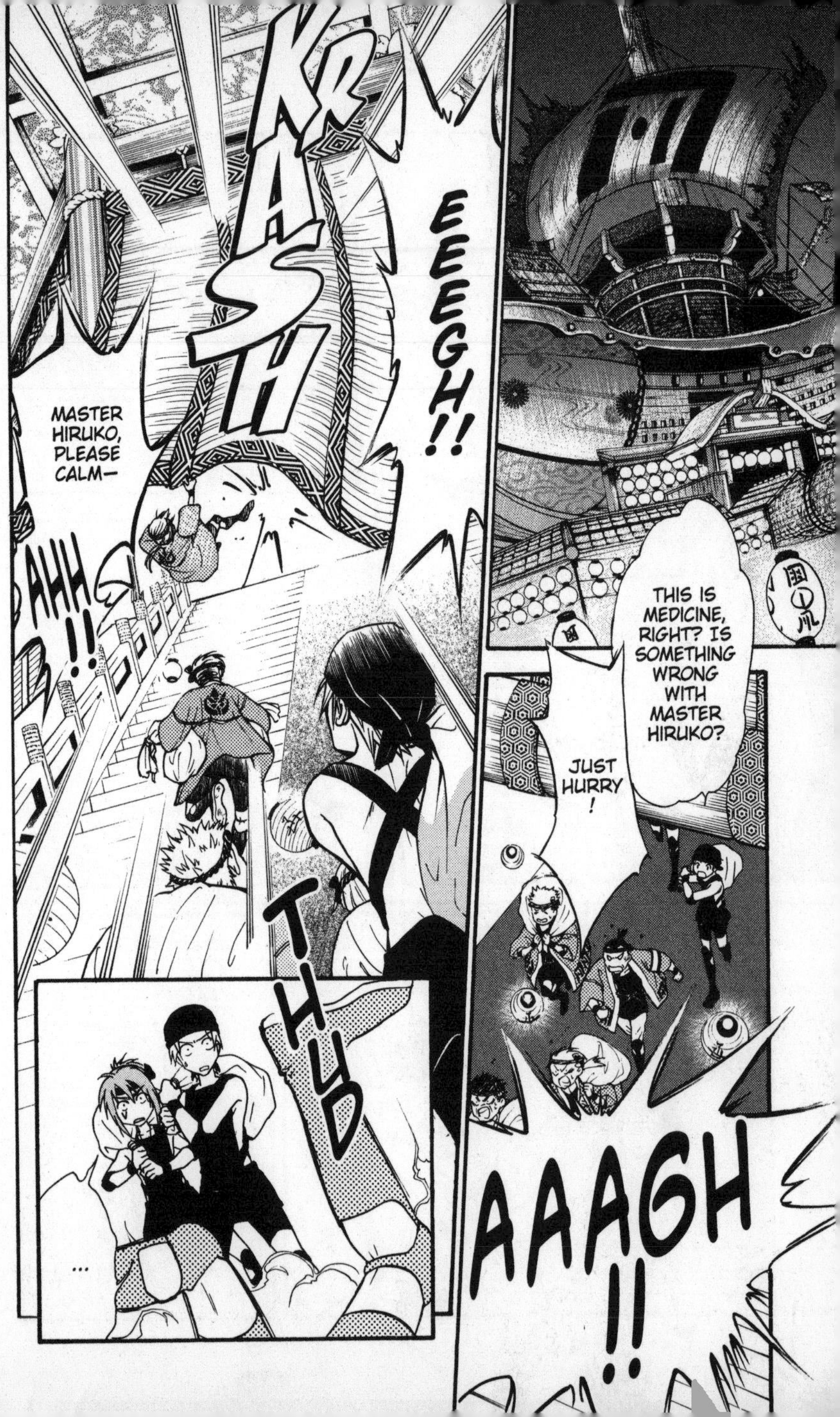
THIS IS MEDICINE, RIGHT? IS SOMETHING WRONG WITH MASTER HIRUKO?
JUST HURRY!
AAAGH!!
KRASH
EEEEGH!!
MASTER HIRUKO, PLEASE CALM—
AHH!!
THUD
...

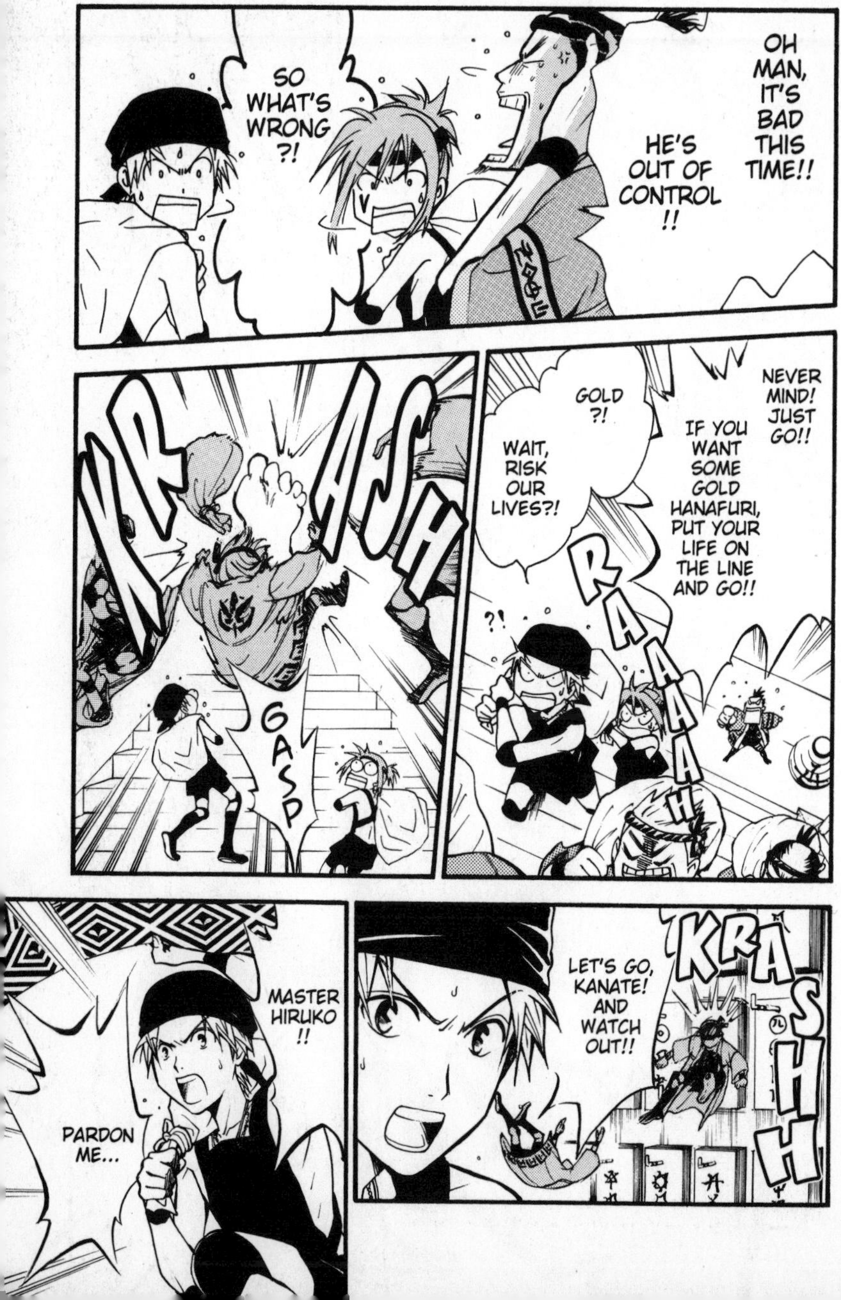
OH MAN, IT'S BAD THIS TIME!!
HE'S OUT OF CONTROL!!
SO WHAT'S WRONG?!
NEVER MIND! JUST GO!!
IF YOU WANT SOME GOLD HANAFURI, PUT YOUR LIFE ON THE LINE AND GO!!
GOLD?!
WAIT, RISK OUR LIVES?!
RAAAAAH
?!
KRASH
GASP
KRASHHH
LET'S GO, KANATE! AND WATCH OUT!!
MASTER HIRUKO!!
PARDON ME...

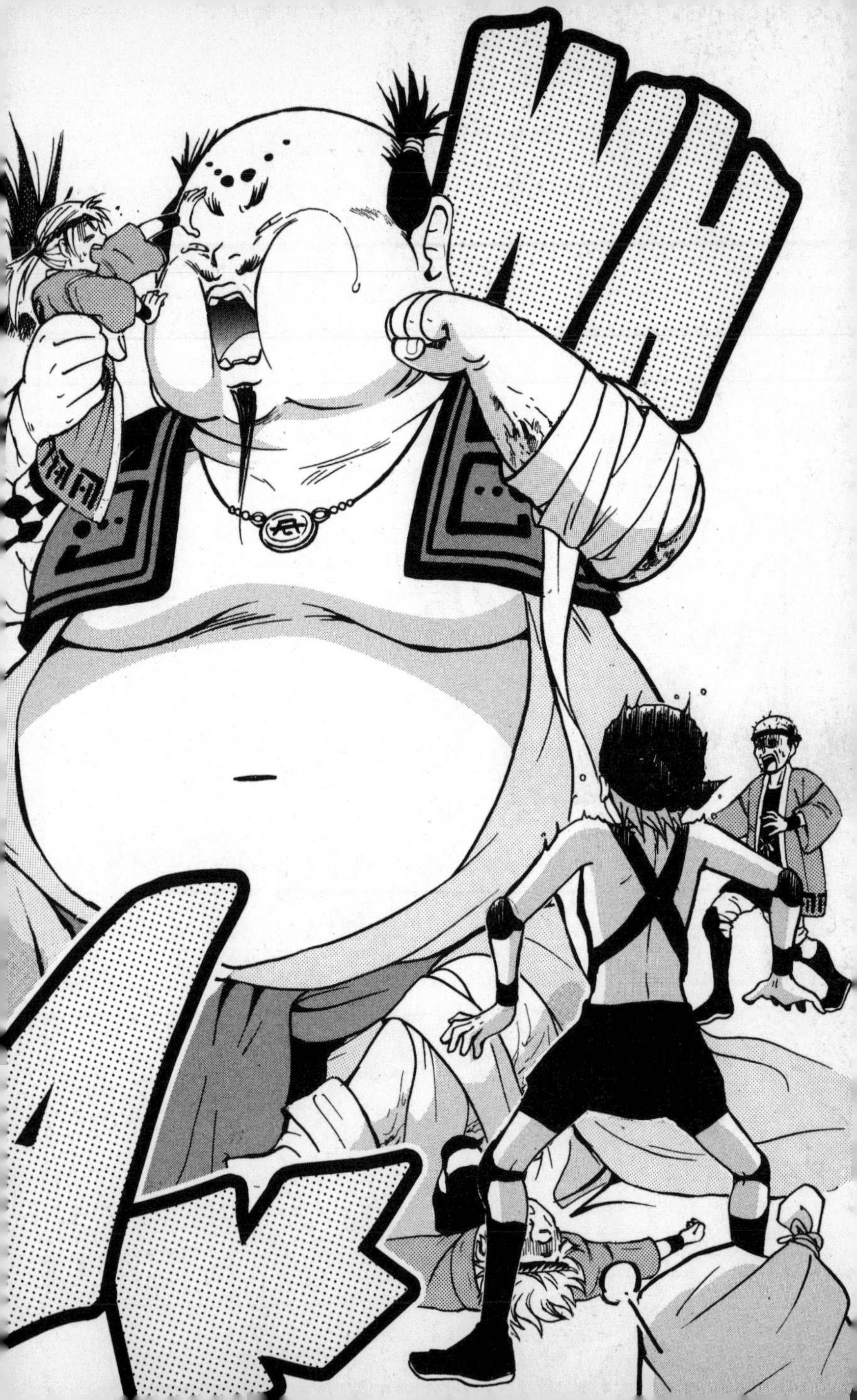

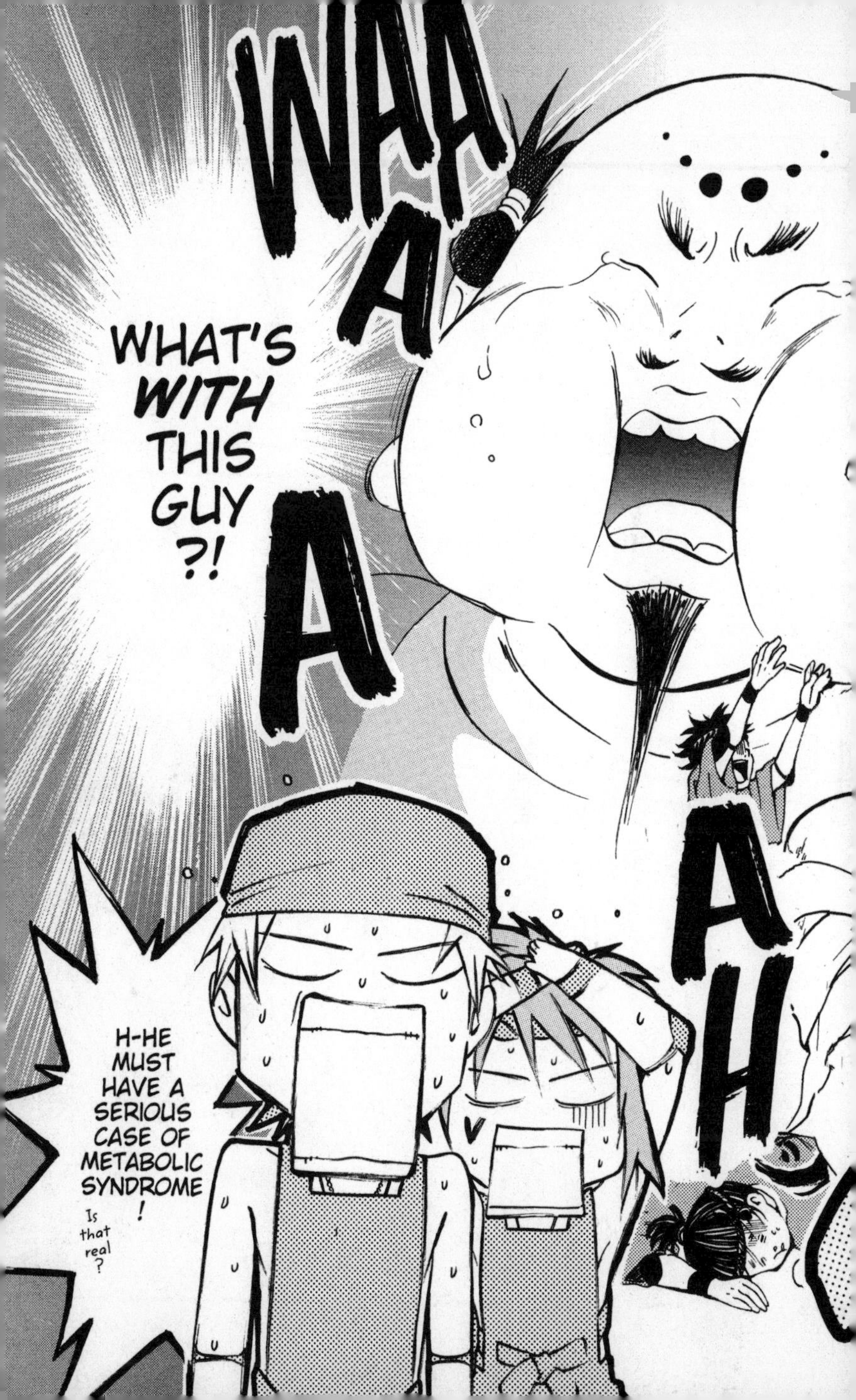
WAAAAAAH
WHAT'S *WITH* THIS GUY ?!
H-HE MUST HAVE A SERIOUS CASE OF METABOLIC SYNDROME!
Is that real?

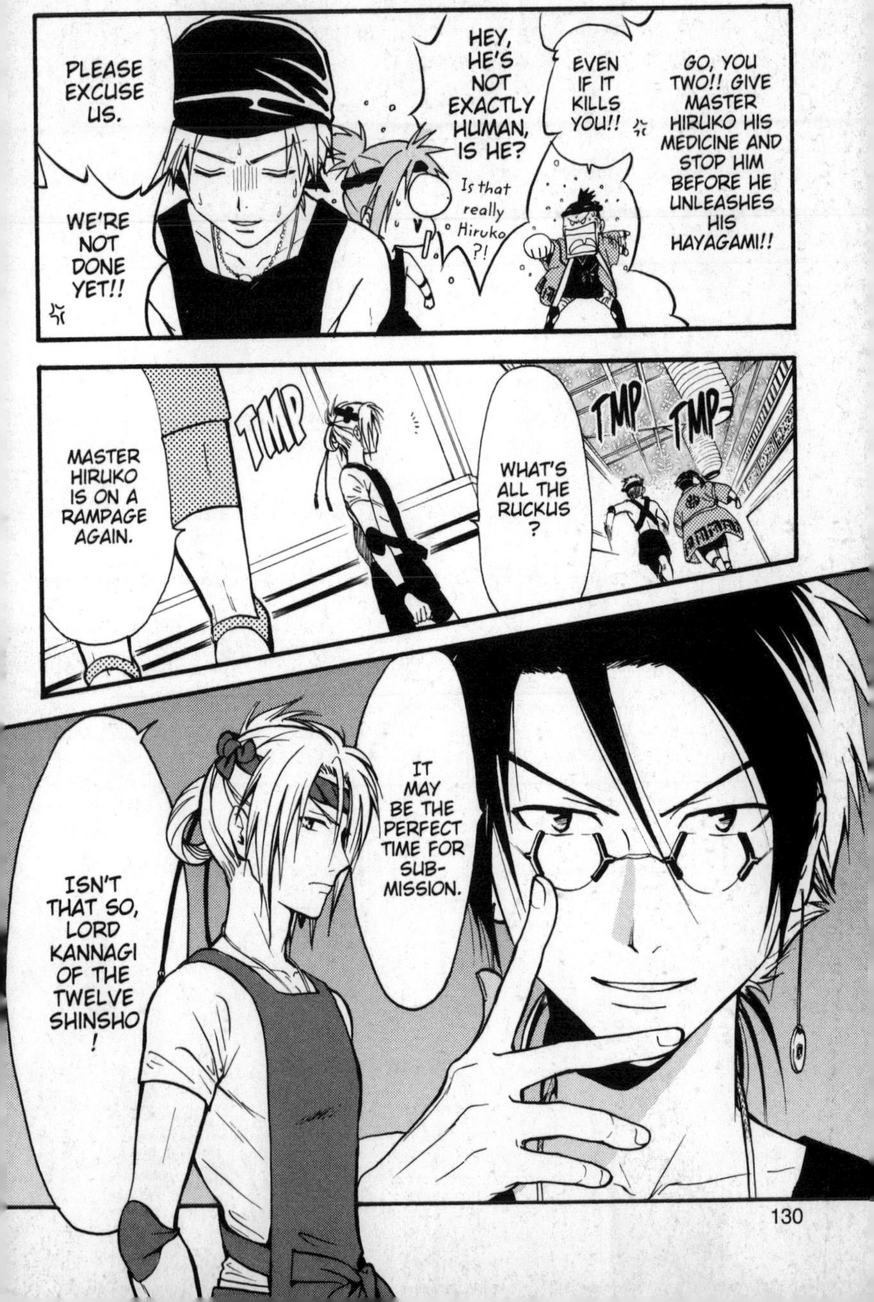
GO, YOU TWO!! GIVE MASTER HIRUKO HIS MEDICINE AND STOP HIM BEFORE HE UNLEASHES HIS HAYAGAMI!!
EVEN IF IT KILLS YOU!!
HEY, HE'S NOT EXACTLY HUMAN, IS HE?
Is that really Hiruko?!
PLEASE EXCUSE US.
WE'RE NOT DONE YET!!
TMP TMP
WHAT'S ALL THE RUCKUS?
TMP
MASTER HIRUKO IS ON A RAMPAGE AGAIN.
IT MAY BE THE PERFECT TIME FOR SUB-MISSION.
ISN'T THAT SO, LORD KANNAGI OF THE TWELVE SHINSHO!

Arata
THE LEGEND

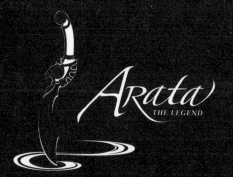

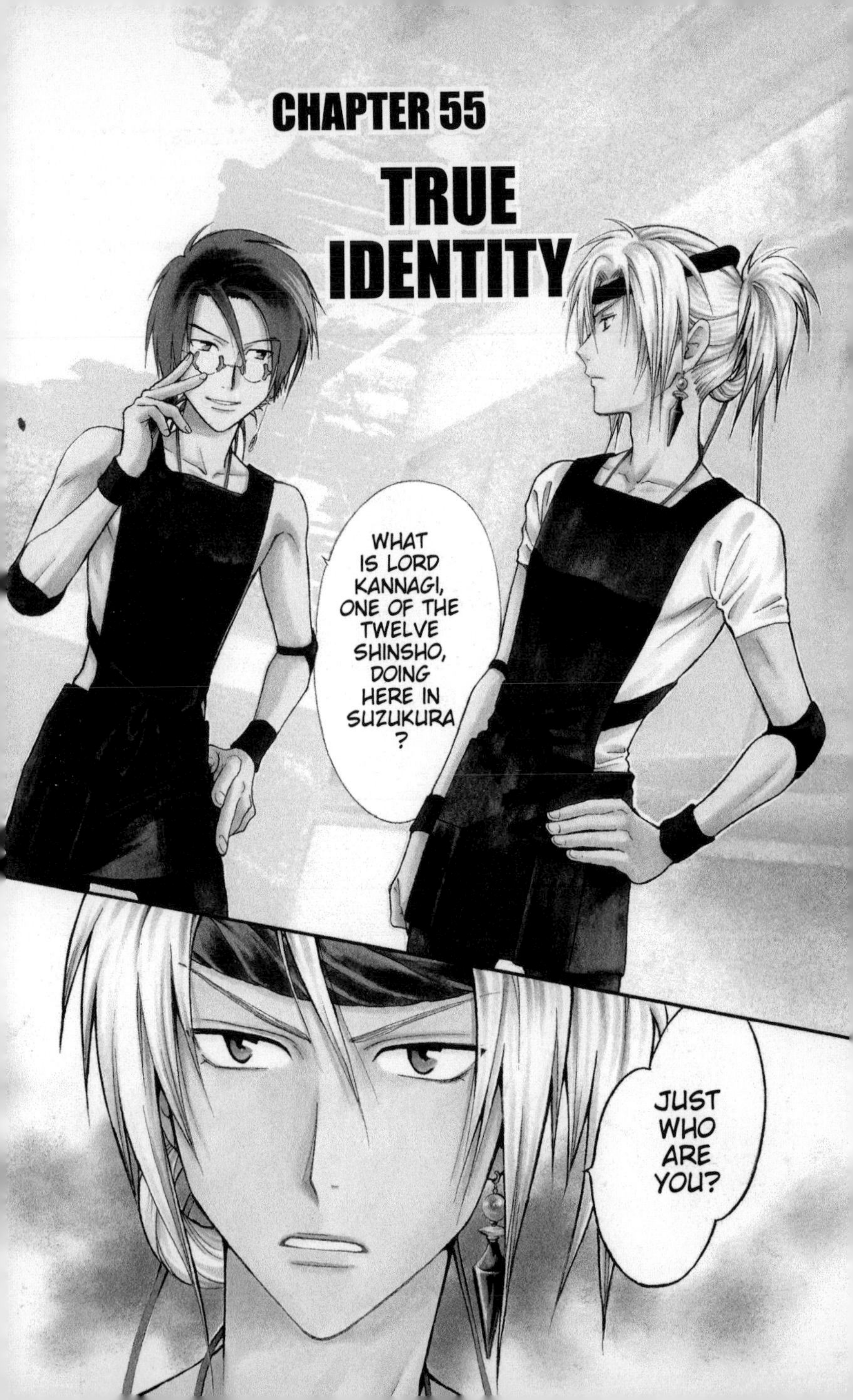
CHAPTER 55
TRUE IDENTITY
WHAT IS LORD KANNAGI, ONE OF THE TWELVE SHINSHO, DOING HERE IN SUZUKURA?
JUST WHO ARE YOU?

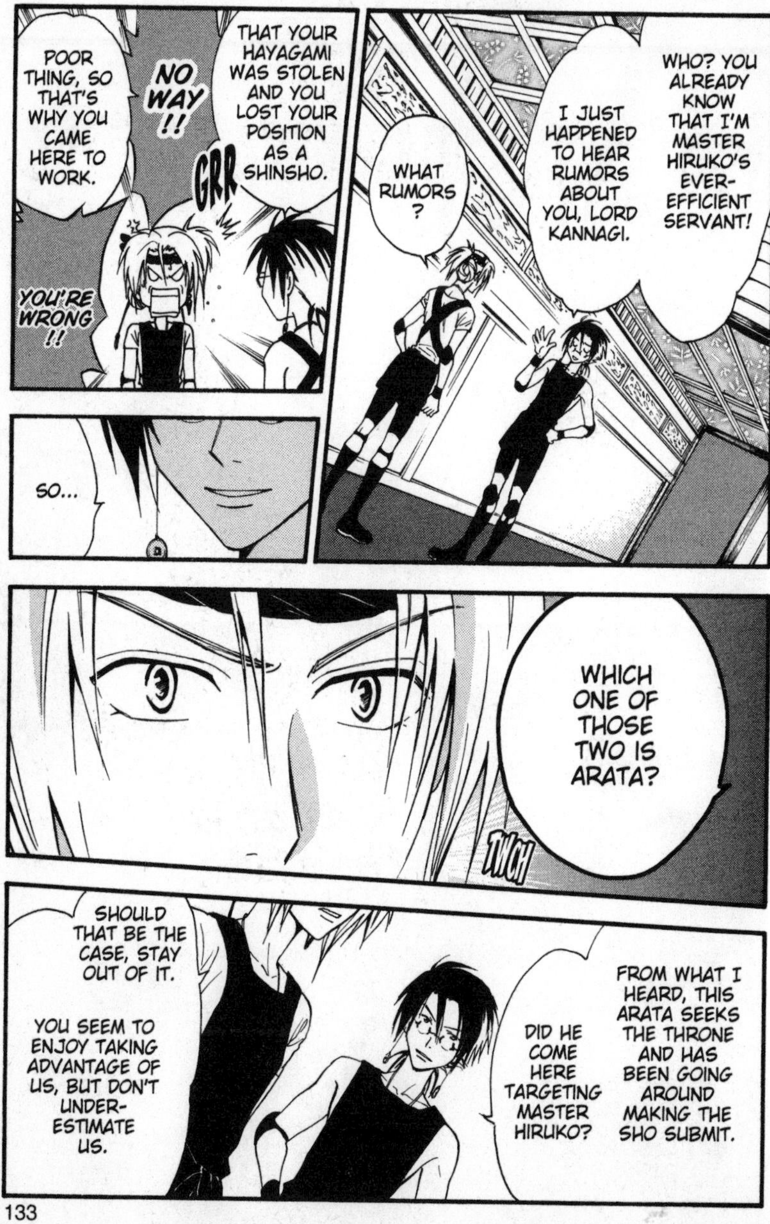
WHO? YOU ALREADY KNOW THAT I'M MASTER HIRUKO'S EVER-EFFICIENT SERVANT!
I JUST HAPPENED TO HEAR RUMORS ABOUT YOU, LORD KANNAGI.
WHAT RUMORS?
THAT YOUR HAYAGAMI WAS STOLEN AND YOU LOST YOUR POSITION AS A SHINSHO.
NO WAY!!
GRR
POOR THING, SO THAT'S WHY YOU CAME HERE TO WORK.
YOU'RE WRONG!!
SO...
WHICH ONE OF THOSE TWO IS ARATA?
TWCH
FROM WHAT I HEARD, THIS ARATA SEEKS THE THRONE AND HAS BEEN GOING AROUND MAKING THE SHO SUBMIT.
DID HE COME HERE TARGETING MASTER HIRUKO?
SHOULD THAT BE THE CASE, STAY OUT OF IT.
YOU SEEM TO ENJOY TAKING ADVANTAGE OF US, BUT DON'T UNDER-ESTIMATE US.

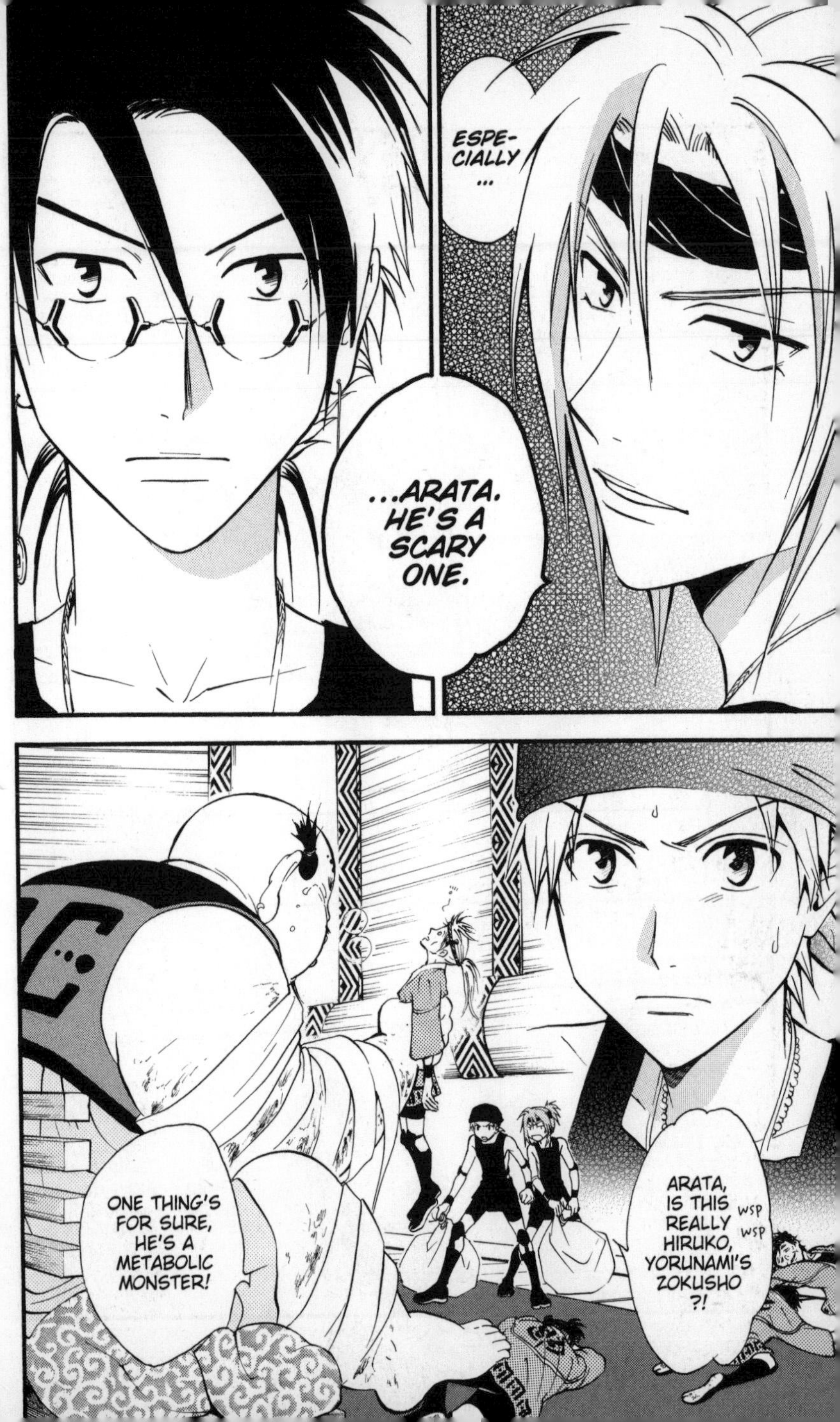
ESPE-
CIALLY
...
...ARATA.
HE'S A
SCARY
ONE.
ARATA,
IS THIS
REALLY
HIRUKO,
YORUNAMI'S
ZOKUSHO
?!
WSP
WSP
ONE THING'S
FOR SURE,
HE'S A
METABOLIC
MONSTER!

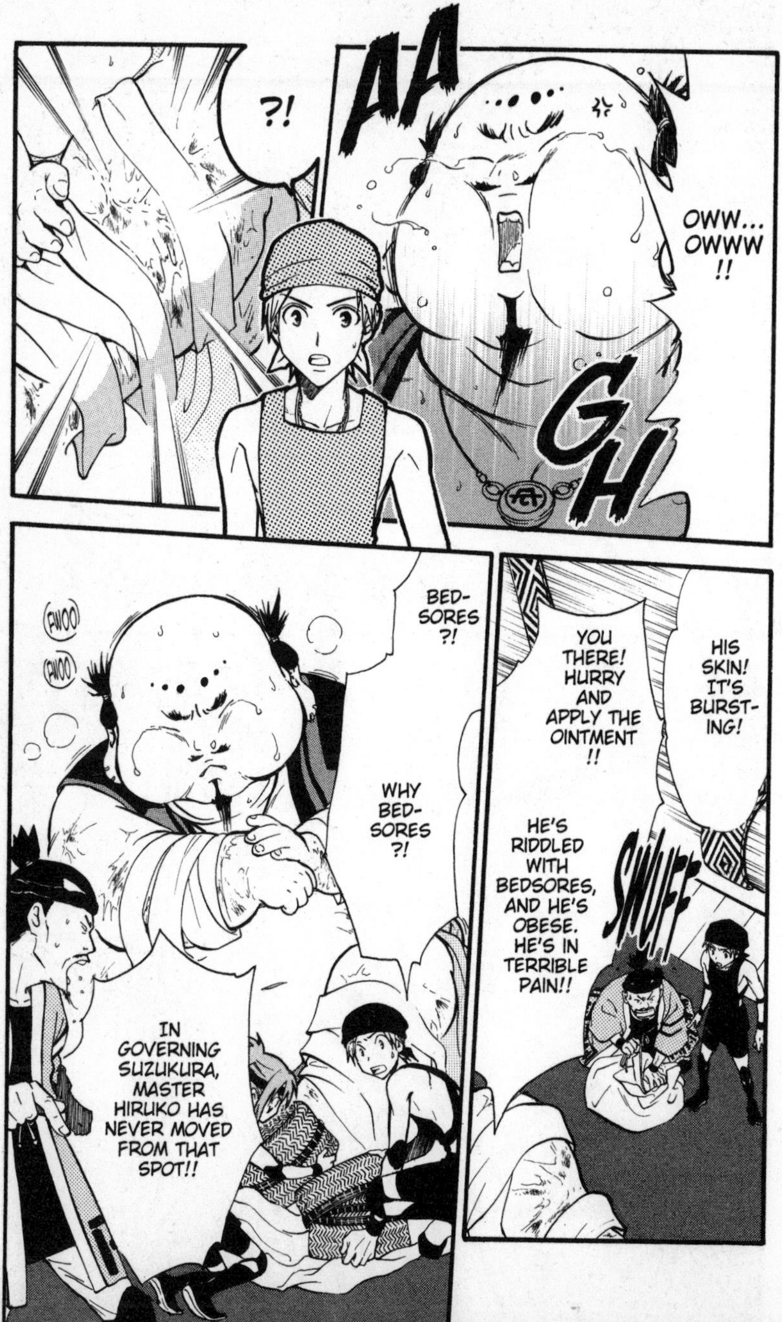

AAGH
OWWW... OWWW!!
?!
HIS SKIN! IT'S BURSTING!
YOU THERE! HURRY AND APPLY THE OINTMENT!!
SNUFF
HE'S RIDDLED WITH BEDSORES, AND HE'S OBESE. HE'S IN TERRIBLE PAIN!!
BED-SORES?!
WHY BED-SORES?!
FWOO
FWOO
IN GOVERNING SUZUKURA, MASTER HIRUKO HAS NEVER MOVED FROM THAT SPOT!!

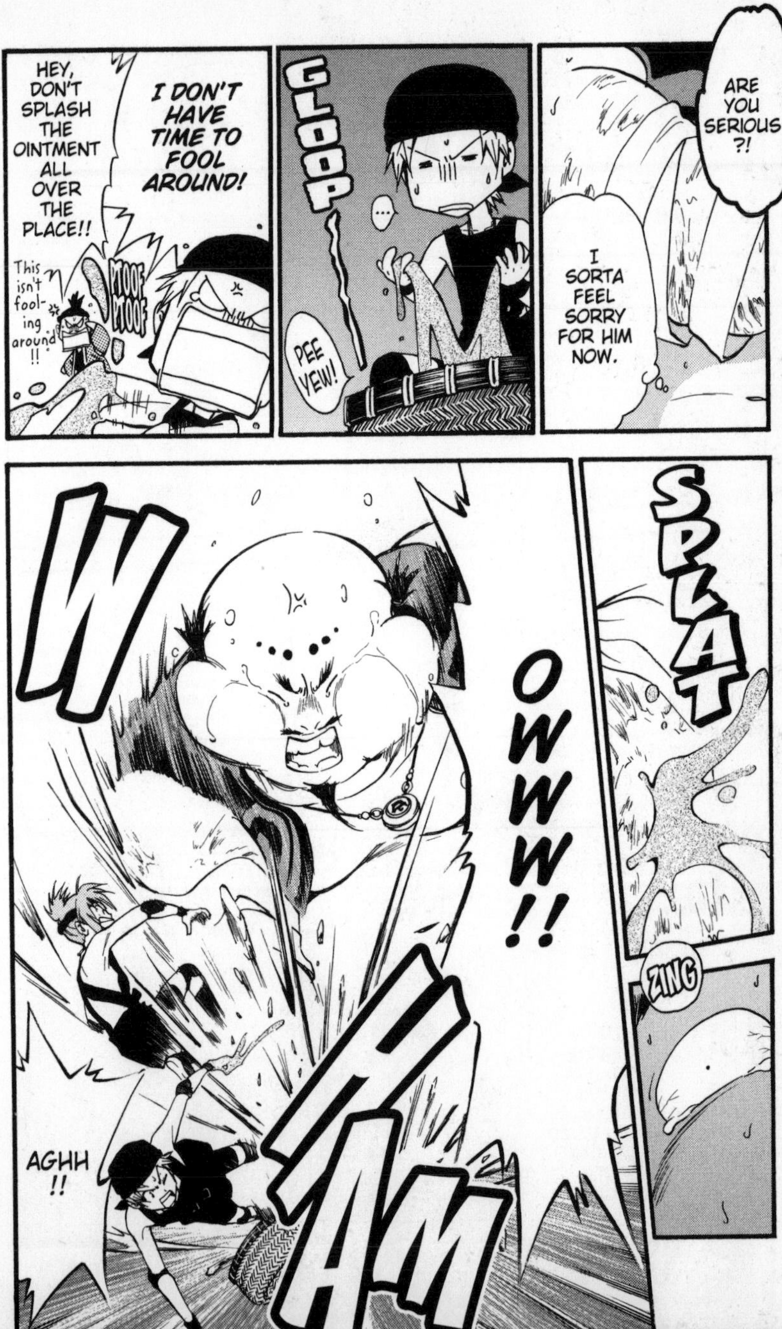
ARE YOU SERIOUS ?!
I SORTA FEEL SORRY FOR HIM NOW.
GLOOP
...
PEE YEW!
HEY, DON'T SPLASH THE OINTMENT ALL OVER THE PLACE!!
I DON'T HAVE TIME TO FOOL AROUND!
PTOOF PTOOF
This isn't fool-ing around!!
SPLAT
ZING
WHAM
OWWW!!
AGHH !!

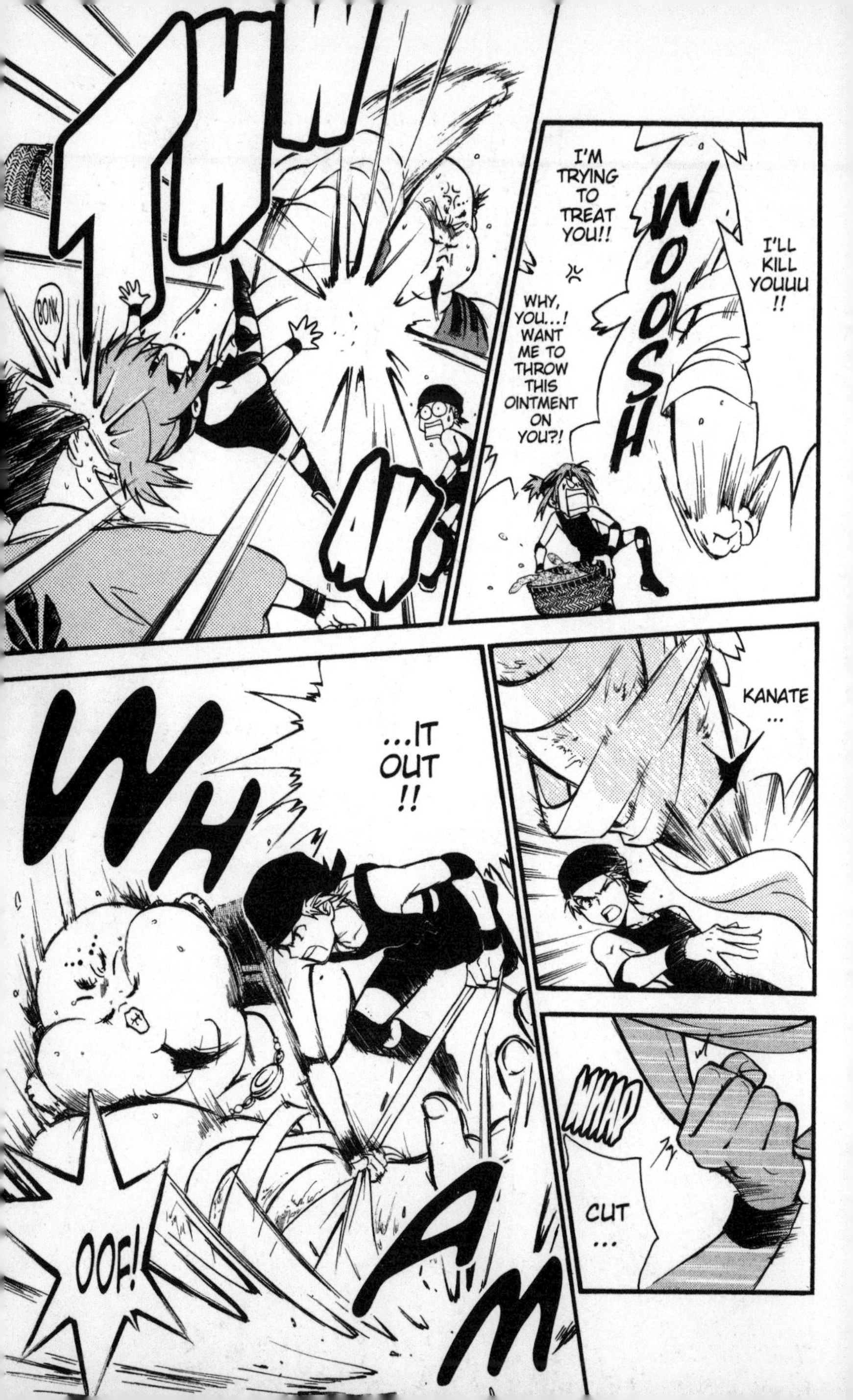
I'LL KILL YOUUU!!
WOOSH
I'M TRYING TO TREAT YOU!!
WHY, YOU...! WANT ME TO THROW THIS OINTMENT ON YOU?!
THWAK
BONK
KANATE...
WHAP
CUT...
...IT OUT!!
WHAM
OOF!

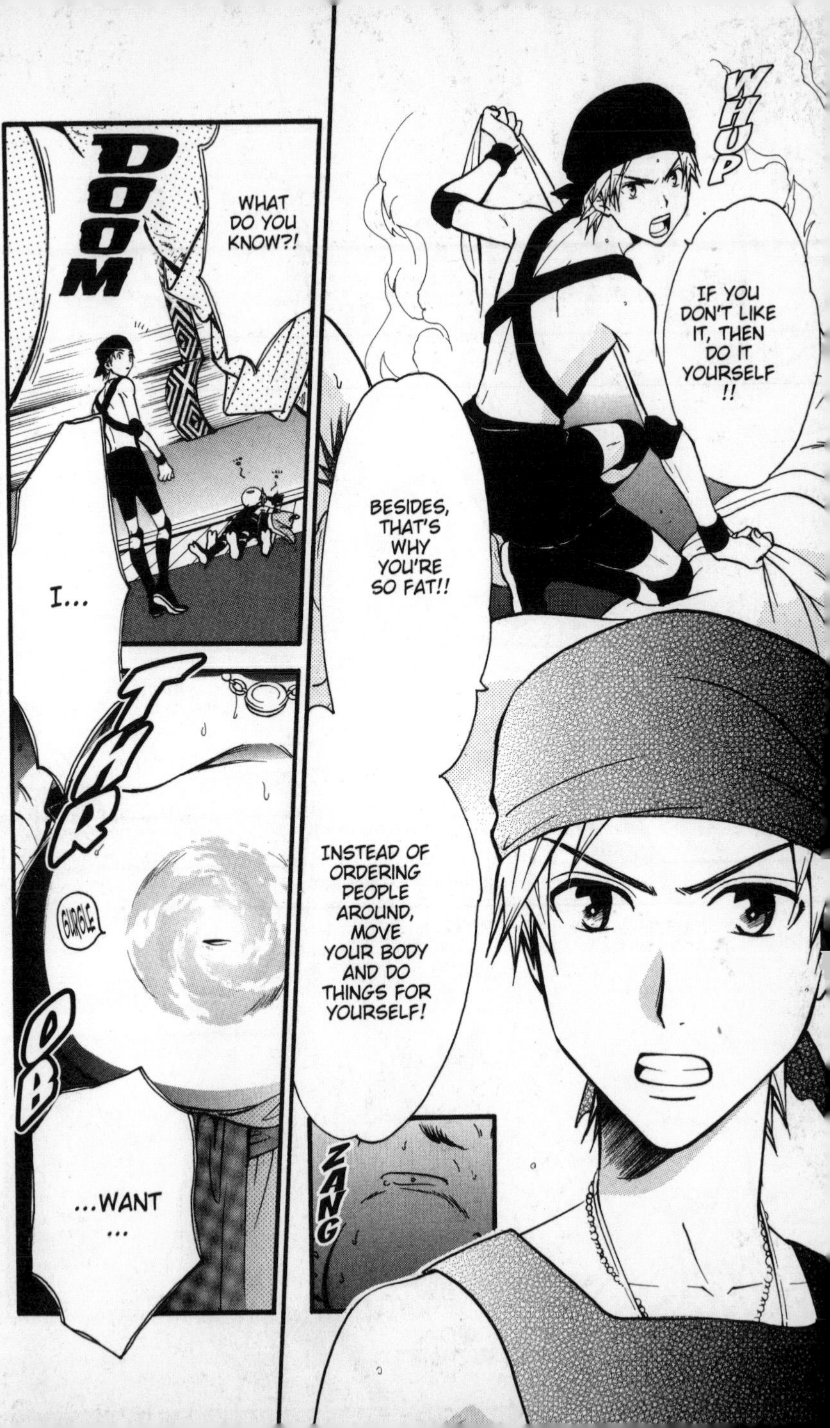
WHUP
IF YOU DON'T LIKE IT, THEN DO IT YOURSELF !!
BESIDES, THAT'S WHY YOU'RE SO FAT!!
INSTEAD OF ORDERING PEOPLE AROUND, MOVE YOUR BODY AND DO THINGS FOR YOURSELF!
ZANG
DOOM
WHAT DO YOU KNOW?!
I...
THROB
GURGLE
...WANT ...

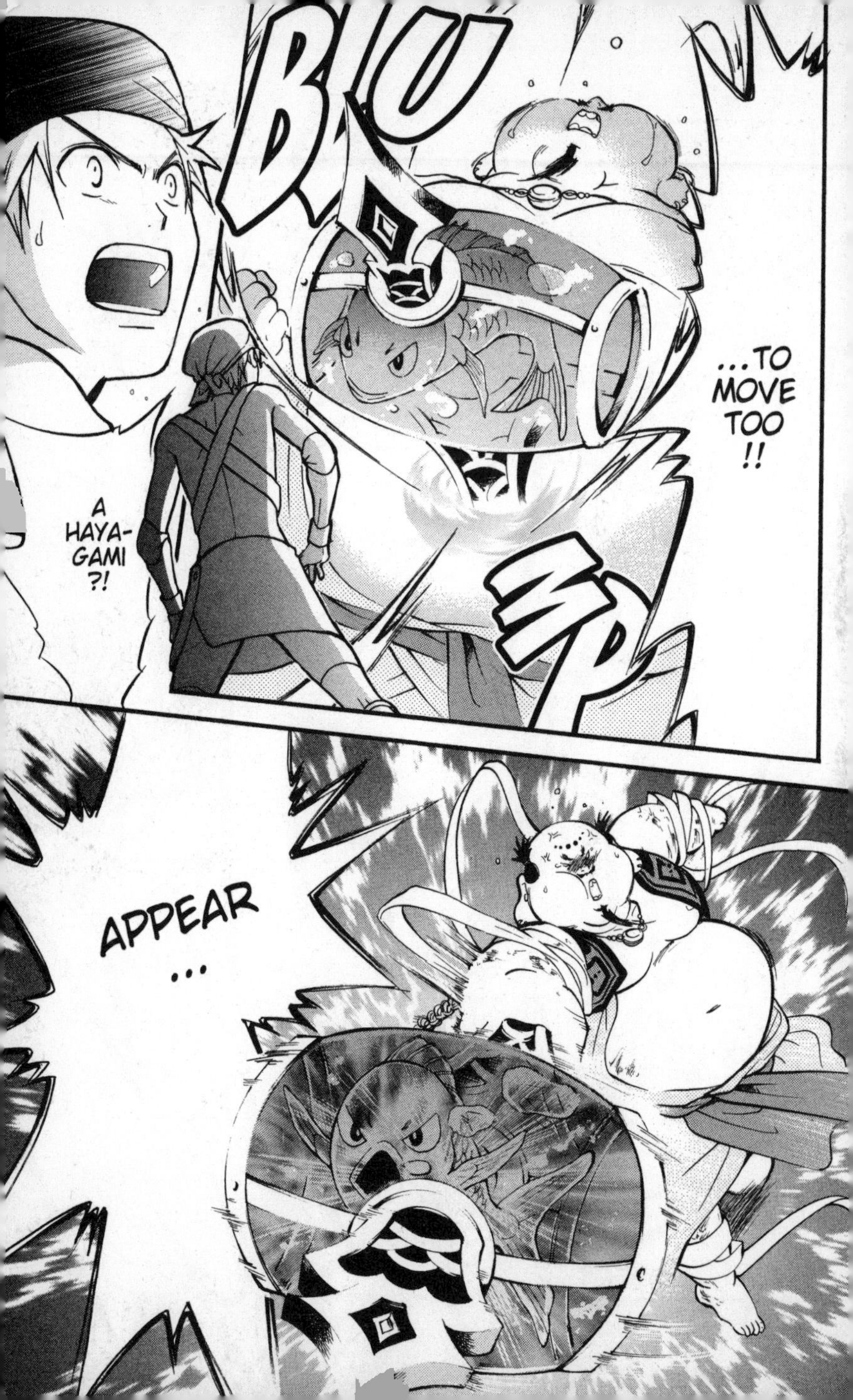
...TO MOVE TOO!!
A HAYA-GAMI?!
APPEAR...

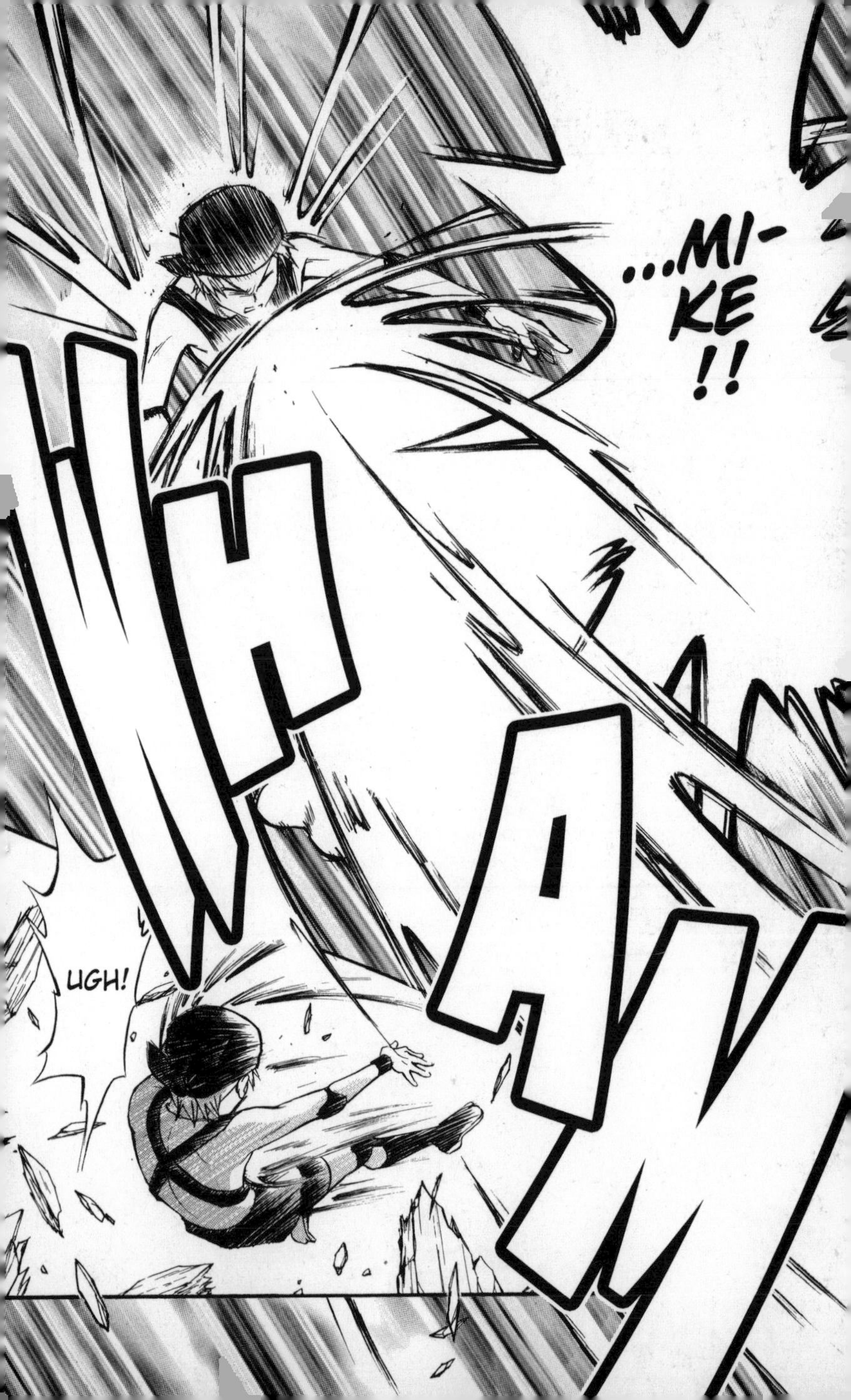
...MI-
KE
!!
WHAM
UGH!

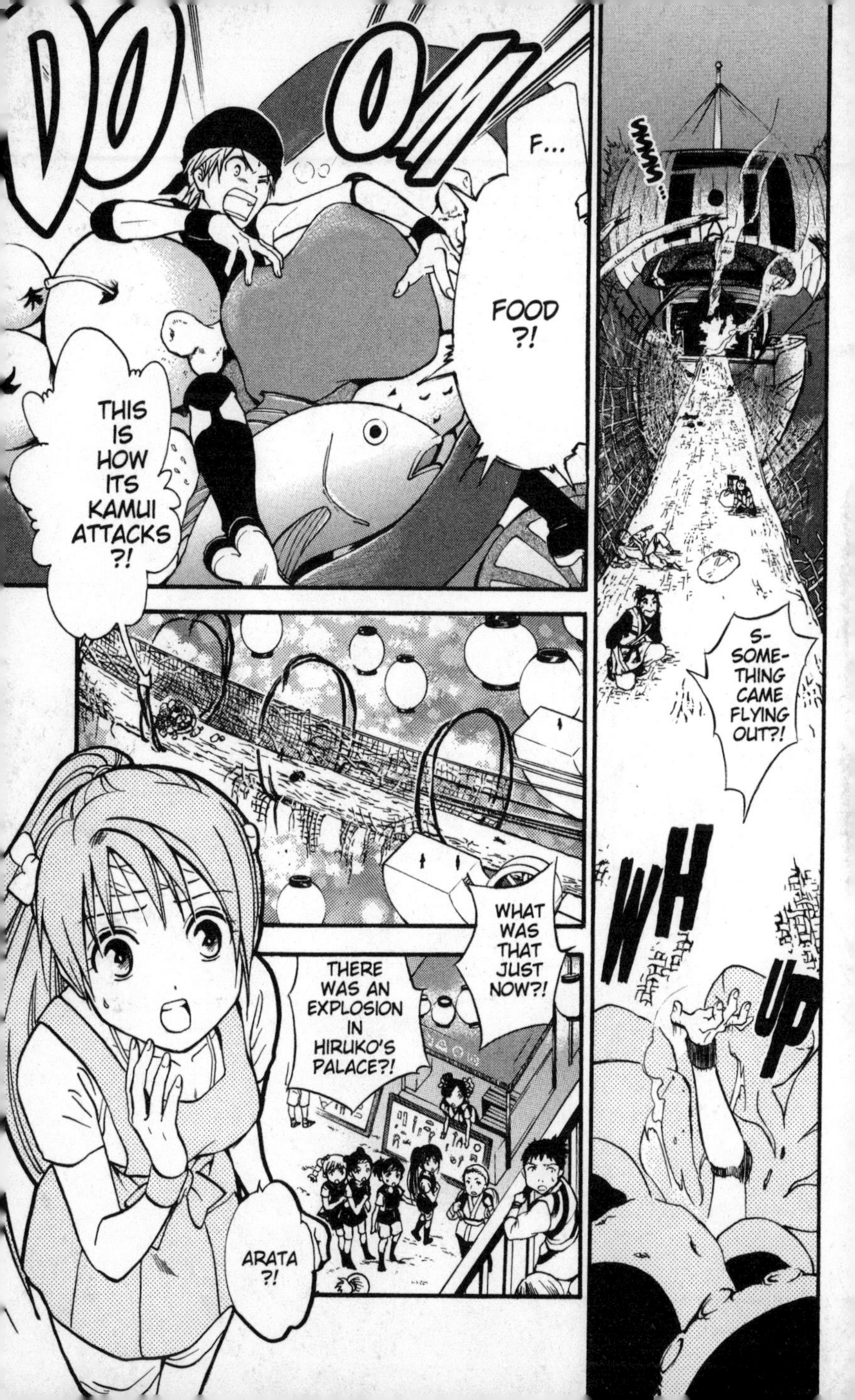

...WWW
S-SOMETHING CAME FLYING OUT?!
WHUP
DOOM
F...
FOOD?!
THIS IS HOW ITS KAMUI ATTACKS?!
WHAT WAS THAT JUST NOW?!
THERE WAS AN EXPLOSION IN HIRUKO'S PALACE?!
ARATA?!

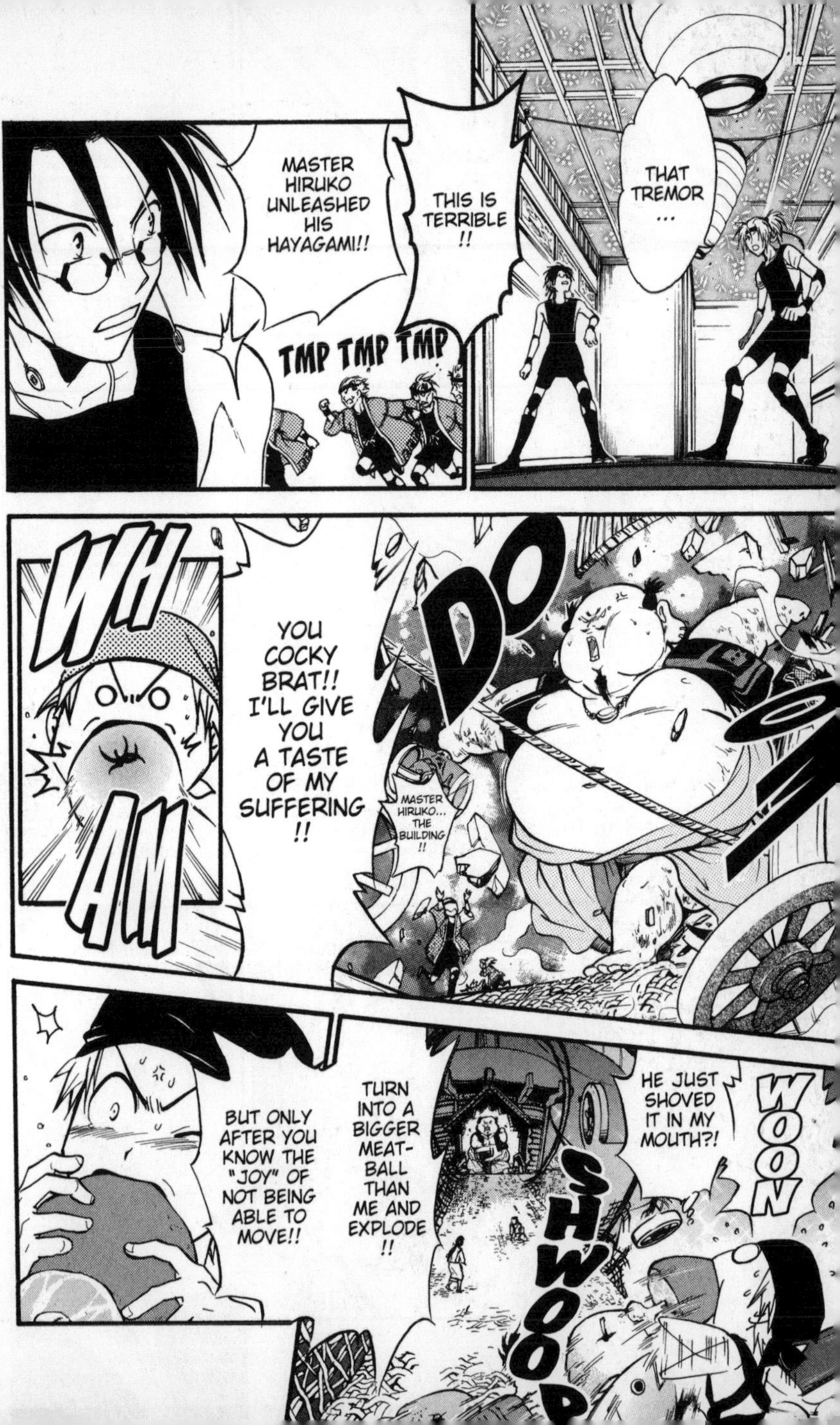
THAT TREMOR ...
THIS IS TERRIBLE !!
MASTER HIRUKO UNLEASHED HIS HAYAGAMI!!
TMP TMP TMP
DOOM
MASTER HIRUKO... THE BUILDING !!
YOU COCKY BRAT!! I'LL GIVE YOU A TASTE OF MY SUFFERING !!
WHAM
WOOON
HE JUST SHOVED IT IN MY MOUTH?!
SHWOOP
TURN INTO A BIGGER MEAT-BALL THAN ME AND EXPLODE !!
BUT ONLY AFTER YOU KNOW THE "JOY" OF NOT BEING ABLE TO MOVE!!

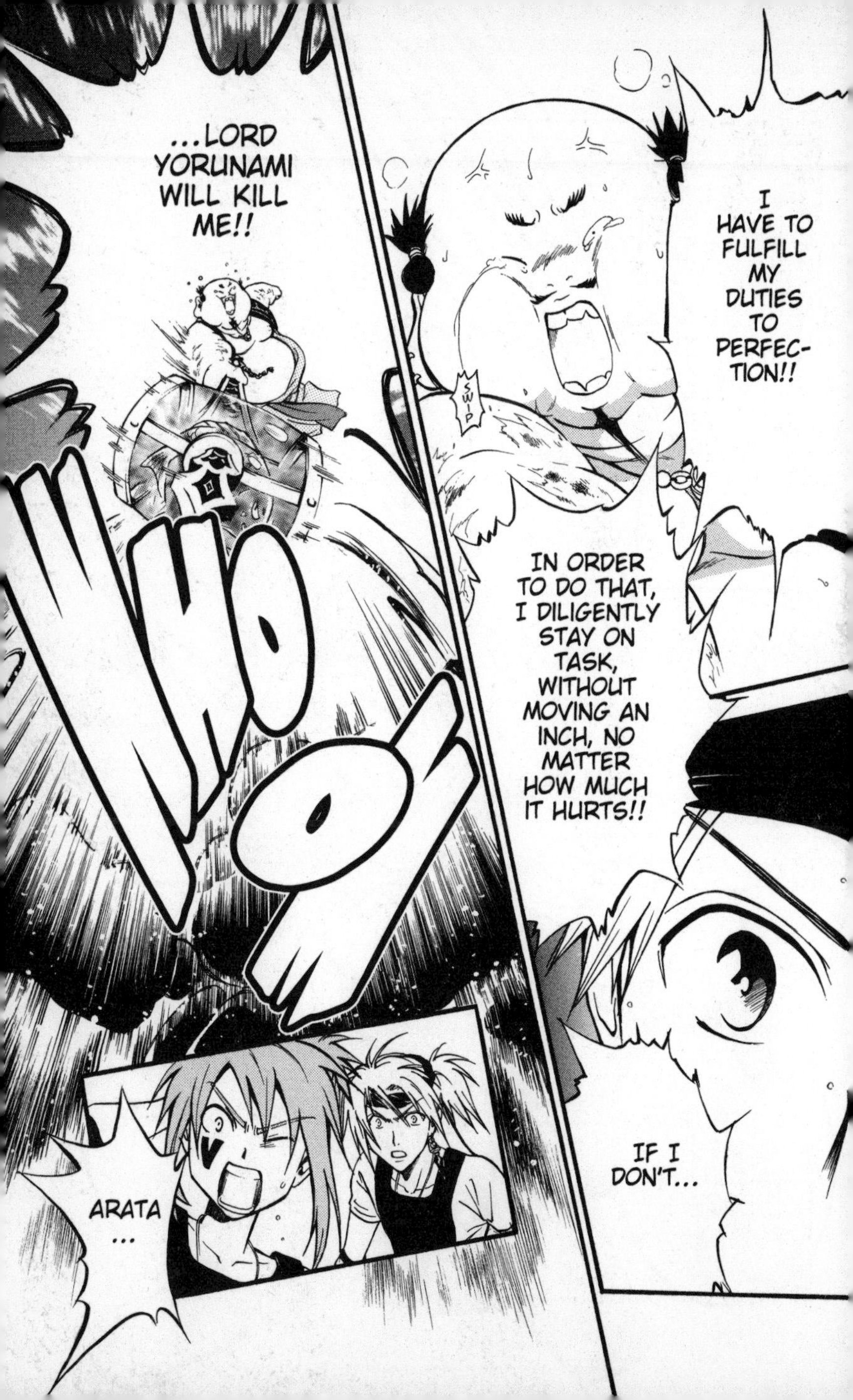
I HAVE TO FULFILL MY DUTIES TO PERFECTION!!
SWIP
IN ORDER TO DO THAT, I DILIGENTLY STAY ON TASK, WITHOUT MOVING AN INCH, NO MATTER HOW MUCH IT HURTS!!
IF I DON'T...
...LORD YORUNAMI WILL KILL ME!!
ARATA ...

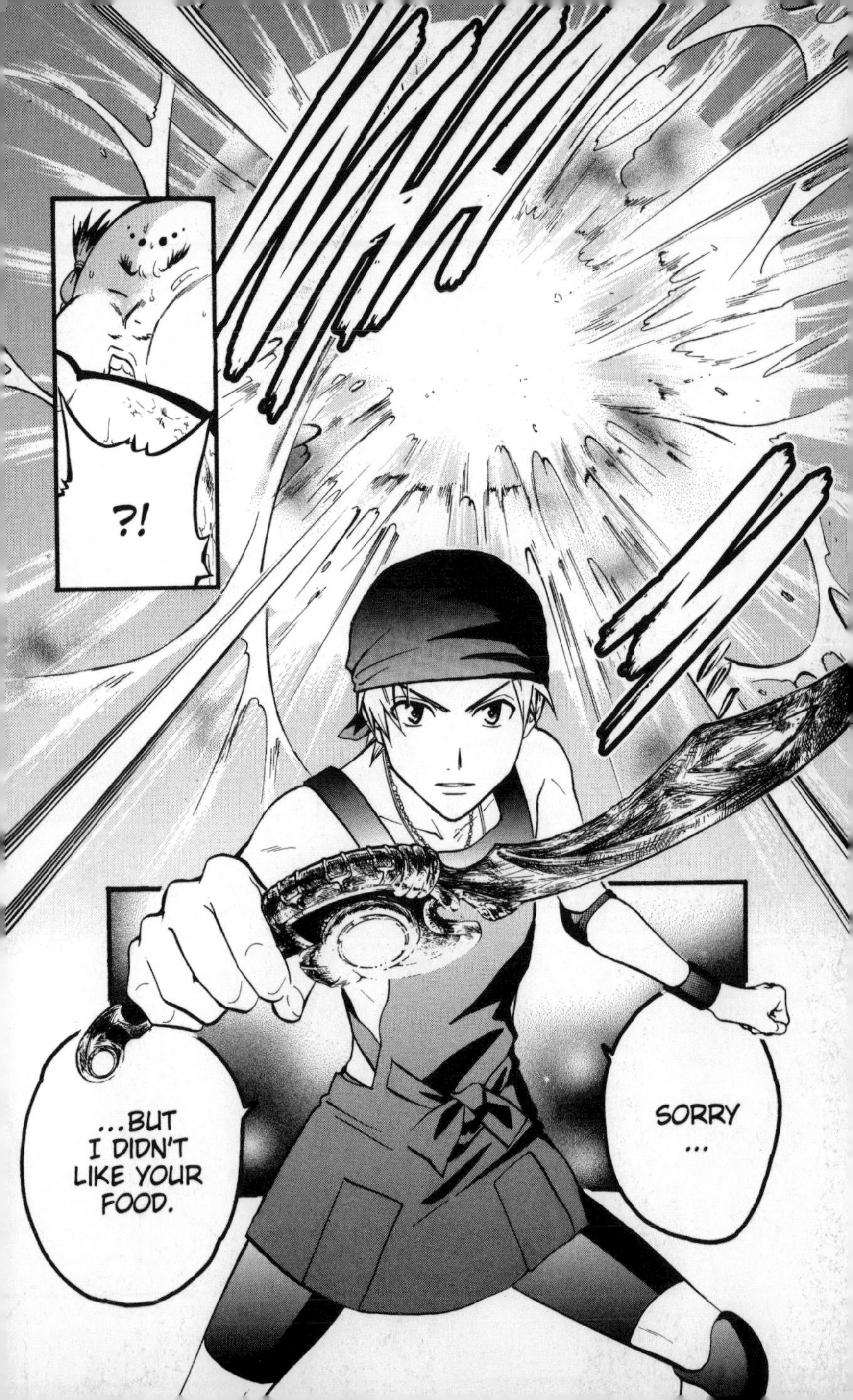
?!
SORRY ...
...BUT I DIDN'T LIKE YOUR FOOD.

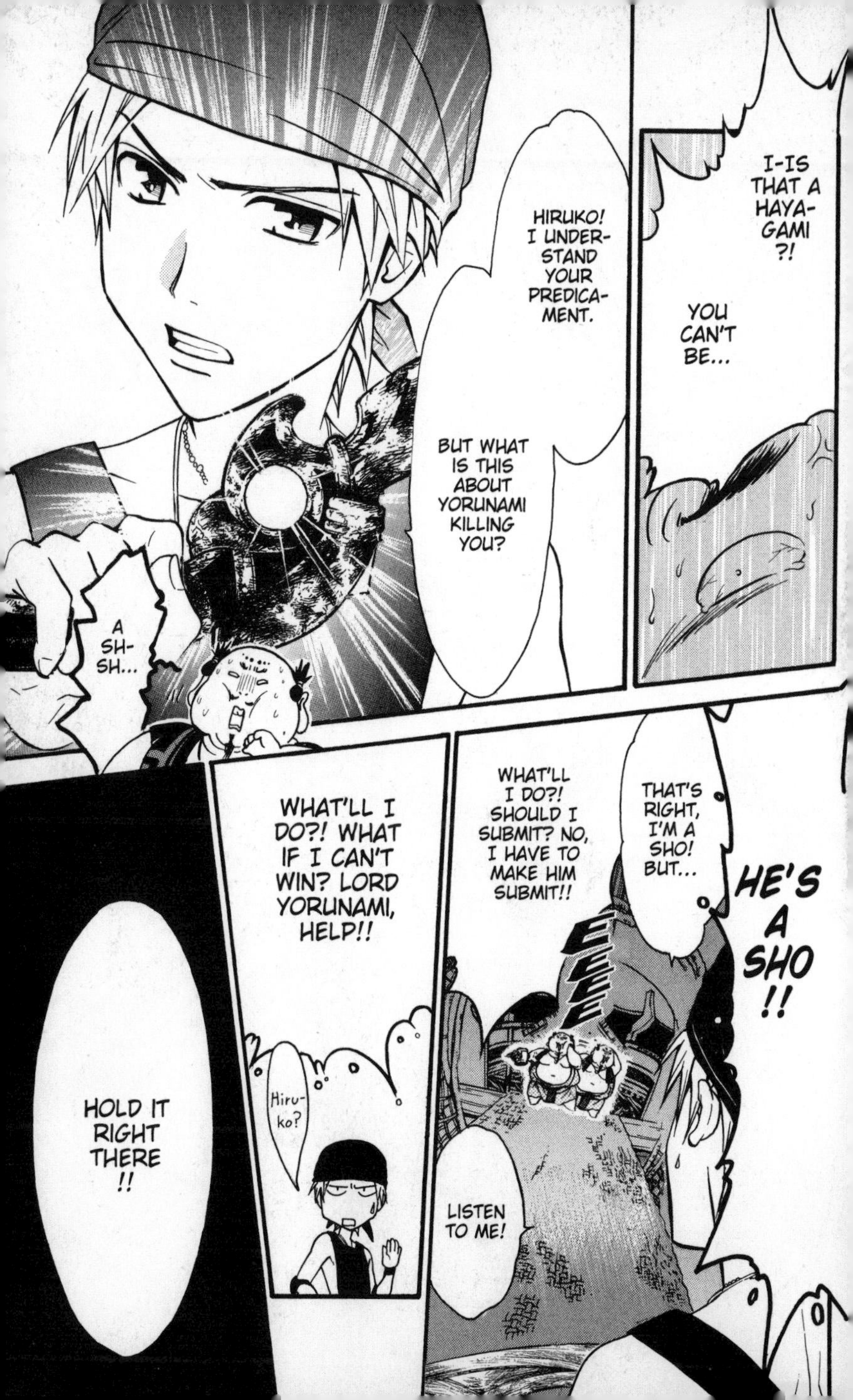
I-IS THAT A HAYAGAMI?!
YOU CAN'T BE...
HIRUKO! I UNDERSTAND YOUR PREDICAMENT.
BUT WHAT IS THIS ABOUT YORUNAMI KILLING YOU?
A SH-SH...
THAT'S RIGHT, I'M A SHO! BUT...
HE'S A SHO!!
WHAT'LL I DO?! SHOULD I SUBMIT? NO, I HAVE TO MAKE HIM SUBMIT!!
LISTEN TO ME!
WHAT'LL I DO?! WHAT IF I CAN'T WIN? LORD YORUNAMI, HELP!!
Hiru-ko?
HOLD IT RIGHT THERE!!

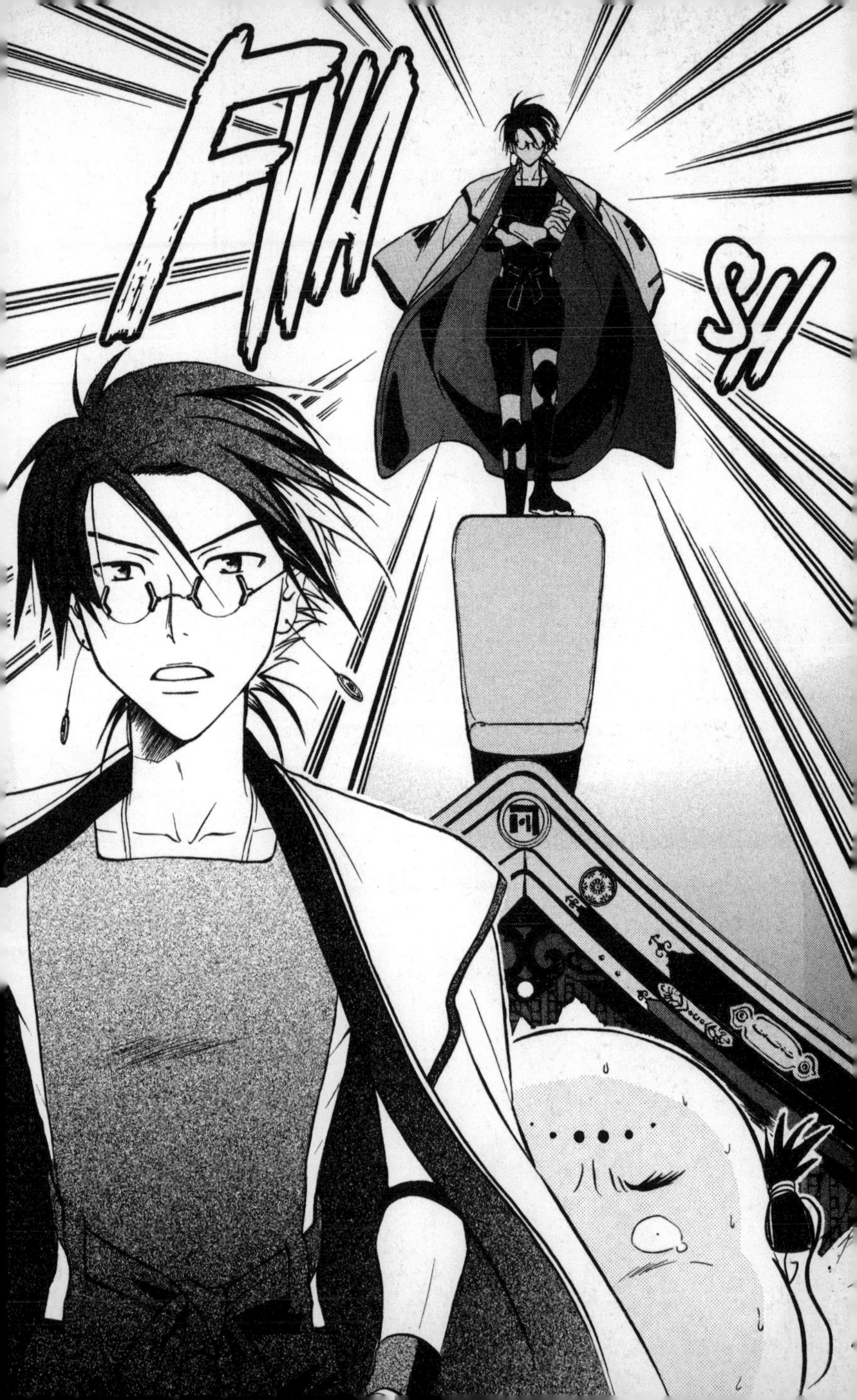
FWA
SH
• • • • •

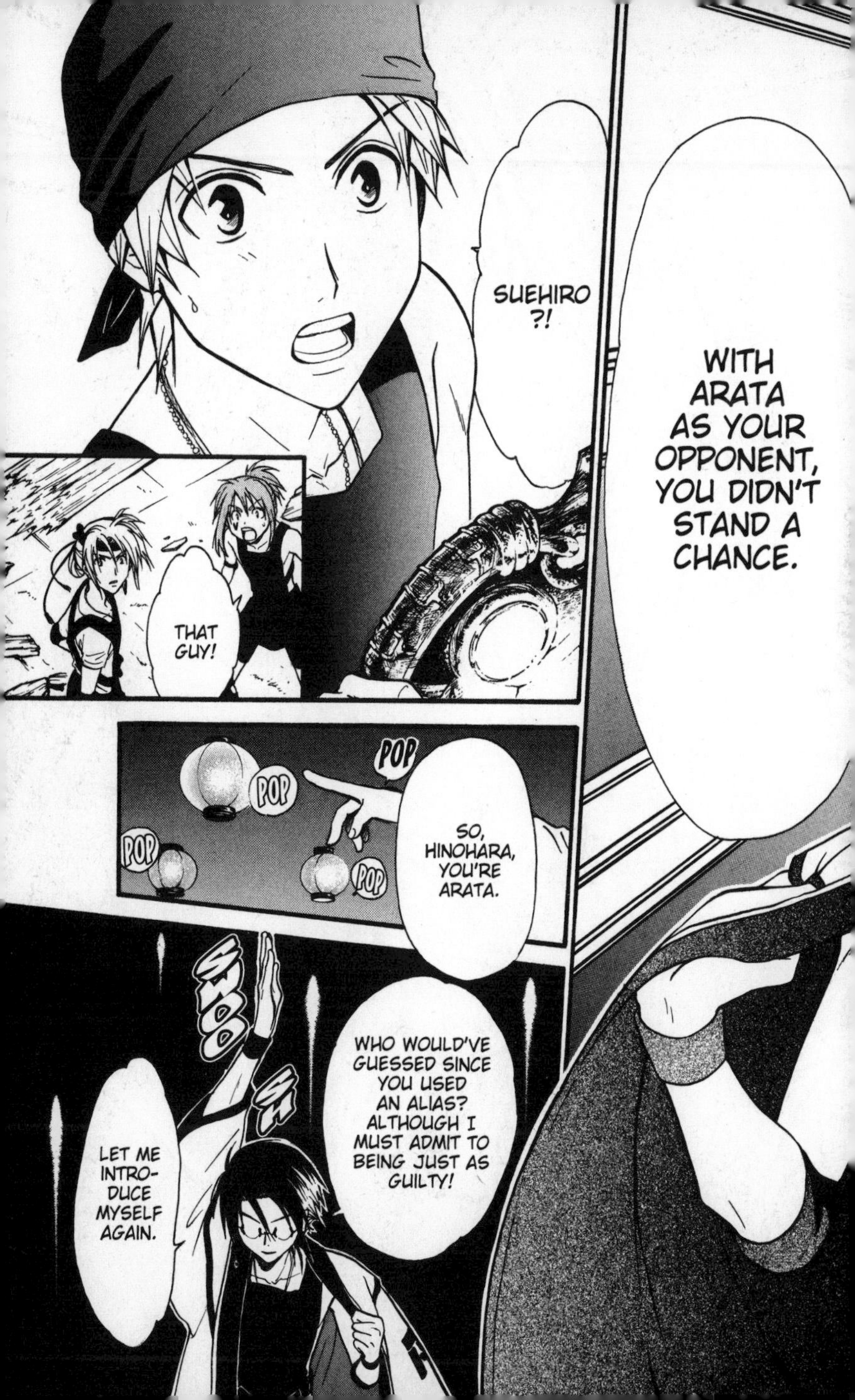
WITH ARATA AS YOUR OPPONENT, YOU DIDN'T STAND A CHANCE.
SUEHIRO ?!
THAT GUY!
POP
POP
POP
POP
SO, HINOHARA, YOU'RE ARATA.
WHO WOULD'VE GUESSED SINCE YOU USED AN ALIAS? ALTHOUGH I MUST ADMIT TO BEING JUST AS GUILTY!
SWOOSH
LET ME INTRO-DUCE MYSELF AGAIN.

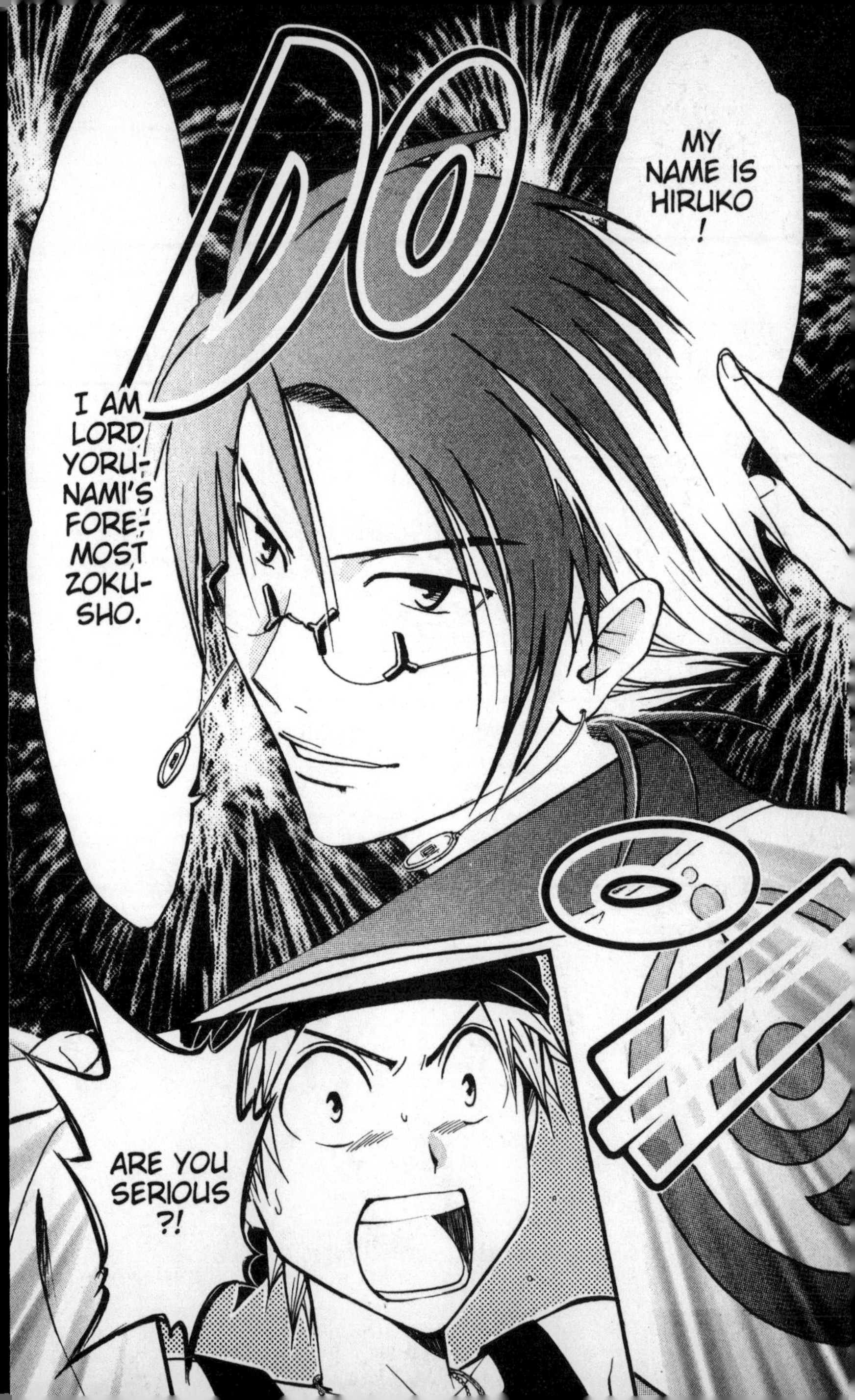
MY NAME IS HIRUKO!
DO
I AM LORD YORUNAMI'S FOREMOST ZOKUSHO.
ARE YOU SERIOUS?!

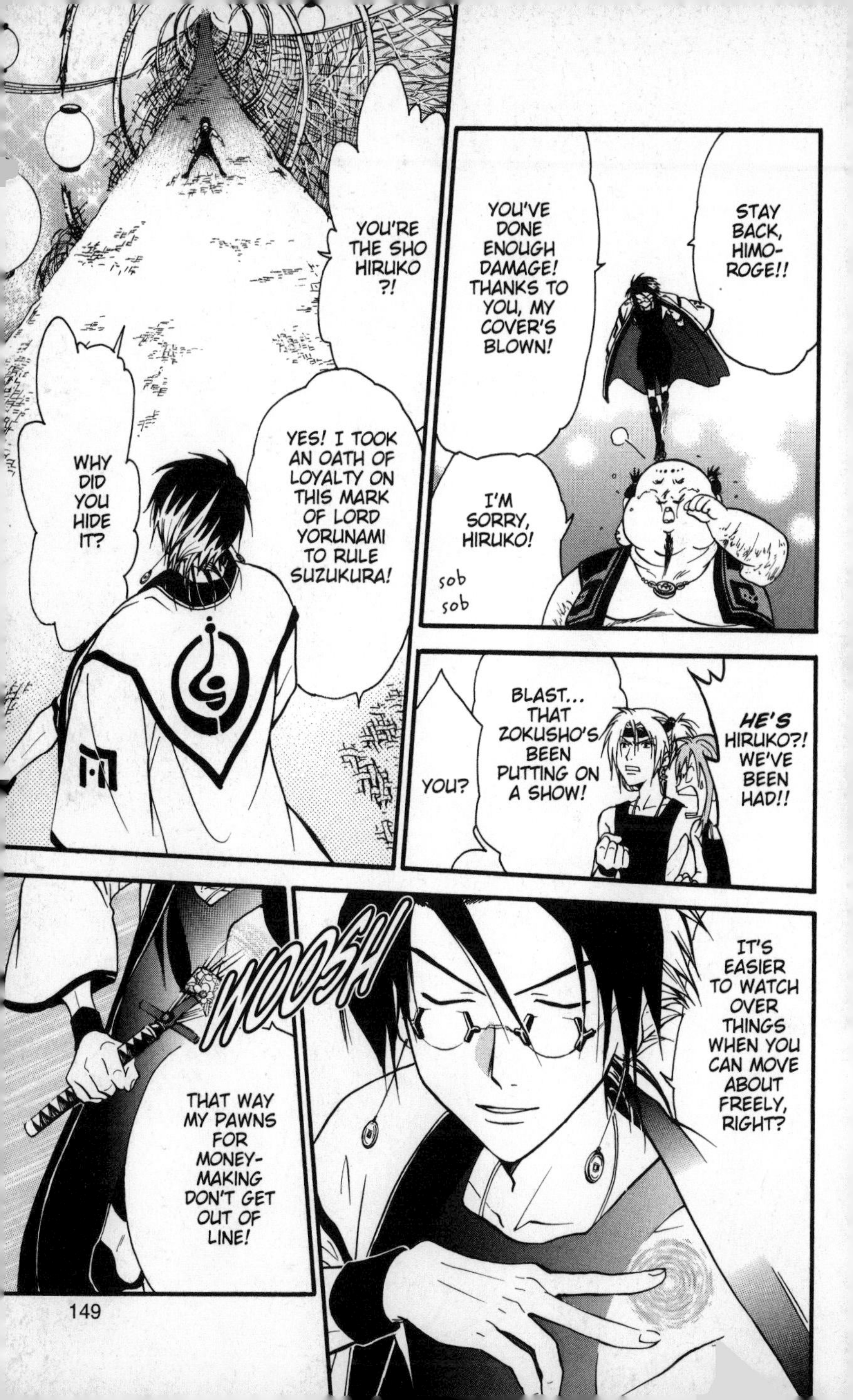
STAY BACK, HIMOROGE!!
YOU'VE DONE ENOUGH DAMAGE! THANKS TO YOU, MY COVER'S BLOWN!
I'M SORRY, HIRUKO!
sob sob
HE'S HIRUKO?! WE'VE BEEN HAD!!
BLAST... THAT ZOKUSHO'S BEEN PUTTING ON A SHOW!
YOU?
YOU'RE THE SHO HIRUKO?!
YES! I TOOK AN OATH OF LOYALTY ON THIS MARK OF LORD YORUNAMI TO RULE SUZUKURA!
WHY DID YOU HIDE IT?
IT'S EASIER TO WATCH OVER THINGS WHEN YOU CAN MOVE ABOUT FREELY, RIGHT?
WOOSH
THAT WAY MY PAWNS FOR MONEY-MAKING DON'T GET OUT OF LINE!

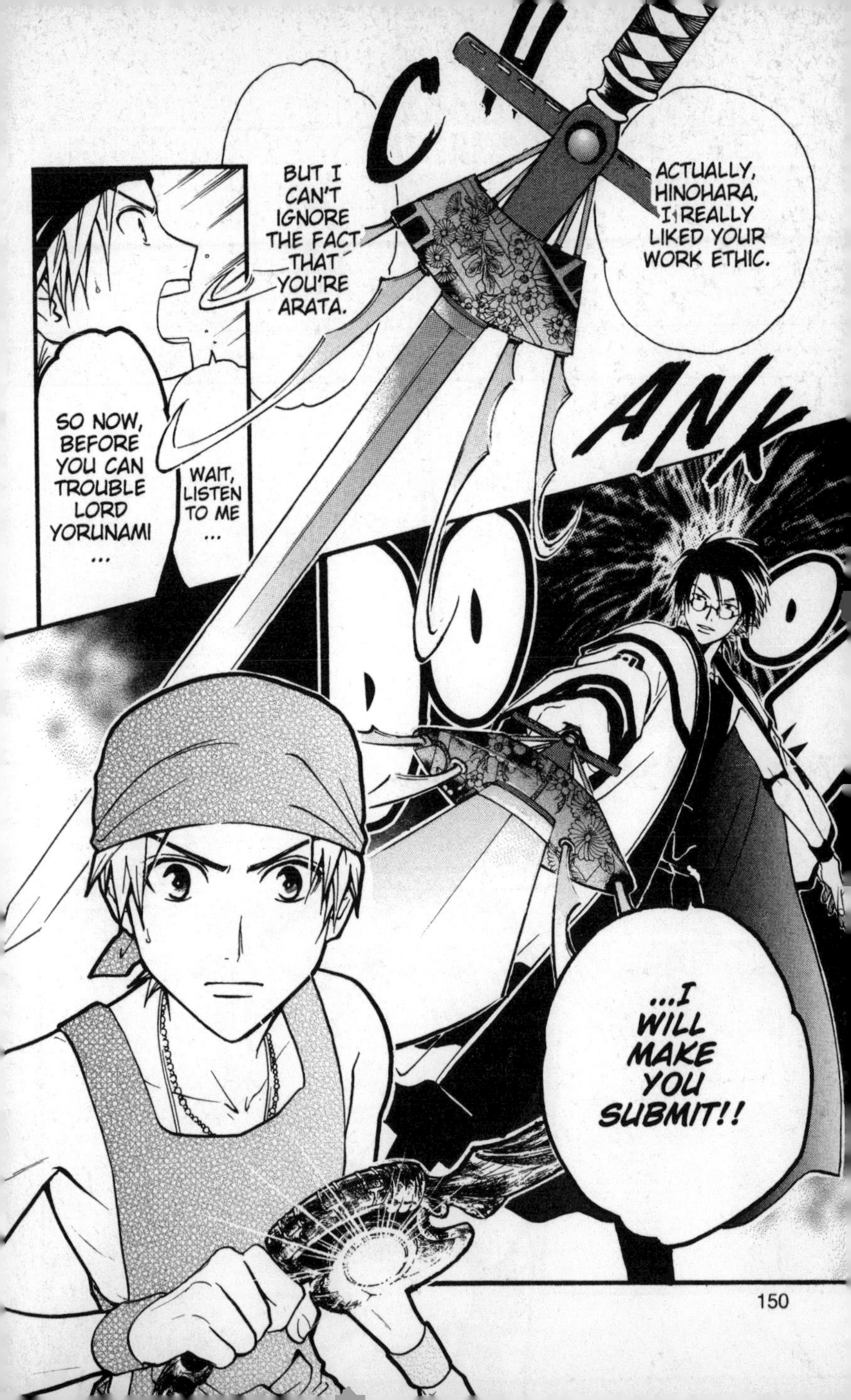
ACTUALLY, HINOHARA, I REALLY LIKED YOUR WORK ETHIC.
BUT I CAN'T IGNORE THE FACT THAT YOU'RE ARATA.
CH
ANK
WAIT, LISTEN TO ME ...
SO NOW, BEFORE YOU CAN TROUBLE LORD YORUNAMI ...
...I WILL MAKE YOU SUBMIT!!

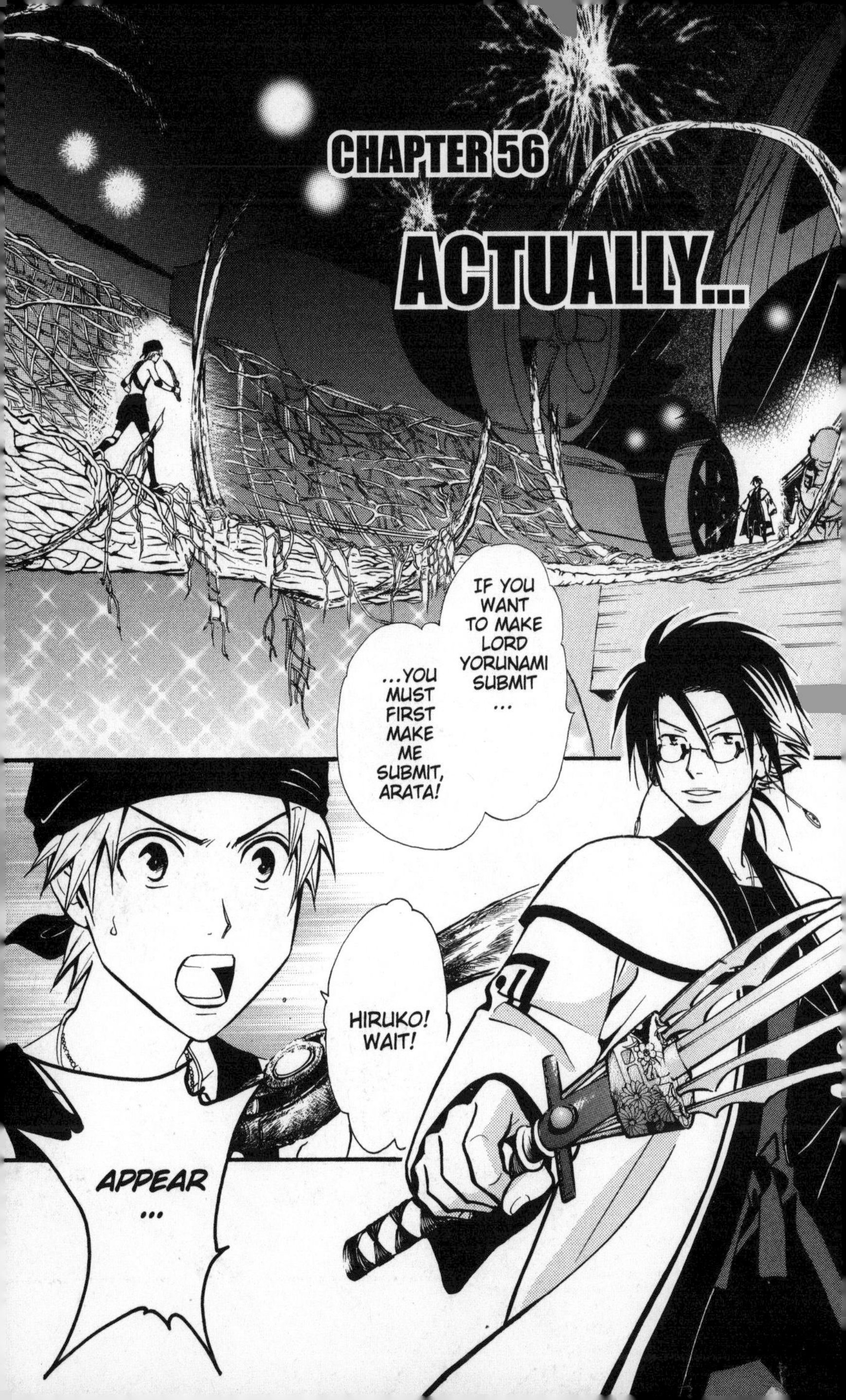
CHAPTER 56
ACTUALLY...
IF YOU WANT TO MAKE LORD YORUNAMI SUBMIT ...
...YOU MUST FIRST MAKE ME SUBMIT, ARATA!
HIRUKO! WAIT!
APPEAR ...

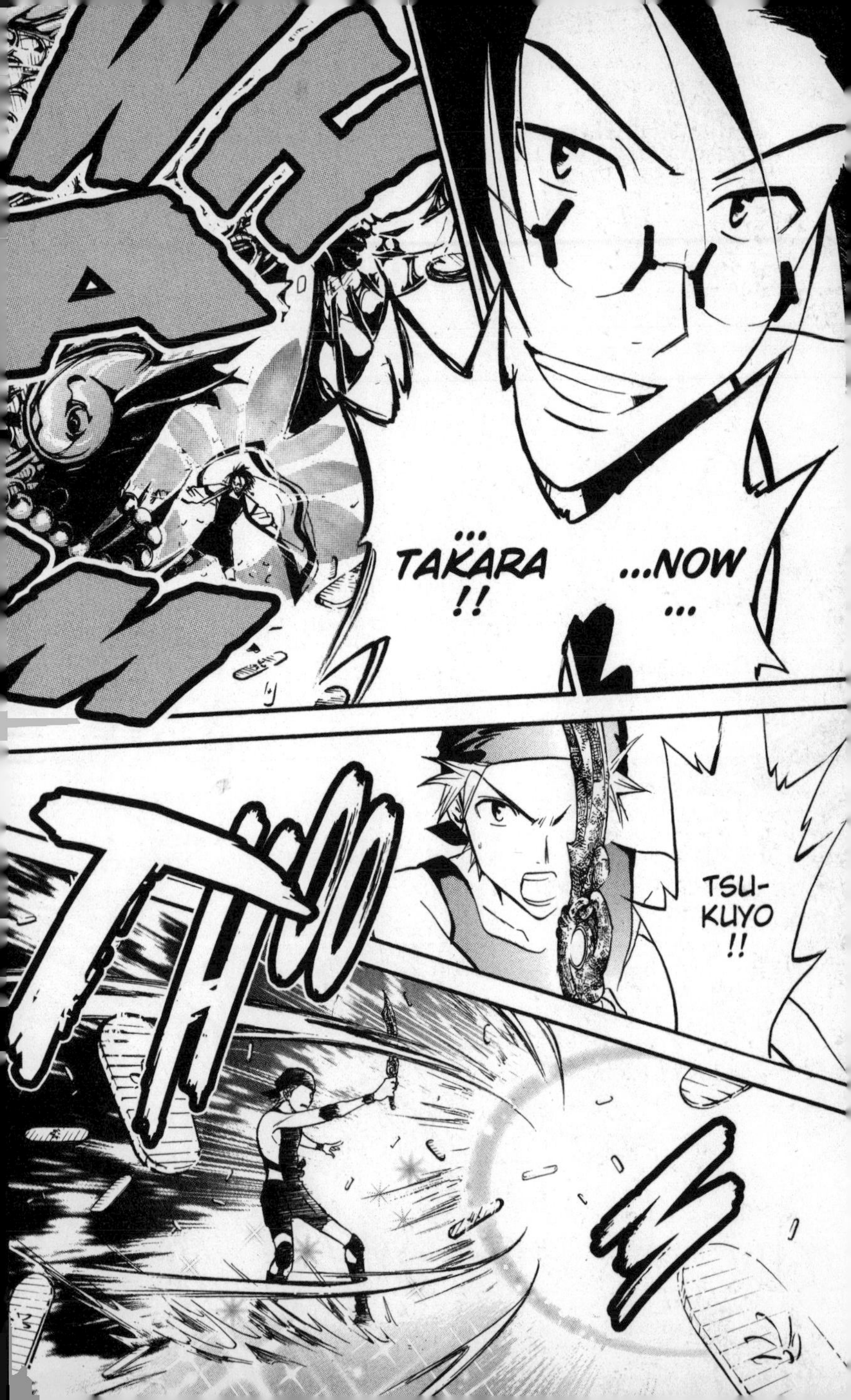
...NOW...
...TAKARA!!
TSU-KUYO!!

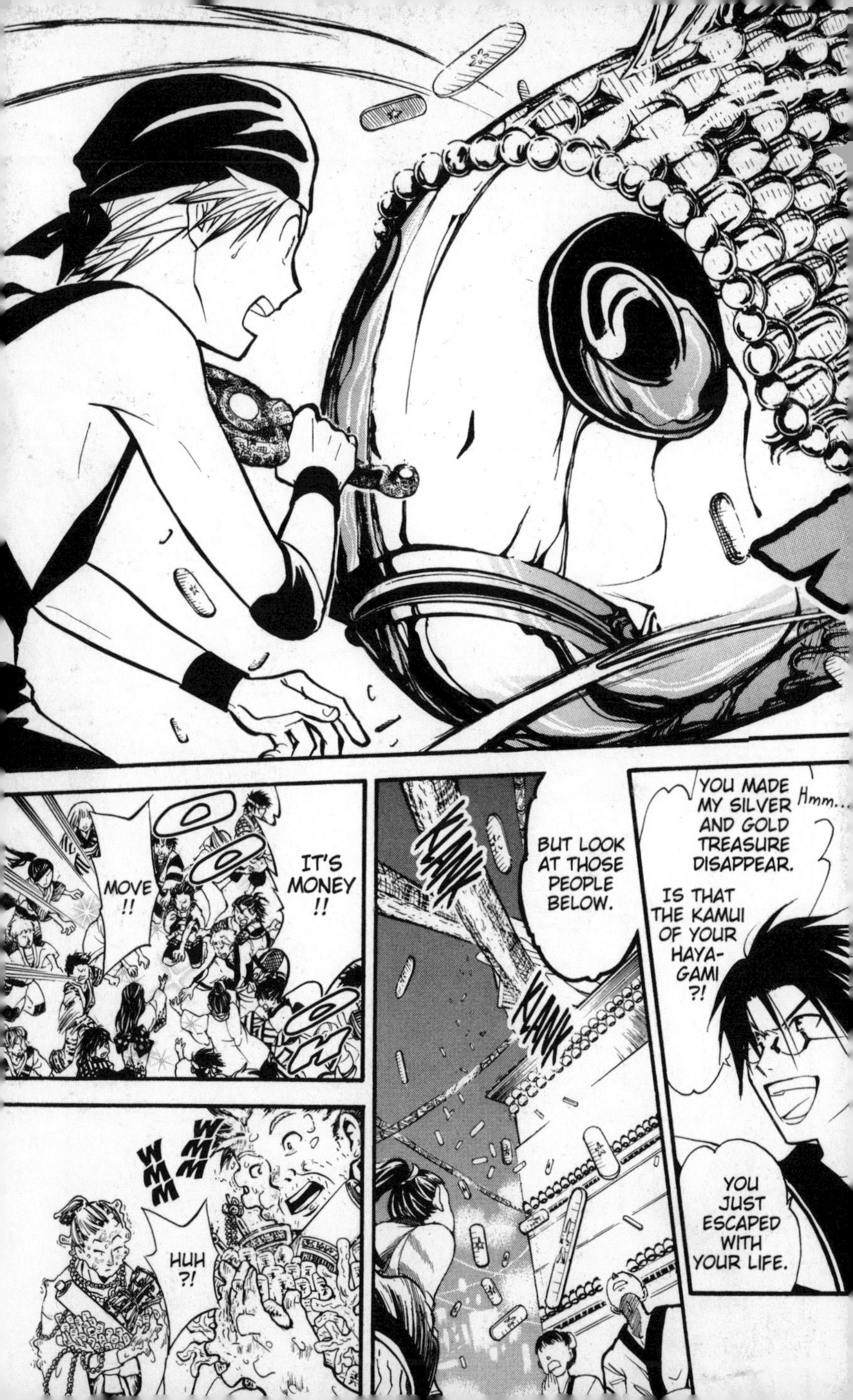
YOU MADE MY SILVER AND GOLD TREASURE DISAPPEAR.
Hmm...
IS THAT THE KAMUI OF YOUR HAYA-GAMI ?!
YOU JUST ESCAPED WITH YOUR LIFE.
KLANK
BUT LOOK AT THOSE PEOPLE BELOW.
KLANK
IT'S MONEY !!
MOVE !!
WMM
WMM
WMM
HUH ?!

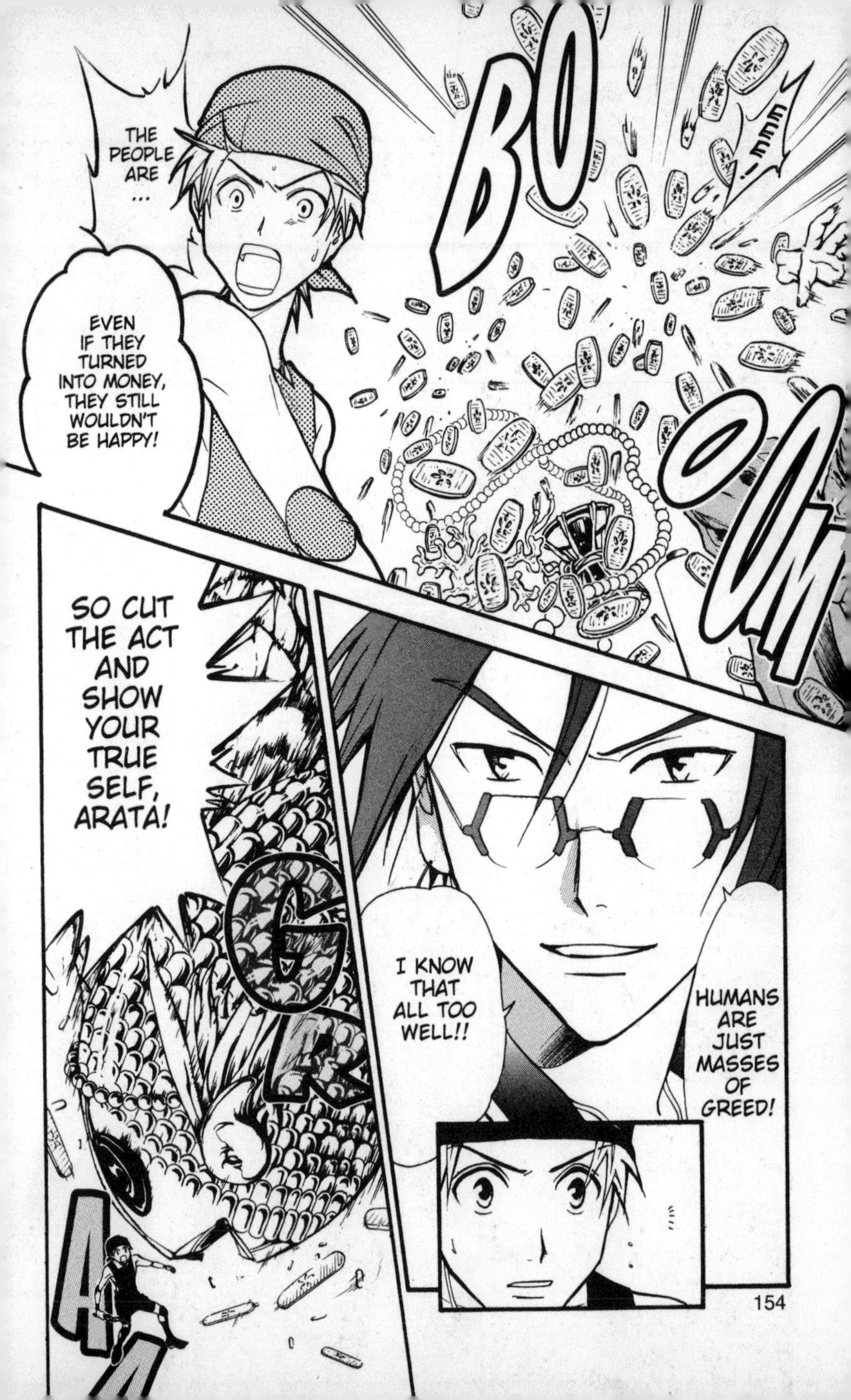
THE PEOPLE ARE ...
EVEN IF THEY TURNED INTO MONEY, THEY STILL WOULDN'T BE HAPPY!
HUMANS ARE JUST MASSES OF GREED!
I KNOW THAT ALL TOO WELL!!
SO CUT THE ACT AND SHOW YOUR TRUE SELF, ARATA!

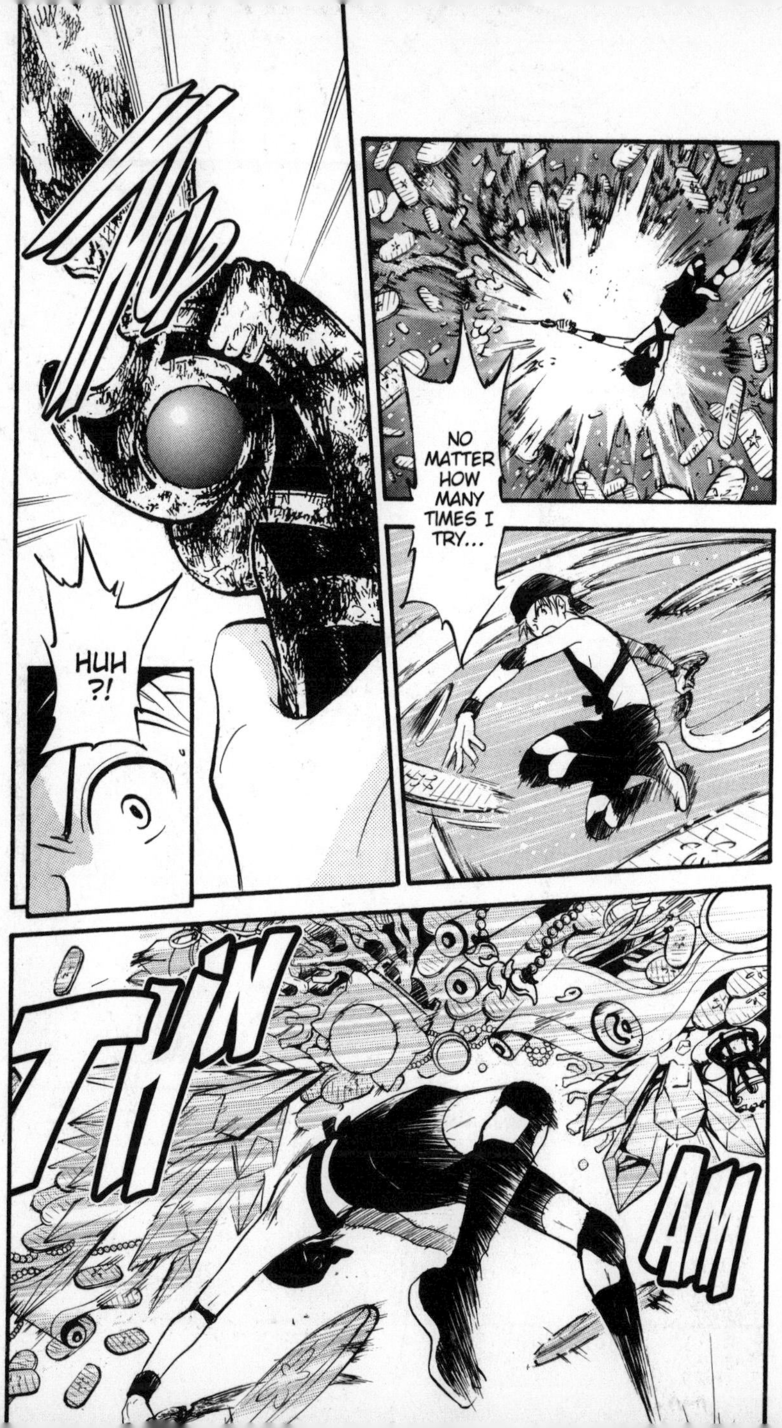
NO MATTER HOW MANY TIMES I TRY...
WHUD
HUH ?!

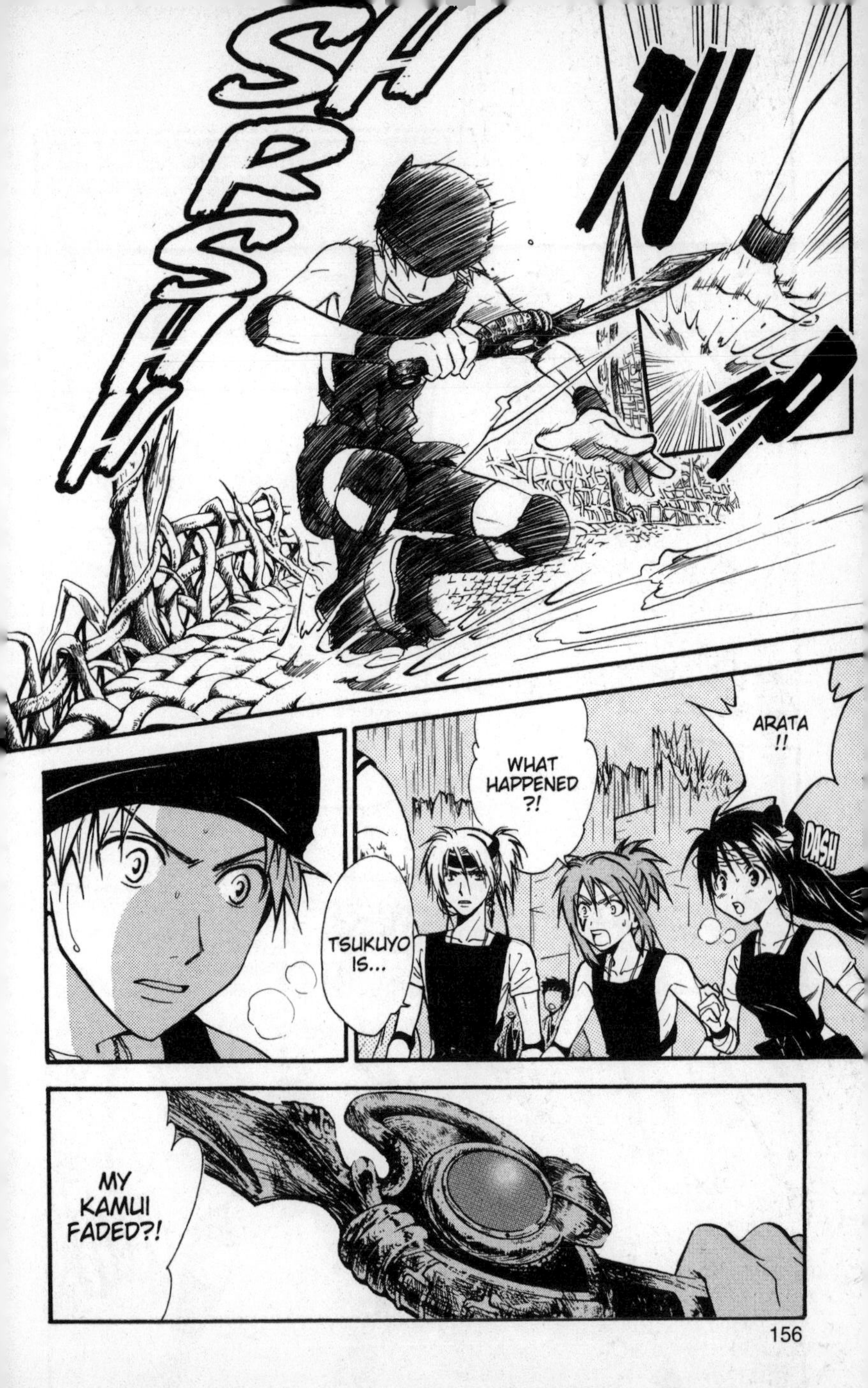
SHRSHH!
ARATA !!
DASH
WHAT HAPPENED ?!
TSUKUYO IS...
MY KAMUI FADED?!

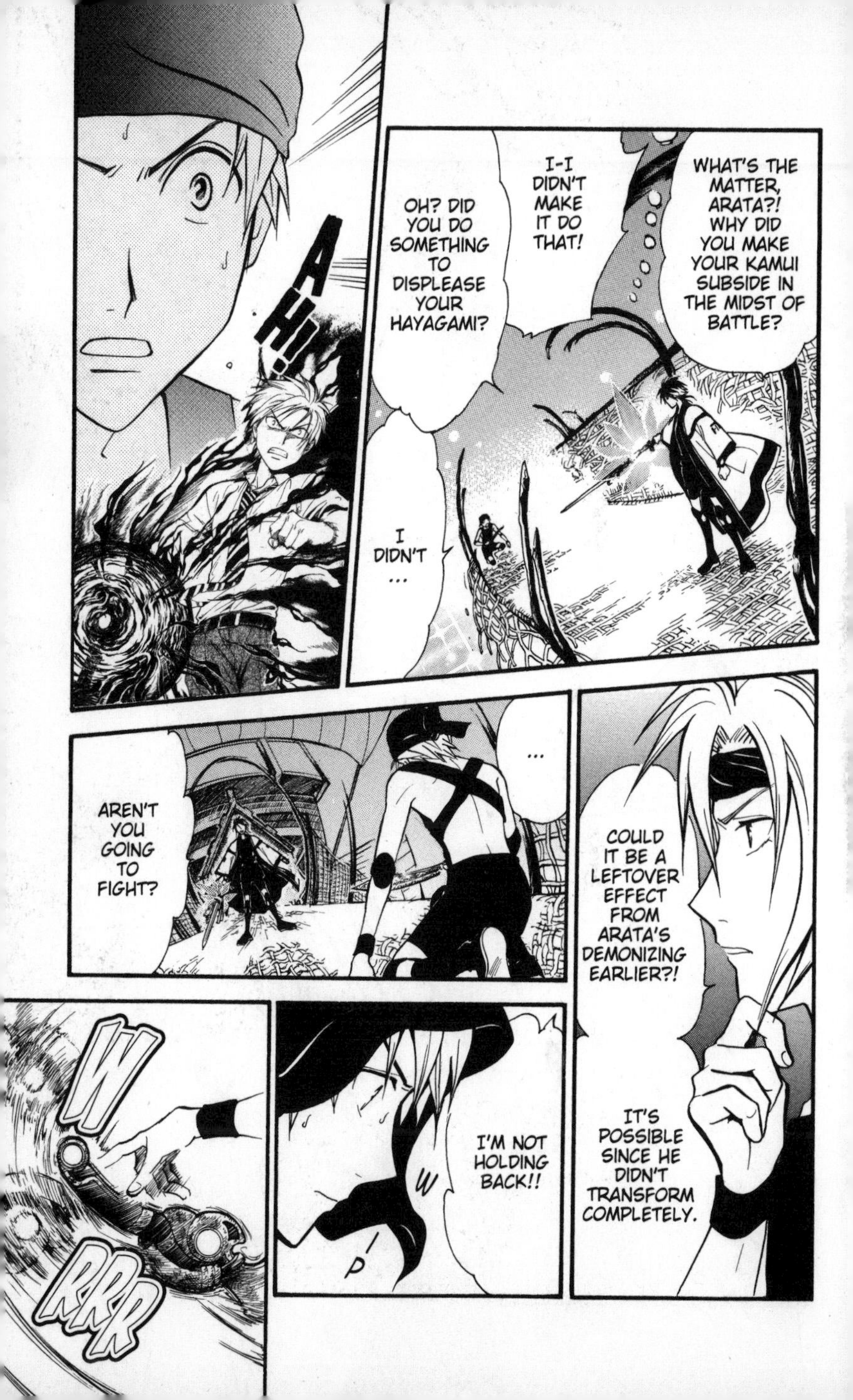
WHAT'S THE MATTER, ARATA?! WHY DID YOU MAKE YOUR KAMUI SUBSIDE IN THE MIDST OF BATTLE?
I-I DIDN'T MAKE IT DO THAT!
OH? DID YOU DO SOMETHING TO DISPLEASE YOUR HAYAGAMI?
I DIDN'T ...
AH!!
COULD IT BE A LEFTOVER EFFECT FROM ARATA'S DEMONIZING EARLIER?!
IT'S POSSIBLE SINCE HE DIDN'T TRANSFORM COMPLETELY.
...
AREN'T YOU GOING TO FIGHT?
I'M NOT HOLDING BACK!!
WRRR

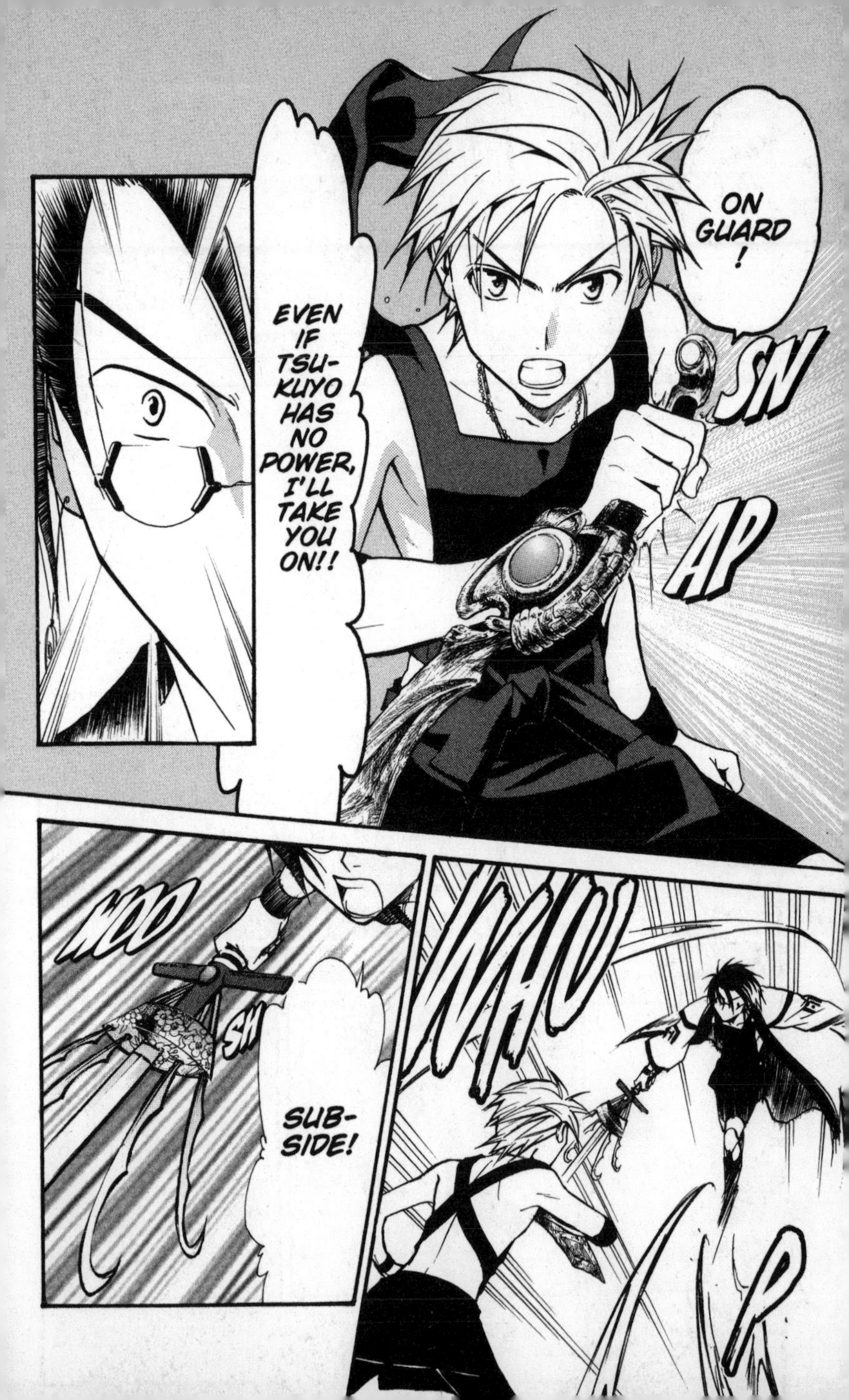
ON GUARD!
SN
AP
EVEN IF TSUKUYO HAS NO POWER, I'LL TAKE YOU ON!!
WHO
P
WHOO
SH
SUBSIDE!

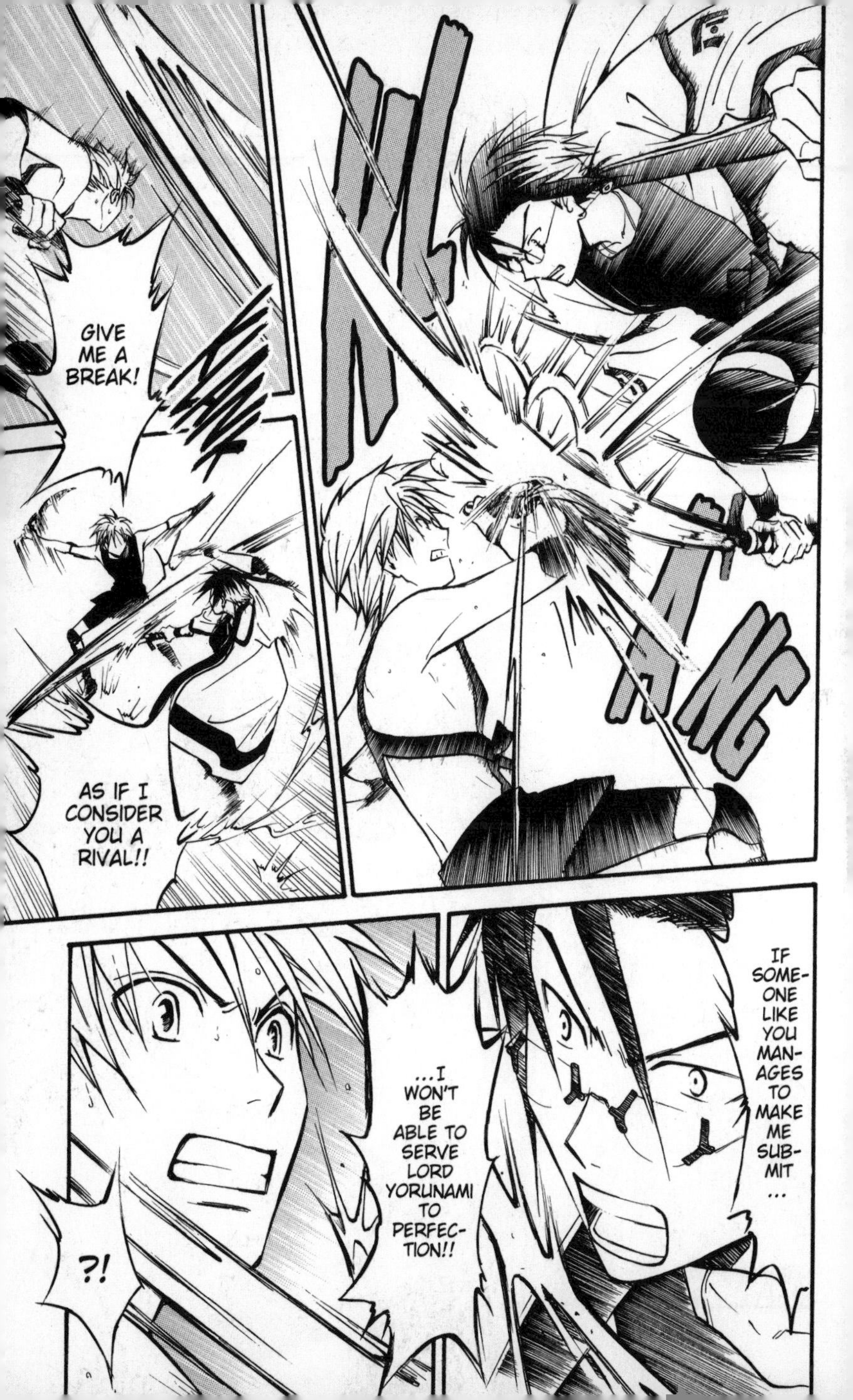
GIVE ME A BREAK!
AS IF I CONSIDER YOU A RIVAL!!
IF SOME-ONE LIKE YOU MAN-AGES TO MAKE ME SUB-MIT ...
...I WON'T BE ABLE TO SERVE LORD YORUNAMI TO PERFEC-TION!!
?!

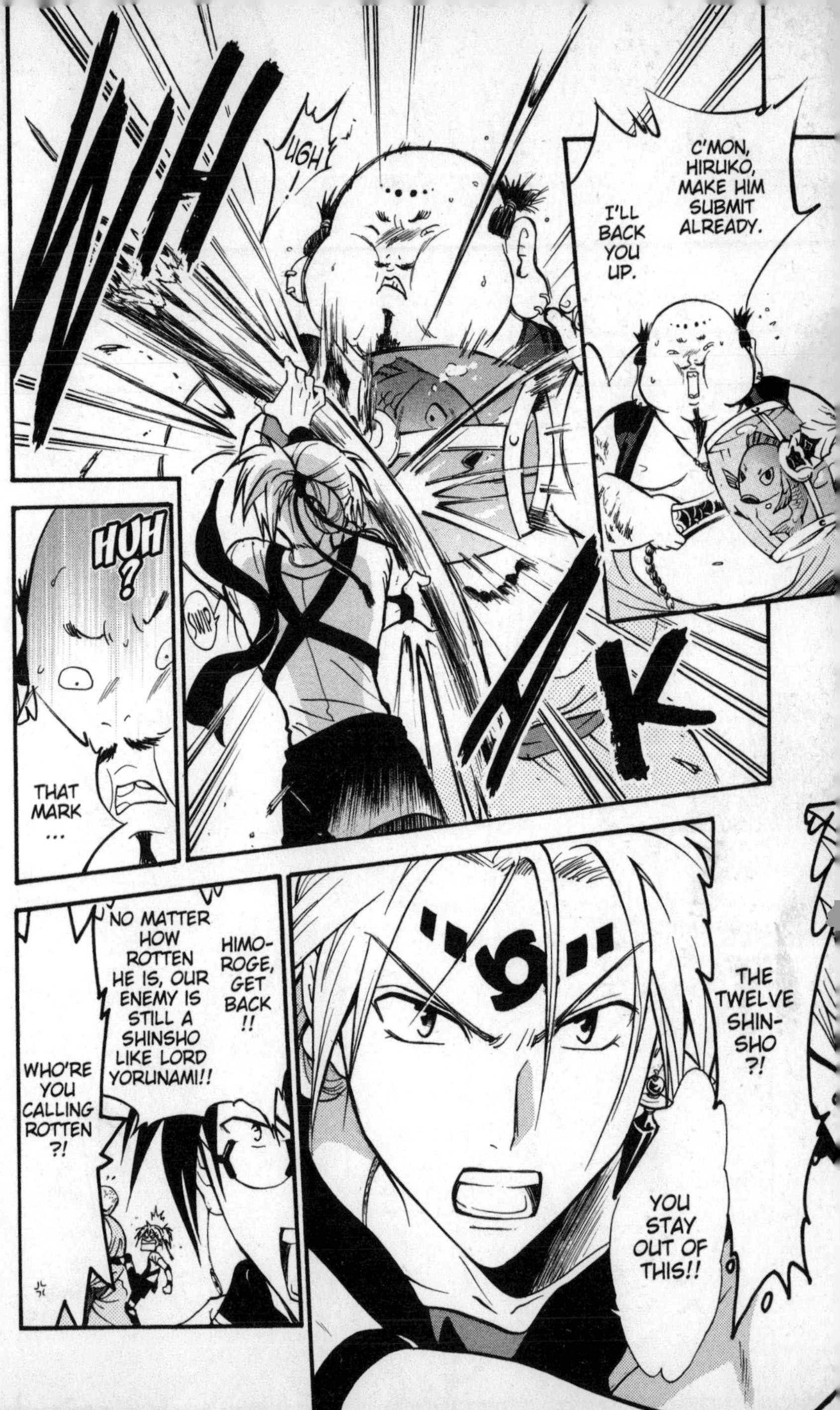
C'MON, HIRUKO, MAKE HIM SUBMIT ALREADY.
I'LL BACK YOU UP.
UGH
WH
AK
SWIP
HUH?
THAT MARK...
THE TWELVE SHIN-SHO?!
YOU STAY OUT OF THIS!!
HIMO-ROGE, GET BACK!!
NO MATTER HOW ROTTEN HE IS, OUR ENEMY IS STILL A SHINSHO LIKE LORD YORUNAMI!!
WHO'RE YOU CALLING ROTTEN?!

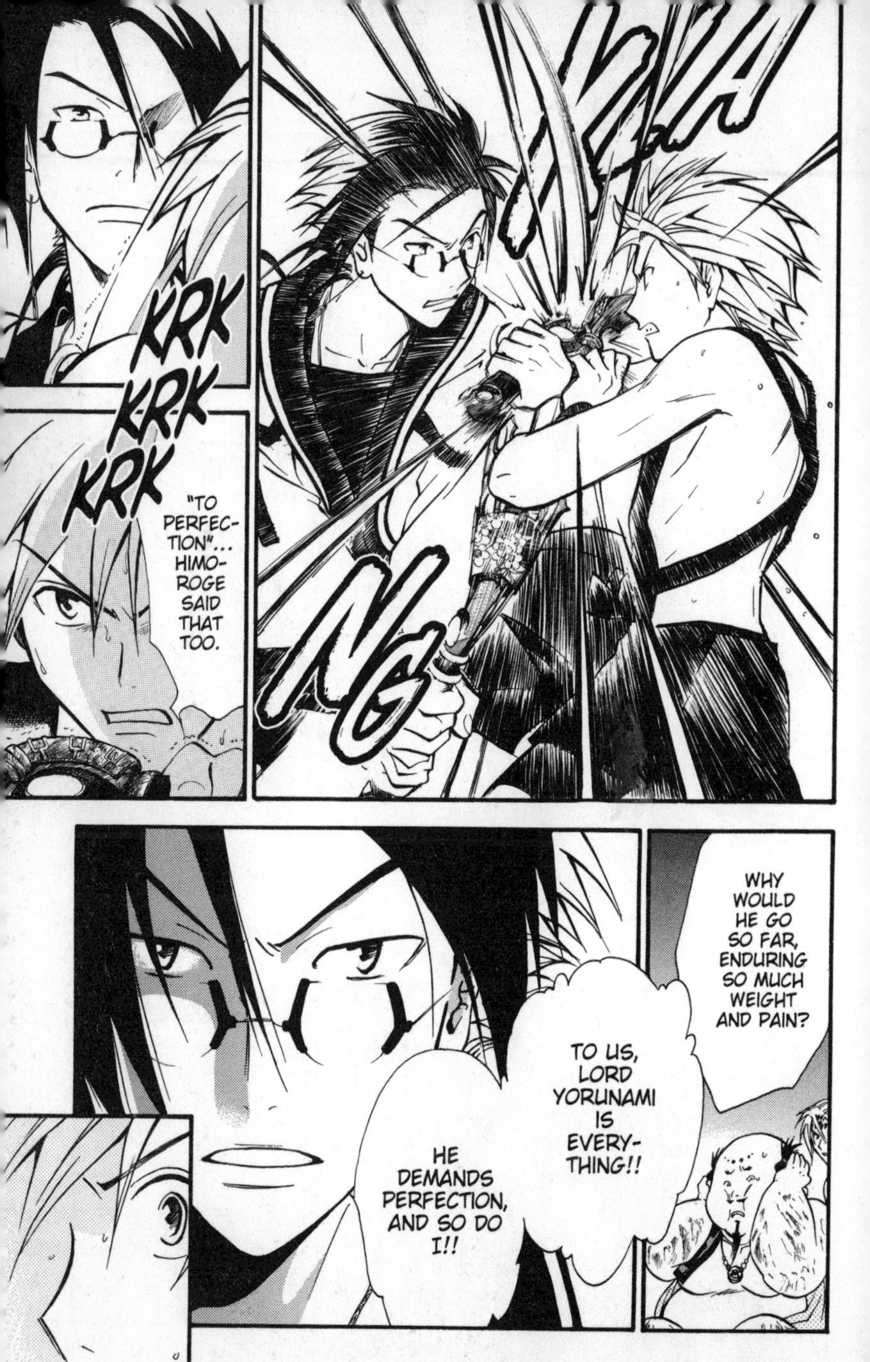
NG
KRK
KRK
KRK
"TO PERFECTION"... HIMOROGE SAID THAT TOO.
WHY WOULD HE GO SO FAR, ENDURING SO MUCH WEIGHT AND PAIN?
TO US, LORD YORUNAMI IS EVERYTHING!!
HE DEMANDS PERFECTION, AND SO DO I!!

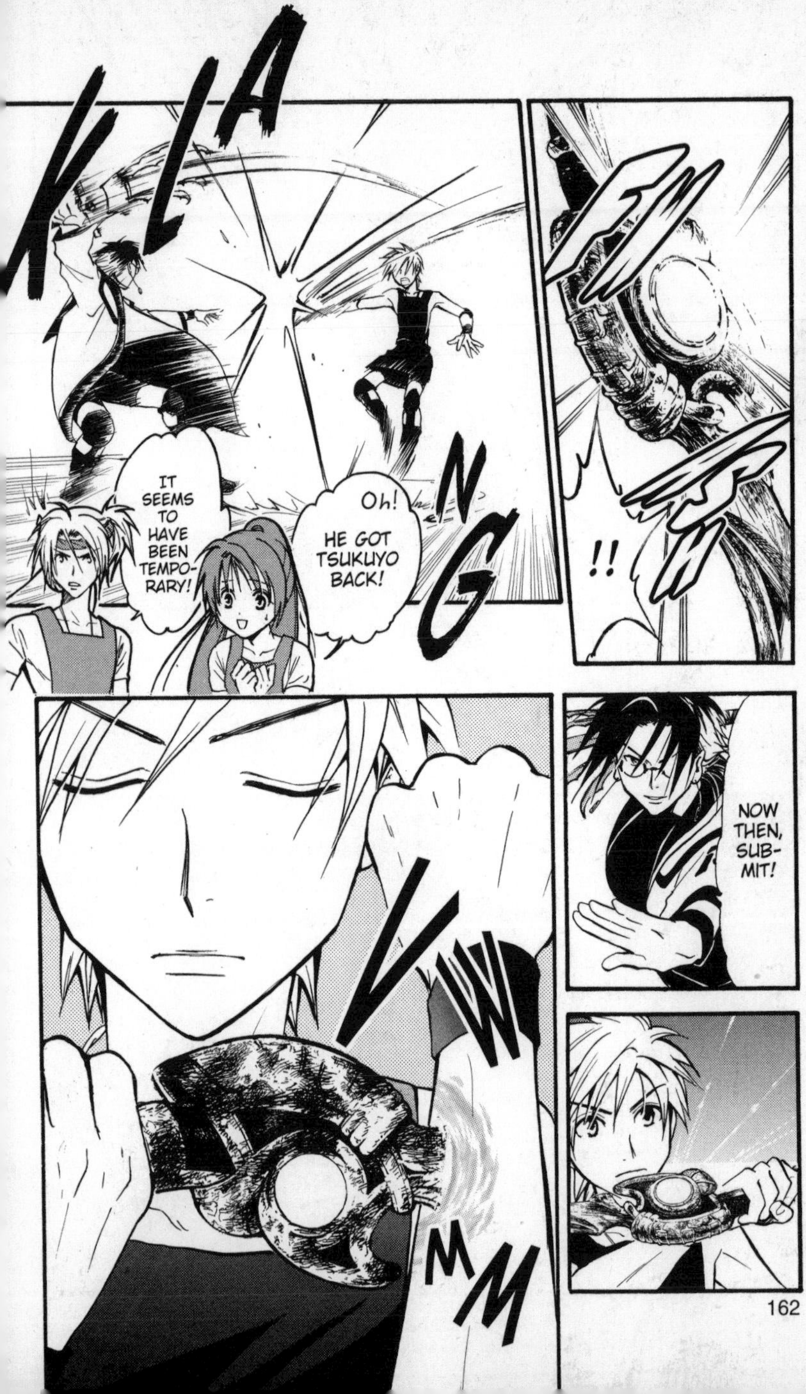
!!
KLANG
Oh! HE GOT TSUKUYO BACK!
IT SEEMS TO HAVE BEEN TEMPORARY!
NOW THEN, SUBMIT!
VWWMM

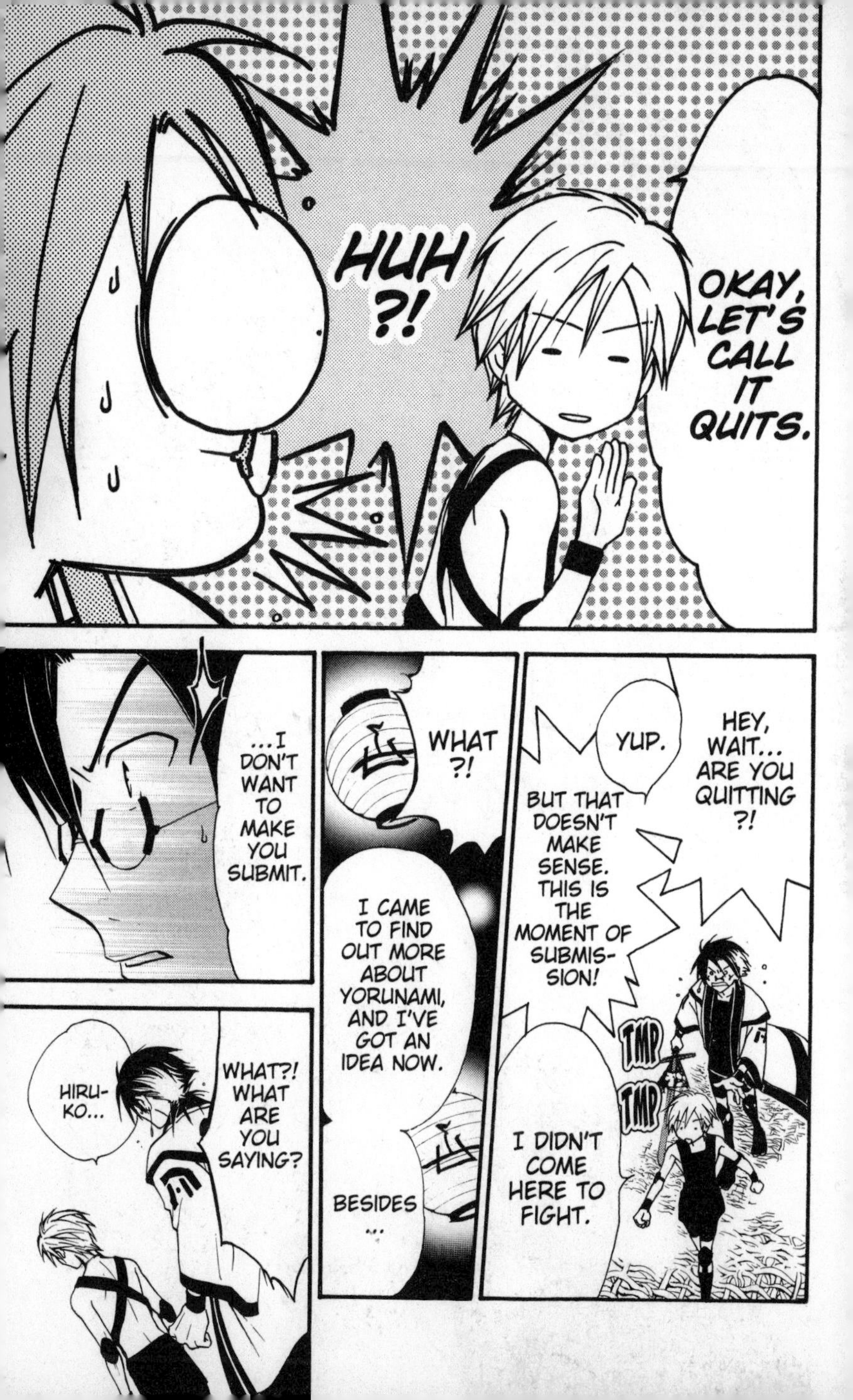
OKAY, LET'S CALL IT QUITS.
HUH?!
HEY, WAIT... ARE YOU QUITTING?!
YUP.
BUT THAT DOESN'T MAKE SENSE. THIS IS THE MOMENT OF SUBMISSION!
TMP
TMP
I DIDN'T COME HERE TO FIGHT.
WHAT?!
I CAME TO FIND OUT MORE ABOUT YORUNAMI, AND I'VE GOT AN IDEA NOW.
BESIDES...
...I DON'T WANT TO MAKE YOU SUBMIT.
WHAT?! WHAT ARE YOU SAYING?
HIRUKO...

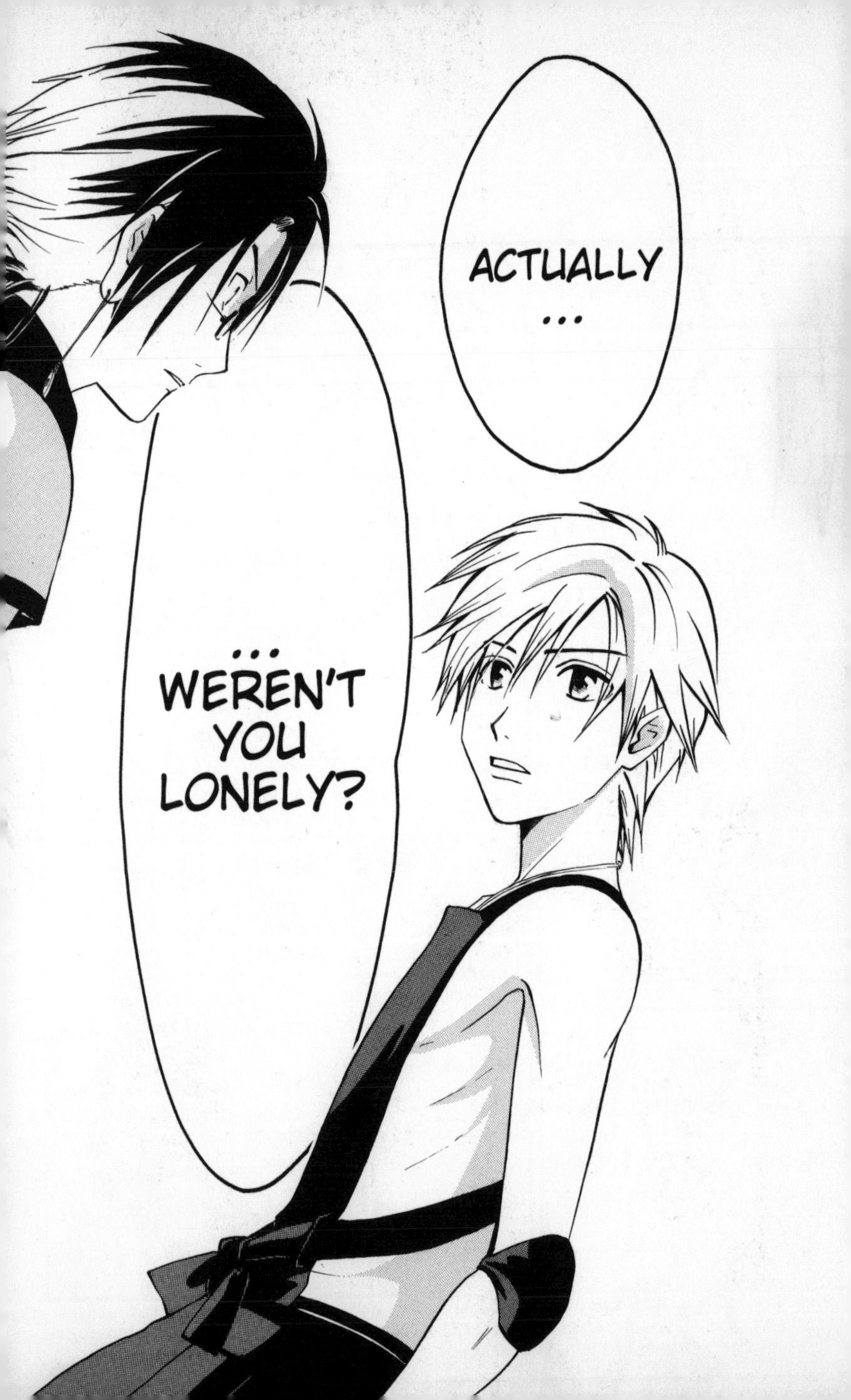
ACTUALLY ...
... WEREN'T YOU LONELY?

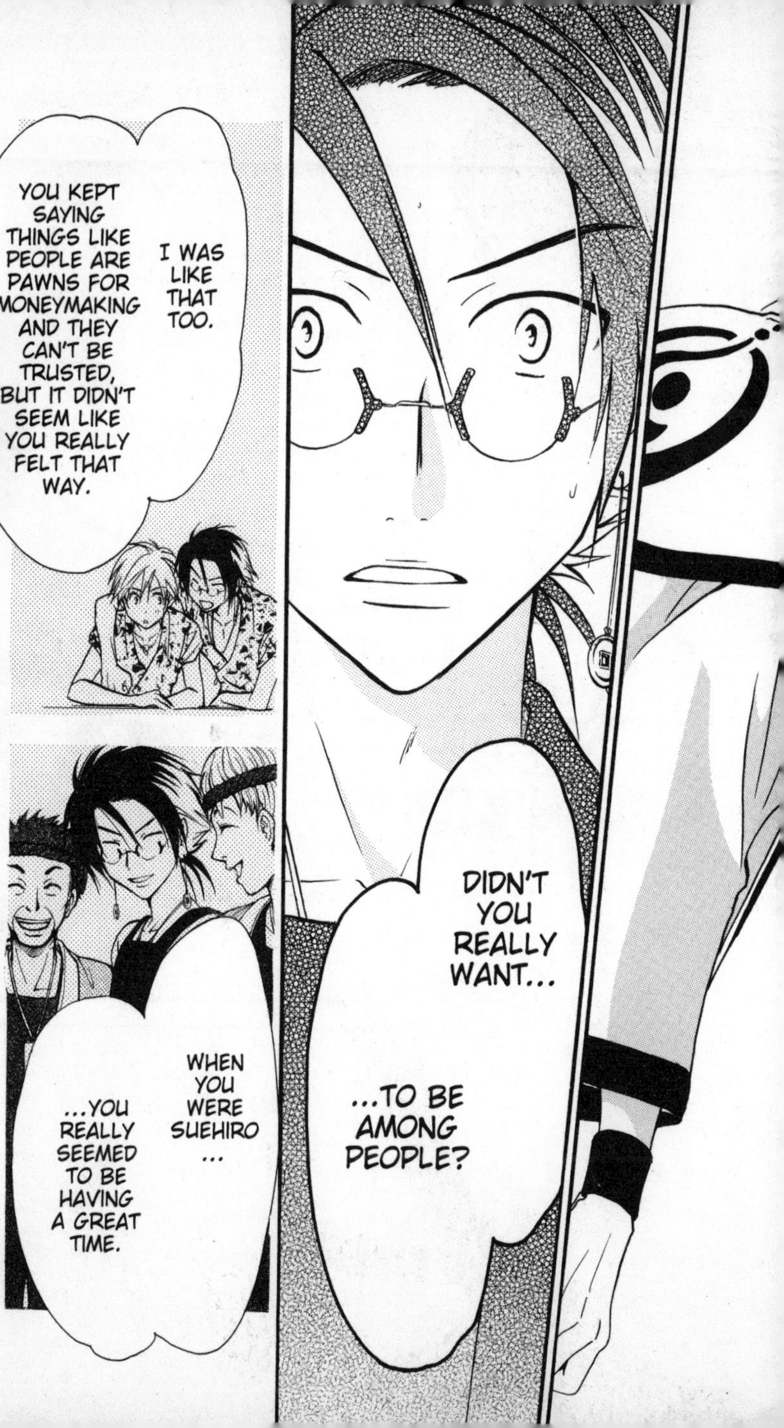
I WAS LIKE THAT TOO.
YOU KEPT SAYING THINGS LIKE PEOPLE ARE PAWNS FOR MONEYMAKING AND THEY CAN'T BE TRUSTED, BUT IT DIDN'T SEEM LIKE YOU REALLY FELT THAT WAY.
WHEN YOU WERE SUEHIRO...
...YOU REALLY SEEMED TO BE HAVING A GREAT TIME.
DIDN'T YOU REALLY WANT...
...TO BE AMONG PEOPLE?

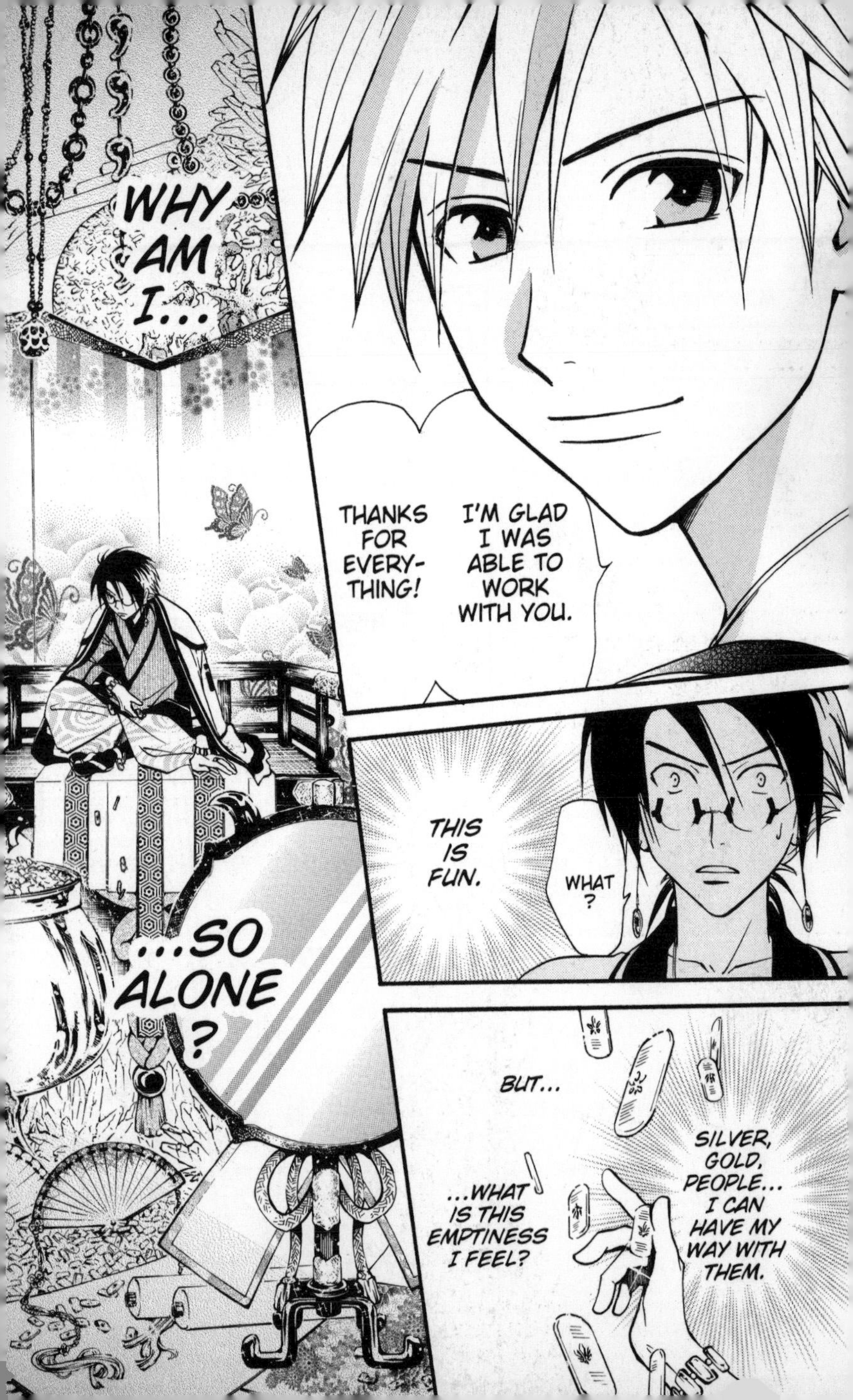
I'M GLAD I WAS ABLE TO WORK WITH YOU.
THANKS FOR EVERYTHING!
THIS IS FUN.
WHAT?
SILVER, GOLD, PEOPLE... I CAN HAVE MY WAY WITH THEM.
BUT...
...WHAT IS THIS EMPTINESS I FEEL?
WHY AM I...
...SO ALONE?

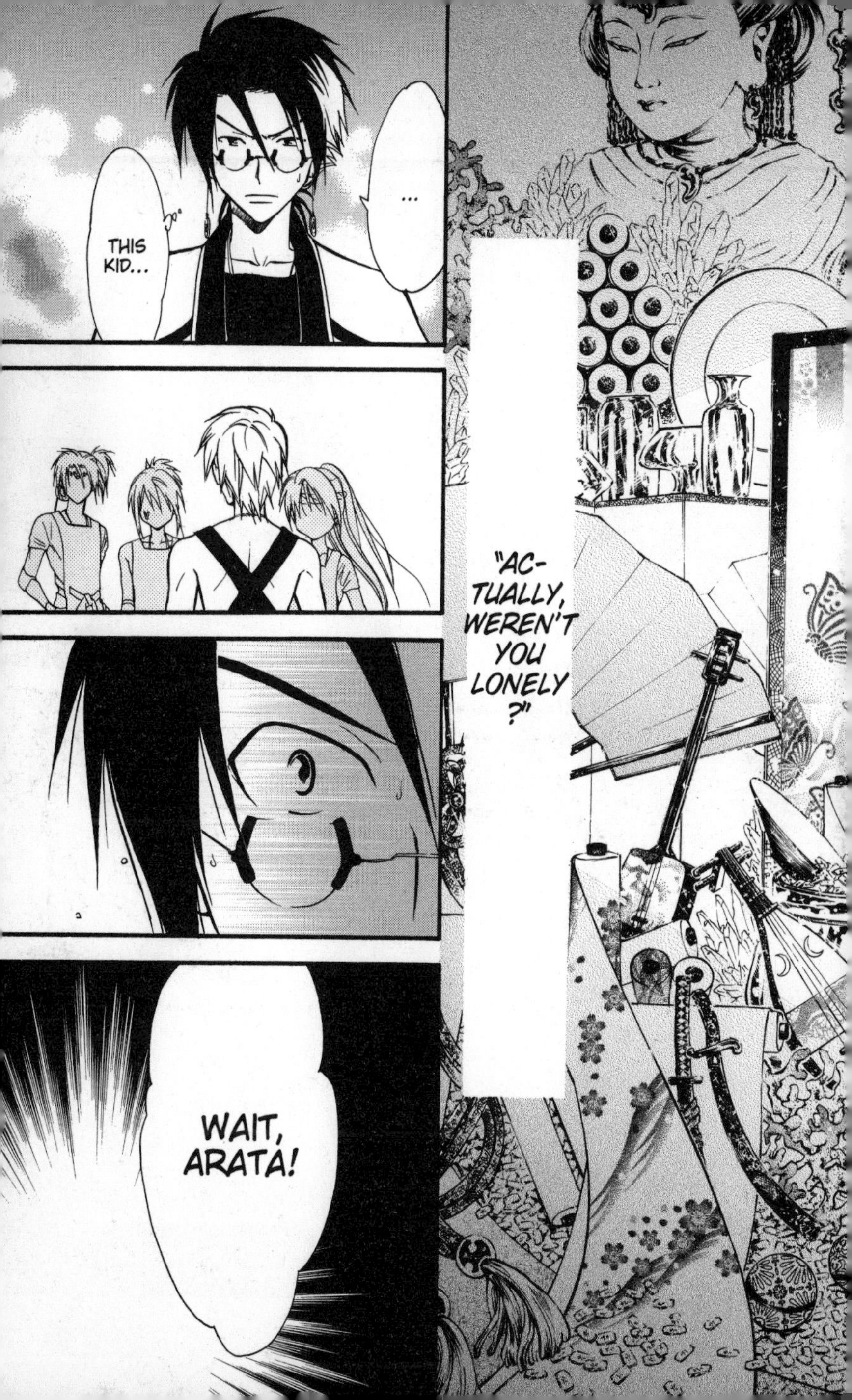
"ACTUALLY, WEREN'T YOU LONELY?"
THIS KID...
...
WAIT, ARATA!

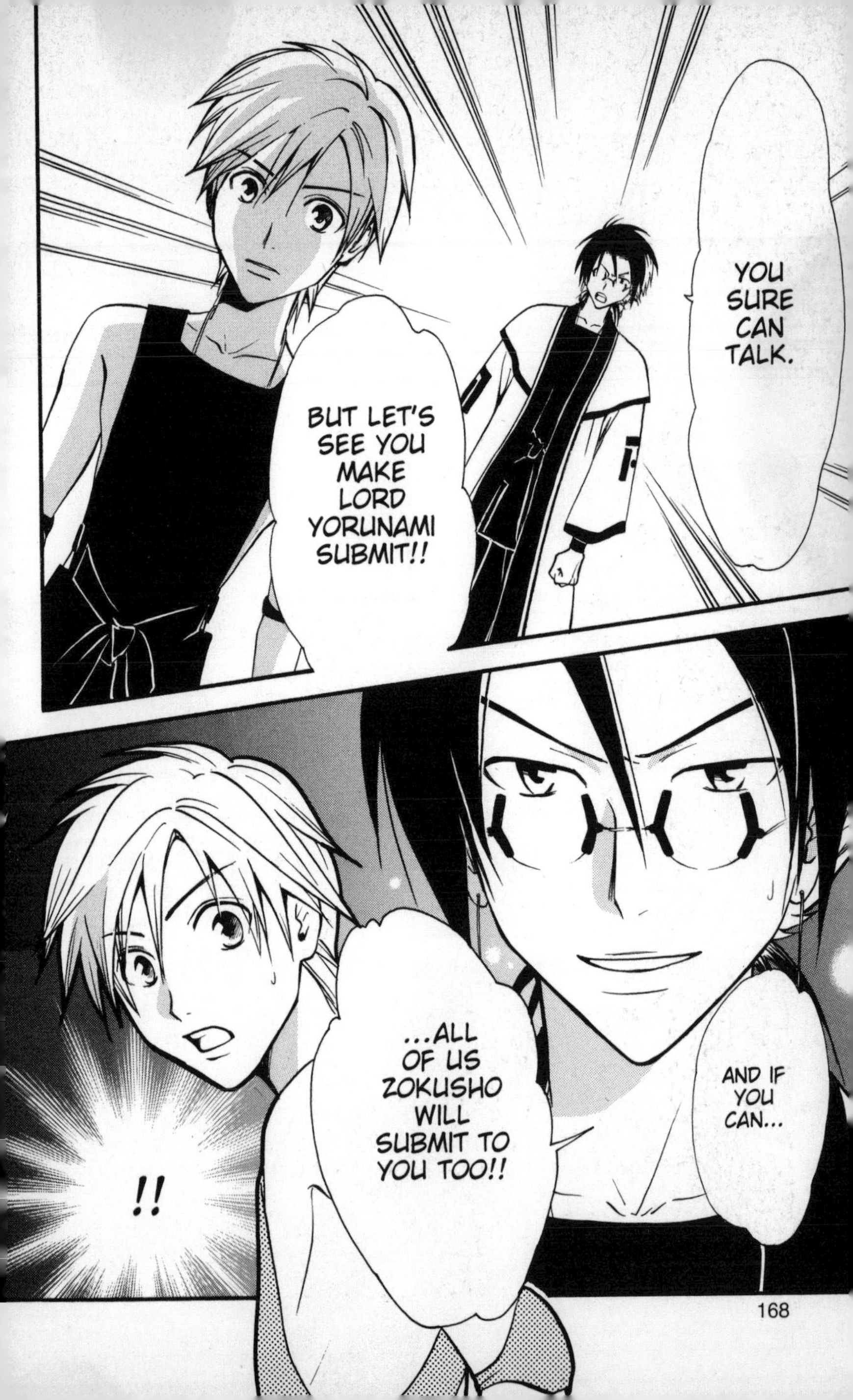
YOU SURE CAN TALK.
BUT LET'S SEE YOU MAKE LORD YORUNAMI SUBMIT!!
AND IF YOU CAN...
...ALL OF US ZOKUSHO WILL SUBMIT TO YOU TOO!!
!!

HIRUKO'S GAMBLE

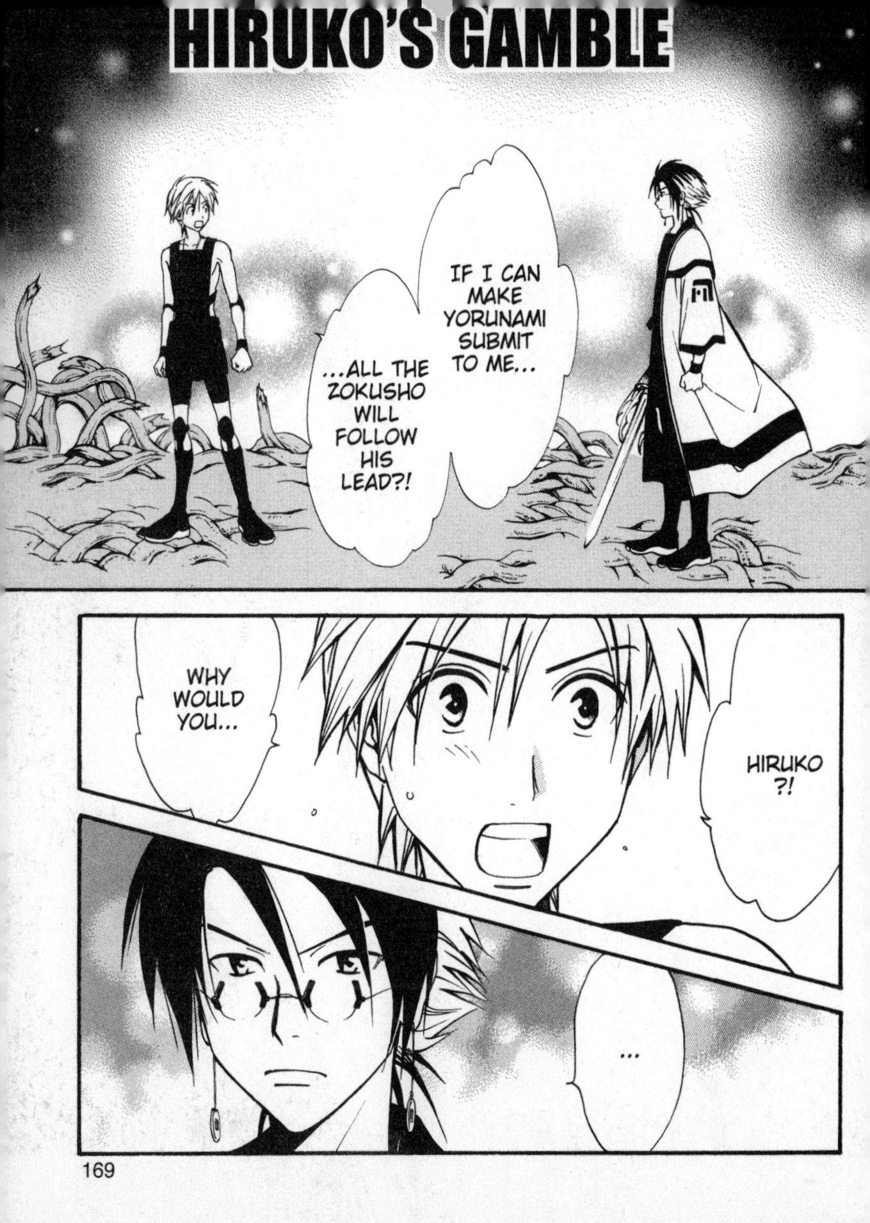

IF I CAN MAKE YORUNAMI SUBMIT TO ME...
...ALL THE ZOKUSHO WILL FOLLOW HIS LEAD?!
HIRUKO ?!
WHY WOULD YOU...
...

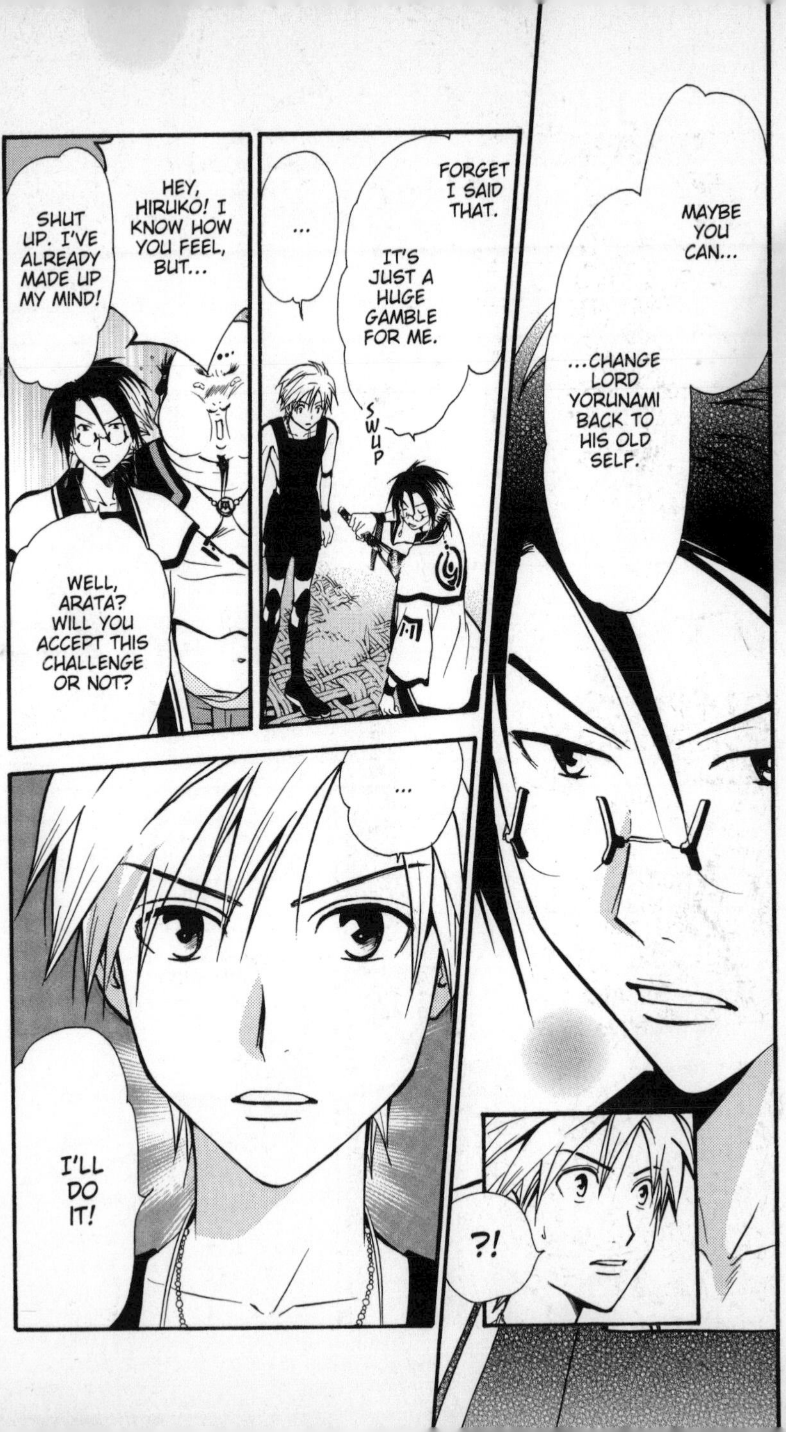
MAYBE YOU CAN...
...CHANGE LORD YORUNAMI BACK TO HIS OLD SELF.
?!
FORGET I SAID THAT.
IT'S JUST A HUGE GAMBLE FOR ME.
...
SWUP
HEY, HIRUKO! I KNOW HOW YOU FEEL, BUT...
SHUT UP. I'VE ALREADY MADE UP MY MIND!
...
WELL, ARATA? WILL YOU ACCEPT THIS CHALLENGE OR NOT?
...
I'LL DO IT!

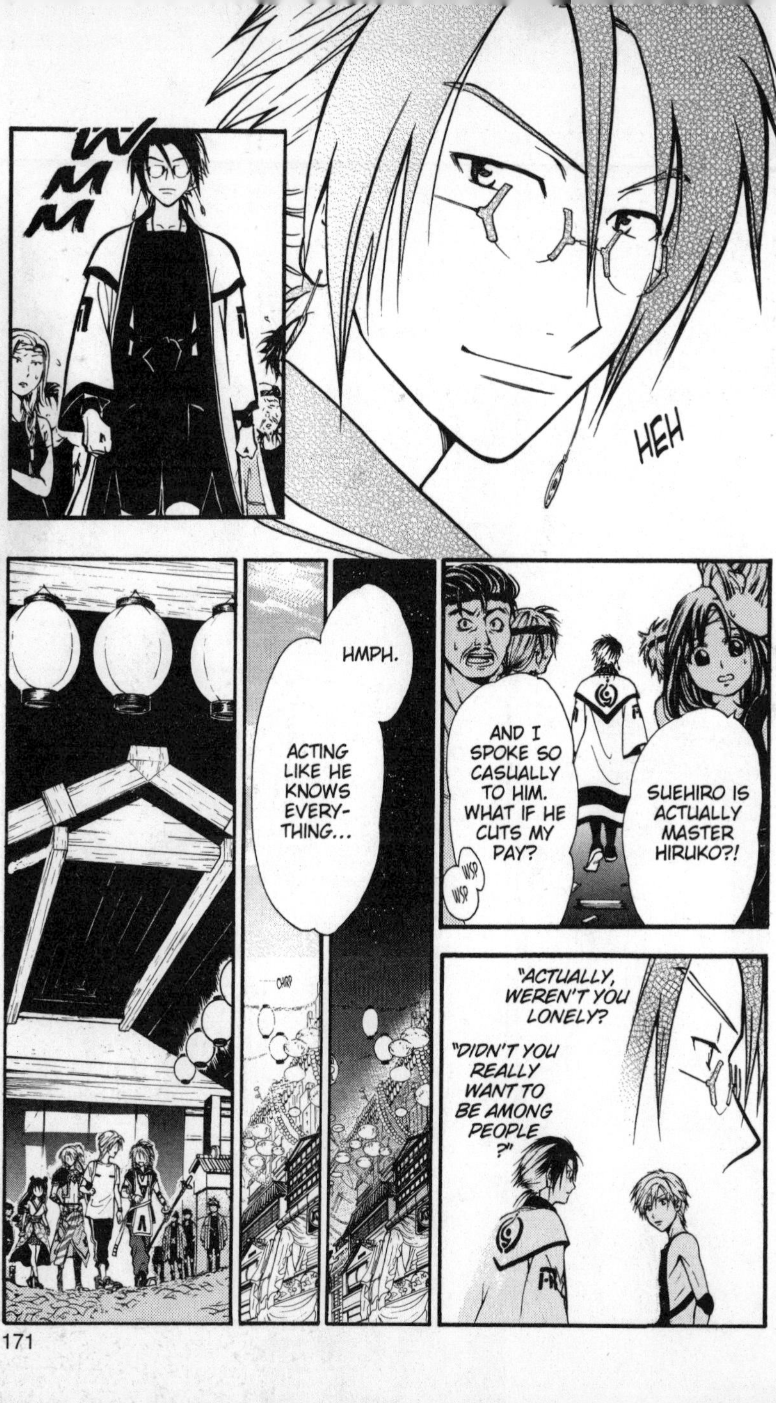
HEH
WMMM
SUEHIRO IS ACTUALLY MASTER HIRUKO?!
AND I SPOKE SO CASUALLY TO HIM. WHAT IF HE CUTS MY PAY?
WSP WSP
"ACTUALLY, WEREN'T YOU LONELY?
"DIDN'T YOU REALLY WANT TO BE AMONG PEOPLE?"
HMPH.
ACTING LIKE HE KNOWS EVERYTHING...
CHIRP

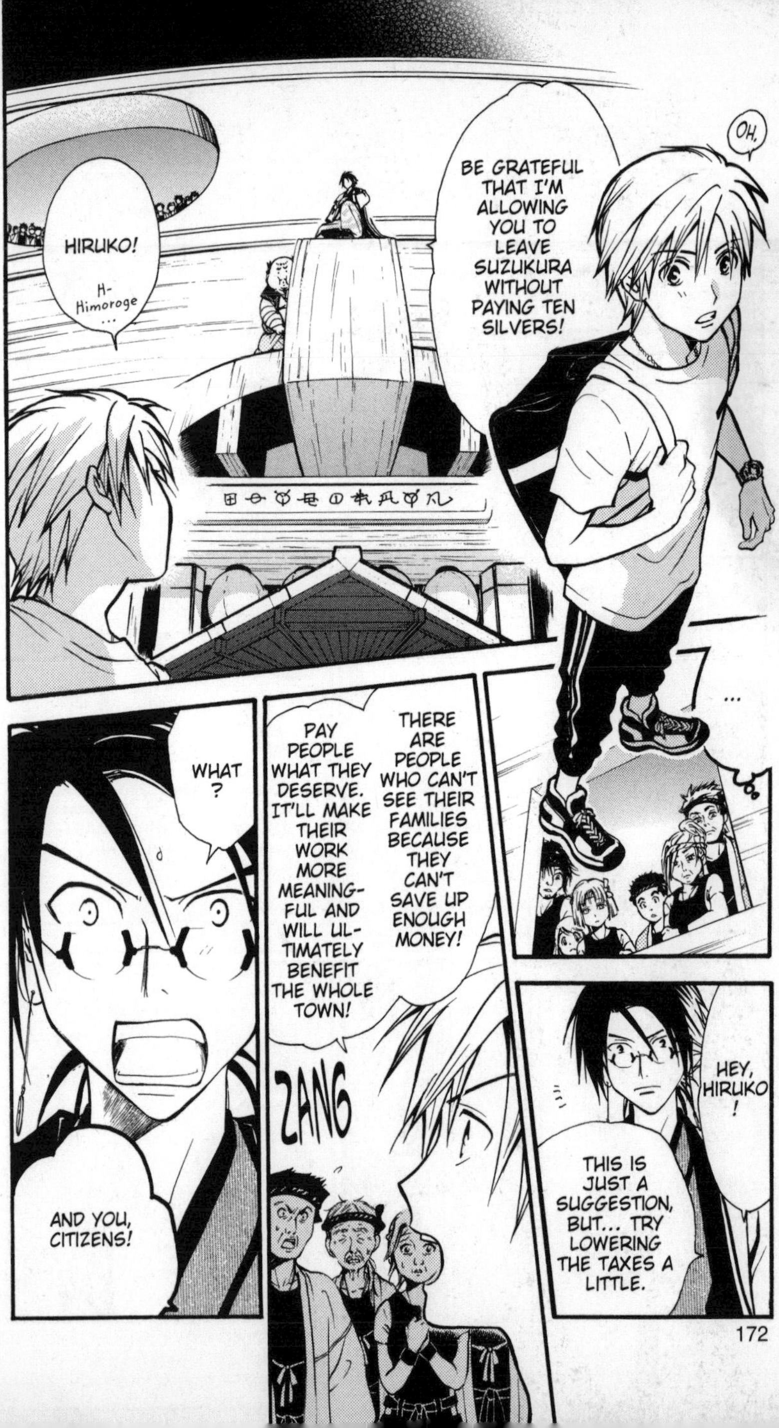
OH,
BE GRATEFUL THAT I'M ALLOWING YOU TO LEAVE SUZUKURA WITHOUT PAYING TEN SILVERS!
HIRUKO!
H- Himoroge ...
...
HEY, HIRUKO!
THIS IS JUST A SUGGESTION, BUT... TRY LOWERING THE TAXES A LITTLE.
THERE ARE PEOPLE WHO CAN'T SEE THEIR FAMILIES BECAUSE THEY CAN'T SAVE UP ENOUGH MONEY!
PAY PEOPLE WHAT THEY DESERVE. IT'LL MAKE THEIR WORK MORE MEANING-FUL AND WILL UL-TIMATELY BENEFIT THE WHOLE TOWN!
ZANG
WHAT?
AND YOU, CITIZENS!

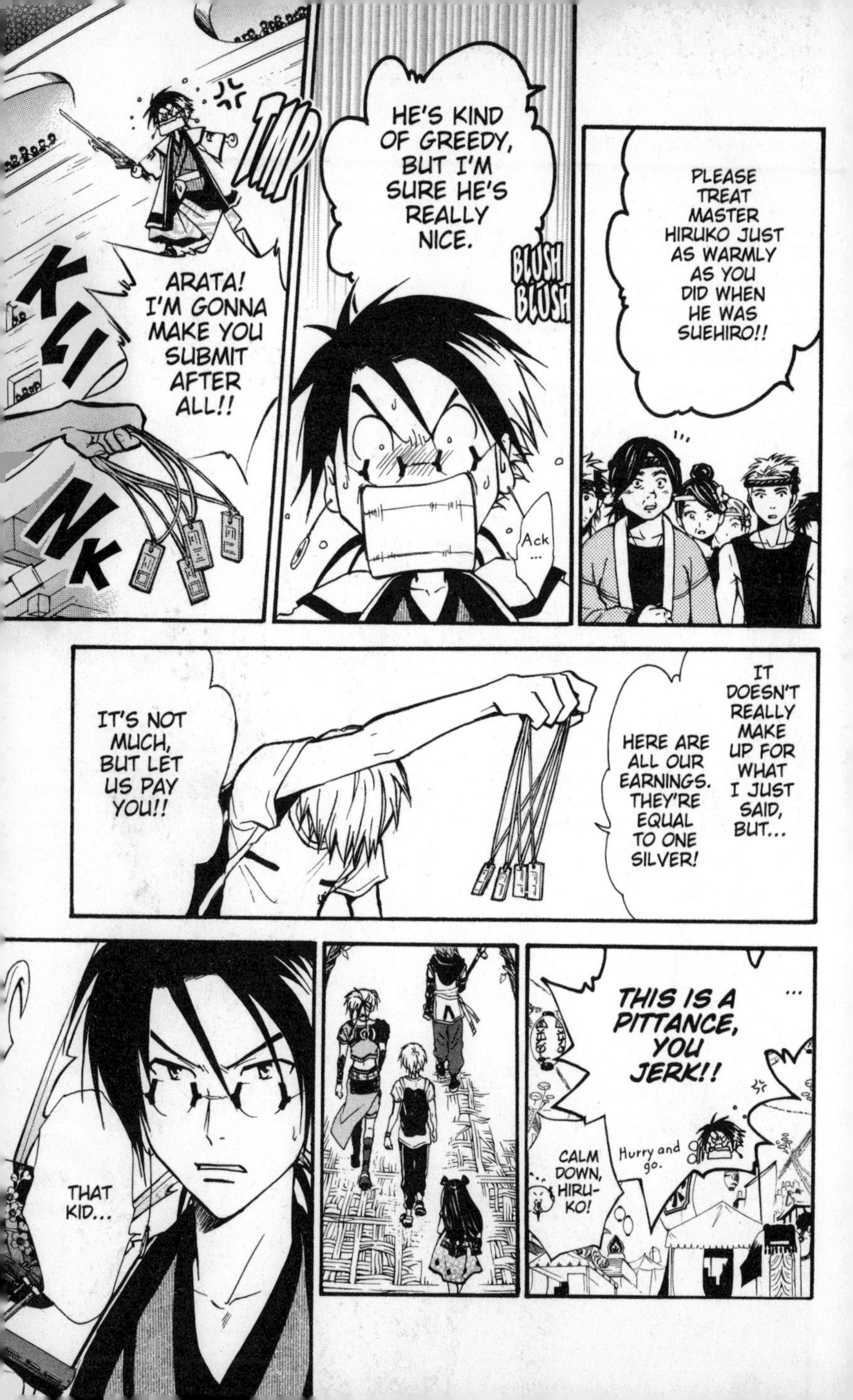
PLEASE TREAT MASTER HIRUKO JUST AS WARMLY AS YOU DID WHEN HE WAS SUEHIRO!!
...
HE'S KIND OF GREEDY, BUT I'M SURE HE'S REALLY NICE.
BLUSH BLUSH
Ack ...
TMP
ARATA! I'M GONNA MAKE YOU SUBMIT AFTER ALL!!
KLINK
IT DOESN'T REALLY MAKE UP FOR WHAT I JUST SAID, BUT...
HERE ARE ALL OUR EARNINGS. THEY'RE EQUAL TO ONE SILVER!
IT'S NOT MUCH, BUT LET US PAY YOU!!
...
THIS IS A PITTANCE, YOU JERK!!
Hurry and go.
CALM DOWN, HIRUKO!
THAT KID...

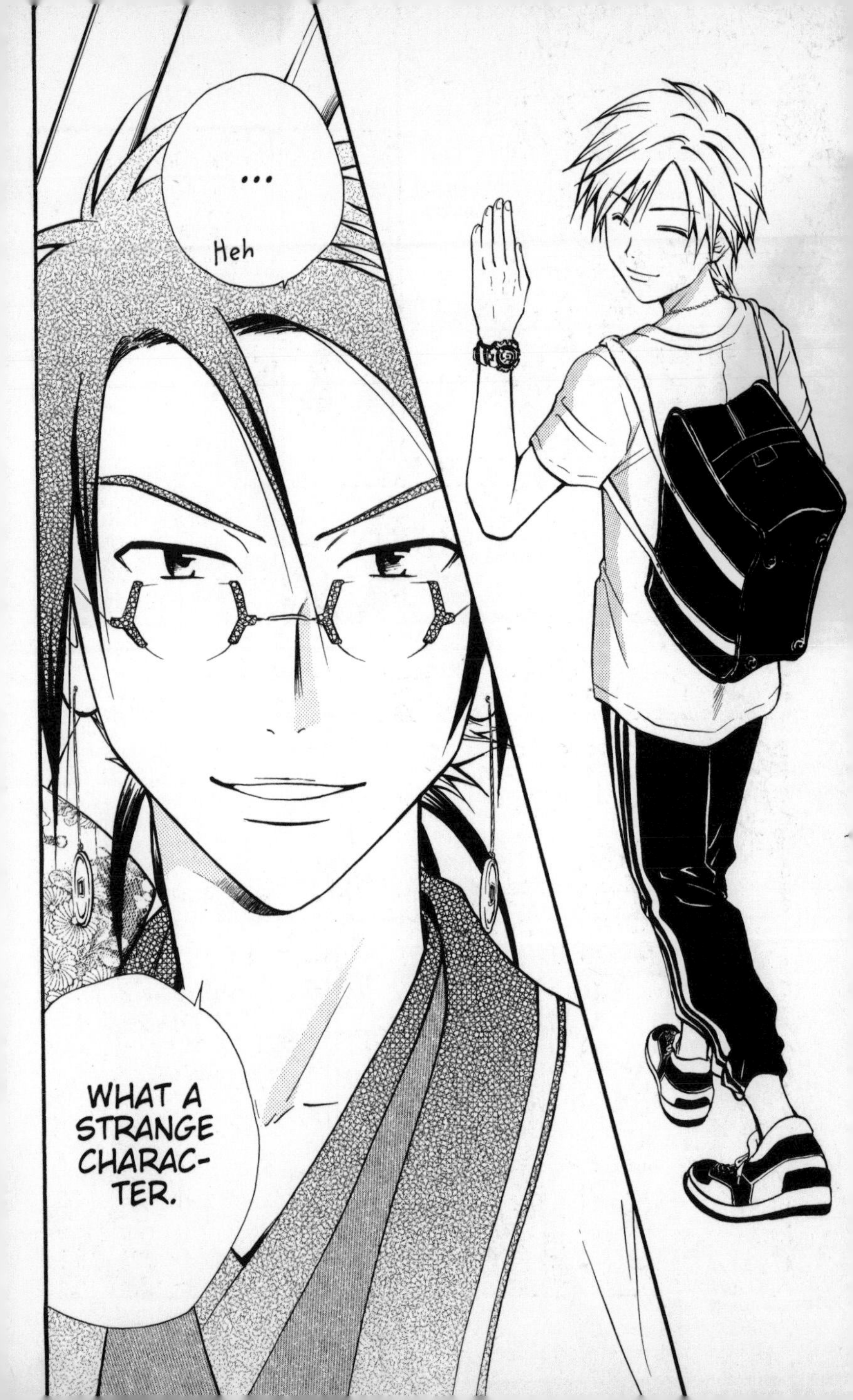
...
Heh
WHAT A STRANGE CHARAC-TER.

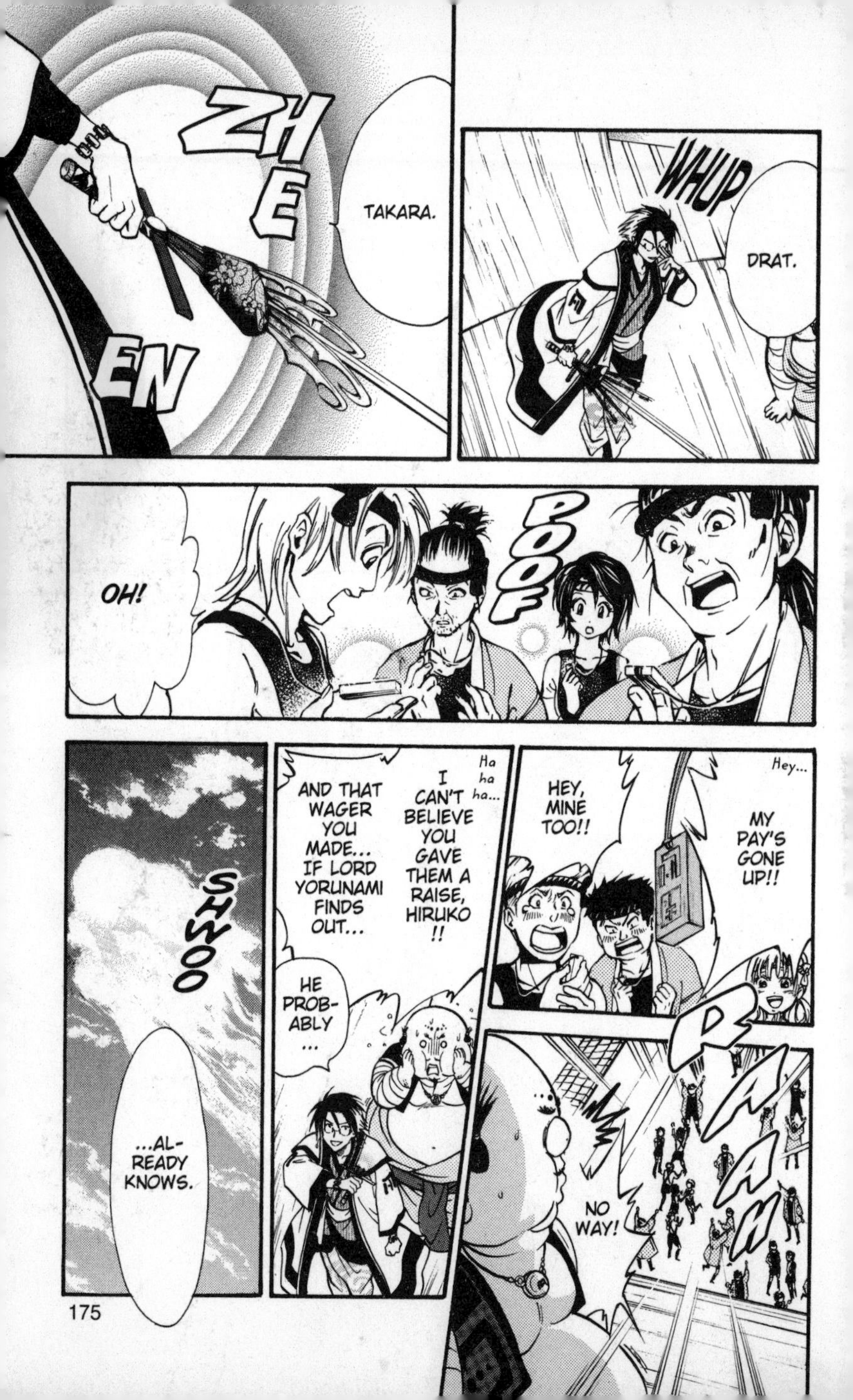
WHUP
DRAT.
ZHE
EN
TAKARA.
POOF
OH!
Hey...
MY PAY'S GONE UP!!
HEY, MINE TOO!!
RAAAH
NO WAY!
Ha ha ha...
I CAN'T BELIEVE YOU GAVE THEM A RAISE, HIRUKO!!
AND THAT WAGER YOU MADE... IF LORD YORUNAMI FINDS OUT...
HE PROBABLY...
SHWOO
...ALREADY KNOWS.

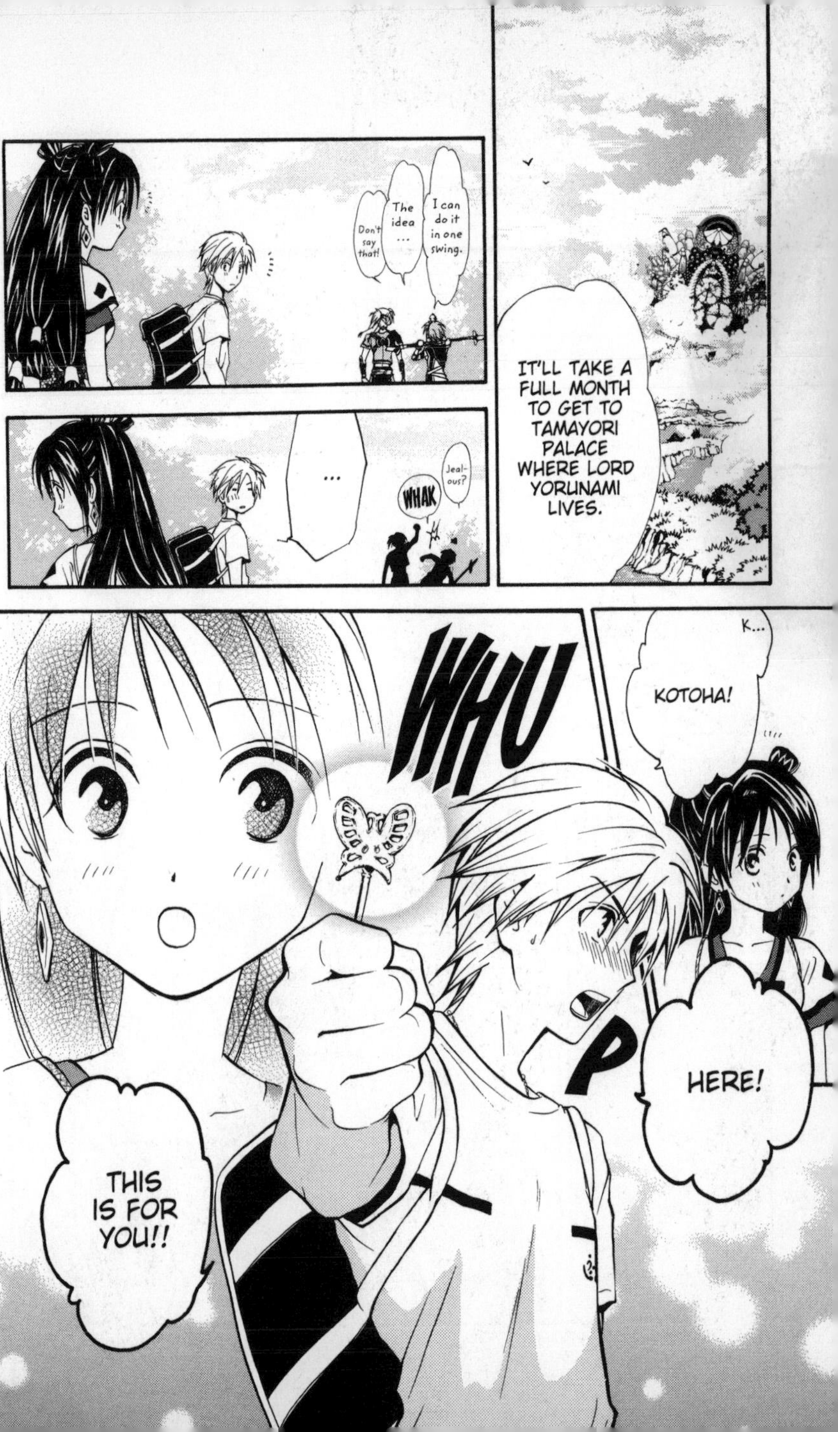
IT'LL TAKE A FULL MONTH TO GET TO TAMAYORI PALACE WHERE LORD YORUNAMI LIVES.
I can do it in one swing.
The idea ...
Don't say that!
Jeal-ous?
WHAK
...
K...
KOTOHA!
WHUP
HERE!
THIS IS FOR YOU!!

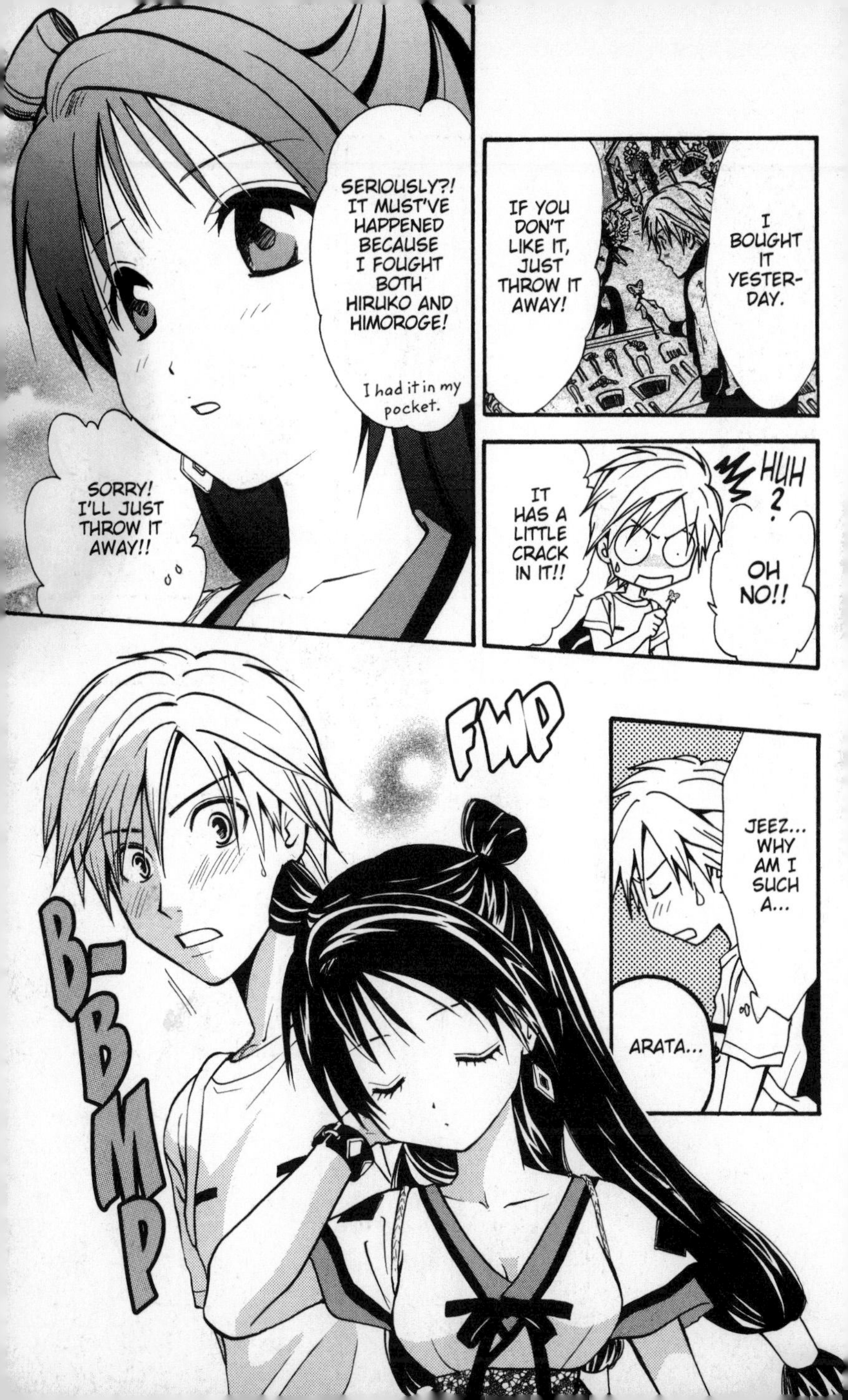
I BOUGHT IT YESTERDAY.
IF YOU DON'T LIKE IT, JUST THROW IT AWAY!
HUH?
OH NO!!
IT HAS A LITTLE CRACK IN IT!!
SERIOUSLY?! IT MUST'VE HAPPENED BECAUSE I FOUGHT BOTH HIRUKO AND HIMOROGE!
I had it in my pocket.
SORRY! I'LL JUST THROW IT AWAY!!
JEEZ... WHY AM I SUCH A...
ARATA...
FWP
B-B-BMP

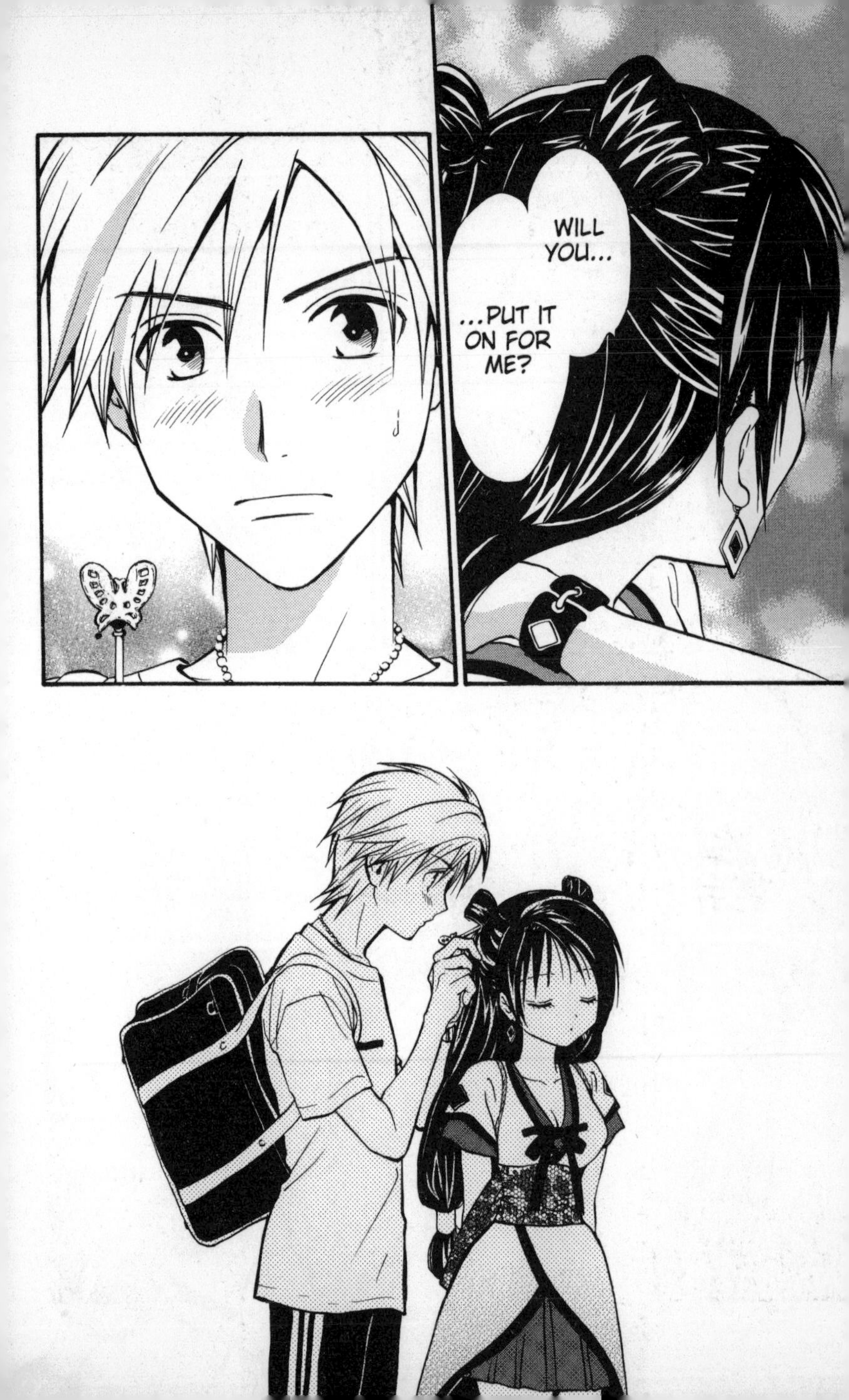
WILL YOU...
...PUT IT ON FOR ME?

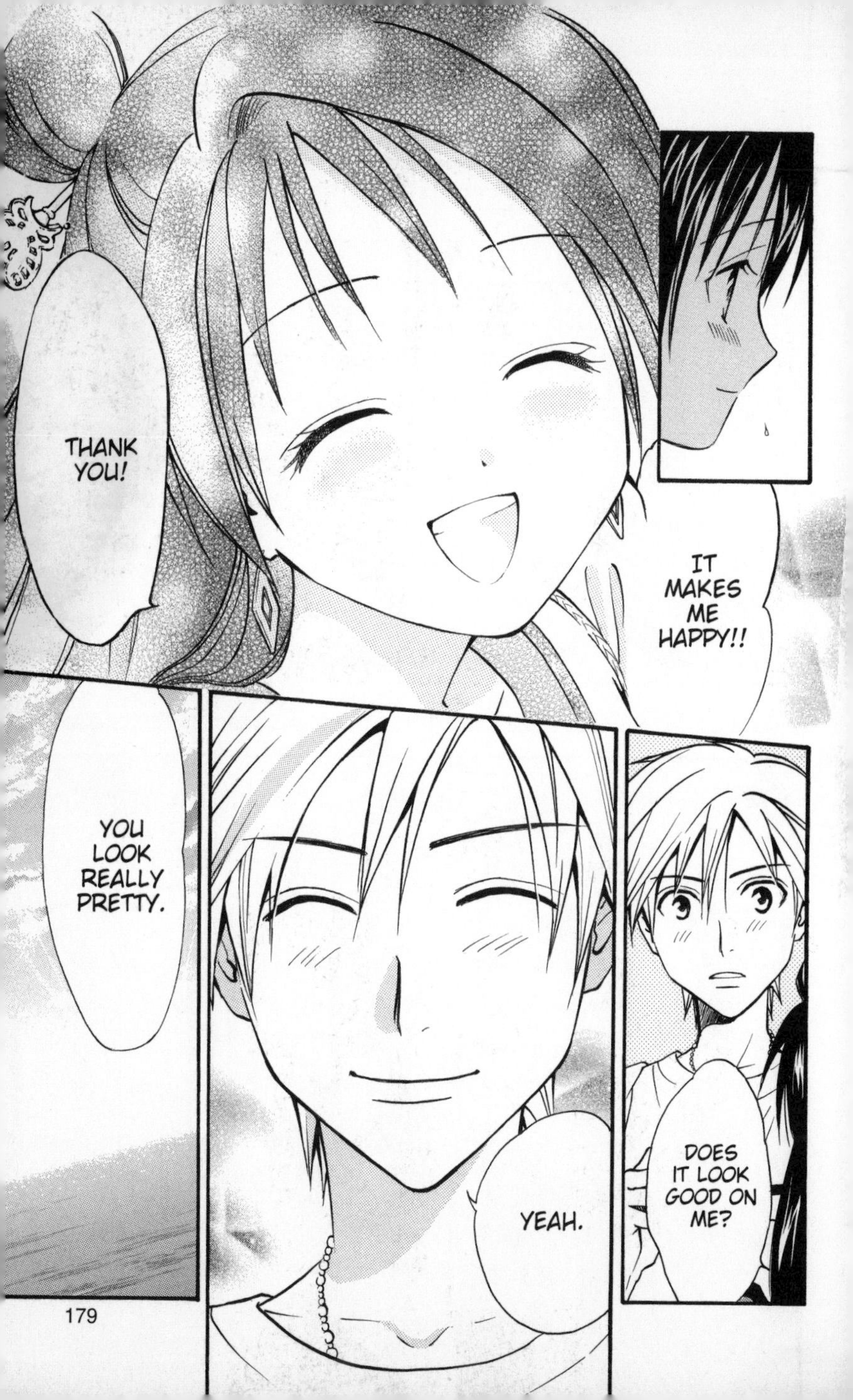
THANK YOU!
IT MAKES ME HAPPY!!
DOES IT LOOK GOOD ON ME?
YEAH.
YOU LOOK REALLY PRETTY.

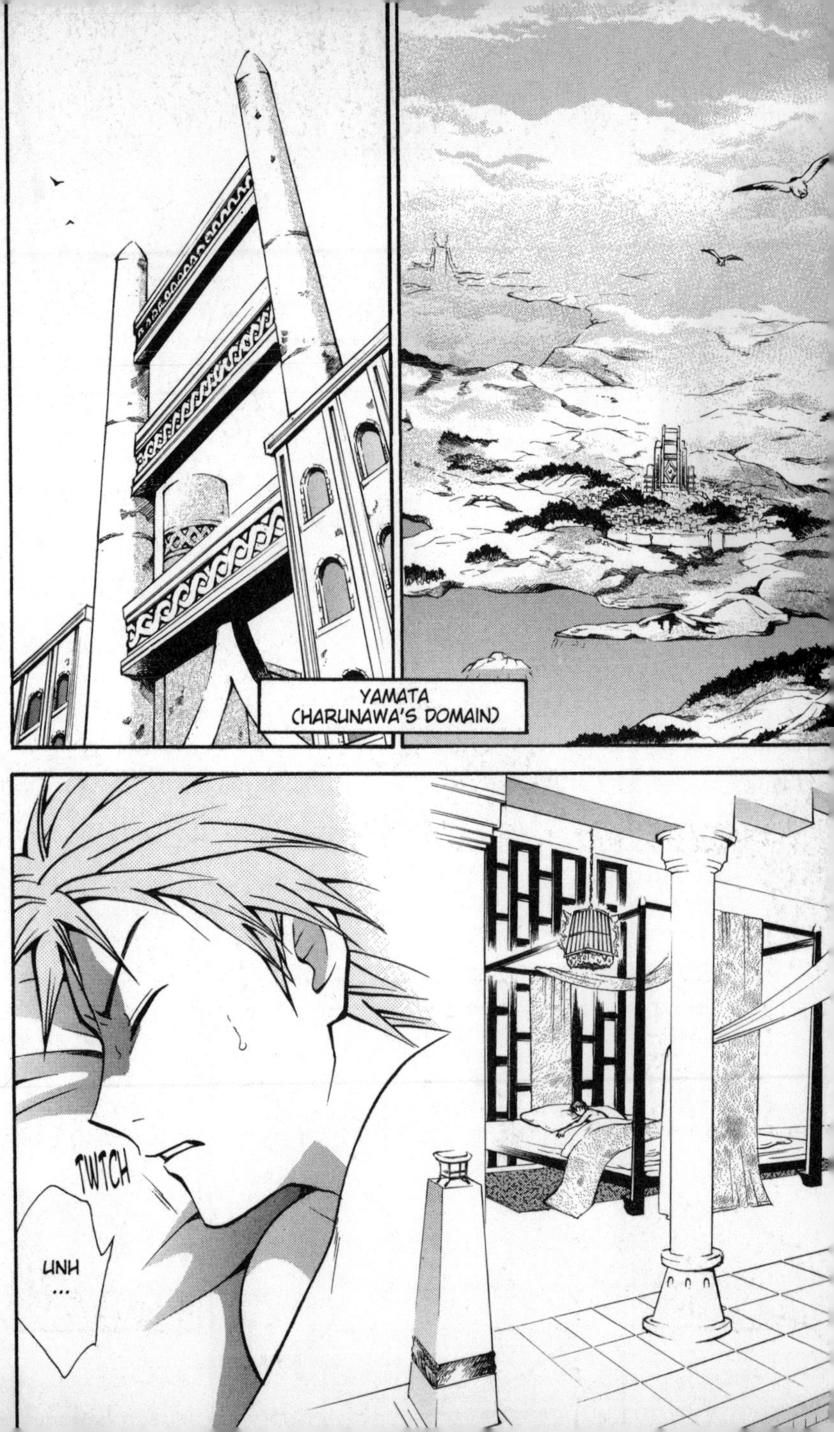
YAMATA
(HARUNAWA'S DOMAIN)
TWTCH
UNH
...

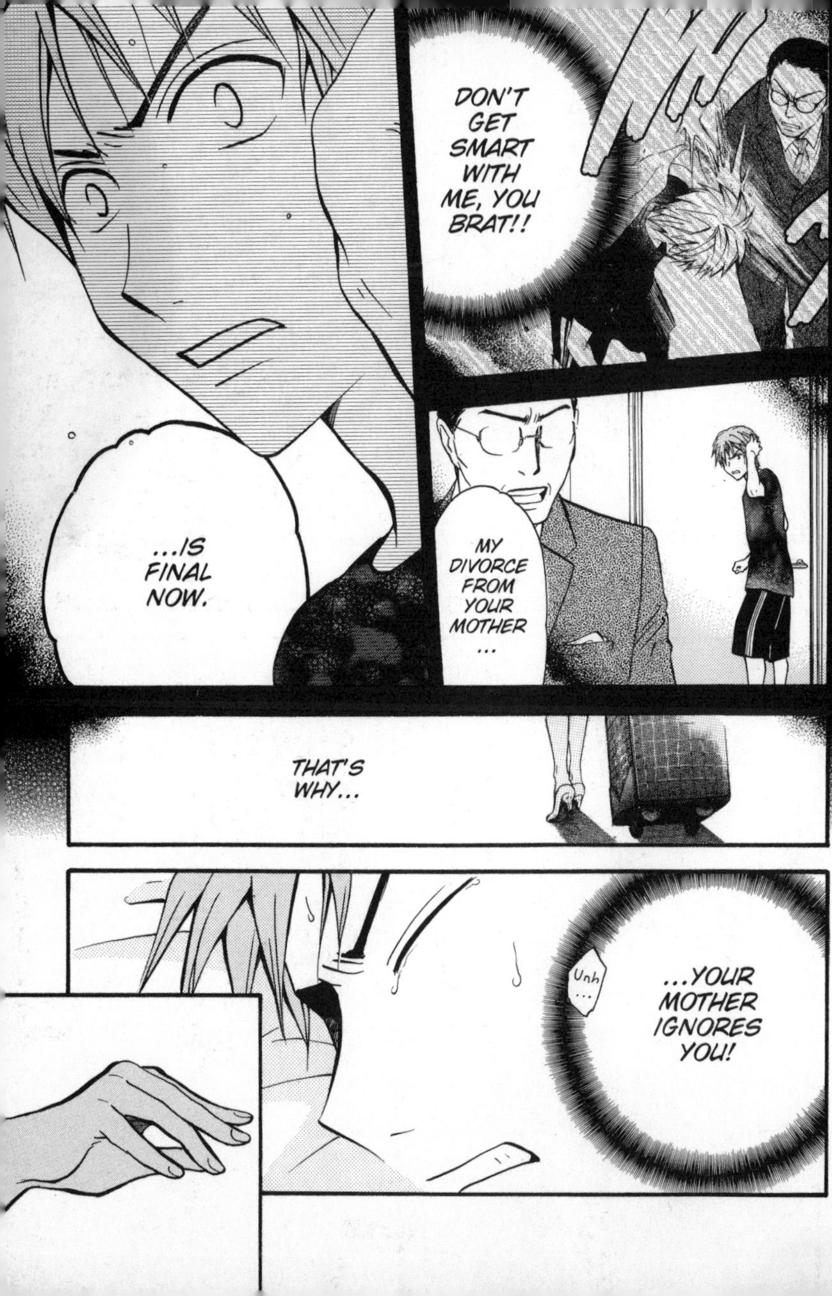
DON'T GET SMART WITH ME, YOU BRAT!!
MY DIVORCE FROM YOUR MOTHER ...
...IS FINAL NOW.
THAT'S WHY...
...YOUR MOTHER IGNORES YOU!
Unh ...

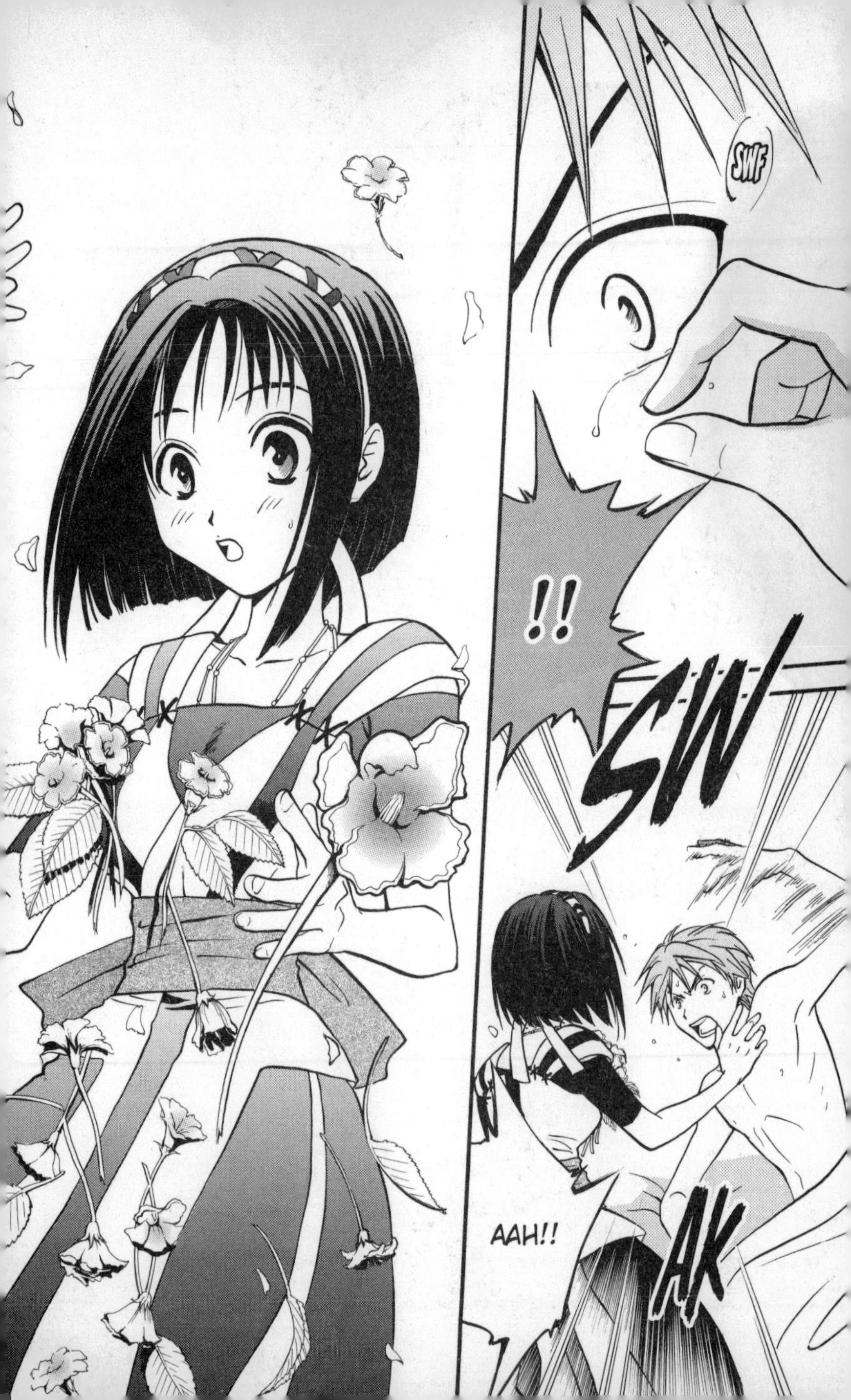
SWF
!!
SWI
AAH!!
AK

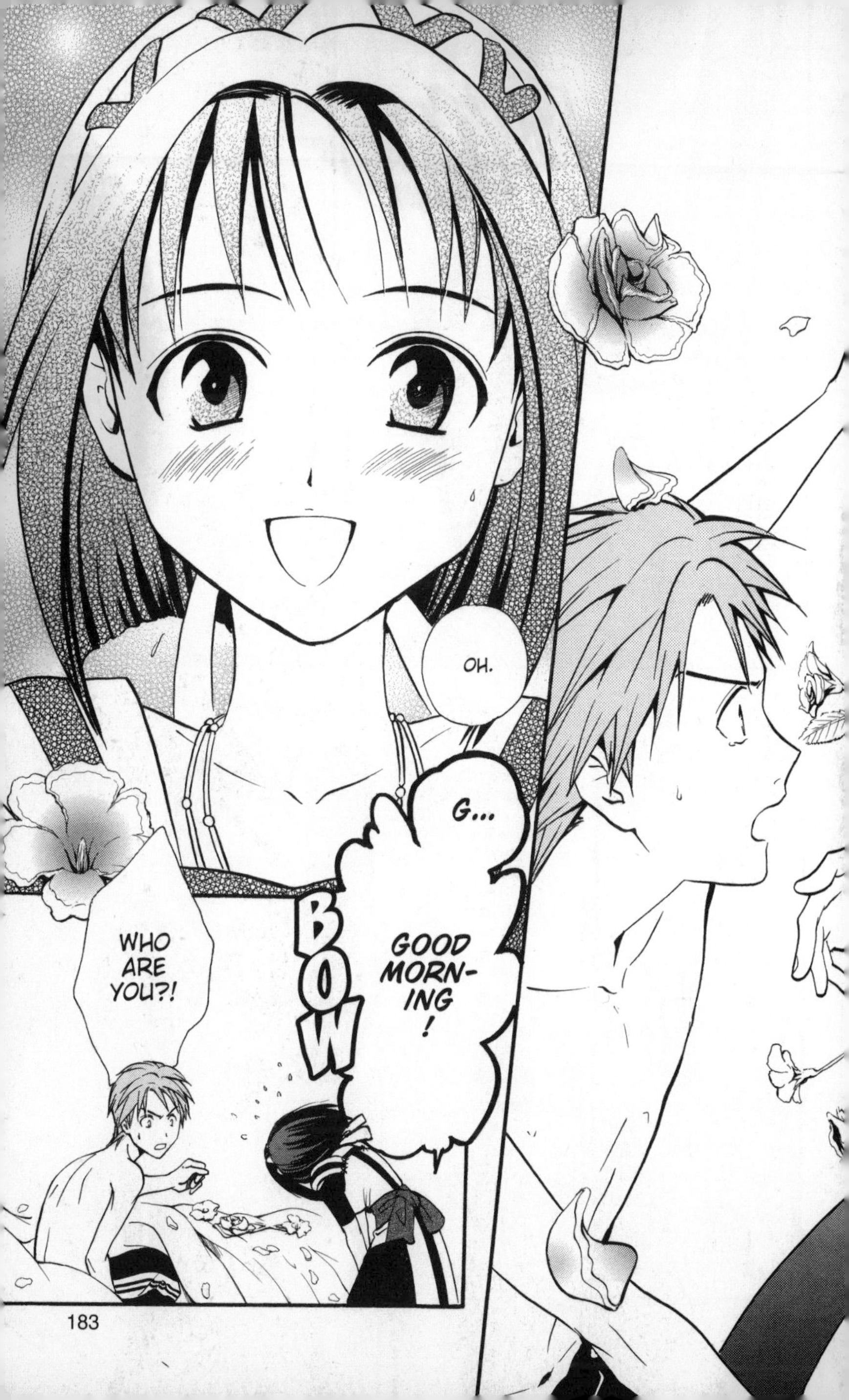
OH.
G...
GOOD MORNING!
BOW
WHO ARE YOU?!

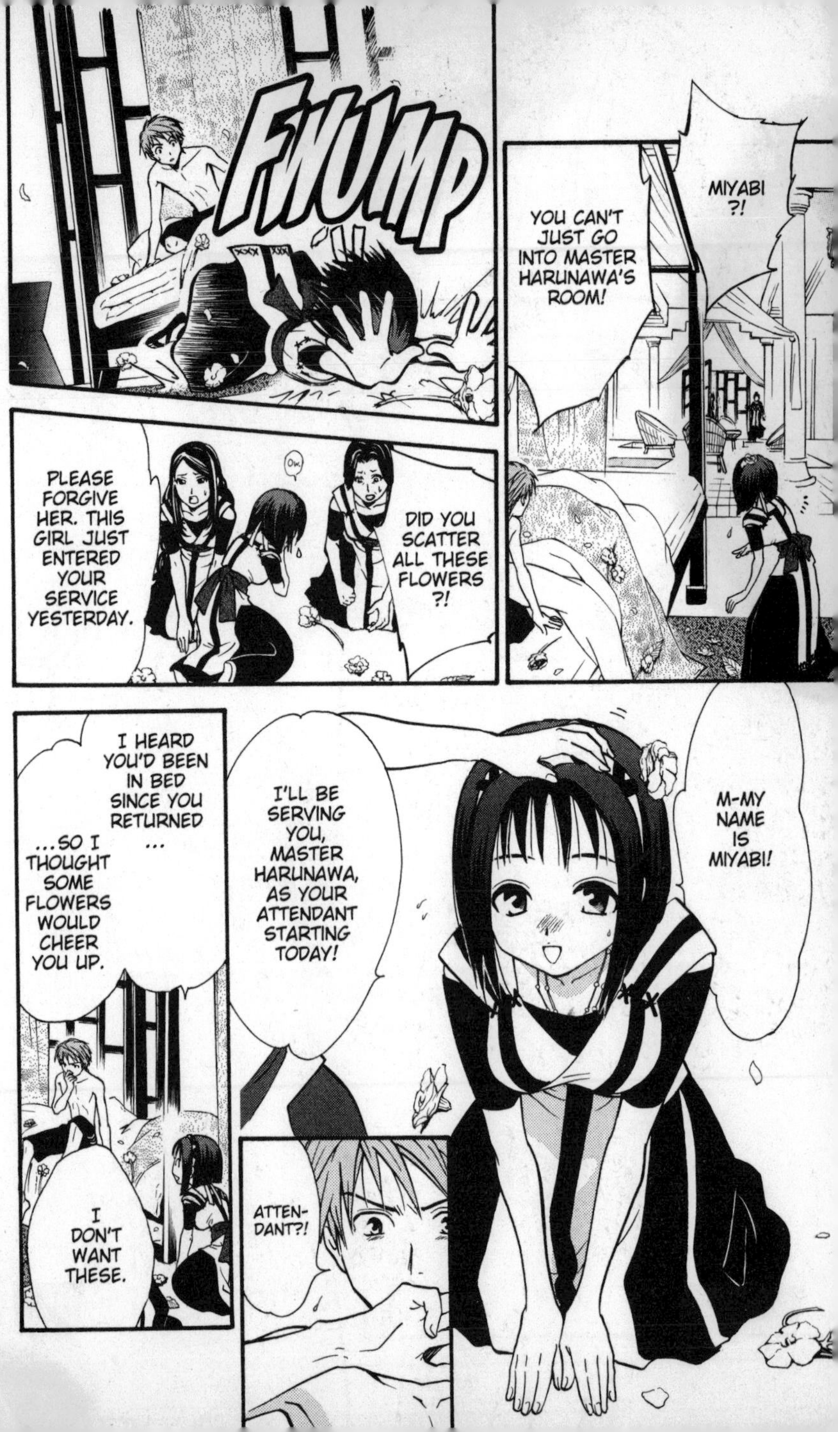
MIYABI ?!
YOU CAN'T JUST GO INTO MASTER HARUNAWA'S ROOM!
FXUMP
DID YOU SCATTER ALL THESE FLOWERS ?!
OK.
PLEASE FORGIVE HER. THIS GIRL JUST ENTERED YOUR SERVICE YESTERDAY.
M-MY NAME IS MIYABI!
I'LL BE SERVING YOU, MASTER HARUNAWA, AS YOUR ATTENDANT STARTING TODAY!
I HEARD YOU'D BEEN IN BED SINCE YOU RETURNED ...
...SO I THOUGHT SOME FLOWERS WOULD CHEER YOU UP.
ATTEN-DANT?!
I DON'T WANT THESE.

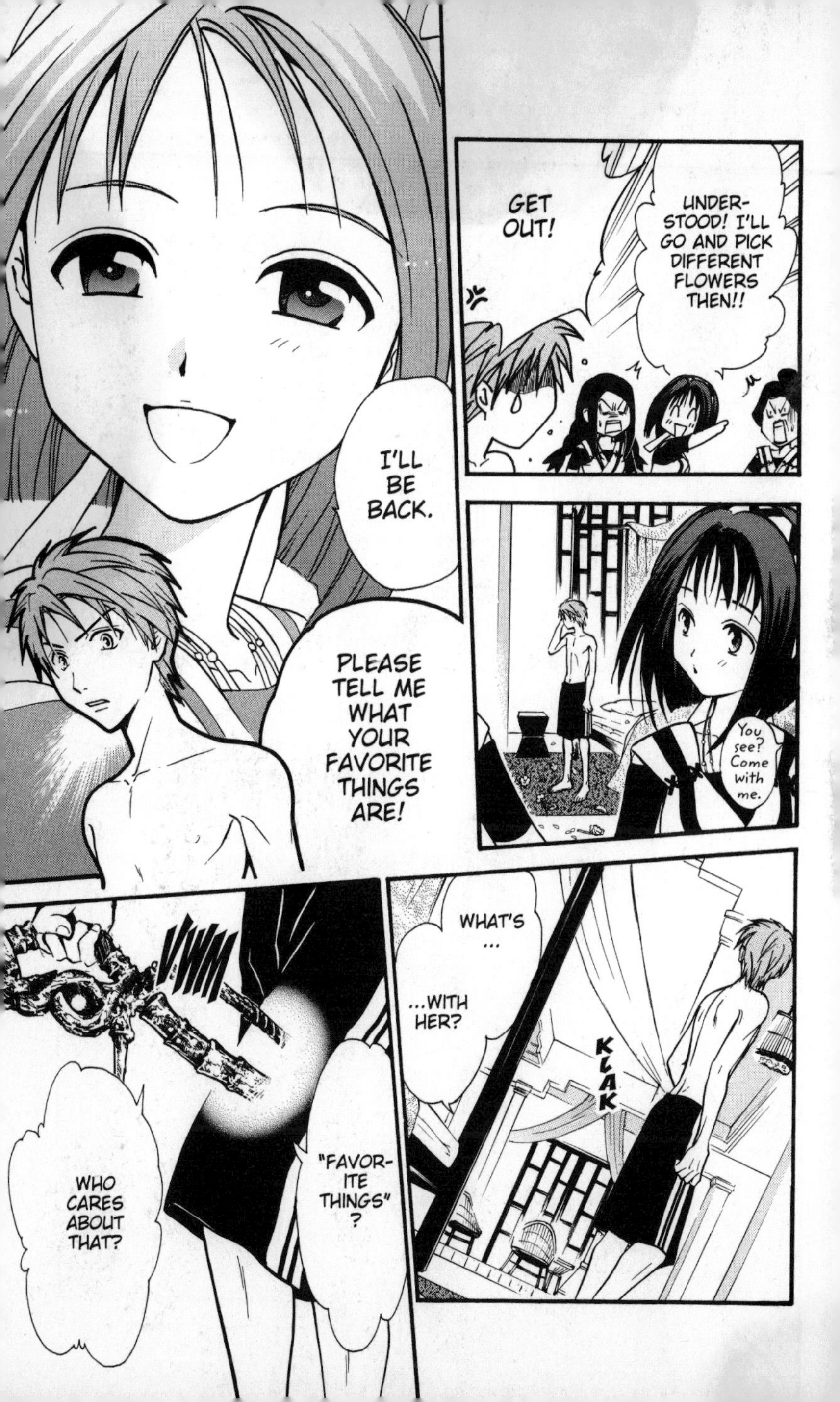
GET OUT!
UNDER-STOOD! I'LL GO AND PICK DIFFERENT FLOWERS THEN!!
You see? Come with me.
I'LL BE BACK.
PLEASE TELL ME WHAT YOUR FAVORITE THINGS ARE!
WHAT'S ...
...WITH HER?
KLAK
VWM
"FAVOR-ITE THINGS"?
WHO CARES ABOUT THAT?

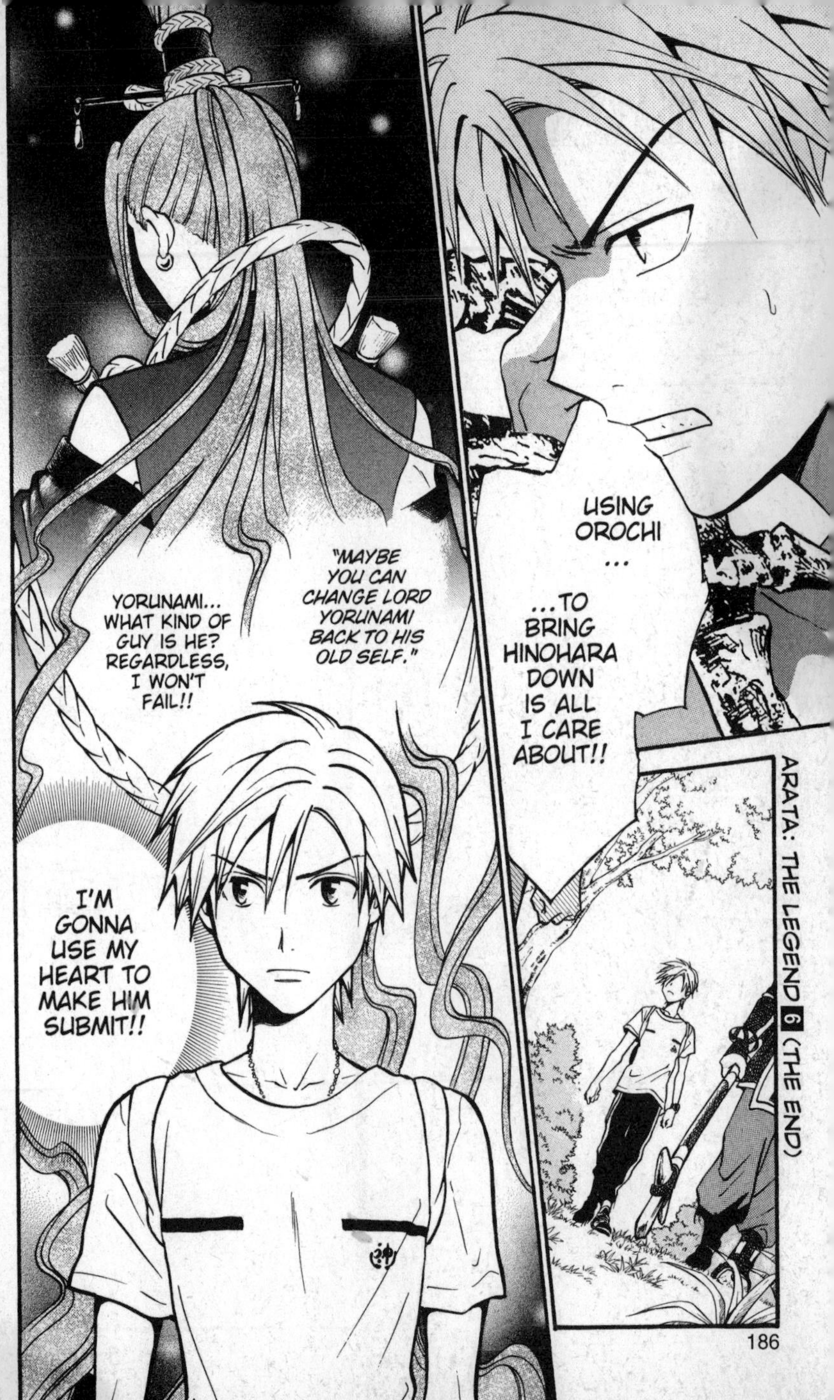
USING OROCHI ...
...TO BRING HINOHARA DOWN IS ALL I CARE ABOUT!!
"MAYBE YOU CAN CHANGE LORD YORUNAMI BACK TO HIS OLD SELF."
YORUNAMI... WHAT KIND OF GUY IS HE? REGARDLESS, I WON'T FAIL!!
I'M GONNA USE MY HEART TO MAKE HIM SUBMIT!!

ARATA: THE LEGEND 6 (THE END)

Arata
THE LEGEND

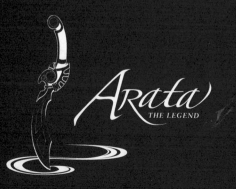

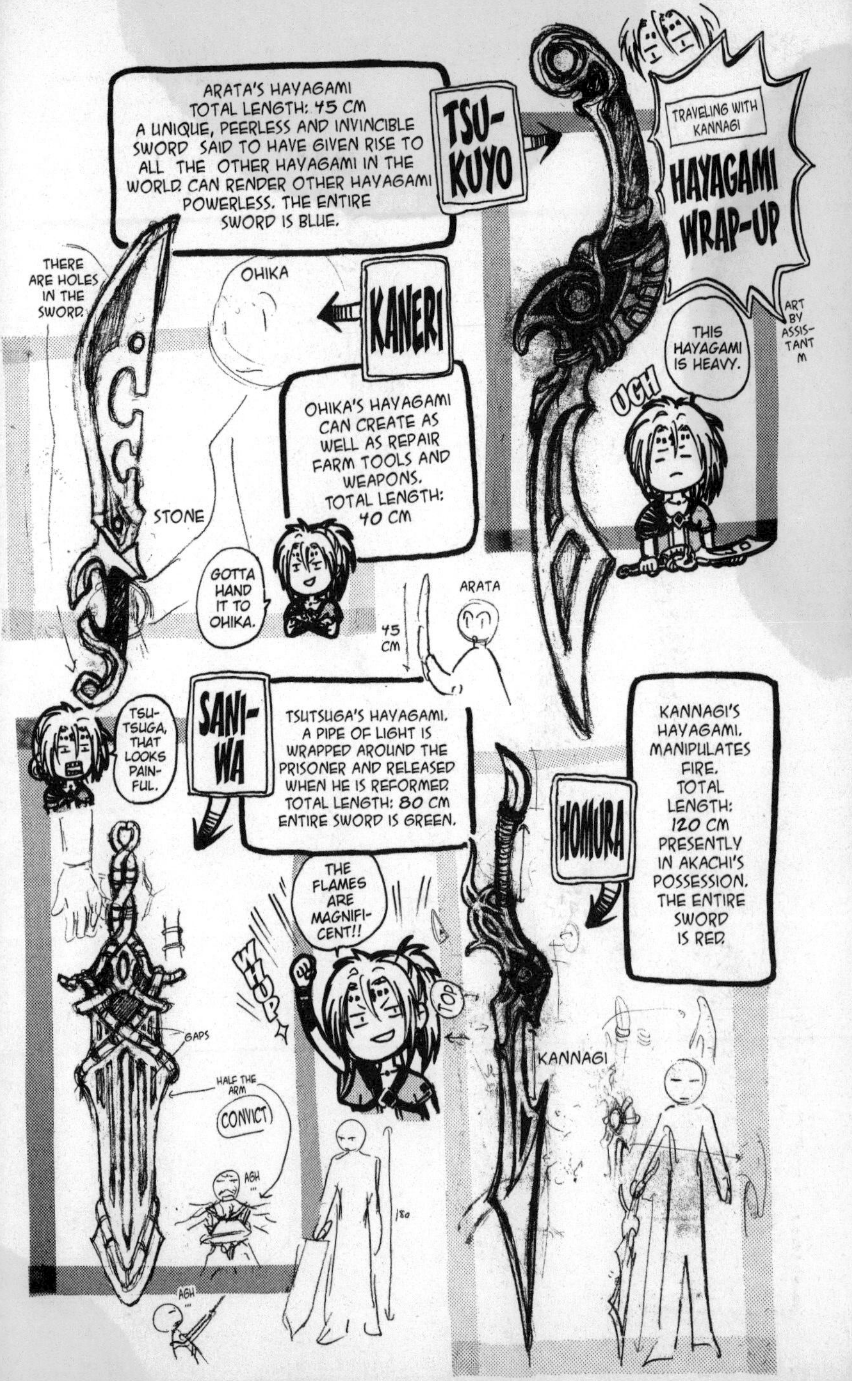
TRAVELING WITH KANNAGI
HAYAGAMI WRAP-UP
TSU-KUYO
ARATA'S HAYAGAMI
TOTAL LENGTH: 45 CM
A UNIQUE, PEERLESS AND INVINCIBLE SWORD SAID TO HAVE GIVEN RISE TO ALL THE OTHER HAYAGAMI IN THE WORLD. CAN RENDER OTHER HAYAGAMI POWERLESS. THE ENTIRE SWORD IS BLUE.
ART BY ASSIS-TANT M
THIS HAYAGAMI IS HEAVY.
UGH
KANERI
OHIKA
OHIKA'S HAYAGAMI CAN CREATE AS WELL AS REPAIR FARM TOOLS AND WEAPONS. TOTAL LENGTH: 40 CM
THERE ARE HOLES IN THE SWORD.
STONE
GOTTA HAND IT TO OHIKA.
ARATA
45 CM
HOMURA
KANNAGI'S HAYAGAMI. MANIPULATES FIRE. TOTAL LENGTH: 120 CM PRESENTLY IN AKACHI'S POSSESSION. THE ENTIRE SWORD IS RED.
SANI-WA
TSUTSUGA'S HAYAGAMI. A PIPE OF LIGHT IS WRAPPED AROUND THE PRISONER AND RELEASED WHEN HE IS REFORMED. TOTAL LENGTH: 80 CM ENTIRE SWORD IS GREEN.
TSU-TSUGA, THAT LOOKS PAIN-FUL.
THE FLAMES ARE MAGNIFI-CENT!!
WHUP
TOP
KANNAGI
GAPS
HALF THE ARM
CONVICT
AGH ...
180
AGH ...

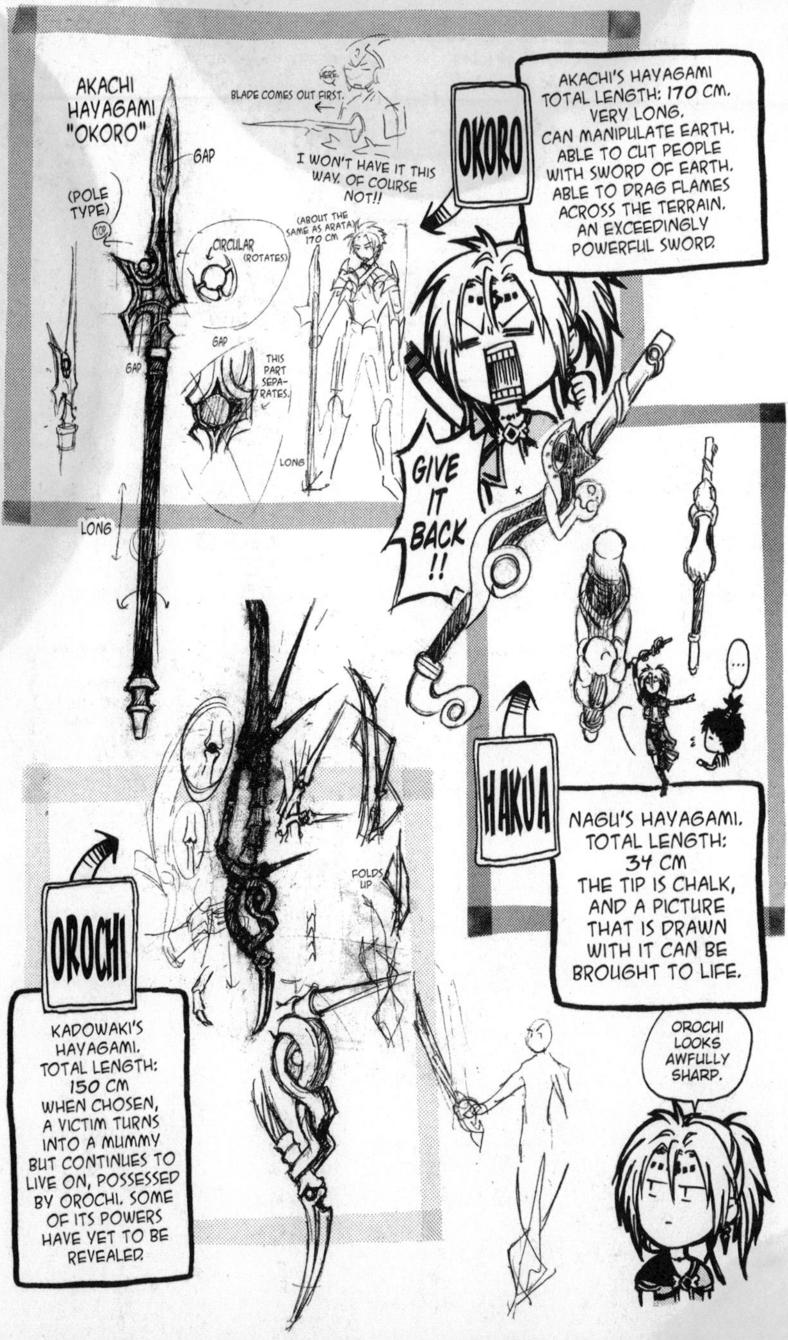
AKACHI HAYAGAMI "OKORO"
GAP
(POLE TYPE)
TOP
HERE.
BLADE COMES OUT FIRST.
I WON'T HAVE IT THIS WAY. OF COURSE NOT!!
(ABOUT THE SAME AS ARATA) 170 CM
CIRCULAR (ROTATES)
GAP
GAP
THIS PART SEPARATES.
LONG
LONG
OKORO
AKACHI'S HAYAGAMI TOTAL LENGTH: 170 CM. VERY LONG. CAN MANIPULATE EARTH. ABLE TO CUT PEOPLE WITH SWORD OF EARTH. ABLE TO DRAG FLAMES ACROSS THE TERRAIN. AN EXCEEDINGLY POWERFUL SWORD.
GIVE IT BACK!!
...
HAKUA
NAGU'S HAYAGAMI. TOTAL LENGTH: 34 CM THE TIP IS CHALK, AND A PICTURE THAT IS DRAWN WITH IT CAN BE BROUGHT TO LIFE.
FOLDS UP
OROCHI
KADOWAKI'S HAYAGAMI. TOTAL LENGTH: 150 CM WHEN CHOSEN, A VICTIM TURNS INTO A MUMMY BUT CONTINUES TO LIVE ON, POSSESSED BY OROCHI. SOME OF ITS POWERS HAVE YET TO BE REVEALED.
OROCHI LOOKS AWFULLY SHARP.

Suzukura is the town that is featured in this volume. Its name means "the condition of being consumed by greed."

I don't think I'm very greedy. It's always better if food tastes good, but I'm satisfied as long as it's nutritious. You know that talk about the three major desires of human beings? One of my staff members said, "Oh, you mean eating, sleeping and eating?" Is eating all she cares about?! She was quite serious. I thought, "How amazing."

–YUU WATASE

AUTHOR BIO

Born March 5 in Osaka, Yuu Watase debuted in the *Shôjo Comic* manga anthology in 1989. She won the 43rd Shogakukan Manga Award with *Ceres: Celestial Legend*. One of her most famous works is *Fushigi Yûgi*, a series that has inspired the prequel *Fushigi Yûgi: Genbu Kaiden*. In 2008, *Arata: The Legend* started serialization in *Shonen Sunday*.

ARATA: THE LEGEND

Volume 6
Shonen Sunday Edition

Story and Art by YUU WATASE

© 2009 Yuu WATASE/Shogakukan
All rights reserved.
Original Japanese edition "ARATAKANGATARI"
published by SHOGAKUKAN Inc.

English Adaptation: Lance Caselman
Translation: JN Productions
Touch-up Art & Lettering: Rina Mapa
Design: Ronnie Casson
Editor: Amy Yu

Printed in the U.S.A.

Published by VIZ Media, LLC
P.O. Box 77010
San Francisco, CA 94107

10 9 8 7 6 5 4 3 2 1
First printing, June 2011

www.viz.com   WWW.SHONENSUNDAY.COM

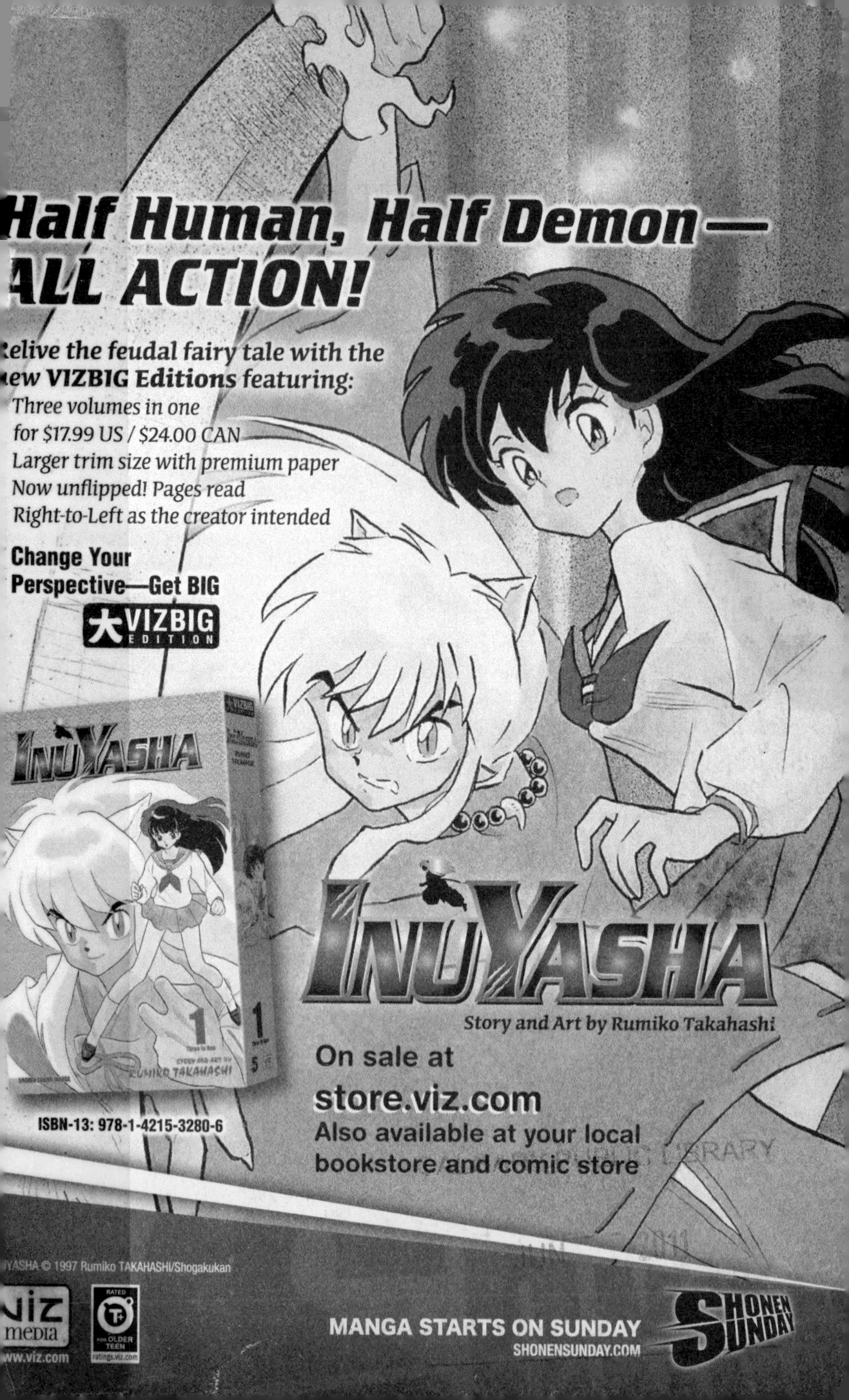
Half Human, Half Demon—
ALL ACTION!
Relive the feudal fairy tale with the new VIZBIG Editions featuring:
Three volumes in one for $17.99 US / $24.00 CAN
Larger trim size with premium paper
Now unflipped! Pages read Right-to-Left as the creator intended
Change Your Perspective—Get BIG
大 VIZBIG EDITION
INUYASHA
ISBN-13: 978-1-4215-3280-6
INUYASHA
Story and Art by Rumiko Takahashi
On sale at
store.viz.com
Also available at your local bookstore and comic store
INUYASHA © 1997 Rumiko TAKAHASHI/Shogakukan
viz media
www.viz.com
RATED T+ FOR OLDER TEEN
ratings.viz.com
MANGA STARTS ON SUNDAY
SHONENSUNDAY.COM
SHONEN SUNDAY